NEW YORK

Herbert B. Livesey

Second
edition
of the
American
Express
Pocket
Guide

Mitchell Beazley

The Author
Herbert B. Livesey, who is also the author of *The American Express Pocket Guide to Spain*, was born in New York and has lived in the area all his life. He also has a home in Spain. He is a novelist and travel writer, and contributes regularly to *Travel & Leisure* magazine.

Acknowledgments
The author and publishers would like to thank the following for their invaluable help and advice: Pamela Fiori, Paul Holberton, Christopher McIntosh, Ila Stanger.

Quotations
Extract on p85 from *My Lost City*: F. Scott Fitzgerald, *The Crack-Up* © 1945 New Directions Publishing Corporation. Reprinted by kind permission of New Directions.

Few travel books are without errors, and no guide book can ever be completely up to date, for telephone numbers and opening hours change without warning, and hotels and restaurants come under new management, which can affect standards. While every effort has been made to ensure that all information is accurate at the time of going to press, the publishers will be glad to receive any corrections and suggestions for improvements, which can be incorporated in the next edition.

Series Editor David Townsend Jones
Editor (first edition 1983) Diana Grant
Editor (second edition 1986) Leonie Hamilton
Researcher Catherine Palmer
Art Editor Eric Drewery
Designer Sarah Jackson
Illustrators Illustrated Arts, Coral Mula
Production Androulla Pavlou

Edited and designed by
Mitchell Beazley International Limited
Artists House, 14–15 Manette Street,
London W1V 5LB

© Mitchell Beazley Publishers 1983, 1986
ISBN   0 85533 600 5

Maps in 4-colour by Clyde Surveys Ltd, Maidenhead, England, based on copyrighted material of Rand McNally & Company. New York City subway map and Manhattan bus map based on copyrighted material of New York City Transit Authority.
Typeset by Vantage Photosetting Co. Ltd, Eastleigh, England.
Printed and bound in Hong Kong by Mandarin Offset International Ltd

Contents

How to use this book

The American Express Pocket Guide to New York is an encyclopaedia of travel information, organized in the sections listed on the previous page. There is also a comprehensive **index** (pages 196–203), which is accompanied by a **gazetteer** (pages 204–208) of the most important streets that are shown in the full-colour **maps** at the end of the book.

For easy reference, all major sections (**Sights and places of interest**, **Hotels**, **Restaurants**) and other sections as far as possible are arranged alphabetically. For the organization of the book as a whole, see *Contents*. For individual places that do not have separate entries in *Sights and places of interest*, see the *Index*.

Abbreviations

As far as possible only standard abbreviations have been used. These include days of the week and months, points of the compass (N, S, E and W), street names (Ave., Pl., Sq., St., St.), Saint (St), century (C), and measurements.

Bold type

Bold type is used in running text primarily for emphasis, to draw attention to something of special interest or importance. It is also used in this way to pick out places – shops or minor museums, for instance – that do not have full entries of their own. In such cases it is usually followed in brackets by the address, telephone number, and details of opening times, printed in italics. Similarly, in *Hotels* and *Restaurants*, it is used to identify places mentioned in one entry which have an entry of their own elsewhere in these sections.

Cross-references

A special type has been used for cross-references. Whenever a place or section title is printed in sans serif italics (for example *Audubon Terrace* or *Basic information*) in the text, this indicates that you can turn to the appropriate heading for further information. For added convenience, the running

---

How entries are organized

Citicorp Center ▥ ☆
153 E 53rd St. (Lexington Ave.), NY 10022 ☎ *559–4259.*
Map 5N4 ⊡ *Open 8.00–24.00.*
Posterity has yet to render its verdict on this building. Its distinctive sloping roof line moves it into the Post-Modernist category of skyscraper design, away from the rectangular glass boxes of the Bauhaus school. The roof was intended to house solar energy collectors, a good intention sacrificed to the gods of cost accounting. Quibbles aside, the 1978 building brought life to a dreary block and accommodated into its design the modest but striking **St Peter's Lutheran Church**. Office floors begin at 127ft (39m), clearing the church steeple and providing a public atrium embracing 22 shops and restaurants. The interior plaza is filled with trees and tables, and live music is often laid on by the management. Co-operating were Hugh Stubbins and Emery Roth & Sons – the latter firm was also partly responsible for such looming local monoliths as the
World Trade Center and *Pan Am Building.*

heads, printed at the top corner of the page, always correspond with these cross-references.

Cross-references always refer either to sections of the book – *Basic information*, *Planning*, *Hotels*, *Shopping* – or to individual entries in **Sights and places of interest**, such as *Audubon Terrace* or *Yorkville*. Ordinary italics are used to identify sub-sections. For instance: see *Architecture* in *Culture, history and background*.

Map references

Each page of the colour maps at the end of the book has a page number (2–16) and each map is divided into a grid of squares, which are identified vertically by letters (A, B, C, D, etc.) and horizontally by numbers (1, 2, 3, 4, etc.). A map reference identifies the page and square in which the street or place can be found – thus **Audubon Terrace** is located in the square identified as Map 8F2.

Price categories

Price categories are denoted by the symbols ☐ ☐☐ ☐☐☐ ☐☐☐☐ and ☐☐☐☐☐ which signify cheap, inexpensive, moderately priced, expensive and very expensive, respectively. In the cases of hotels and restaurants these correspond approximately with the following actual prices, which give a guideline at the time of printing. Although actual prices will inevitably increase, in most cases the relative price category – for example expensive or cheap – will be likely to remain more or less the same.

Price categories	Corresponding to approximate prices	
	for **hotels**	for **restaurants**
	double room with bath; single slightly cheaper	*meal for one with service, taxes and house wine*
☐ cheap	under $75	under $10
☐☐ inexpensive	$75–$95	$10–25
☐☐☐ moderate	$95–$110	$20–35
☐☐☐☐ expensive	$110–$150	$30–50
☐☐☐☐☐ very expensive	over $150	over $50

--- Bold blue type for entry headings.

--- Blue italics for address, practical information and symbols, encapsulating standard information and special recommendations. For list of symbols see p6.

--- Black text for description. Bold type used for emphasis.
--- Sans serif italics used for cross-references to other entries.

Entries for hotels, restaurants, shops, etc. follow the same organization, and are usually printed across a narrow measure.
In hotels, symbols indicating special facilities appear at the end of the entry, in black. ---

Howard Johnson's ✿
851 8th Ave. (near 51st St.), NY 10019 ☎ 581–4100 ✆ 147183. Map 4N3 ☐☐☐ ☎ 300 ☐ 300 ☐ ☐ ☐ AE CB ◆ ◎ VISA
Location: w of the midtown Theater District. One of a trio of relatively new midtown motels, it shares the virtues and the liabilities of the others – ready access by car, walking distance from the major theatres and moderate tariffs; but charmless rooms and a bleak neighbourhood.
‡ ☐ ☐ ✇

Key to symbols

- ☎ Telephone
- ⑦ Telex
- ★ Not to be missed
- ☆ Worth a visit
- ✿ Good value (in its class)
- ➡ Car parking
- ⌂ Simple (hotel)
- ⌂ Luxury (hotel)
- ☐ Cheap
- ☐☐ Inexpensive
- ☐☐☐ Moderately priced
- ☐☐☐☐ Expensive
- ☐☐☐☐☐ Very expensive
- ◱ Number of rooms
- ⌸ Rooms with private bathroom
- ▦ Air conditioning
- ⌂ Residential terms available
- AE American Express
- CB Carte Blanche
- ⓓ Diners Club
- ⓜ Master Card
- VISA Visa
- ▱ Secure garage
- ⇒ Own restaurant
- ⌂ Quiet hotel
- ⬍ Lift
- ♿ Facilities for the disabled
- ☐ TV in each room
- ◪ Telephone in each room
- ✷ Dogs not allowed

- ⬳ Outstanding views
- ⇌ Swimming pool
- ✍ Tennis court(s)
- ⛌ Conference facilities
- Ⓡ Restaurant
- ⌣ Simple (restaurant)
- ⌣ Luxury (restaurant)
- ⌷ A la carte available
- ▰ Set (fixed price) menu available
- ⬄ Good for wines
- ⌂ Open-air dining available
- �𝗆 Building of architectural interest
- † Church or cathedral
- ▣ Entrance free
- ▣ Entrance fee payable
- ▣ Entrance expensive
- ⌘ Photography not permitted
- ⟋ Guided tour available
- ⟋ Guided tour compulsory
- ⬛ Cafeteria
- ✳ Special interest for children
- ⵦ Bar
- ● Disco dancing
- ◪ Nightclub
- ♫ Live music
- ◡ Dancing
- ⬃ Revue

6

Before you go

Documents required
Canadians, Mexicans, and British subjects living in Canada, Bermuda, the Bahamas, and the Cayman Islands need only a proof of place of birth and residence to enter the US, and a passport serves this purpose. Other UK citizens must have a passport and visa. Apply to the nearest US embassy or consulate with your passport and one passport-sized photo. You will also need to produce evidence that you intend to return home following your visit. This could be a dated return ticket or a letter from your employer. Your passport must be valid for six months beyond the end of your visit. At present, no vaccinations are required for entry.

To hire a car, you need a passport and a valid driving licence. Some firms ask to see your return ticket. If you are arriving by private car from other states and countries, you should bring the car registration document and certificate of insurance with you.

Travel and medical insurance
Medical care in the US is good to excellent, but very expensive. Medical insurance is therefore strongly recommended. UK travel agents usually have the necessary forms, and tour operators frequently include medical cover in their packages.

Money
The basic unit is, of course, the dollar ($). It is divided into 100 cents (¢). Coins are the penny 1¢, nickel 5¢, dime 10¢, quarter 25¢ and half dollar 50¢. Bank notes (bills) are in denominations of $1, $5, $10, $20, $50 and $100. Some $2 bills are in circulation. Any amount of money can be imported or exported, but when the total exceeds $5,000 you must inform the US Customs Service.

Cash or travellers cheques in foreign currencies are not as easily converted as in Europe. For that reason, purchase travellers cheques in dollars, in advance and do exchange adequate amounts of money upon arrival. Travellers cheques issued by American Express, Bank of America, Barclays, Citibank and Thomas Cook are widely recognized, and MasterCard and Visa have also introduced them. Make sure you read the instructions included with your travellers cheques. It is important to note separately the serial numbers of your cheques and the telephone number to call in case of loss. Specialist travellers cheque companies such as American Express provide extensive local refund facilities through their own offices or agents. Credit cards are honoured by most hotels, airlines, car hire agencies, restaurants and many shops. American Express, Diners Club, MasterCard (Eurocard) and Visa are the most common cards. Carte Blanche has less coverage.

Customs
First clear passport control, collect your baggage, and then move on to a customs official. The combination of three jumbo jets disgorging at once and government concern over smuggling can slow things down to a crawl. It may take no more than 30min from plane to street, but an hour or more is not unusual.

Non-residents can bring in any items clearly intended for personal use, duty-free, with the exceptions noted overleaf.

Basic information

Tobacco goods   Adults over 18 are allowed 200 cigarettes *or* 50 cigars *or* 3lb (1.5kg) tobacco. (Cuban tobacco products are prohibited.)
Alcoholic drinks   1 quart (1 litre) spirits.
Other goods   Non-residents may also import up to $100 in gifts without tax or duty. Returning residents are granted a duty-free allowance of $300.
Families travelling together can pool their allowances to cover joint purchases.

For more information on customs regulations, ask at the nearest US embassy or consulate for a copy of the brochure *US Customs Hints*.

Getting there

Three airports serve the New York area: Kennedy, LaGuardia and Newark. Most international flights arrive at Kennedy, which is about an hour's drive from Manhattan. LaGuardia is the smallest and closest to the centre (30min), and Newark is on the other side of the Hudson River in New Jersey (45min).

Long distance and commuter trains arrive at Pennsylvania Station (7th Ave. and 32nd St.) or Grand Central Terminal (Park Ave. and 42nd St.). Buses from the suburbs and other states use the Port Authority Bus Terminal (8th Ave. and 41st St.).

From the W and S, interstate highways I-78, I-80 and I-95 connect with Manhattan via the George Washington Bridge, the Lincoln Tunnel and the Holland Tunnel. From the N, I-87 (Governor Thomas E. Dewey Thruway) and I-95 (New England Thruway) lead to the Triborough Bridge and other Harlem River and East River crossings. Most of these funnel into the FDR Drive, which parallels the East River. Tolls across the Hudson River are paid when entering the city, but not when leaving.

Climate

May, June, Sept and Oct are the agreeable months. Spring and autumn are short and unpredictable. Extended periods of oppressive humidity and temperatures over 32°C (90°F) characterize July and Aug, while Dec, Jan and Feb feature cold rains, occasional snow, and readings at or near freezing point.

Clothes

A raincoat with a detachable lining is a good investment for an Oct–Apr visit, as are folding rubber boots and a waterproof hat. The winds that accompany rain often turn umbrellas inside-out. Foreigners may be surprised by high levels of central heating and air conditioning. 'Layering' of clothes is appropriate, permitting easy removal or addition of garments.

New Yorkers have grown less formal in dress in recent years. Men feel most comfortable with a jacket at medium-priced and luxury restaurants, but a tie is obligatory at relatively few establishments. Denim clothing is sometimes barred by smarter discos and clubs.

Poste restante

A letter marked 'General Delivery' c/o any US post office should be held until collected. Certain commercial firms also provide a poste restante service – available to customers only.
American Express   150 E 42nd St., New York, NY 10017
Central Post Office   42 8th Ave., New York, NY 10001
Thomas Cook   18 E 48th St., New York, NY 10017

Getting around

From the airport to the city
Express buses depart Kennedy and LaGuardia every
20–30min between early morning and midnight, less
frequently at other times. They stop at Grand Central
Terminal. Fares from Kennedy and LaGuardia are similar.
Neither is expensive. Some hotels provide transportation from
the airports if advance arrangements are made.

Similar service is provided from Newark to the Port
Authority Bus Terminal. Abbey buses run directly from
Newark to selected Manhattan hotels every 30min between
7.00–24.00. Major hotels between 33rd and 63rd St. are
served.

Taxis from Kennedy and LaGuardia to destinations within
the city are metered. The average fare from Kennedy is about
50% more than from LaGuardia. During rush hours the cost
can double. From Newark, the fare is twice the meter toll.
Bridge and tunnel tolls are extra.

Helicopters fly between the three airports and between
Kennedy and the heliport at 34th St. and the East River.

Private limousines often cost little more than taxis, and cars
can be hired at airports (see *Other transport p11*).

Public transport
Undergrounds ('subways') and buses are dirty, noisy, defaced
by graffiti and subject to unexplained delays. But a single fare
lets you journey for as far as you like along any one line.
Subways operate 24hr a day, with reduced frequency
between 24.00–6.00. Peak rush hours are 8.00–9.00 and
17.00–18.00.

For information on subways and buses ☎330–1234.

Subways
Buy a token at the booth near the entrance and insert it in the
turnstile. Free transfers can be made at 25 intersections with
other lines. Getting on the right train in the right direction can
be complicated. First note whether you must go uptown,
downtown or crosstown, and whether your final station is a
local or express stop (*Map **14–15***). Insert token in turnstile.
Follow directional signs to correct platform. Once there, look
for signs to indicate whether express and local trains stop on
same or opposite sides of platform.

Buses
Upon boarding, deposit subway token or equivalent in coins in
box next to driver. He cannot give change, but sells 'Add-a-
ride' transfers to intersecting lines. Routes roughly follow the
major N–S avenues (*Map **16***). E–W crosstown routes serve as
connections between subway lines, which are primarily N–S.

Taxis
Licensed taxis are painted yellow and, in most cases, have
electronic digital meters. Drivers are required to take
passengers to any destination in the city. Within the five
boroughs, fares are standard for the first ninth of a mile, with
supplements for each additional ninth. There is also a surcharge
between 20.00–6.00 for some cabs during the week and all day
Sun. Bridge and tunnel tolls extra. Tip 20% of total fare.
For lost articles ☎825–0416.

Basic information

Getting around by car

Most cross streets and many avenues are alternately one-way. Unlike the rest of the state, right turns are not permitted at red traffic lights unless specifically stated. Speeds are sign-posted, usually 35mph or less. Do not exceed the time limit in a metered parking space, or your car will probably be towed away to a pound.

Hiring a car

A credit card can be presented in lieu of a deposit, in which case the driver may be as young as 18. Otherwise, a cash deposit is required, and the driver must be over 21. Rent-it-here-leave-it-there, weekend and unlimited mileage packages are available. Comprehensive insurance is optional, but recommended. If you are arriving by private car from other states and countries, check with your insurance company about short-term extra cover.

Getting around on foot

The best way to cover short distances in Manhattan is on foot. Above 14th St., it is difficult to lose your way. Streets are laid out in a straight grid. Named and numbered avenues run N–S, from 1st Ave. in the E to 11th Ave. in the W. Cross streets run northward from 14th in the S to 225th in the N. 5th Ave. is the dividing line between E and W. Building numbers mount from one to the mid-hundreds to the E, and in the same way to the W. On the avenues, numbers increase as they proceed N. Because the avenues and Broadway are so long, the nearest cross street is often mentioned when asking for a main street address. Ave. of the Americas is always spoken of as 6th Ave., although the grander name is still used for postal addresses.

The Manhattan grid is not perfect, of course. Broadway cuts diagonally across the island from Park Ave. and 14th St. to the W of Central Park. Below 14th St., in the older part of the city, the grid goes awry. Down there a map is essential.

Railway services

Both long distance and commuter trains arrive at Grand Central Terminal (Park Ave. and 42nd St.) and Pennsylvania Station (7th Ave. and 32nd St.). The Harlem, Hudson and New Haven commuter lines feed into Grand Central from up to 100 miles N, while the Long Island and New Jersey commuter lines use Penn Station. Amtrak trains from Canada, Boston, Chicago, Washington and Florida use both terminals.

Amtrak ☎736–3967 (Metroliners – US equivalent of Intercity), ☎736–4545 (all others)
Metro North (commuter) ☎532–4900 (Westchester County and Connecticut)

Domestic airlines

Domestic flights leave all three airports. The Eastern Airlines shuttle to Washington and Boston has a separate terminal at LaGuardia. This service has hourly flights by day and early evening. New York Air runs a similar shuttle, with low fares. PEOPLExpress operates cheap flights from Newark to the East Coast and Mid-West.

Air Canada 600 Madison Ave. ☎935–4141
American 405 Lexington Ave. ☎557–1234
Braniff 135 E 42nd St. ☎949–0750
Delta 1 Pennsylvania Plaza ☎868–2300

Eastern   10 Rockefeller Plaza ☎397–4610
New York Air   LaGuardia Airport ☎565–1100
Northwest   537 5th Ave. ☎594–0320
Pan Am   200 Park Ave. ☎880–1234
PEOPLExpress   Newark Airport ☎772–0344
Piedmont   1290 Ave. of the Americas ☎765–7088
Republic   630 5th Ave. ☎489–0784
TWA   2 Pennsylvania Plaza ☎695–6000
United   1221 Ave. of the Americas ☎764–2800
US Air   535 5th Ave. ☎736–3200

Ferry services
America's favourite boat ride – the Staten Island Ferry – is still
the biggest bargain in town, serving up spectacular views and
bracing breezes for a minimal sum. It departs from the
Whitehall St. pier at downtown Battery Park every 20–30min,
24hr, seven days a week. Check to see whether ferries are
running to Ellis Island during its renovation.

Other transport
Hourly rates for private limousines are high but there are
special airport and theatre-dinner flat rates that can total little
more than taxi fares. Among the reputable firms:
Alex Limousines   500 E 77th St. ☎535–5553
Cooper Rolls Royce   132 Perry St. ☎929–0094
Dav-El   219 W 77th St. ☎580–6500
London Towncars   40–14 23rd St. (Long Island City)
☎988–9700
Manhattan Limousine   13–05 43rd Ave. (Long Island City)
☎786–0800
Villela Limousine   30 E 40th St. ☎225–5227

Hire a rowing boat or bicycle at the 72nd St. boathouse in
Central Park. Bicycles and mopeds can be hired from the
following firms:
Metro Bicycles   1311 Lexington Ave. (88th St.) ☎427–4450
6th Ave. Bicycles   546 Ave. of the Americas (15th St.)
☎255–5100
Stuyvesant Bicycle   349 W 14th St. ☎254–5200
West Side Bicycle   231 W 96th St. ☎663–7531
Rides in horse-drawn hansom cabs begin from near the 5th Ave.
and 59th St. corner of Central Park, day or night. Most rides
take 30min. Establish the rate in advance.

On-the-spot information

Public holidays
Jan 1; Martin Luther King Day, third Mon in Jan; President's
Day, a three-day weekend in mid-Feb; Memorial Day,
a three-day weekend at the end of May; Independence Day,
July 4; Labor Day, first Mon in Sept; Columbus Day, second
Mon in Oct; Election Day, first Tues in Nov; Veterans Day,
Nov 11; Thanksgiving, last Thurs in Nov; Dec 25.
    Shops, schools, post offices and most public services are
usually closed on these days, although some shops stay open on
the three-day weekends.

Basic information

Time zones

New York is in the US Eastern Time Zone, 5hr behind GMT in winter, 4hr behind GMT from last Sun in Apr to last Sun in Oct during Daylight Saving. Because British Summer Time operates almost concurrently with Daylight Saving, the local time difference is nearly always 5hr.

Banks and currency exchange

Customary business hours for banks are 9.00–15.00, Mon–Fri, but some are open until 16.00, or Thurs evenings, or Sat mornings. Most banks take hours to exchange foreign currencies. For this type of transaction, try one of Citibank's currency exchange offices, Bank Leumi Trust, or Deak-Perera. Otherwise, travel services such as American Express and Thomas Cook have exchange desks.

Shopping hours

Department stores and clothes and sports equipment shops usually open between 9.00–10.00 and close at 18.00. Late night shopping is on Thurs, usually until 20.00 or 21.00. Although many fast-food stands, coffee shops and delicatessens open by 8.00 and don't close until 20.00 or later, more formal restaurants confine themselves to 12.00–15.00 and 18.00–23.00, with slight variations. Bars and discos do not have to close until 4.00. In Greenwich Village and SoHo, boutiques and galleries may not get going until 12.00.

Rush hours

Driving or using public transport between 8.00–9.00 and 17.00–18.00 could be considered an exercise in masochism, and the situation is almost as bad for an hour before and after these times. Avoiding lunch between 12.00 and 14.00 is canny, as is making dinner reservations before 19.30 or after 21.00.

Post and telephone services

Post offices are open 8.00–17.00 Mon–Fri, 8.00–12.00 Sat. The main post office at 8th Ave. and 33rd St. is open 24hr.

Telephones are everywhere. Try to use those in shops or public buildings – the ones installed on street corners are often vandalized. Lift the receiver, wait for the dialling tone, and deposit the amount indicated. Manhattan and The Bronx are in area code 212, so merely dial or push-button any local seven-digit number. When calling an out-of-town number or Brooklyn, Queens or Staten Island, dial 1, then the area code, and finally the seven-digit number. ITT is the main service for international telegrams: ☎797–3311.

Public lavatories

These are to be avoided at all times in subway stations. Those in museums and public buildings are usually satisfactory. In extremis, duck into the nearest hotel. Ask for the 'restroom', 'men's room', 'ladies' room' or 'bathroom'.

Electric current

Current is 110–120V, 60 cycles AC. All lamps and small household appliances use standard two-pronged plugs.

Laws and regulations

The selling of drugs is a far more serious offence than possession of small amounts. Laws on jaywalking and littering are rarely enforced. But dog owners are expected to pick up and discard pet droppings. Smoking is not permitted in subways, on buses, in lifts, or in most shops and theatres. Hitch-hiking is illegal.

Customs and etiquette
New Yorkers are demonstrative when meeting friends and acquaintances. In some circles, kissing on one or both cheeks is thought appropriate on second meeting. Use of first names upon introduction or shortly afterwards is common.

Tipping
In restaurants, tip the waiter at least 15% of the bill before tax. An easy way to work out the minimum is to double the 8% tax. Bellmen are given a large coin or a small note for each bag carried, depending on size and distance. Doormen get the same for hailing a taxi. Barmen, barbers, hairdressers and beauticians are normally given 15%. Lavatory attendants get a few coins. When there is no stated fee for leaving coats and parcels, give much the same per item. Tour guides expect a note or two.

Disabled travellers
Many restrooms provide special facilities for the disabled and certain buses are equipped with motorized platforms. Most hotels provide specially converted rooms. Subways are nearly impossible to negotiate without help, however. Guide dogs are permitted everywhere.

Local publications
Arts and leisure sections appear on Fri and Sun in *The New York Times* and in the weekly magazines *New York* and *The New Yorker*. They provide reviews and listings of current plays, concerts, films, exhibitions, ballets and operas. *The Village Voice* weekly newspaper emphasizes off-beat arts.

Addresses and telephone numbers
Tourist information
American Express Travel Service   150 E 42nd St. ☎323–2000 is a valuable source of information for any traveller in need of help, advice or emergency services.
NY Convention and Visitors Bureau   2 Columbus Circle
☎397–8222
Times Square Information Center   Broadway (42nd St.)
☎221–9869

Main post offices
8th Ave. (33rd St.)
Lexington Ave. (45th St.)

Telephone services
Daily events ☎976–2323
Free daily cultural events ☎755–4100
Time ☎976–1616

Consulates
Australia   636 5th Ave. ☎245–4000
Austria   31 E 69th St. ☎737–6400
Belgium   50 Rockefeller Plaza ☎586–5110
Canada   1251 Ave. of the Americas ☎581–2280
Denmark   280 Park Ave. ☎697–5101
Finland   540 Madison Ave. ☎832–6550
France   934 5th Ave. ☎535–0100
Germany (West)   410 Park Ave. ☎752–5020
Greece   69 E 79th St. ☎988–5500
Ireland (Eire)   580 5th Ave. ☎245–1010
Italy   690 Park Ave. ☎737–9100

Basic information

Japan   280 Park Ave. ☎986–1600
Netherlands   1 Rockefeller Plaza ☎246–1429
New Zealand   630 5th Ave. ☎586–0060
Norway   825 3rd Ave. ☎421–7333
South Africa   425 Park Ave. ☎838–1700
Spain   150 E 58th St. ☎355–4090
Sweden   825 3rd Ave. ☎751–5900
Switzerland   444 Madison Ave. ☎758–2560
United Kingdom   845 3rd Ave. ☎752–8400

Tour operators

Circle Line   Pier 83, end of W 43rd St. ☎563–3200.
(Three-hour boat cruises around Manhattan, Apr–Nov)
Crossroads Sightseeing   900 8th Ave. (47th St.) ☎581–2828
Gray Line   900 8th Ave. (54th St.) ☎397–2600
Greenwich Village Walking Tours   ☎226–1426
Island Helicopter   Heliport at end of E 34th St. ☎895–5374
Manhattan Sightseeing Bus Tours   150 W 49th St. ☎245–6641
New York Big Apple Tours   162 W 56th St. ☎582–6339
Penny Sightseeing Company   303 W 42nd St. ☎247–2860
ShortLine   166 W 46th St. ☎354–5122

Major places of worship

Baptist   Calvary Baptist Church, 123 W 57th St.
Catholic   St Patrick's Cathedral, 5th Ave. (51st St.)
Episcopal   St Thomas' Church, 1 W 53rd St. (Entrance on 5th Ave.)
Jewish   Temple Emanu-El, 5th Ave. (65th St.)
Lutheran   Holy Trinity, Central Park West (65th St.)
Methodist   Lexington United Methodist Church, 150 E 62nd St.
Presbyterian   Presbyterian Church, 5th Ave. (55th St.)

Conversion tables

Length

cm	0		5		10		15		20		25		30
in	0	1	2	3	4	5	6	7	8	9	10	11	12

metres	0		0.5		1		1.5		2
ft/yd	0	1ft	2ft	3ft(1yd)				2yd

Distance

km	0	1	2	3	4	5	6	7	8	9	10	11	12	13	14	15	16
miles	0	1		2		3		4		5		6		7	8		9	10

Weight

			(¼kg)		(½kg)		(¾kg)		(1kg)
grammes	0	100	200	300	400	500	600	700	800	900	1,000
ounces	0	4 (¼lb)	8 (½lb)	12 (¾lb)	16 (1lb)	20	24 (1½lb)	28	32 (2lb)

Fluid measures

litres	0	1	2	3	4	5	litres	0	5	10		20		30
imp.pints	0	1	2	3	4	5	6	7	8	imp. gallons	0	1	2	3	4	5	6
US pints	0	1	2	3	4	5	6	7	8	US gallons	0	1	2	3	4	5	6	7

Temperature chart

°C	−15	−10	−5	0	5	10	15	20	25	30	35	36.9 40		100
°F	0	10	20	30 32	40	50	60	70	80	90	98.4 105		212

Emergency information

Emergency services

Police
Ambulance } ☎911 (10¢ needed from a call box)
Fire

Hospitals with casualty departments

Ambulances called on 911 carry the patient to the nearest municipal hospital. Private hospitals are generally preferable, however, so if possible take a taxi to one of these: *Financial District*, Beekman Downtown Hosp., 170 William St. ☎233–5300. *Greenwich Village*, St. Vincent's Hosp., 7th Ave. (11th St.) ☎790–7000. *Lower East Side*, Bellevue Hosp., 1st Ave. (29th St.) ☎561–4141. *Midtown East*, New York University Med. Center, 1st Ave. (30th St.) ☎340–1999. *Midtown West*, Roosevelt Hosp., 9th Ave. (58th St.) ☎554–7000. *Upper East Side*, New York Hosp., York Ave. (70th St.) ☎472–5454. *Upper East Side and East Harlem*, Flower-Fifth Ave. Hosp., 5th Ave. (103rd St.) ☎860–8000. *West Harlem*, Columbia Presbyterian Med. Center, 622 W 168th St. ☎694–2500.

Other emergencies

Doctors Emergency Service   ☎328–1000
Dentists Emergency Service   ☎679–3966 (9.00–20.00)
                                 ☎679–4172 (20.00–9.00)

Late-night chemists (pharmacies)

Kaufman   557 Lexington Ave. (50th St.) ☎755–2266
Manhattan Garden   1632 Broadway (W 50th St.)
☎265–3546

Help lines

Crime Victim Hotline   ☎577–7777
Drug problems   ☎488–4274
Help Line (personal counselling)   ☎481–1070
Rape Help Line   ☎233–3000
Traveller's Aid Society   ☎679–0200

Motoring accidents

— Call the police immediately.
— If car is hired, call number in rental agreement.
— Do not admit liability or incriminate yourself.
— Ask witnesses to stay and give statements.
— Exchange names, addresses, car details, insurance
   companies and three-digit insurance company codes.
— Remain to give your statement to the police.

Car breakdowns

Call one of the following from nearest telephone.
— Number indicated in car rental agreement.
— Local office of AAA (if you are a member).
— Nearest garage or towing service.

Lost passport

Contact the police and your consulate (see p13/14), where you will be issued with emergency travel documents.

Lost travellers cheques

Notify the local police immediately, then follow the instructions provided with your travellers cheques, or contact the issuing company's nearest office. Contact your consulate or American Express if you are stranded with no money.

Introduction

New York is not America. A world city – *the* world city, by any reasonable measure – it cannot be contained within geopolitical boundaries. Every language is spoken in New York, every cuisine prepared, every nation and race represented, every dream conjured, every depredation performed. If an idea, an object, a hope, a taste, a scent, a sin cannot be found here, the likely conclusion is that it does not exist. The only emotion New York cannot arouse is indifference. No other place created by man provokes such adoration and abhorrence, often at the same time, in the same individual. Few words applied to this city can be dismissed as hyperbole. It is an entity of exhilarating, numbing, horrifying, glorious excess.

Ethnic diversity

Although among the greatest of cities, it can no longer claim to be the largest. New York covers nearly 300 square miles and has a population of over 7,000,000 people. A recent census recorded 4,293,695 whites, 1,784,124 blacks, 11,824 Native Americans, 231,505 Asians, and an astonishing 749,882 regarded as racially unclassifiable.

The largest ethnic minority is probably that of Hispanic origin, but there is no ethnic majority. People of Italian, Irish and East European origins are present in enormously influential numbers. Germans and other North Europeans were among the earliest immigrants and were quickly assimilated. Puerto Ricans and others of Caribbean background continue as largely unified groups, as do the Chinese. Refugees from Southeast Asia, Haiti, Central America, Greece and the Indian subcontinent are becoming increasingly apparent.

City of villages

Water-girt New York is comprised of five distinct divisions called boroughs, only one of which – The Bronx – is situated on the North American continent. The island of Manhattan is, of course, the central borough. Brooklyn (largest in population) and Queens (largest in area) take up the western tip of Long Island, which itself stretches 125 miles into the Atlantic. Staten Island, to the S of its sisters, snuggles up to New Jersey.

When approached from the E through the outlying industrial dross, the famous Manhattan skyline appears somehow diminutive. At the southern tip of the island, the concrete spires and glass slabs of the Financial District are dominated by the twin pillars of the World Trade Center. The profile then dips to the lower heights of converted warehouses ('loft' buildings) and tenements, lifting gradually once more to midtown and the peak of the instantly recognizable Empire State Building. After another two miles, the skyline dips again, nearly meeting the rising ground that continues for another six miles, terminating at the lip of the inky tidal course known as the Spuyten Duyvil.

Once you plunge into the street canyons, warring stimuli battle for attention: the noise of the traffic seems trapped between the high walls of buildings. From time to time, clouds of steam billow from manholes as if from an inferno just below. Rivers of people press forward on apparently urgent tasks. Traffic jerks and clogs along congested arteries. All the senses are staggered, and continue to be bombarded even when the newcomer has begun to adapt to the pace.

But there are quiet places, too. Side streets end in shaded

cul-de-sacs, over 50 museums muffle the clamour beyond their thick walls, and there are nearly 37,000 acres of parks. The most important of these is Central Park, in the heart of Manhattan. Two Monacos could be contained within its borders, with room left over for a chunk of Nice.

A brief history

The broad protected harbour was first discovered in 1524, but permanent settlement did not take place until a century later. The English took New Amsterdam from the Dutch in 1664, and the city was renamed New York. Resentment against British rule culminated in the War of Independence in 1775 and New York was for a time the capital of the infant nation.

The population was then slightly over 30,000. It multiplied dramatically with the mass immigrations of the 19thC, and those who prospered moved uptown. In the 40 years following the Civil War (1861–65), Central Park was finished and the first skyscrapers erected. In 1898, the four outer boroughs were annexed to Manhattan, instantly fashioning the largest city in the world. The population was now over 3 million.

Despite the Wall Street Crash of 1929, construction of the Empire State Building began. Twenty years later, the city's population reached 8 million, and the United Nations moved into its new headquarters on the East River. The city was at its zenith – the capital of the world, untouched by war.

Since then there has been a gradual decline, evidenced by fiscal crises, deteriorating public services, accelerating crime rates and loss of industry and workers. But signs of recovery are visible. Tourism continues to grow, as Americans and foreigners alike rediscover New York. And while the demise of Broadway has been proclaimed with tedious regularity since the Depression and The Talkies, it continues to flourish. New York remains the centre for those intent on careers in publishing, finance, advertising, ballet, opera and the visual arts.

Safety first

To avoid a visit to New York on the basis of out-of-proportion stories of crime is akin to denying oneself Naples because of rubbish in the streets. Still, prudence is in order. After dark, for example, women and older people are wise to travel in groups or with escorts. Although the odds are that a nightly walk across the nearest park or along deserted streets would be uneventful, there is no reason to tempt fate. Expensive-looking jewellery and clothing should be avoided when travelling by foot. Grip handbags firmly and keep wallets in a safe place. When in the subways at night, ride in the crowded central cars.

New Yorkers

The reputation New Yorkers have earned for rudeness and pugnacity is not without foundation. Yet beneath their often brusque exterior lies an enviable openness to new experiences and relationships. There is no fad, art form, lifestyle or ideology that they will not sample, or at least tolerate. Out of working hours – and, in a 24hr city, that means any time – they can be seen jogging, cycling, flipping Frisbees, roller- or ice-skating, dancing in nightclubs, demonstrating at the UN, taking the sun on Hudson piers or watching it set from Riverside Park. Of all the surprises of a first visit to this city, one of the most agreeable can be the New Yorkers themselves.

Time chart

1524 Italian explorer Giovanni da Verrazano discovered New York Bay while searching for a NW passage.

1609 Henry Hudson sailed his *Half Moon* up the river that was eventually given his name.

1623 New Netherland became a province of the Dutch West India Company and the cluster of huts at the S tip of Manhattan was called New Amsterdam.

1626 Provincial Director-General Peter Minuit bought the island from the Algonquin Indians.

1643 Population grew to about 500 people speaking 18 different languages. During the tenure of Governor Peter Stuyvesant, settlements were established in the areas eventually known as The Bronx, Queens, Brooklyn and Staten Island.

1664 The Duke of York sent a fleet into the harbour. Abandoned by the burgomasters who chafed under his authoritarian rule, Stuyvesant surrendered the city to the English. It was renamed New York.

1674 After extended hostilities between the English and Dutch – and one brief reoccupation by the Dutch – the city and province were ceded by treaty to the English.

1689 A German merchant, Jacob Leisler, led a revolt against oligarchic trade monopolies when he learned of the overthrow of James II. He was hanged for treason.

1712 Slaves now constituted a substantial segment of the population. Despite ordinances denying them weapons and the right of assembly, a number of blacks set fire to a building near Maiden Lane and killed nine whites who attempted to stop the blaze. When soldiers arrived, six of the blacks committed suicide; 21 others were captured and executed.

1725 The New York *Gazette* was founded.

1734 John Peter Zenger, publisher of the *New York Weekly Journal*, was charged with libel of the Government. He was acquitted in the first test of the principle of freedom of the press in the colonies.

1754 Population now 16,000. King's College founded.
–63 Benjamin Franklin proposed union of the colonies for common defence during the French and Indian War, but was rejected. A force led by George Washington was defeated by the French at Fort Necessity in Pennsylvania. The conflict, part of the worldwide Seven Years War, ended with the Treaty of Paris. English sovereignty over most of explored North America was thereby conceded.

1764 Colonial grumbling over British rule escalated into
–70 sporadic demonstrations and protests with the passage of the punitive Sugar, Stamp, and Colonial Currency Acts. The Quartering Act permitted British troops to requisition private dwellings and inns, their rent to be paid by the colonies. At the Stamp Act Congress held in Manhattan, delegates of nine colonies passed a Declaration of Rights and Liberties. Skirmishes between soldiers and the insurrectionist Sons of Liberty culminated in January 1770 in the killing of a colonial and the wounding of several others. The Boston Massacre, in which British troops fired upon taunting protesters, occurred seven weeks later.

1775 –83	The American Revolution. The Continental Congress appointed Washington Commander-in-Chief and, on July 4, 1776, adopted the Declaration of Independence. After early battles ranging from Manhattan to Long Island, most of which he lost, Washington withdrew. New York was occupied by the British for the remainder of the War. With the Treaty of Versailles in September 1783, the British troops left the city.
1789	Washington was sworn in as first President at Federal Hall in New York, the first capital of the Federal Government.
1790	An official census recorded the population at 33,000.
1807 –09	Robert Fulton made a round trip from New York to Albany in his steamboat *Clermont*. In reaction to British and French seizure of American ships at sea, Congress prohibited export of most goods. This Act did more harm to New York and New England agriculture and commerce than to the other side, and was repealed.
1812	War declared against Britain. New York blockaded.
1814	Peace treaty signed at Ghent.
1825	Erie Canal opened, enhancing New York's role as a port.
1832	New York and Harlem railway completed.
1830 –60	The influx of immigrants – largely German and Irish – rose to flood proportions. Epidemics of yellow fever and cholera ensued, exacerbated by poor water supplies, insanitary conditions and the poverty of most of the newcomers. Yet on the eve of the Civil War, the population neared 750,000.
1861 –65	Civil War, caused by growing differences between northern and southern states, notably the slavery issue. New York on the side of the Union (N) against the Confederates (S).
1863	Draft Riots, following a conscription law that permitted the rich to buy deferment. New Yorkers set fire to buildings and looted shops and homes. Over 1,000 died.
1868 –98	The first waves of Italian and East European immigrants arrived, many of them working on the new elevated railway, Brooklyn Bridge and early skyscrapers. The Statue of Liberty, a Franco-American project, was inaugurated in 1886. At the culmination of a period of annexation and expansion, New York assumed its present boundaries. There were now more than 3 million inhabitants.
1900 –29	Immigration continued unabated, despite growing pressure for its curtailment. The railway system was extended, now underground as well as above. The decade after World War I brought Prohibition, women's suffrage, economic prosperity, and a Federal Act cutting immigration (1924).
1929 –39	The Wall Street Crash and the start of the Great Depression. The worst of the Depression was over by 1936, but it did not end until 1939 when the country began to prepare for war.
1941 –45	Apart from rationing, blackouts and shortages, New York was not greatly affected by World War II. It grew more prosperous, as did the rest of the country.
1948	Idlewild Airport opened in Queens (renamed Kennedy in 1963).
1952	United Nations headquarters complex opened.
1973	World Trade Center opened.

Architecture

Were the existing 18thC structures of New York grouped together, they would constitute a sizeable and quite handsome village. As it is, they are scattered throughout the city, largely neglected survivors of the Great Fires of 1776 and 1835. Most are Georgian Colonial or Federal, corresponding to the style prevalent in England during the successive reigns of the four Georges.

Although Georgian was itself imitative of Classical Greco-Roman themes, the first half of the 19thC saw a heightened enthusiasm for Greek and Gothic Revival. These overlapping modes dominated from 1830–55, manifest in the Athenian 'temple' that is the Federal Hall National Memorial (1842), and that homage to medieval workmanship, Trinity Church (1846). In the increasingly popular terraced town houses, Greek Revival was largely confined to decorative facades.

After the Civil War, an unabashed exuberance for virtually all European styles took hold. Motifs ranging from Venetian Renaissance to French Second Empire to Tudor to

◄ **St Paul's Chapel (1766)** The only Colonial church left in New York. Interior is noted for its fluted Corinthian columns and Palladian window.

Morris-Jumel Mansion (1768) Georgian Colonial, remodelled in Federal style in 1810. Tuscan-columned portico and wooden quoins are typical Federal features.

Trinity Church (1846) A landmark at the end of Wall Street, Richard Upjohn's church is the city's best known example of Gothic Revivalism.

Federal Hall National Memorial (1842) This Neo-Greek temple is perhaps the purest example of Greek Revival architecture in New York.

Romanesque were used, not infrequently all on the same building. The result was often called 'Kitchen Sink', for obvious reasons. The fashionable architectural firm of the time was McKim, Mead and White, whose fondness for the Italian Renaissance is best seen in the Villard Houses (1886).

Technology was prompting fresh looks at old design assumptions. The Brooklyn Bridge (1883) employed Gothic granite towers, but also spidery cables of woven steel. The invention of the hydraulic elevator and the presence of a sturdy bedrock known as 'Manhattan schist' made skyscrapers possible. By 1900, commercial buildings of 20 floors and higher were routine.

Terraced houses persisted as the favoured residential mode, however, now embellished with Italianate carving around arched doors and pediments. Red sandstone, widely used as a facing material, gave this style the name of brownstone. Blocks of brownstone terraces remain throughout Manhattan and Brooklyn, lending a Parisian flavour to their neighbourhoods. Luxury high-rise apartments made their appearance with the Chelsea and the Dakota in 1884, but that innovation was

Washington Square North (c. 1832) Ionic porticos reflect the mid-19thC rage for Greek Revivalism.

Villard Houses (1886) Now incorporated into the Palace Hotel, a complex of six houses inspired by the Palazzo della Cancelleria in Rome.

Flatiron Building (1902) The revolutionary steel frame is disguised by rusticated stone facades.

Metropolitan Museum of Art (1902) Rich, Neo-Classical decoration typical of the Beaux Arts movement.

resisted by the wealthy for decades. The turn of the century brought a flirtation with the voluptuous Beaux Arts style and related neo-chateau fancies, best seen in the Metropolitan Museum of Art (1902).

Meanwhile commercial architecture was entering the Modernist phase with the form-follows-function theories of Louis Sullivan. His work in Chicago proved to his successors that tall structures need not simulate stacked neo-Georgian or Romanesque tiers. The next major influence was Art Deco, applied to spectacular effect in the steel-arched tower of the Chrysler Building (1930). With the Empire State Building (1931) and RCA Building (1932), the Chrysler represents the apogee of the first phase of the skyscraper phenomenon.

Further developments were delayed until economic recovery in the late 1940s. A technique was developed in which walls of glass without a weight-bearing function were literally hung on the sides of steel skeletons. Among the first and most enduring realizations of this International Style were Lever House (1952) and the Seagram Building (1958).

More recently, sculptural planes and masses have shaped both small and large buildings, such as the Whitney Museum (1966) and the Waterside Houses (1974). The latest, Post-Modernist trend shows a revival in decorative interest.

Chrysler Building (1930) The world's tallest building until overtaken by the Empire State in 1931.

Whitney Museum (1966) A return to sculptural solidity.

Lever House (1952) One of the earliest glass-and-steel curtain wall constructions.

AT & T Building (1978–82) The Chippendale cornice shows a Post-Modernist trend. ▶

The arts in New York

Creativity found a foothold as soon as the city emerged from the early settlement period. The first theatre opened its doors on Maiden Lane in 1732, to be followed by dozens more. But New York was chiefly a commercial centre, and artists who achieved prominence – painters Benjamin West and John Singleton Copley, for example – went off to Europe, setting a pattern that was to prevail for nearly two centuries.

Impressionism and the other 'isms' that reverberated around Europe in the later 19thC had little influence across the Atlantic. The aesthetic ferment did not spill over to the United States until the New York Armory Show of 1913, when Duchamp's *Nude Descending a Staircase* scandalized public opinion. By then, however, most of the men who were to form the first generation of post-World War II Radical Abstractionists were already alive. Encouraged by such artist-teachers as Hans Hofmann, who fled the gathering European tragedy in the 1930s, these artists champed under the restraints of the Depression and War, exploding after 1945 into what seemed to be a movement already mature at the instant of birth.

The controlled 'splash-and-dribble' canvasses of Jackson Pollock were no less shocking than the earlier Cubist fantasies which now seemed sedate by comparison. Pollock died young, but compatriots Robert Motherwell, Clyfford Still, Mark Rothko, Willem de Kooning, Philip Guston, James Brooks, Jack Tworkov, Franz Kline and Sam Francis all contributed to the importance of the movement. All were associated with the city, and together they became known as the 'New York School'. They gathered in the same bars, summered on Long Island, and inspired a new row of galleries along E 10th St. It was a zesty era, enhanced not inhibited by its coexistence with the conformist Eisenhower-McCarthy period.

Art, like life, should be free, since both are experimental.
George Santayana

New York, which had long regarded itself as an oasis on the edge of a cultural wasteland, was the natural wellspring of what proved to be a surge to international pre-eminence in the arts. As the only major city to emerge unscathed from the global conflict, it could indulge its artists with almost unlimited support. The Guggenheim Museum, Frank Lloyd Wright's only commission in the city, was intended to serve as a repository for modern painting and sculpture. It was completed in 1959. The Lincoln Center for the Performing Arts was conceived in 1955 to house the Metropolitan Opera, the Philharmonic Orchestra, the City Opera and Ballet companies, a repertory theatre, a concert hall for small classical and popular groups, and the Juilliard School for actors, musicians and dancers. The five principal buildings were finished between 1962 and 1966. Additions to the Metropolitan Museum and the Museum of Modern Art, and the erection of a new home for the Whitney, maintained the pace.

During the last decade, creative endeavour in the visual arts has been highly experimental: Conceptual, Minimal, Neo-Constructivist, Optical – all executed in wildly mixed media: neon, ferro-concrete, forged metal, shaped canvas, boxes and heaps of earth ... The descendants of Pollock are as unrestrained and every bit as provocative.

Culture, history and background

Guide to the galleries

In this vibrant and ever-changing playground of creativity, gallery-hopping is not surprisingly a cherished pastime among culture-conscious New Yorkers. Although the galleries are in the business of selling works of art, browsers are welcome. All galleries are open Tues–Sat, a few on Mon as well, usually from 10.00–17.00 or 18.00. Summer is the slow season, with various closing periods, often July or Aug, or both. The galleries cluster in three distinct areas, 57th St., Madison Ave. and SoHo, and each of these can be explored easily on foot. A walking tour is, in fact, the most practical way to get to know them.

57th St.

Start at Park Ave. and walk w on the s side of 57th St.

Brooks Jackson Gallery Iolas
52 E 57th St. ☎ *755–6778*
Modern European and American paintings and sculpture.

Washburn Gallery
42 E 57th St. ☎ *753–0546*
Eclectic selection of American photographs, paintings, prints, drawings and sculpture of the last 100yr.

Multiples/Marian Goodman Gallery
38 E 57th St. ☎ *755–3520*
Reproductions and unusual contemporary pieces.

Gruenebaum Gallery
38 E 57th St. ☎ *838–8245*
Sculptures, collages, paintings, mostly by living Americans.

Pace Gallery
32 E 57th St. ☎ *421–3292*
Influential representative of luminaries Louise Nevelson, Jim Dine, Piet Mondrian. Non-objective to Photo Realist.

Dorsky Galleries
4 W 57th St. ☎ *489–1020*
Contemporary paintings, graphics, drawings, sculptures.

Gallery Denise Rene
6 W 57th St. ☎ *765–1330*
Closely associated with colourist Constructivist Victor Vasarely. Other Europeans and Latin Americans of that inclination.

Sidney Janis Gallery
6 W 57th St. ☎ *586–0110*
Superstars of American Abstract Expressionism, as well as their Modernist European forefathers.

Brooke Alexander
20 W 57th St. ☎ *757–3721*
American painters since 1960.

Kornblee Gallery
20 W 57th St. ☎ *586–1178*
Living American and British painters and sculptors.

Betty Parsons Gallery
24 W 57th St. ☎ *247–7480*
Potent force in cause of abstract art, international in scope.

Alonzo Gallery
30 W 57th St. ☎ *586–2500*
Contemporary American paintings, sculptures, drawings.

Kennedy Galleries
40 W 57th St. ☎ *541–9600*
American graphics and figurative paintings of last three centuries.

Marlborough Gallery
40 W 57th St. ☎ *541–4900*
19th and 20thC works of many styles and media.

Terry Dintenfass
50 W 57th St. ☎ *581–2268*
Recent representational work.

Allan Frumkin Gallery
50 W 57th St. ☎ *757–6655*
Active New York and California figurative artists.

Kathryn Markel Fine Arts
50 W 57th St. ☎ *581–1909*
Contemporary drawings and graphics.

Getler-Pall Master Prints
50 W 57th St. ☎ *581–2724*
Contemporary American drawings and graphics.

Cross to the N side of 57th St. and walk E.

Arras Gallery
29 W 57th St. ☎ *421–1177*
Multimedia works by Europeans and Americans.

Tibor de Nagy Gallery
29 W 57th St. ☎ *421–3780*
Non-objective, representational paintings, sculpture.

Rosa Esman Gallery
29 W 57th St. ☎ *421–9490*
Experimental young Americans.

Fischbach Gallery
29 W 57th St. ☎ *759–2345*
Primarily American painters of the last 25yr.

Marilyn Pearl Gallery
29 W 57th St. ☎ *838–6310*
New salon for avant-gardists.

A.M. Sachs Gallery
29 W 57th St. ☎ *421–8686*
Established and lesser-known Americans.

Zabriskie Gallery
29 W 57th St. ☎ *832–9034*
Sculpture and photography of post-War period.

Midtown Galleries
11 E 57th St. ☎ *758–1900*
Frequent group shows of traditionalist Americans.

Wally Findlay Galleries
17 E 57th St. ☎ *421–5390*
One of the chain focussing on French Impressionists, contemporary European and American.

Andre Zarre Gallery
41 E 57th St. ☎ *752–0498*
Current Americans, geometric and colourist idioms.

Andrew Crispo
41 E 57th St. ☎ *758–9190*
Large-scale paintings and constructions, smaller oils and watercolours, mostly by Americans.

Andre Emmerich Gallery
41 E 57th St. ☎ *752–0124*
Early supporter of Abstract Expressionists and those who followed. Large format pieces at SoHo branch.

Marisa del Re Gallery
41 E 57th St. ☎ *688–1843*
Abstractionists.

Pierre Matisse Gallery
41 E 57th St. ☎ *355–6269*
International artists of 20thC, including Chagall and Giacometti. Owner is the son of Henri.

Witkin Gallery
41 E 57th St. ☎ *355–1461*
Historical and contemporary photography.

Hammer Galleries
51 E 57th St. ☎ *644–4400*
Impressionists, Post-Impressionists, 19th and 20thC American.

Madison Ave.
Many of these galleries are on cross streets, but near Madison. From 59th St., walk N on the w side of Madison. Return to that Ave. after each short detour, continuing N.

Frank Rehn Gallery
14 E 60th St. ☎ *753–4694*
American Realists.

Wildenstein & Company
19 E 64th St. ☎ *879–0500*
17th to 20thC paintings, sculpture, antique furniture.

Davis & Long Company
746 Madison Ave. ☎ *861–2811*
Three centuries of English and American paintings, drawings.

Christopher Gallery
766 Madison Ave. ☎ *737–3224*
Naïve and Realist paintings.

ACA Galleries
21 E 67th St. ☎ *628–2440*
Every major American school, from early Realists to Abstract Expressionists.

Babcock Galleries
20 E 67th St. ☎ *535–9353*
American paintings of the last 100yr.

Helios Arts
18 E 67th St. ☎ *988–5593*
Vintage photography, supplemented by post-War prints.

Hirschl & Adler Galleries
21 E 70th St. ☎ *535–8810*
Three centuries of English and American masters.

M. Knoedler & Company
19 E 70th St. ☎ *794–0550*
Old masters; vanguardists such as Motherwell.

Monique Knowlton Gallery
19 E 71st St. ☎ *749–9700*
Assemblage, painted sculpture.

Culture, history and background

Lerner-Heller
956 Madison Ave. ☎ *861–9010*
Contemporary canvasses of marked social comment.

Blum Helman Gallery
13 E 75th St. ☎ *249–5350*
Abstract Expressionism onwards.

Cordier & Ekstrom
980 Madison Ave. ☎ *988–8857*
On the fifth floor of the former Sotheby Parke Bernet building. International contemporary art.

David Findlay
984 Madison Ave. ☎ *249–2909*
American and European works of the last two centuries.

Lee Ault & Company
25 E 77th St. ☎ *861–2317*
Includes Latin American works, African sculpture.

Castelli Graphics
4 E 77th St. ☎ *288–3202*
Prints by artists represented at SoHo sister gallery.

Aberbach Fine Art
988 Madison Ave. ☎ *988–1100*
Paintings with a Surrealist emphasis.

Weintraub Gallery
992 Madison Ave. ☎ *879–1195*
Europeans of early Modernist schools.

F. Rolin & Company
1000 Madison Ave.
☎ *879–0077*
Primitive art from Asia, Africa and the Americas.

Paul Rosenberg & Company
20 E 79th St. ☎ *472–1134*
Primarily painters of the French School.

Acquavella Galleries
18 E 79th St. ☎ *734–6300*
Chagall, Braque, Cézanne, Degas. Also Lichtenstein, Motherwell, Frankenthaler.

Graham Gallery
1014 Madison Ave.
☎ *535–5767*
American Realists and illustrators prior to 1940.

Perls Galleries
1016 Madison Ave.
☎ *472–3200*
Picasso, Rouault, Utrillo, and their colleagues.

Grace Borgenicht Gallery
1018 Madison Ave.
☎ *535–8040*
Influential in promotion of the New York School and recent movements.

Brewster Gallery
1018 Madison Ave.
☎ *472–9481*
Miró, Chagall, Braque, Calder graphics.

Saidenberg Gallery
1018 Madison Ave.
☎ *288–3387*
Focus on Picasso, but many examples of important Europeans and Americans of his time.

Gimpel & Weitzenhoffer Gallery
1040 Madison Ave.
☎ *628–1897*
Abstract Expressionist paintings and sculpture, current prints.

Carus Gallery
1044 Madison Ave.
☎ *879–4660*
Bauhaus, Constructivists, Russian Modernists.

FAR Gallery
22 E 80th St. ☎ *734–7287*
Representational American painters and sculptors.

La Boetie
9 E 82nd St. ☎ *535–4865*
Expressionists, Dadaists, Surrealists.

Cross Madison Ave.

Coe Kerr Gallery
49 E 82nd St. ☎ *628–1340*
American Realists, with examples of Hudson River School.

Return to Madison and turn S on E side.

Robert Elkon Gallery
1063 Madison Ave.
☎ *535–3940*
Favours non-objective styles, but not exclusively.

Sid Deutsch Gallery
43 E 80th St. ☎ *861–4429*
All manner of quality 20thC work – no discernible preferences.

Serge Sabarsky Gallery
987 Madison Ave. ☎ *628–6281*
Scholarly presentations of German and Austrian Expressionism.

Lefebre Gallery
47 E 77th St. ☎ *744–3340*
Post-War European paintings and
prints, some sculpture.

Staempfli Gallery
47 E 77th St. ☎ *535–1919*
Contemporary European, North
and South American art.

Xavier Fourcade
36 E 75th St. ☎ *535–3980*
Eclectic modern collection.

Ronald Feldman Fine Arts
33 E 74th St. ☎ *249–4050*
Experimental works and events
that defy classification.

Robert Schoelkopf Gallery
825 Madison Ave. ☎ *879–4638*
Abstractionists to Realists.

Marcuse Pfeifer Gallery
825 Madison Ave. ☎ *737–2055*
Photography from the Civil War to
the present.

SoHo

The artists exhibited here work without ideological labels. Except as
noted, anticipate the unimaginable. Walk s on w Broadway from
Houston St.

Buecker & Harpsichords
465 W Broadway ☎ *260–3480*
Vorpal Gallery
465 W Broadway ☎ *777–3939*
Westbroadway Gallery
431 W Broadway ☎ *966–2520*
Nancy Hoffman
429 W Broadway ☎ *966–6676*
John Weber Gallery
420 W Broadway ☎ *966–6115*
Andre Emmerich Gallery
420 W Broadway ☎ *431–4550*
Leo Castelli Gallery
420 W Broadway ☎ *431–5160*
Mary Boone
420 W Broadway ☎ *966–2114*
Sonnabend Gallery
420 W Broadway ☎ *966–6160*
Edward Thorp
419 W Broadway ☎ *431–6880*
Elise Meyer
410 W Broadway ☎ *925–3527*
Heiner Friederich
393 W Broadway ☎ *925–9380*
Holly Solomon
392 W Broadway ☎ *925–1900*
John Gibson Gallery
392 W Broadway ☎ *966–9808*
Susan Caldwell
383 W Broadway ☎ *966–6500*
O.K. Harris
383 W Broadway ☎ *431–3600*
Cayman Gallery
381 W Broadway ☎ *966–6699*
Hispanic films and concerts as well
as paintings.
Chuck Levitan Gallery
42 Grand St. ☎ *966–2782*

Return to Broome St. and turn E.

Frank Marino Gallery
489 Broome St. ☎ *431–7888*
Leslie-Lohman
485 Broome St. ☎ *966–7173*
The Kitchen
484 Broome St. ☎ *925–3615*
Landmark Gallery
469 Broome St. ☎ *966–1173*

Numeroff Gallery
451 Broome St. ☎ *925–2894*
Folk art.
Women in the Arts
435 Broome St. ☎ *966–5894*

Return to Greene St. and turn N.

Makers Gallery
124 Spring St. (Greene St.)
☎ *966–7224*
Crafts in all media.
Pinder Gallery
127 Greene St. ☎ *533–4881*
Women's cooperative.
Green Mountain
135 Greene St. ☎ *674–2390*
Representational work.
The Drawing Center
137 Greene St. ☎ *892–5266*
Max Hutchinson Gallery
138 Greene St. ☎ *966–3066*
Sculpture Now
142 Greene St. ☎ *966–3066*
Same ownership as Max
Hutchinson Gallery (above).
Sperone Westwater Fischer
142 Greene St. ☎ *431–3685*

Turn w into Houston St., then s
into Wooster St.

Paula Cooper Gallery
155 Wooster St. ☎ *677–4390*
Pleiades Gallery
152 Wooster St. ☎ *475–9658*

Turn w into Prince St.

Prince Street Gallery
106 Prince St. ☎ *226–9153*
Ward-Nasse
131 Prince St. ☎ *475–9125*
Jack Gallery
138 Prince St. ☎ *966–4235*
Louis K. Meisel
141 Prince St. ☎ *677–1340*
Alexander F. Milliken
141 Prince St. ☎ *674–3131*

PLANNING

Orientation map

Major places of interest

1. American Museum of Immigration
2. American Museum of Natural History
3. Audubon Terrace
4. Bronx Zoo and New York Botanical Garden
5. Carnegie Hall
6. Cathedral Church of St John the Divine
7. Chrysler Building
8. City Hall
9. Cloisters
10. Cooper-Hewitt Museum
11. Empire State Building
12. Federal Hall National Memorial
13. Flatiron Building
14. Fraunces Tavern Museum
15. Frick Collection
16. Guggenheim Museum
17. Hall of Fame for Great Americans
18. Lincoln Center
19. Madison Square Garden
20. Metropolitan Museum of Art
21. Morris-Jumel Mansion
22. Museum of Modern Art
23. New York Public Library
24. Pan Am Building
25. Pierpont Morgan Library
26. Rockefeller Center
27. St Patrick's Cathedral
28. South Street Seaport Museum
29. Statue of Liberty
30. Trinity Church
31. Union Square
32. United Nations Headquarters
33. Washington Square
34. Whitney Museum of American Art
35. Woolworth Building
36. World Trade Center

US Highway

Interstate Highway

State Highway

N

Calendar of events

See also *Public holidays* in *Basic information* and *Sports and activities* for further information.

January

Mid-Jan for two weeks. Boat Show. New York Coliseum, Columbus Circle. Same motives and same lavish display as the Auto Show, but the subject is pleasure craft, both power and sail

Between mid-Jan and early Feb. Chinese New Year. Chinatown, lower Manhattan. Ten days of fireworks and celebrations feature silk lions and a fearsome dragon that snakes and dances along Mott St. to frighten evil spirits ☎ 267–5780 for details

Late Jan for one week. Auto Show. New York Coliseum, Columbus Circle. A vast glittery exhibition of foreign and American-made cars: antique, classic, custom and brand new

Late Jan. Winter Antiques Show. 7th Regiment Armory, Park Ave. and E 67th St. This exhibition of superior antiques is also an excuse to see the grand interiors by Stanford White and Louis Comfort Tiffany, usually closed to the public

February

Feb 12–22. Lincoln and Washington Birthday Sales. Department stores. On the days around these national holidays the large stores mount enormous sales

Mid-Feb. Westminster Dog Show. Madison Square Garden, 7th Ave. and 33rd St. Two days of intense competition

Mid-Feb for one week. National Antiques Show. Madison Square Garden, 8th Ave. and 32nd St. Perhaps the largest show of antiques and related objects in the world ☎ 564–4400 for dates

Late Feb. Lantern Day. Chinatown and City Hall, lower Manhattan. On the night of the fifteenth day of the Chinese Lunar New Year, children form a parade to present paper lanterns to the Mayor. There are martial arts demonstrations, dancing and singing ☎ 267–5780 for details

March

For Easter events, see *April*
St Patrick's Day, Mar 17. St Patrick's Day Parade. 5th Ave. from 44th St. to 86th St. All New Yorkers are Irishmen on this day. Beer is green, clothing is green, even the line down the middle of 5th Ave. is green. Irish taverns and St Patrick's Cathedral are the centres of activity

Usually around Mar 25. Greek Independence Day Parade. 5th Ave. above 59th St. Less universal than St Patrick's Day, the growing Greek population nevertheless provides a substantial parade each year, with floats and bands

Late Mar for two months. Ringling Brothers and Barnum & Bailey Circus. Madison Square Garden, 7th Ave. and 33rd St. A small parade of elephants and wagons heralds the opening

April

Two weeks preceding Easter. Easter Egg Exhibition. Ukrainian Museum, 2nd Ave. (12th St.). A specially mounted display of hand-painted eggs, a staple of this small museum ☎ 228–0110 for details

Week before Easter. Easter Flower Show. Macy's Department Store, Herald Sq. The nation's largest department store blooms on several floors

Week before Easter. Easter Lilies Display. Channel Gardens, Rockefeller Center

Easter Sunday. Easter Parade. 5th Ave., from 49th St. to 59th St. Not an organized parade at all, but a promenade of celebrants showing off their new spring finery, some of it extraordinary

May

Weekend in mid-May. Ninth Avenue International Festival. 9th Ave. from 36th St. to 59th St. Once known as 'Paddy's Market', this stretch of 9th Ave. specializes in prosaic and exotic foods – an annual gustatory orgy of *kielbasa*, quiche, *falafel*, *knishes*, *tacos*, Belgian waffles, *zeppoli*, *baklava*, *souvlaki* and every fast food conceived by man. Crafts, merchandise and entertainment

May 18. Martin Luther King Jr. Memorial Parade. 5th Ave. above 59th St.

Last weekend in May. Memorial Day Weekend. Official opening of city beaches; antiques show at 7th Regiment Armory; women's 10,000 metre L'Eggs Marathon

Late May–early June. Washington Square Outdoor Art

Exhibition. Washington Sq. and adjacent streets. Artists, amateur and otherwise, fill walls and fences with watercolours (landscapes, tigers on velvet, sedate nudes), metalwork, tooled leather and wire jewellery. Everything is for sale and bargaining is expected. The event is repeated in early Sept

June

Early June–late Aug. Summer Festival. Parks and plazas throughout the city. Leading groups and companies perform outdoors, in Central Park, at the Rockefeller Center, in the Sculpture Garden of the Museum of Modern Art, at the South Street Seaport Museum and at the World Trade Center. Music and other cultural events, many of them free. There is dance, Shakespeare, opera, jazz, pop and folk music ☎755–4100 for a daily recorded announcement

Sun in early June. Puerto Rican Day Parade. 5th Ave. above 59th St. Colourful, well-attended, sprightly celebration associated with the patron saint of the Puerto Rican capital, San Juan

Early June for two weeks. Festival of St Anthony. Little Italy, lower Manhattan. Sullivan St. below Houston St. is lined with booths selling games of chance, sizzling sausages, *calzone*, pizza and flavoured ices. Religious observances dominate during the day, secular entertainments take over after dusk. Go hungry, for the aromas are irresistible

Early June. Rose Day Weekend. New York Botanical Garden, The Bronx. Stunning demonstration of the horticulturist's craft, with tours and lectures

Mid-June. Salute to Israel Parade. 5th Ave. above 59th St.

Late June–early July. Kool Jazz Festival. Concert halls and outdoor locations around Manhattan. Jazz in all its permutations, from Dixieland to atonal, takes over from midday to midnight. Some events are free. Check newspapers for details

July

July 4th (Independence Day)
Festivities
Battery Park, lower Manhattan. Old New York Harbor Festival takes place in the afternoon and evening, with patriotic ceremonies, food, music and performers.
Richmondtown Restoration,

Staten Island. Celebrations matching the Colonial and Federalist ambience.
Riverside Park, West Side Manhattan. This is the best vantage point for the spectacular fireworks over the Hudson River, sponsored by Macy's Department Store. The display starts around 21.30, but check newspapers.
South Street Seaport Museum, lower Manhattan. Tall ships and sailing vessels from other nations and ports often visit. Street festival has music, crafts and food

July–Aug. Summer Festival. Snug Harbor Cultural Center, Staten Island. Music and art exhibitions at weekends throughout the summer

Mid-July through Aug. Mostly Mozart Festival. Lincoln Center, West Side Manhattan. This treasured event commences with a free outdoor concert, then proceeds through the rest of the summer indoors, primarily in Avery Fisher Hall. Ticket prices are unusually low ☎874–2424 for details

Jul–Aug. Washington Square Music Festival. Washington Square Park, Greenwich Village. Chamber music by the fountain on Tues evenings ☎473–8321

Late July to mid-Aug. New York Philharmonic Parks Concerts. Various park locations in all boroughs. The famed symphony orchestra performs beneath the stars, for free ☎755–4100 for details

August

Mid-Aug to early Sept. Lincoln Center Out-of-Doors. Lincoln Center, West Side Manhattan. Free live entertainment on the plaza from noon to sunset ☎877–1800 for details

September

Early Sept for two weeks. Washington Square Outdoor Art Exhibition. Washington Sq. and adjacent streets. A duplicate of the spring event (see *May*)

Sun in mid-Sept. 'New York is Book Country' Street Fair. 5th Ave. from 47th St. to 57th St. and adjacent blocks.

Mid-Sept. Steuben Day Parade. 5th Ave. from 59th St. to Yorkville. Exuberant small-scale commemoration of the German officer who aided the Revolutionary cause

Late Sept for 11 nights. *Festa di San Gennaro*. Little Italy, lower

31

Planning

Manhattan. Blocks of gaming and eating booths tempt with the possibility of sudden modest riches and the certainty of excessive calorie consumption. It is becoming an increasingly inter-cultural event, Sicilian sausages being augmented by Cantonese egg rolls

Sun in late Sept. Atlantic Avenue Antic. Southern edge of Brooklyn Heights. This predominantly Syrian neighbourhood asserts its individuality with displays of crafts, foods, and Middle Eastern dancing ☎783–4469 for details

Mid-Sept to early Oct. New York Film Festival. Alice Tully Hall, Lincoln Center. Serious film buffs revel in three weeks of afternoon and evening showings, with no need of questionable awards and overheated publicity

October

On or about Oct 5. Pulaski Day Parade. 5th Ave. The Polish community takes its turn

On or about Oct 12. Columbus Day Parade. 5th Ave. Second only to the St Patrick's Day Parade in intensity and numbers, and along the same route

Early Oct for one week. National Arts and Antiquities Festival. 7th Regiment Armory, Park Ave. and 67th St.

3rd Sun in Oct. Old Home Day. Richmondtown Restoration, Staten Island. Crafts demonstrations, dancing and entertainment in this re-created old-time village

Last Sun in Oct. New York City Marathon. From Staten Island to Central Park. Not the oldest, but the biggest marathon, with nearly 16,000 runners following a route from the w end of the Verrazano Narrows Bridge through all five boroughs

Oct 31, late afternoon. Halloween Parade. Greenwich Village, lower Manhattan. Villagers in outlandish costumes wind through the streets of their district, with ghoulish happenings along the route and a party at Washington Sq.

November

Early Nov for six days. National Horse Show. Madison Square Garden. Equestrian competition of jumping and dressage

Last Thurs in Nov. Macy's Thanksgiving Day Parade. Broadway, 77th St. to 34th St.

Traditional 3hr morning event with bands, celebrities and huge helium-filled balloons in the shapes of Kermit the Frog, Snoopy, Superman and Mickey Mouse, among others

Nov 26 – Jan 6. Star of Wonder Show. Hayden Planetarium. The night sky of Bethlehem is vividly reproduced with music and commentary ☎873–8828

Thanksgiving to New Year's Day. Lord & Taylor Christmas Windows. 424 5th Ave. (39th St.). All the big stores vie with each other in Christmas decorations, but this one is the perennial champion, managing to outdo itself every year

December

Late afternoon in early Dec. Rockefeller Center Tree-Lighting Ceremony. 5th Ave. between 50th St. and 51st St. The huge tree rising above the ice-skating rink and the gilded statue of *Prometheus* is illuminated by dignitaries and celebrities to the accompaniment of Christmas carols. Extravagantly decorated trees are also set up in the American Museum of Natural History and the Metropolitan Museum of Art

First Sun in Dec. Christmas in Richmondtown. Richmondtown Restoration, Staten Island. Period Christmas celebration in the restored village, complete with costumed guides ☎351–1611

First night of Chanukah. Lighting of Chanukah Candles. City Hall, lower Manhattan. 92nd St. YM-YWHA, 1395 Lexington Ave.

Dec. Nutcracker Ballet. Lincoln Center. Traditional performance by the New York City Ballet ☎879–5500 for details

The two Suns before Christmas, 11.00–15.00. Fifth Avenue Holiday Mall. 5th Ave., 34th St. to 57th St. The Ave. is closed to traffic and public entertainments draw shoppers past sublime and gaudy windows

Dec 31. New Year's Eve. All over the city. A 'Big Apple' slides down a flag pole above Times Sq., reaching the bottom at the first second of the New Year to the cheers of thousands of witnesses. Cars sound their horns, boats in the harbour blow their whistles, and celebrants kiss each other in the ballrooms of dozens of hotels. There is also a 5-mile run in Central Park, commencing at midnight, accompanied by fireworks.

When and where to go

Before the 1960s, the conventional advice was to avoid New York in its relentlessly humid summer. Probably for that reason, the theatre and concert season did not begin until Oct, when most of the new plays opened. That is still one of the best months to visit, when the gathering energy of the city is palpable. But the widespread adoption of air-conditioning in the last two decades now makes July bearable, and major new musicals and dramas hold their premieres throughout the year. While affluent New Yorkers still flee to summer cottages by the sea or in the New England hills, there is never that impression of an abandoned city given by, say, Paris in Aug. Some of the de luxe restaurants lock up for two or three weeks, but most remain open for business, as do the museums and landmark buildings. Concerted efforts under the 'New York is a Summer Festival' rubric have brought about a full schedule of established cultural events, as a glance at the *Calendar of events* on the previous pages reveals. Many of these events feature front-rank performing groups at little or no cost – which is decidedly not the case from Oct–May. There is a marked shirt-sleeved looseness in New Yorkers themselves in the hot months, a departure from their inclination towards dressy formality during the rest of the year. Visitors devoted to art should avoid July and Aug, when most galleries are closed.

Apr and May, Sept and Oct are the best months in terms of weather. For that reason, hotels are heavily booked at those times. Demand slackens in Jan and Feb, but although there will be some bone-chilling days, winters are usually not too severe and snowfalls of more than four inches are rare.

Those intent on a shopping holiday will encounter large crowds and frayed tempers in the weeks between Thanksgiving and Christmas. The biggest sales are in Jan and Feb. Sports enthusiasts find that the seasons of the eight major professional teams overlap in early autumn. Allowing for these few caveats, little will be missed no matter what time of year is chosen.

New York is an island city, with four of its five administrative units, called boroughs, separated by water from the North American continent. They are linked with each other and the mainland by 65 bridges and 19 tunnels. Every likely tourist destination is within reach of the extensive public transportation system – by subway, bus, or a combination of the two. Many out-of-town locations can be reached by rail or bus as well, although a car is often preferable.

At the spiritual and geographical centre is Manhattan. Even residents of the other boroughs refer to it as "The City", a reality made official by the Postal Service: all addresses in Manhattan are 'New York, NY', while the others are designated Brooklyn, Queens, The Bronx and Staten Island. Nearly all visitors stay in Manhattan. The major hotels are there, as are about 15,000 restaurants and most of the theatres, concert halls, art galleries, landmarks, corporation headquarters, libraries, universities and best-known churches and department stores.

The outer boroughs, although largely residential and industrial, are by no means bereft, however. The Bronx has its Zoo and Yankee Stadium; Queens has Shea Stadium and the Aqueduct Racetrack; Brooklyn has its beaches and a fine museum; and Staten Island has a Tibetan temple and two complexes of restored architectural treasures.

Area planners

Manhattan

Manhattan is 12 miles along its N–S axis and about 3 miles across at its widest point. The roll of history and fashion flows northwards, for development started with a Dutch settlement at the S tip and spread in the only direction available.

Financial District (Map 2U4). This neighbourhood long ago assumed the role evident in its present name, and now bristles with concrete and glass monuments to capitalism, among which are a few public buildings surviving from the late Colonial and early Federalist periods. They constitute a captivating history lesson enhanced by vistas of New York's rivers and harbour. Despite the frenetic business activity, however, there is only one hotel of consequence and few first-class restaurants.

Chinatown and *Little Italy* (*Map 2–3S-T4–5*). In the Financial District, when space began to run out, corporation rulers transferred their building mania to midtown. In doing so, they leapfrogged a band of small residential communities, former villages that still cling to very specific identities. While neither Chinatown, S of Canal St., nor Little Italy, a block or two to the N, are postcard-pretty, their ethnic vitality persists.

Lower East Side (*Map 3R5*). This lies to the E, and historically was the first land-fall of impoverished immigrants. A dreary area of rubbish-filled streets and sagging tenements – then and now – its only touristic significance is the frenetic Sunday shopping along Orchard St., when startling bargains in high-style apparel can be plucked from heaps of used and poorly-made clothing and shoes.

SoHo and *TriBeCa* (*Map 2S4*). In the 1960s, the warehouses and lofts of SoHo were 'discovered' by artists seeking larger spaces at lower rents. Inevitably, they drew gallery owners and restaurateurs, until boutiques and stockbrokers began to supplant the painters and sculptors. So the artists moved on to nearby TriBeCa, where a similar transformation is under way.

Greenwich Village (*Map 2R4*). This area also knows the cycle well. After a time as an upper-middle-class suburb, it too became an artist's enclave. Experimental theatres, art galleries and the new Bohemia flourished here in the early 20thC, and many of the theatres remain. Rows of terraced brownstones and carriage-house mews alternate with tacky commercial streets and the restaurants of SoHo and Greenwich Village blanket the entire field of price and achievement.

Chelsea, *Gramercy Park* and *Murray Hill* (*Map 4–5P4,Q3–4*). North of 14th St., the planned gridwork of streets and avenues takes hold. On the W is Chelsea, at an early stage of gentrification, as growing numbers of antique shops and trendy bars and eateries show. East of Park Ave. and N of 42nd St. are the contiguous neighbourhoods of Gramercy Park and Murray Hill, where pockets of 19thC elegance persist. Several quiet and relatively small hotels provide alternatives to the flashy behemoths farther N and the restaurants and nightspots give fair value without sacrifice of elbow room.

The Midtown district, from 42nd St. to 59th St. and Hudson River to East River, and particularly *Midtown East* (*Map 5*) contains a disproportionate share of the attractions for which New York is known. Most of the major hotels, theatres, shops and world-class restaurants are within its elastic boundaries, as well as the *United Nations Headquarters*, Times Square, *Rockefeller Center*, *St Patrick's Cathedral*, the *Museum of*

Modern Art, *Grand Central Terminal*, and dozens of examples of New York's most renowned contribution to architecture, the skyscraper. The pace is swifter here, crowds thicker, rooms and meals more costly, aggravations greater.

By comparison, the Upper *East Side* is relatively tranquil. Along 5th Ave., its western border, are most of the major museums of art and history, dominated by the *Metropolitan Museum of Art*. Mingled with the private townhouses of the side blocks are eclectic galleries and shops; and towards the East River, upwardly mobile young married couples and single people, who favour the post-War highrises, keep the many pubs and discos filled to the walls.

Upper West Side (*Map 6J – K2 – 3*). This is an area in transition. It is not as sleek as the Upper East Side, and has large concentrations of low income families, but is enjoyed by professionals who find the area and its people less superficial. The *Lincoln Center* for the Performing Arts and the *American Museum of Natural History* are the centrepieces. Between the Upper East and Upper West Side is *Central Park*.

Harlem (*Map 8 – 9H3 – 4*). The area stretches river to river immediately to the N of these two neighbourhoods. Despite its substandard housing, poverty and attendant ills, it boasts a number of important cultural institutions, especially the four specialized museums of *Audubon Terrace*.

The high, narrow neck of land at the NW corner of Manhattan Island has the sanctuary of *Fort Tryon Park* and a remarkable assemblage of medieval chapels and gardens from European monasteries known as *The Cloisters*.

Even in combination, the other four boroughs cannot match this panoply, though each has its charms nevertheless.

The Bronx

The only borough on the mainland. A full day can be profitably spent at the *Bronx Zoo and New York Botanical Garden*, with a side trip to the *Van Cortlandt Mansion and Museum*.

Brooklyn

Had it resisted annexation in 1898, Brooklyn would now be the fourth largest city in the United States. It is still self-contained, with its own civic and cultural centres, concert halls, downtown shopping district, beaches, colleges, and residential neighbourhoods both elite and prosaic. Among its inducements are the *Brooklyn Museum*, *New York Aquarium*, *Brooklyn Heights* and the promenade that overlooks an extraordinary panorama of the Manhattan skyline from the *Statue of Liberty* to the *Empire State Building*.

Queens

This borough has both LaGuardia and JFK airports. Sports fans take the subway to the *Aqueduct Racetrack* for thoroughbred racing, and to *Shea Stadium* for Jets football and Mets baseball games. (See *Sports and activities*.)

Staten Island

Despite the 1964 *Verrazano Narrows Bridge*, which connects it with Brooklyn, Staten Island remains somewhat isolated from the other boroughs. Those who take the time to look around, however, will discover pockets of bucolic solitude, notably: *Richmondtown Restoration*, a village of Colonial and 19thC homes and shops; *Snug Harbor Cultural Center*, a living museum of buildings in every 19thC style; the re-created temple that is the *Tibetan Museum*; and the small but remarkable *Staten Island Zoo*.

35

Planning

Walks in New York

Many parts of Manhattan, and Brooklyn Heights across the East River, have a surprisingly intimate character, which can be best appreciated on foot. The following walks serve as samples.

Walk 1/An introduction to New York

Tourists and natives alike find themselves passing through the *Rockefeller Center* and its immediate surroundings repeatedly. They come for the shopping along 5th Ave., the views from atop the *RCA Building*, Radio City Music Hall, the city's tallest Christmas tree, and the Easter Parade.

Begin at the **Channel Garden** entrance on the w side of 5th Ave. between 49th St. and 50th St., perhaps after a visit to *St Patrick's Cathedral*, one block N. The Channel itself, with, appropriately, **La Maison Française** on the s and the **British Empire Building** on the N, has long, raised flower beds, where the plantings are changed with seasons. At the end of this walkway, a golden statue of *Prometheus* hovers above a sunken rectangular plaza that is an outdoor cafe from Apr–Sept and an ice-skating rink from Oct–Mar.

Circle around, glancing up at the narrow limestone slab that is the RCA Building with Art Deco details over and around the high portals. Inside, heroic murals in sepia tones depict muscular workers striding across walls and ceilings. Take the lift beyond the front lobby to the **observation deck** for what many believe is the best viewpoint in Manhattan – more central and less lofty than the *Empire State Building* or *World Trade Center*. Depending on the time of day, a drink in the lounge of the Rainbow Room might then be welcome. Afterwards descend to the subterranean concourse, one floor beneath ground level. A village of small shops thrives down there, along arcades that connect buildings from 6th Ave. to 5th Ave., and from 48th St. to 53rd St.

Return to Rockefeller Plaza at the front of the RCA Building and turn right, s, then right again, w, into 48th St. The amiable mock-Dublin pub **Charlie O's Bar & Grill**, at no. 33, is a good place to stop for a hamburger or a platter of oysters. Continue w to Ave. of the Americas (known to all as 6th Ave.). The wall of intimidating skyscrapers on the opposite side is technically part of the Rockefeller Center, although the buildings were erected in the 1960s. Cross the Ave. and walk down one level at the base of the McGraw Hill Building. The fast-paced multi-media production called the *New York Experience* is there, with performances on the hour from late morning to early evening. Return to 6th Ave. and walk N. Sidewalk vendors with food preparation carts line this route in all seasons. If they tempt, take your snack to the marble bench around the fountain in front of the **Time-Life Building** at the corner of 6th St. and 50th St. Directly opposite is the **Radio City Music Hall**. For 50yr it featured big Hollywood 'family' films interspersed with stage shows that focused on the precision dance troupe known as The Rockettes. Business fell off in the 1970s and the hall nearly closed, but was saved by a new policy of special events, rock and pop concerts, and limited-run revues. The ornate vaulted interior must be seen to be believed.

Tickets for guided tours of the Rockefeller Center may be purchased at the RCA Building. They leave about every 30min, Mon–Sat 9.30–17.30, and include the observation deck and a backstage look at the Music Hall.

Walk 2/Financial District

From the day the first Dutch settlers crept into hastily
constructed bark shelters, the foremost business of New York
was commerce. Gradually merchants became financiers, ever
more distant from the commodities they bartered, and as ever
greater space was needed to contain the people who
administered the system, so the present thicket of skyscrapers
emerged, a 20thC metropolis built to the edges of a 17thC street
plan.

By 1850 few people actually lived below Chambers St. and
the *Brooklyn Bridge*, the approximate northern border of
what was 'Little Old New York' and is now the *Financial
District*. From Mon–Fri 8.00–18.00 the streets teemed with
millions of workers, then at dusk and on weekends the dark
canyons heard only the sigh of winds and the rustle of blown
refuse. That is less true today, for New Yorkers are starting to
move back, and restaurateurs and retailers are following close
behind them. So whether a Fri or a Sat is chosen to look around
depends on the tastes of the visitor. Most buildings of note are
open both days, but most eating places lock up as soon as the
last commuter has downed his Martini and headed for
home.

A walking tour logically begins with the observation deck of
the south tower of the *World Trade Center*, the easiest
structure to find in New York City. Exit on to Liberty St. Turn
left, to the E, then right, S, on Broadway. Three blocks down is
Trinity Church. The Gothic Revival third version (1846) of a
1696 original, it stands out from its towering neighbours by
virtue of a layer of city grime so black it glistens. After a stroll
through the surrounding graveyard, continue S on Broadway to
Bowling Green. Directly beyond that undistinguished patch of
lawn is the **Custom House**, usually cited as one of the city's best
examples of the florid Beaux Arts style popular at the turn of
the century. The four sculptures in front are by Daniel Chester

French. They represent the continents of Africa, America, Asia and Europe.

Turn right, SW, into *Battery Park*, following the main path to the semicircular *Castle Clinton National Monument*. An 1807 fortress that never fired on an enemy ship, it served instead as a concert and exposition hall, an immigrant processing centre and an aquarium. After a look, walk to the promenade at the water's edge for a panorama that includes *Ellis Island*, the *Statue of Liberty*, **Governors Island** (a military base) and, to the E, *Brooklyn Heights*. Passing the Statue of Liberty ferry dock, turn inland, keeping the park on the left. At the mounted cannon, look across State St. The **Georgian-Federal mansion**, at no. 7, with its inset columned porch, is the last of a row of such homes that once bordered this avenue. Further along is the **Seaman's Church Institute**, a refuge for retired sailors. The public is welcome to use its cafeteria and tour the collections of nautical memorabilia. Cross over to it, afterwards continuing E along bordering Pearl St. In two short blocks, at the corner of Broad St., is the *Fraunces Tavern Museum*, a recreation of a Colonial Georgian residence. It has a museum of Revolutionary War artefacts upstairs, a pleasant restaurant down. Breakfast is the best meal served, but there is also afternoon tea. Proceed along Pearl St. The next corner is Coenties Slip, so named because it was once a docking bay for merchant ships. Long since filled in, it now has Jeanette Park, contributed by the builders of the office building on the N side. Turn left, W, into Coenties Alley, which connects with narrow Stone St., the first paved pathway in the Dutch colony, and ends in Hanover Sq. To the right is the 1854 **India House**, Italian Renaissance in style to serve the merchant princes that were its earlier occupants. It is now a private club, but members of the public are welcome to use the restaurant. Turn left, curving N along William St., then left, to the W, into Exchange Pl. Turning right, N, into Broad St., watch for the **New York Stock Exchange**, no. 8, on the left. It's readily identified by the Neo-Grecian facade. Inside, the seemingly inchoate frenzy in the pit of the main floor can be observed, if not necessarily understood, from the second floor balcony (*Mon – Fri 10.00 – 16.00* 📧).

Where Jews and Gentiles most are wont
To throng for trade and last quotations.

E.C. Stedman, *Pan in Wall Street*

At the next corner, glance left down Wall St., its concrete canyon framing Trinity Church. The Greek Revival 'temple' directly across the street is *Federal Hall National Memorial*.

Continue E down Wall St., named for the wood stockade erected there in 1653 to protect the Dutch colonists from attack by Indians or the British. Turn left, N, on Water St., crossing Maiden Lane, where young women once washed their laundry in a brook. Continue to Fulton St., and walk E along Schermerhorn Row. Built around 1812 as a block of warehouses and now rehabilitated, it is essentially Federalist in spirit, albeit with subsequent stylistic overlays. Upstairs, at no. 2, is **Sweet's** seafood restaurant, opened in 1842 and, by some accounts, resting on its laurels since 1900. That doesn't stop the files of customers who dutifully queue for lunch every weekday. Just round the corner is the entrance to **Sloppie Louie's**, an historic spot that treats its patrons as cavalierly as its competitors but produces better fish. Sailing vessels of a more romantic era are moored at the piers of the *South Street Seaport Museum* across the way. When it is fine, there are concerts, puppet shows, buskers and chairs in which to sit and admire the view of the Brooklyn Bridge.

Leave along the N side of Fulton St. turning right, N, into Water St. A restored stationer's shop is followed by the **Seaport Gallery** with maritime exhibits and helpful maps of the neighbourhood. New shops open (and close) frequently with the ongoing development of the area. At the corner with Peck Slip, look towards the river at the amusing *trompe-l'oeil* painting that covers the entire side wall of a brick building, complete with a reproduction of a bridge tower duplicating the real one just beyond. At the end of Water St. is a forerunner of the sprightly new bar-restaurants beginning to spring up in the district, the **Bridge Cafe**.

Walk 3/Civic Center–Chinatown–Little Italy

Contrasts are endemic to New York, sometimes jarring, sometimes poignant. They tumble over each other, person by person, structure by structure; overweening power and grinding need, harsh modernity and mellowed history, optimism and despair, cosmopolitanism and parochialism. This walk is illustrative.

Start at the juncture of Broadway, Park Row and Vesey St., at *St Paul's Chapel*. Completed in 1766, it is the oldest church and public building in Manhattan. Back on Broadway turn left, to the N. Two blocks up is the *Woolworth Building*, the cathedral-like lobby of which deserves a detour.

Cross Broadway to **City Hall Park**, with the approaches to the *Brooklyn Bridge* in the background. Municipal architecture is more often dreary than inspired, but the 1811 *City Hall*, with a handful of nearby governmental buildings, is exceptional. Its elegant facade faces S, an evocation of the palaces of the Sun King. Pass City Hall on the right, continuing to the NE corner of the park. Across Chambers St. is the marvellously Baroque **Hall of Records**, and to the right is the towering **Municipal Building**. An agglomeration style that was the hallmark of the McKim, Mead & White firm, it employs a concave facade, a forest of Corinthian columns before a triumphal arch that pierces the base, and 34 storeys of statues, carvings and embellishment that owe debts to every European architectural fancy of the last 600yr. Glimpsed through the arch is a monumental steel sculpture that announces the entrance of the aggressively contemporary **Police Headquarters**.

Cross Chambers St., keeping right of the Hall of Records. The street opens into Foley Sq. On the E is an odd structure that can be said to signal the end of the Classical vogue in Federal architecture. Sombre, massive and intimidating, the 1936 **United States Courthouse** mocks the often pleasing 'temples' of a century earlier. Pass in front of this exercise in failed monumentality and its adjacent, marginally more graceful sister, the **New York County Courthouse**, still bearing right, then walk E along Worth St. to the small Columbus Park on the opposite side. Cross over and take Park St., angling off Worth St. and bordering the park.

This, it will be instantly apparent, is *Chinatown*. A Cantonese enclave for over 100yr, it is home to as many as 100,000 Chinese, and spiritual centre for ten times as many relatives who have scattered along the East Coast. Evenings and weekends, they all seem to have returned. The musty sterility of the Civic Center is instantly replaced by a barrage of visual and olfactory stimuli (most of them agreeable or at least intriguing).

Stroll across Mulberry St. and turn right into Mott St. where shades of crimson and yellow flare against the dark backdrop of the upper storeys of grimy brick. In just these short blocks, window displays and maddening aromas inspire an irresistible urge to eat, but before snatching up the nearest egg roll, enter the *Chinese Museum* (*8 Mott St.*). It's upstairs, past the dancing chicken and above the amusement arcade. At the end of Mott St., turn left, E, on to *The Bowery*. At no.6 is **Olliffee's Pharmacy**, the oldest (1803) chemist in America, and at no. 18, an off-track betting parlour (OTB) in a restored house of the Revolutionary War era.

But Chinatown is not about landmarks. First, to eat. That can be bewildering, for there are over 200 restaurants in these few streets. To surmount the language and gastronomic barrier, try a *dim sum* parlour where you will be served a limitless variety of tasty oddments, each nestling in a small dish. Just look and point and eat, as often as required. At the end, the bill is calculated by the number of empty dishes. **Hee Seung Fung** (*46 Bowery, open 7.30–2.00 daily*) is one such place.

Afterwards, double back to Pell St. and turn right, W. Tucked between grocery stores and restaurants are shops offering satin shoes, kites, jade, fans, woks, kimonos, medicinal herbs, paper lanterns, embroidered silks, chopsticks, candles, cricket cages and Buddha figurines; often all together. Narrow staircases lead up to clubrooms whence can be heard gongs and drums and the clack of *mah-jong* tiles. Telephone boxes have pagoda roofs, and banners flutter overhead. In the midst of all this, at Pell St. and Mott St., is the Georgian-Gothic *Church of the Transfiguration.* Turn right, N, into Mott St., shortly passing a Buddhist temple on the right.

At Canal St., turn left, W, one block, crossing over, N, at Mulberry St. For many years, Canal St. was an unofficial *cordon sanitaire* between Chinatown and *Little Italy*, but the former community is expanding N and E, the latter shrinking. Little Italy persists, however, despite the advancing age of its remaining inhabitants, still a Neapolitan-Sicilian bubble of trattorias and cafes and scrupulously fervent allegiances to church and family.

As in Chinatown, uptown and suburban relatives stream back for every native celebration and holiday. There, the big one is Chinese New Year (mid-Jan–early Feb); here, the *Festa di San Gennaro* (Sept). Try to be there, for floats, parades, dancing and miles of sizzling sausage and *calzone*. During the rest of the year the preservation of ethnicity is the draw, largely as regards food, although neighbourhood *ristorani* are consistently surpassed by Italian eateries in other parts of the city. Nevertheless, fair value is given by **Puglia** (*corner of Hester St. and Mulberry St.*), **Angelo's** (*146 Mulberry St.*), and **Grotta Azzurra** (*corner of Broome St.*). All are open for lunch and dinner, Tues–Sun. After, or instead, turn right, E, along Grand St. for a *cappuccino* and a pastry at **Ferrara's** at no. 195. It has sidewalk tables in summer. Alternatively, turn left W into Broome St. from Mulberry St. for a similar treat at **Cafe Roma** at no.385. From here, it is only a few blocks W on Broome St. into the creative ferment of SoHo. See *Guide to the galleries* in *Culture, history and background* for a tour that doubles as a walk in this district.

```
        0   200   400   600 yd
        0   200   400   600 m

Walk 3 ————
Walk 4 - - - -
```

SoHo
Little Italy
Houston St.
Orchard St.
Essex St.
Broome St.
Delancey St.
Mulberry St.
Grand St.
Church of the Transfiguration
Hester St.   Hester St.
Canal St.
East Broadway
Chinatown
Columbus Park
Worth St.
Rutgers St.
Foley Sq.
Mott St.
City Hall
Bowery
Pell St.
Chambers St.
Chinese Museum
Park Row
New York County
Courthouse
United States
Courthouse
Police
Headquarters
Broadway
Vesey St.
Park Row
Hall of Records
Municipal
Building
St Paul's
Chapel
City Hall Park
Brooklyn Bridge
Woolworth
Building

N

Walk 4/Lower East Side

When the first boatloads of East Europeans squeezed into the
Lower East Side in the 1880s, they found choked streets,
deprivation and cramped, cold flats. Little has changed, except
that Spanish is now more often heard than Yiddish and there are
bathtubs in the kitchens. Two kinds of tourists now stop by –
those seeking cultural roots and those seeking bargains. Sun is
best; Fri and Sat worst; and on weekdays the absence of crowds
leaves the streets less safe and less interesting.

From the subway station at the intersection of Delancey St.
and Essex St., walk w on Delancey. Turn right, N on Orchard St.
This is the liveliest block on the Lower East Side, so jammed
with shoppers, residents and merchants on Sun that cars are
banned. Pick your way along the E side, among the sights and
sounds of blasting salsa and disco music, clothing hung above
like heraldic banners, signs in four languages, people of every
hue. Cross back and forth as whim dictates. You may find
designer clothes with discounts of 20–50%, if you will accept
the inconveniences of communal changing rooms, harried and
often brusque sales people and shabby fixtures. Check out
Breakaway Fashions, at no.125, **Feminique**, no.143½, **JBZ**,
no.121, **Fine and Klein**, no.119, **Lace Up**, no.119, **Sosinsky &
Son**, no.143 and **Samuel Backenstein**, no.130. The bargains in
luggage, fabrics, bathing costumes and handbags as well as
clothes, continue as far N as Houston St. Turn around and work
s, comparing prices. Continue past Hester St., the narrow
thoroughfare brought to prominence by a recent film of the
same name. Along the way, consider the wares of **Arnie's
Place**, no.37, for jeans, **Opium**, no.52 and no.104, for dresses,
P.J. Goodstuff, no.104, for men's clothing, **Flair's Edge**,
no.110, for shoes, and **Alaska**, no.41, for shearling coats.

Turn left, E, on Canal St. All along this route is evidence of
the declining Jewish population, in abandoned synagogues and

converted tailors' shops, but at the corner of E Broadway and Rutgers St. the old ways persist at the garden-less and strictly kosher **Garden Cafeteria**. Bearded men squabble good-naturedly or lecture their children over plates of *borscht* and *blintzes*, and gruffly paternalistic waiters cock disapproving eyebrows at the sight of uneaten scraps of *gefilte* fish or the surpassing cheesecake.

Walk N along Essex St., past purveyors of religious articles. Hassidim decked in black, ringlets of hair hanging before their ears, negotiate purchases of prayer shawls, *yarmulkes* and Torah scrolls. Turn left W into Grand St., proceeding to *Little Italy* and *SoHo*, where you can end the walk or join *Walk 3* or the gallery tour in *Culture, history and background*.

Walk 5/Greenwich Village

"The Village isn't the same," say those who prospered, matured and moved away. They are correct, but it doesn't matter. The neighbourhoods of New York are not static. They shrink, or expand, or divide, or deteriorate, or adjust, or rally. Next year, or tomorrow, The Village will have changed again, but the past and provocative present remain.

Begin a tour at the University Pl. end of Washington Mews, one-half block N of the NE corner of *Washington Square*. To the left is **La Maison Française**, to the right, **Deutsches Haus**. Both are units of *New York University*, which owns much of the property in this area. Proceed down the cobblestoned Mews. Once servant quarters and stables for the grand houses on Washington Sq. North and 8th St., most of the buildings are now private homes.

Turn left into 5th Ave., towards **Washington Arch**. A wooden version of the monument was first erected in 1886 to commemorate the centennial of George Washington's inauguration. It became an instant landmark, so the architect Stanford White designed this marble rendition, completed in 1892. The statue of *Washington* on the left was carved by A. Stirling Calder, father of Alexander Calder.

Turn left along Washington Sq. North. This block of Greek Revival terraced houses was built in the 1830s. No. 16 was the site of Henry James's novel, *Washington Square*. Note the bronze lions bracketing the steps of no.6, which now houses university offices and seminar rooms. Painter Edward Hopper maintained a studio at no.3, but the upper floors burned away in the early 1970s. Continue along as the street becomes Waverly Pl., turning right into Greene St.

At the foot of Greene St. is **Tisch Hall**, with its flower-and-tree-filled plaza. It is the second of Philip Johnson's commissions for the university. Turn right into W 4th St., which soon becomes Washington Sq. South. On the left is a one-block mall popularly referred to as 'Bobkin Lane', after the bordering buildings, the **Bobst Library** and **Shimkin Hall**. The controversial library is Johnson's first design for N.Y.U. Step inside to see the twelve-storey balconied atrium. Outside, turn left, then left again on La Guardia Pl., and walk S as far as Bleecker St. Turn left, E, to see the three high-rise apartment houses on the right, which are the university-owned **Silver Towers**. In the plaza at their base is a monumental rendering of Picasso's *Silvette*, one of only two exterior sculptures by the influential artist in North America. Return to Bleecker St., now heading W, and continue to Sullivan St. This intersection is the centre of the long-established Italian community of the South

Village. Walk N, past poultry stores, dim cafes and unusual shops. Some have been there for almost a century, others change hands and functions with dizzying rapidity.

Turn left on W 3rd St. for a short block, then left again into MacDougal St. The **Cafe Reggio** (*119 MacDougal St.*) is an authentic throwback to the legendary Bohemian and beatnik days of The Village, dark and smoky, with a well-used espresso machine hissing at one side. Continue S and turn right into Bleecker St., crossing 6th Ave. and picking up Bleecker St. again on the other side.

Turn left into Leroy St., which becomes St. Luke's Pl. on the other side of 7th Ave. The houses on the right-hand side of this peaceful tree-shaded block date from the 1860s. Turn right into Hudson St., right again into Morton St., to 7th Ave., then left into Bedford St. where Edna St Vincent Millay, the poet and actress, resided for a time, at no.75½. Only 8ft wide, it is the narrowest house in The Village. The oldest is probably no.77, built in 1799.

Just beyond, turn left into Commerce St. At the end of the short block is the **Cherry Lane Theater**, one of several in which the energetic Ms. Millay had a hand. Turn right into Barrow St., then left into Bedford St. Ahead are the double-gabled houses known as the 'Twin Sisters', reputedly built by a seafaring father whose daughters would not live under the same roof. At the next intersection, take a few paces left into Grove St. to peer through the gate to the courtyard. Among the bordering houses, built in the 1840s, are some of the few surviving wood houses in Manhattan.

Return to Bedford St., continue along Grove St. and turn right into Bleecker St., a commercial artery, dominated by abundant displays of foodstuffs. Turn left into Cornelia St., and left again into W 4th St. for more shops of even greater diversity. Make a right turn at 7th Ave. and continue as far as Charles St., then turn right again and walk to Greenwich Ave. Turn left, window-gazing, then cut across and backtrack down the other side. The triangular garden between 10th St. and 6th

Ave. was made possible by the demolition of the unlamented Women's House of Detention. The adjacent structure with the fanciful brick tower is the **Jefferson Market Courthouse Library**, a mouthful that describes its sequential uses.

Turn right into Christopher St., walking away from 6th Ave., then left into Gay St., which was home (at no.14) to two sisters from Ohio, one of whom wrote *My Sister Eileen*. In a classic case of cultural recycling, her novel begat a play that was transformed into a musical that started the whole thing over again, complete with remakes and a television series. At the end of this crooked street, turn left into Waverly Pl. and follow it to the NW corner of Washington Square. Make one last detour – a half-block to the left. On the right is **MacDougal Alley**, a quaint relic of the privileged past. It is a deceptively ramshackle variation of Washington Mews, its former carriage houses now serving as expensive residences.

Return to the square. Two blocks s, chess and domino players and *kibitzers* form knots around the cement games tables installed there. Back at the central fountain, which is intended more for splashing than beauty and functions on an unpredictable schedule, several musical groups are bound to be performing, at least on fine days. Further E is a statue of *Garibaldi*. Consistent with campus legends everywhere, *Il Signore* is said to unsheath his sword whenever a virgin passes. Finally, stroll over to the *Grey Art Gallery* on the E side, another university facility, featuring exhibitions more lively than the name suggests.

Walk 6/Central Park

An amenity without which life in New York is unimaginable, the park is a product of mid-19thC vision and expediency. At that time, the land N of 59th St. was a place of mosquito-infested swamps, malodorous meat-rendering factories, and the festering hovels of thieves and the homeless. Prompted by poet-journalist William Cullen Bryant and his supporters, the city authorities launched a design competition that was won by landscapist Frederick Law Olmsted and the British architect Calvert Vaux. The squatters were evicted, the swamps drained or reshaped into lakes, 100,000 trees planted, tons of rock and earth pushed about to supplement existing topographical features and create new ones. After 20yr it was complete, with gravel carriageways, bridle paths, secluded glades, lakes for boating and fishing, and playing fields. Most of these remain, despite the trampings of generations of New Yorkers, periods of neglect, vandalism and intrusions both well-intentioned and profane.

Olmsted and Vaux envisioned a people's park, a place of refuge for poor and privileged citizens alike, not an enclosed chunk of ersatz wilderness. To enhance circulation and fantasy, they incorporated bridges, fountains, promenades and even a castle. Ever since they completed their commission, however, would-be benefactors and entrepreneurs have proposed 'improvements'. Most are turned away before the predictable firestorms of protest, but over the decades a number of projects both grand and irrelevant have squeezed through the screen. As a result, there are more structures and monuments within the park than even natives can enumerate, constituting an agreeable walking tour of surprising diversity. One reluctant caveat, however: the stories about Central Park at night are true. Apart from those frequent evening occasions – concerts and plays – that provide the security of large crowds, it is statistically unwise to visit after dusk.

Enter the park at 79th St. and 5th Ave., walking W along the path to the N of the Transverse Rd. This hugs the S wing of the *Metropolitan Museum of Art*, continues over a low rise and heads down under an arched stone bridge. Go through, bearing right, N. A few steps further on is *Cleopatra's Needle*, an Egyptian obelisk given to the city and erected in 1881. Turn about, taking the first footpath to the right. The level green to the N called **The Great Lawn** was once a reservoir, drained and filled in the 1930s and now busy with softball and football players. Above the small lake on the left, S, is **Belvedere Castle**, presently in the later stages of renovation. At the end of the lake is the open-air **Delacorte Theater** (check newspapers for current performances or ☎ 755–1400). Beyond the ticket booth, bear left, S, up the hill to the castle. Paths at the back cross over the Transverse Rd. Take the one to the right, proceeding SW, then SE. Eventually, it winds past the Loeb Boat House. Bicycles, roller-skates and rowing boats are available for hire. There is a fast-food counter with a patio. Follow the same pathway due E until it soon reaches the concrete oval of **Conservatory Pond**. At its N end is a statue of *Alice in Wonderland*: on the W, one of *Hans Christian Andersen*. Children clamber all over them, especially when stories are told at the Andersen monument on Sat mornings (May – Sept).

Take the walkway that goes W from the S end of the pond, under the Park Drive and along the bank of the lake. **Bethesda Fountain** is just ahead, the most grandiose element of the Vaux contributions. A winged angel surmounts a gaggle of cherubim and, when the plumbing is in order and New York is not having a water crisis, there is pretty splashing in the pool at the base.

Take the exit path leading W along the lake shore to the lovely cast-iron **Bow Bridge**. Another Vaux design, it was restored in 1974, and crosses the lake into **The Ramble**, a cat's cradle of footpaths that curl through low trees, patches of grass and plantings of bush and flower. The section is favoured by serious birdwatchers. Return across the bridge to the Bethesda Fountain and walk S along The Mall. On the left, E, is a bandshell, site of summer evening concerts.

Continue S on The Mall, passing bronze portraits of *Columbus*, *Shakespeare* and *Robbie Burns* that are less than compelling. Runners, skate-boarders, eaters and musicians compete for space all the way to the end. Once there, bear right to **The Dairy** (*open Tues – Sun 10.00–16.30*) from where walking tours depart. Recent restoration of the building was faithful to its Victorian Gothic origins, and the vaulted interior is now an information centre with appropriate exhibitions and a slide show. Plans are approved to recreate the loggia that was removed in the 1950s.

Cross over the nearby Transverse Rd., still heading S. The zoo (see *Central Park Zoo*) is within a stone's throw, on the left, E, and it might be time to have a snack in its cafeteria, if the ongoing restoration is complete. The **Children's Zoo** is 50yd to the N. That can be the end of a tour, but if energy and curiosity remain, leave the zoo through the S gate, bearing right under the drive. Pass the **Wollman Memorial Rink** on your right. At the edge of the pond encountered there, choose the path to the left around the edge of the pond. At the road that enters the park from Central Park South head W, following the Park Drive as it curves N along the W side of the park. This is the final leg of the New York Marathon in Oct, with the finish line at about 66th St. The expanse of lawn to the right, E, is the recently reseeded Sheep Meadow. A road to the left, W, passes the **Tavern On The Green** restaurant – once the barn for the sheep that grazed on the Meadow until the 1930s – and exits on Central Park West.

Children's playgrounds are located at intervals along the E and W borders of the park (see *New York for children*). From May–Oct park roads are closed to vehicular traffic, Mon–Fri 10.00–15.00, Mon–Thurs 19.00–22.00, Fri at 19.00 until Mon 6.00, holidays 19.00–6.00 in the morning of the next working day. From Nov–Apr only the weekend closings apply.

Walk 7/Upper East Side

The wealthy and super-rich made the Upper East Side their habitat in the late 19thC, pushing aside the squatters and farmers then in residence. They erected Italo-Franco-Anglo chateaux and palazzi one after the other, each grander than its neighbour. Those were the last decades before enactment of income tax, however, and even these privileged folk couldn't maintain their 50-room retreats long after that blow. But the rest of us profited, for many of those mansions now serve the public as schools and museums. The result is 'Museum Mile', along 5th Ave., bordering Central Park, a string of public repositories of arts and antiquities of astonishing diversity stretching from 70th St. to 103rd St. This suggested walk links many of those museums, which are described in detail in *Sights and places of interest*. The walk can be broken off at any point and returned to another day, as interest and energy dictate.

Start at the headquarters of the *Asia Society*, at the NE corner of Park Ave. and 70th St. Opened in 1981, the handsome red granite structure houses galleries of Far Eastern artefacts. Exhibits are changed two or three times yearly.

Cross Park Ave. continuing W on 70th St. Several buildings along the next two blocks are interesting. The **Explorer's Club**, at no.46, reflects the waning Gothic Revival enthusiasm of the pre-World War I years, and no.32 has Florentine detailing of the same period.

This district is home to at least a third of the city's important art galleries, and **Knoedler & Co.**, at no.19, dealing in 20thC moderns and some earlier masters, is one of the most influential. Keeping to the N side of the street, watch for the entrance to the *Frick Collection* on the right. Industrialist

Henry Clay Frick intended to have his 1914 mansion converted to a museum upon his death, and with that prospect in mind he filled it with paintings of the Renaissance and the French and English 18thC.

From the Frick Collection, turn right, w, into 70th St., then right, n, into 5th Ave., where it forms one of the grand boulevards of the city, the green of *Central Park* to the left and placid residences to the right. At 75th St., turn right, e. On the n side is a Romanesque mansion surrounded by an unusual iron fence, formerly the Harkness House, now a foundation headquarters. Continue to Madison Ave. The striking cantilevered structure on the se corner is the *Whitney Museum of American Art*, suggesting a fortress, complete with moat and fixed bridge. The leafy cafeteria on the glassed-in sub-street level provides a welcome place to sit down and relax, in full view of lyrical Calder mobiles and stabiles.

Walk N on Madison Ave., intimate by contrast with Park
Ave. and 5th Ave., with shoulder-to-shoulder art and antiques
galleries and compact shops of idiosyncratic mien. Along 76th
St. is the exclusive **Carlyle** hotel, choice of John F. Kennedy
when he was in town. Military buffs are drawn to **The Soldier
Shop** (*1013 Madison Ave.*), with its fascinating collection of
painted lead soldiers and assorted paraphernalia of many wars.

Go on to 78th St. and walk W to 5th Ave. to the family home
that tobacco heiress Doris Duke bequeathed to New York
University. It now houses the highly regarded **Institute of Fine
Arts**. At 5th Ave., turn right, N, once again. A cultural annexe
of the French Embassy is housed within the building at no.972,
designed by the omnipresent McKim, Mead & White (see
Stanford White, *Biographies*).

The Gothic Revival house (1899) at the next corner is
the **Ukrainian Institute of America** (*open Tues–Fri
14.00–18.00*), which shelters a collection of contemporary
Ukrainian paintings and folk art and costumes. The choices
here are to spend the next 2–3hr in the *Metropolitan Museum
of Art*, just across 5th Ave.; to pick up the Central Park walk
(see *Walk 6*) along the pathway at the S end of the Met; or to
continue N along 5th Ave. to visit, in sequence, the
Guggenheim Museum, the *Jewish Museum*, the
International Center of Photography and the *Museum of the
City of New York*.

Should those alternatives seem daunting, have a coffee at the
sidewalk cafe of the **American Stanhope Hotel** (*81st St.*), then
go to 82nd St. and turn right. This tree-lined, unblemished
block of terrace houses serves as a fitting approach to the Met,
seen to good advantage from Madison Ave. Turn left, N, into
Madison, then right, E, into 86th St. Across Lexington Ave.
you are in *Yorkville*. Although once a village of Germans and
Slavic immigrants, little is left to lend any middle-European
distinction, apart from a *bierstube* or two, with the exception of
the **Cafe Geiger** on the S side of 86th St. between 3rd and 2nd
Ave., which evokes the authentic atmosphere of a Viennese
konditorei.

Continue E on 86th St. After York Ave., cross to the N side.
Near the end of the block is **Henderson Place**, a mews with
little houses of symmetrical lines, rare in New York. Stroll
to the end and back, then continue along 86th St. to end the
walk in *Carl Schurz Park*, at the lip of the East River. At the N
end is *Gracie Mansion*, home of the Mayor and unfortunately
closed to the public. On the opposite bank is Queens; to the
right, Roosevelt Island; to the left, the Triborough Bridge. The
nearest subway station for your return journey is back at 86th
St. and Lexington Ave.

Walk 8/Brooklyn Heights

Manhattan's first suburb and the first neighbourhood to come
under the protection (in 1965) of the Landmarks Preservation
Commission, Brooklyn Heights is meant for leisurely
meandering. Smaller than *Greenwich Village*, which it
resembles in part, it is less flawed by commercial shabbiness
and modern architectural intrusions. Street after street is lined
with restored brownstone terrace houses with hardy plane trees
in front and gardens at the back. Lovingly maintained details of
cast-iron fences, chandeliered vestibules and flower boxes on
the windows are contrasted with the spectacular panorama of

harbour and skyline provided by the pedestrian esplanade that hangs above the East River docks.

Start from the BMT or IRT subway stations on Court St., walking S one block to turn right, W, on Remsen St. Prominent among the first buildings encountered are the elegant **Brooklyn Club**, at no.131, and **Brooklyn Bar Association**, no.123. Turn left, S, into Henry St. In the middle of the block, on the left, is **Hunt's Lane**, an alley of carriage houses converted to residences. Continue along Henry St. to Joralemon St., turn right, then right again into Hicks St. After a few steps, wander into **Grace Court Alley** on the right. It is far more handsomely preserved than Hunt's Lane, a true mews with upper-storey hay cranes still in place above the stables where horses were once kept. Go N again along Hicks, then left, W, into Remsen, and right, N, into Montague Terrace. Unlike the terrace houses already seen, commissioned individually by their first owners, this grouping of attached residences was designed as a set in 1886 and retains its original look. Author Thomas Wolfe lived a while at no.5. At the end, turn right, E, into Montague St. proper. In the last 10yr, this main shopping and eating street has blossomed with boutiques, craft shops, bookstores and gourmet and health-food emporia. None of the eating places are likely to attract the attention of highbrow Manhattan restaurant critics, but they cover a range of ethnic proclivities and some have sidewalk tables. Consider **Leaf & Bean**, no. 136, **Old Hungary**, no. 142, **Foffe**, no.155 and **Cafe Galleria**, no.174.

After three blocks along Montague St. turn left, N, into Clinton St. then left, W, again into Pierrepont St. **The Long Island Historical Society** building on the corner, erected in 1880, shows the Classical influences in vogue at the time. Exhibits of books, paintings and artefacts related to the heritage of Long Island and New York are open to the public. Continue W along Pierrepont St. The **Unitarian Church** at the corner of

Monroe Place was designed by the influential early 19thC architect Minard Lafever. Look up to the enchanting turret on no.114. It is hard to believe that the Renaissance Revival pile beneath it was once the duplicate of the Greek Revival mansion at no.108.

Follow Pierrepont St. to the end. Until 1950, it ran downhill to the river's edge. A plan to run the Brooklyn–Queens Expressway through the heart of the Heights was resisted by residents, and the compromise that evolved was to stack the highway in two tiers and divert it along the westerly edge of the neighbourhood. As a final fillip it was roofed over, smothering traffic noises and exhaust fumes, and providing a five-block promenade that bestows a glorious, unobstructed vista from the *Statue of Liberty* northwards past the spires of lower Manhattan, to the *Brooklyn Bridge* and Manhattan Bridge and all the way to the *Empire State Building*. Take it all in while strolling N, noting the trellised gardens and balconies of the narrow houses that border the promenade. Sunset is a good time, for the heavens blaze behind that famous skyline in a manner that cannot be duplicated on film.

Every river has, moreover, its influence over the people who pass their lives within sight of its waters.

H.S. Merriman, *The Sowers*

Take the next exit right, E, into Clark St., glancing both ways as you cross Columbia Heights and then Willow St., for you might be drawn to explore them further. Beyond Hicks St., pass the former (1885) **St George Hotel**, turning left, N, on Henry St., then left again, W, into Orange St. **Plymouth Church** is in mid-block, a chunky 1847 edifice of little physical distinction. Its importance lies with its founder and first preacher, Henry Ward Beecher. An ardent opponent of slavery, he attracted the attention of Abraham Lincoln, who worshipped here, as did Charles Dickens and Mark Twain. His sister, Harriet Beecher Stow, was the author of *Uncle Tom's Cabin*.

Proceed to Hicks St. and turn right, N. The private wooden residence at the corner of Cranberry St. is one of the oldest (1820) structures in the Heights. At Middagh St., named after a local burgher of the early 18thC, turn left, W. Most of the buildings along this block have been altered beyond recognition, but the splendid 1829 Federalist clapboard house, at no. 24, is an exception; its streetside fence enclosing a garden with a willow tree and connecting with a former servants' cottage. Step close to examine the carvings and leaded windows around the main door.

Continue to Columbia Heights and turn right, N, as it dips towards the base of the Brooklyn Bridge, framed beneath a walkway connecting two sections of the Watchtower Building. This passage leads into Cadman Plaza W, formerly Fulton St. From 1814–1924 this Fulton St. was linked to the one in Manhattan by ferry.

Turn towards the river. A former fireboat house stands on the site of the old ferry terminal. Now it is a **maritime museum** (*open daily 12.00–18.00*). Sailing ships often put in at the dock.

For a grand finale, amble N into the **Fulton Ferry Park**. Ever-improving food and unimprovable views are the staples of the **River Cafe**. They'll call a taxi for you for the return to your hotel.

Sights and places of interest

New York has first-class museums covering a phenomenal range of subjects. Try to squeeze in some of the more specialized ones besides the usual star attractions. Huge collections necessitate frequent rotation of exhibits and several museums (notably the Metropolitan Museum of Art) are currently undergoing major reorganization. Modern art collections are in a constant state of flux, due to ever-shifting emphases. For all these reasons, detailed cataloguing is impossible and descriptions are intended to convey a general impression. Fortunately, organization is excellent, with clear labelling and helpful floor plans. Note that the ground floor is known as the first and leads directly up to the second. Use the lists below to identify sights by type.

Bridges and tunnels
Brooklyn-Battery Tunnel
Brooklyn Bridge
George Washington Bridge
Holland Tunnel
Lincoln Tunnel
Queensboro Bridge
Queens-Midtown Tunnel
Verrazano Narrows Bridge

Churches and synagogues
Brotherhood Synagogue
Cathedral Church of St John The Divine
Church of the Ascension
Church of the Transfiguration
Grace Church
Judson Memorial Baptist Church
Marble Collegiate Church
Riverside Church
St Bartholomew's Church
St Mark's Church In-The-Bowery
St Patrick's Cathedral
St Paul's Chapel
Temple Emanu-El
Trinity Church

Colleges and universities
Columbia University
Cooper Union
New York University
Yeshiva University

Districts
Bowery, The
Brooklyn Heights
Chelsea
Chinatown
Coney Island
East Side

Financial District
Garment Center
Gramercy Park
Greenwich Village
Harlem
Little Italy
Lower East Side
Midtown East
Murray Hill
SoHo
Theater District
TriBeCa
Upper West Side
Yorkville

Exhibition halls
Burlington House
Guinness World Records Exhibit Hall
New York Coliseum
New York Experience

Historic buildings
Abigail Adams Smith Museum
Castle Clinton Monument
Chelsea Hotel
City Hall
Dakota Apartments
Dyckman House
Ellis Island
Federal Hall National Memorial
Gracie Mansion
Grand Central Terminal
Morris-Jumel Mansion
Old Merchant's House
Richmondtown Restoration
Snug Harbor Cultural Center
Theodore Roosevelt Birthplace
Van Cortlandt Mansion and Museum
Villard Houses

Libraries
Bible House
New York Public Library
Pierpont Morgan Library
Monuments
Cleopatra's Needle
General Grant National Memorial
Hall of Fame for Great Americans
Statue of Liberty
Museums of art
African-American Institute
American Academy and Institute of Arts and Letters
American Craft Museum
Asia Society
Audubon Terrace
Center for Inter-American Relations
Cloisters
Cooper-Hewitt Museum
Downtown Whitney Museum
Frick Collection
Grey Art Gallery
Guggenheim Museum
International Center of Photography
Metropolitan Museum of Art
Museo del Barrio
Museum of American Folk Art
Museum of American Illustration
Museum of Modern Art
Puerto Rican Museum for the Arts
Tibetan Museum
Whitney Museum of American Art

Museums of history and culture	New York Historical Society	New York Botanical Garden
	Police Academy Museum	Paley Park
		Prospect Park
American Museum of Immigration	South Street Seaport Museum	Riverside Park
		Union Square
American Museum of Natural History	Ukrainian Museum	Washington Square
	Museums of science and technology	**Skyscrapers and modern architecture**
American Numismatic Society	Hayden Planetarium	Chrysler Building
Aunt Len's Doll and Toy Museum	Museum of Broadcasting	Citicorp Center
		Empire State Building
Brooklyn Museum	Museum of Holography	Flatiron Building
China House		Ford Foundation Building
Chinese Museum	**Music and sports halls**	
Fire Department Museum	Carnegie Hall	Lever House
		Pan Am Building
Fraunces Tavern Museum	Lincoln Center	RCA Building
	Madison Square Garden	Rockefeller Center
French Institute		Seagram Building
Goethe House	**Parks and gardens**	United Nations Headquarters
Hispanic Society of America	Battery Park	
	Bowling Green	Waterside Houses
Japan House Gallery	Brooklyn Botanic Garden	Woolworth Building
		World Trade Center
Jewish Museum	Bryant Park	**Zoos and aquarium**
Museum of the American Indian	Carl Schurz Park	Bronx Zoo
	Central Park	Central Park Zoo
Museum of the City of New York	Fort Tryon Park	New York Aquarium
	Greenacre Park	Staten Island Zoo

Abigail Adams Smith Museum 🏛

421 E 61st St. (1st Ave.), NY 10021 ☎ 838–6878. Map 5N5
▨ ✗ Open Mon–Fri 10.00–16.00. Closed Sat, Sun.
Discounts for senior citizens; free entry for children under 12.

An unexpected retreat amid the feverish pace of the East Side, this 1799 carriage house sits on a slope behind stone retaining walls, a fetching remnant of the Federalist era. The estate it served was owned by William Stephens Smiths, but the titular tenant was his wife, the daughter of the eventual second President of the United States. She didn't stay long. After dismemberment of the property, the building became a residence in 1826. It remained in private hands until its purchase in the early 20thC by the Colonial Dames of America. That organization is still headquartered here, and maintains several exhibition rooms. Most of the furnishings are of the early 19thC, although they are not traced to the original owners.

Academy and Institute of Arts and Letters   See
American Academy and Institute of Arts and Letters.

African-American Institute

833 United Nations Plaza (47th St.), NY 10017
☎ 949–5666. Map 5O5 ▢ 🅿 Open Mon–Fri 9.00–17.00,
Sat 11.00–17.00. Closed Sun.

Appropriately positioned within sight of the *United Nations Headquarters*, this small gallery strives to promote interest in African arts and crafts, both past and present. Frequently changing exhibitions can feature sand paintings, wood carvings, bronze figures, and intricately woven fabrics in unpredictable array.

American Academy and Institute of Arts and Letters Part of the *Audubon Terrace* museum complex, this is primarily a society of prominent artists and thinkers. Exhibitions of an eclectic nature are laid on at certain times.

American Craft Museum ☆
44 W 53rd St. (6th Ave.), NY 10019, and 77 W 45th St. (6th Ave.), NY 10036 ☎ *397–0630. Map* **5N4&04** ▨ *53rd St. branch open Tues–Sat 10.00–18.00, Sun 11.00–17.00. Closed Mon. 45th St. branch open Mon–Fri 11.00–19.00. Closed Sat, Sun. Half-price entry for senior citizens, students, under-16s.*
Wit, panache, and impeccable workmanship mark the ever-changing one-person and group shows of this two-part museum. Exhibits are generally shared between the two locations. Over the course of a season, works in every material are represented: metal, paper, clay, plastic, fibre, glass, wood. The focus is on American artisans of the 20thC, but other times and cultures are sometimes explored.

A little strip of an island with a row of well-fed folks up and down the middle, and a lot of hungry folks on each side.   Harry Leon Wilson, *The Spenders*

American Museum of Immigration
Liberty Island, NY 10004 ☎ *732–1236. Map* **12D3** ▣ *✗* � *Open 9.00–17.00 Extended hours in summer. Ferry from Battery Park.*
Housed in the base of the *Statue of Liberty*, this relatively new museum understandably emphasizes the contributions – rather than the travails – of the immigrants who created a nation. Taped reminiscences, slide shows, dioramas, photographs, and displays of clothing, furnishings, and folk art combine to tell the story.

American Museum of Natural History ▦ ★
Central Park W (79th St.), NY 10024 ☎ *873–4225. Map* **6L3** ▨ *✗* ▨ ✚ *Open Mon, Tues, Thurs, Sun 10.00–17.45, Wed, Fri, Sat 10.00–21.00.*
Beloved by generations of schoolchildren for its realistic animal dioramas and models of Indian villages, the museum interprets its mission in the broadest terms. Appealing as the exhibits of mounted Alaskan bears and African lions unquestionably are, adults are drawn to the halls highlighting the crafts, costumes, jewellery, masks, and artefacts of the peoples of Asia, Mexico, and pre-colonial North America. The collections, begun in 1874, include 34 million items, from a 94ft (29m) model of a blue whale to the fabled Star of India.

Calvert Vaux, who shared credit for Central Park, worked with Jacob Wrey Mould on the first building (1877). So many additions were made from then until 1933, however, that only a portion of it is still visible from the rear. Critics cite the southern red granite facade as a superior example of the Romanesque Revival. Perhaps so, if one's notion of romantic architecture derives from ponderous Teutonic fortresses. The main entrance, dominated by a 1939 equestrian statue of *President Theodore Roosevelt*, is even less graceful. Yet in spite of the forbidding exterior, this great museum qualifies as an obligatory stop.

American Museum of Natural History

First (ground) floor

Meteorites & Gems

Biology of Man

Education Hall

Entrance

Northwest Coast Indians

West 77th St.

Parking area

Man and Nature

Biology of Fishes

North American Mammals

Entrance

Hayden Planetarium

Biology of Invertebrates

Entrance Hall

Biology of Birds

Central Park West

Second (main) floor

Mexico and Central America

Closed to the public

Birds of The World

Man in Africa

Hall of Asian Peoples

African Mammals

Asiatic Mammals

Entrance Hall

Oceanic Birds

For maximum impact, choose the W 77th St. entrance rather than the one on Central Park W. Directly beyond the door leading to the first (ground) floor is an impressively scaled ocean-going canoe of a British Columbian tribe. Adjoining rooms are devoted to North American mammals, birds and invertebrates, meteorites and gems.

From the second (main) floor hall, turn left, continuing past animal exhibits to the Gardner D. Stout **Hall of Asian Peoples**, the newest and most ambitious section of the museum. In a masterful mix of scholarship and showmanship, it charts the progress of Eurasian cultures from prehistory to the recent past, employing every imaginable device to delineate evolutionary stages of religion, commerce, language, art and science. A gallery of **Birds of the World** leads on to another incorporating monumental stelae and terra cotta funeral urns, sculptures, and

ornaments from pre-Columbian Mexico and Central America.
Close by, **Man in Africa** brings to life the diverse societies of
African forest and desert. The rest of this floor and the third
floor feature reptiles, primates and birds of several continents.
Reassembled **dinosaur skeletons** are the attraction on the
fourth floor, especially the awesome Tyrannosaurus Rex that
figures in so many Grade B fantasy films.

In addition to the basement cafeteria, there is a cocktail
lounge in the lobby, and tables set around hot-dog carts on the
front steps in summer. Travelling shows, lectures, and music
and dance programmes augment the permanent exhibitions.

Hayden Planetarium ☆

Central Park W (81st St.), NY 10024 ☎ 873–8828 ▦ ✳
Shows: Mon–Fri 13.30, 15.30, Sat 11.00, 13.00, 14.00,
15.00, 16.00, 17.00, Sun as Sat except 11.00, Wed extra
show 19.30. Fewer shows July–Sept. Admission includes
American Museum of Natural History.

Since 1935, the artful technology of the Hayden Planetarium
has reproduced on its domed ceiling the movements of
constellations, planets, and meteor showers. Seasonal shows
focus on the 'Star of Wonder', nebulae and stellar formations,
and the projected end of the world through astronomical
accident. Music and commentary supplement the 1hr
presentations, and there are 'cosmic laser concerts'
(☎724–8700 for times and prices). Observing the 2½-ton
projector in action is worth the admission.

American Numismatic Society

Housing a large
collection of coins and medals, this is part of the *Audubon
Terrace* complex.

Aquarium

See *New York Aquarium*.

Ascension, Church of the

See *Church of the
Ascension*.

Asia Society ▥

725 Park Ave. (E 70th St.), NY 10021 ☎ 288–6400. Map
7M4 ▦ ✗ Open Tues–Sat 10.00–17.00, Thurs
10.00–20.30, Sun 12.00–17.00. Closed Mon.

A striking addition to a bland stretch of Park Ave., the new
1981 headquarters of the Asia Society echoes imperial palaces of
India with its facing of alternately polished and textured red
granite. The gallery floors house one of the many benefactions
of the Rockefeller family: in this case, the collection of Nepalese
and Chinese artefacts assembled by John D. 3rd. That is not the
extent of the holdings, however, and there are supplementary
loan exhibitions three or four times a year, as well as films,
lectures and recitals. As this is not a formal museum operating
within the strictures of scholarship, objects on display reflect
the tastes of the contributors. Fortunately, those predilections
are disciplined and educated. Sculptured metal and
polychromed ceramics mingle with ancient many-armed
buddhas from Kampuchea and fierce feline temple guardians.

Audubon Terrace ▥ ☆

Broadway at 155th St. Map 8F2. Subway 1 to 157th St;
AA, B to 155th St.

Gathered around a Neo-Classical plaza in a NW precinct of
Harlem is a remarkable complex of four museums and

associated societies. While they are not all individually of great importance, as a group they rival all but a handful of the city's cultural repositories. Only their location denies them the recognition they deserve.

Ornithologist John James Audubon owned this property at the crest of the slope above the Hudson River and intermittently lived here from 1825 until his death in 1851. It was purchased by a speculator convinced that the steady northward thrust of the city would eventually make him rich. When it became clear that growth had stabilized at a point 5 miles s, the tract changed hands. A master plan was drawn up in 1908, and the present buildings were completed by 1926. They can be characterized as of the Beaux Arts mode, with a typical Greco-Renaissance mix. All the buildings are clustered in the block abutting Broadway between W 155th St. and W 156th St.

Museum of the American Indian ☆
☎ 283–2420 ▨ ✷ *Open Tues–Sat 10.00–17.00, Sun 13.00–17.00. Closed Mon.*

The largest repository of Native American artefacts anywhere, with over four million items on display and in storage, this museum is of particular interest to overseas visitors who plan to go no farther w than Manhattan. Even three large, crammed (if skilfully organized) floors can contain no more than a small portion of the acquisitions. These are rotated from a storage annex in seemingly inexhaustible numbers. 'American' here refers to the entire Western Hemisphere, with Eskimo carvings, Hopi kachina dolls, Chilean silverwork, and tools, funeral urns, tomahawks, jewellery, pottery, beadwork, feather head-dresses and costumes, and fetishes from many Indian tribes and empires. The shrunken bodies (not mere heads) of captives of the Ecuadoran Jivaros are a macabre revelation. This museum deserves to be ranked among the best in the city, at least in terms of comprehensiveness.

Hispanic Society of America
☎ 926–2234 ▨ *Open Tues–Sat 10.00–16.30, Sun 13.00–16.00. Closed Mon.*

The entrance is marked by an equestrian bronze of *El Cid*, the 11thC Spanish hero – a fitting choice for a museum that concerns itself with Iberian rather than Latin American culture and history. At the very minimum, step into the splendid **main hall** ☆ and savour the rosy blush of terra cotta Renaissance arches and ornamentation. During certain hours, light through the two-storey skylight heightens the play of intricate shadow on carved scrollwork and panels. Of conventional interest are the canvasses and drawings of El Greco, Velazquez and Goya. But the Spain of the Catholic kings is upstaged by that of the earlier Moors, with tiled chambers and relics of exquisite workmanship. The Roman and Visigothic occupations are represented as well, and there is a substantial library of pre-1700 books.

American Numismatic Society
☎ 234–3130 ▨ *Open Tues–Sat 9.00–16.30, Sun 13.00–15.00. Closed Mon. Ring bell for entry.*

The ground floor is given over to a large display of coins, medals and banknotes, the second floor to a specialist library.

Puerto Rican Museum for the Arts
☎ 222–2966 ▨ *Visits by appointment only.*

What was until recently the home of the American Geographical Society now features permanent and rotating exhibitions of photographs, prints, paintings and sculpture, all with Puerto Rican associations.

American Academy and Institute of Arts and Letters
☎ 368–5900 🖸 *Open Mar–June, Nov–Dec, Tues–Sun 13.00–16.00. Telephone first to confirm hours and exhibitions.*
Primarily an association of celebrated artists and intellectuals, not unlike its French counterpart, this institution mounts periodic exhibitions covering a wide range of subjects, from ancient manuscripts to architectural themes.

Aunt Len's Doll and Toy Museum
6 Hamilton Terrace (141st St.), NY 10031 ☎ *281–4143. Map 8G3* 🖾 *Ҟ Open Tues–Sun. Closed Mon. Telephone first for an appointment. Subway 1 to 137th St.*
An enthusiasm for collecting has a way of getting out of hand – in this case, to the delight of parents and children alike. 'Aunt Len' was a local schoolteacher who gathered over 3,000 dolls, miniature houses with scale furniture, mechanical and clockwork toys, dolls' prams and accessories. When she saw what she had done, she decided to give everyone else a chance to share it. Every corner and surface is crowded with her acquisitions, and the effect is magical. A visit might be combined with a trip to the several museums of *Audubon Terrace*, some 14 blocks to the N.

Battery Park
Battery Pl. and State St. (foot of Broadway). Map 2V4.
Named for a rank of cannon that defended the old town from uncertain foes – presumably British – after the Revolution, the present 21 acres occupy the western rim of the extreme southern tip of Manhattan. Financial District workers eat their packed lunches in view of the *Statue of Liberty* and the now diminished but no less beguiling harbour traffic. Other attractions are the **Verrazano Memorial**, commemorating the Italian explorer who first saw New York Bay in 1524, and the *Castle Clinton National Monument*, once on an islet but later joined by landfill to what is now the park. The ferry to the Statue of Liberty departs from a pier at the edge of the park and the one to Staten Island is nearby.

Bible House
1865 Broadway (61st St.), NY 10023 ☎ *581–7400. Map 4N3* 🖸 *Ҟ for groups. Open Mon–Fri 9.00–16.30. Closed Sat, Sun.*
Over 38,000 volumes are on permanent display, including scraps of the Dead Sea Scrolls, pages from the 15thC Gutenberg Bible, and Braille editions once owned by Helen Keller.

The Bowery
Map 3S5.
A country road from the time of the original Dutch colony, the 'Bouwerie' retained its bucolic status into the 19thC. It went downhill from there – apart from a brief revival in the 1890s as a place for bawdy music halls – and rapidly slid into utter despair. Now it is a grimy concentration of dosshouses and bars, the last stop for derelict men and women made homeless by alcoholism, madness and misfortune. There are a handful of discount kitchenware and home furnishing stores, but the persistence of The Bowery as a tourist attraction is a mystery.

Bowling Green
Battery Pl. (foot of Broadway). Map 2U4.
This triangular bit of lawn once hosted early Colonial bowlers
and a statue of *George III.* True to revolutionary tradition, the
monument was pulled down in 1776. The fence that protected
the memorial is all that remains of even minor historical and
visual interest.

Bronx Zoo and New York Botanical Garden
These adjacent and spectacular sights constitute two of the best
reasons for venturing over the Harlem River.
Bronx Zoo ★
Southern Blvd. (185th St.), Bronx, NY 10460
☎ *220–5100. Map 13B–C4* ☒ *Tues–Thurs* ☒ *Fri–Mon in
winter* ☒ *Fri–Mon in summer. Modest extra charges for a
few special sections, also tractor train, aerial tram and
monorail* ✗ *free by appointment* ☎ *220–5141* ▣ ✱ ⬤
*Open Mon–Sat 10.00–17.00, Sun and hols 10.00–17.30.
Most outdoor exhibits closed in winter, roughly Oct–Apr.
Subway 2,5 to Pelham Parkway.*
Many New York attractions are as engaging as ever, others are
in decline, but few have actually improved in recent years. The
Bronx Zoo falls into this last felicitous category. Known
officially as the New York Zoological Park, it was inaugurated
in 1899 and now has over 3,000 animals of 800 species, deployed
in imaginative settings carved out of the hills and meadows of
the original 252 acres. Because such diversity can cause
indecision, the management have provided the means to obtain
overviews and thereby make choices. A tractor train with guide
makes a complete circuit of the grounds, an aerial tram glides
over the African Plains section, and a monorail meanders about
Wild Asia, where tigers and elephants roam free.

To proceed in an orderly manner on foot, begin at the Pelham
Parkway extrance. This leads to the earliest part of the zoo, the
formal Baird Court, centring on the **Seal Pool**, around which
are arranged the **Aquatic Birds**, **Carnivores**, **Monkeys**,
Elephants, and a giant bird enclosure called the **Flying Cage**.
Pause by the 3-acre **Bison Range** for a look at the beasts that
once roamed over thousands of square miles of the Old West.
Beyond that is the 1972 **World of Birds**, through which you can
pass in the company of over 500 birds, with no interceding
screens. South of the Elephant House is a popular group of
buildings sheltering the **Reptiles**, **Penguins** and **Gorillas**.
Nearby is the fascinating **World of Darkness**, where a variety
of nocturnal creatures are fooled by artificial lighting into
believing that day is night.

Apart from these necessary structures, animals are at liberty
in much of the park, in simulated habitats. Cleverly
camouflaged moats keep them apart and protect the public.
The Skyfari tramway carries observers above the remarkably
convincing veldt of the **African Plains**, and you can look down
on moving lion prides, antelope and deer.

The park embraces a stretch of the Bronx River, wide enough
here to be called a lake. Most exhibits are to the w, but **Wild
Asia** takes up the E bank. The concept is similar to the African
Plains area, but the Bengali Express monorail follows a looping
route around the perimeter and over the river. Fences
separating clusters of rare animals from the Asian Subcontinent
are the only element detracting from the carefully staged
natural environment.

Bronx Zoo and New York Botanical Garden

Museum

Entrance

Rhododendrons

Magnolias

New York Botanical Garden

Conservatory

Entrance

Bronx River

Dogwoods

Azaleas

Old Lorillard Snuff Mill

Lilacs

Entrance

Pelham

Parkway

Entrance

Flying Cage

Rare Animal Range

Aquatic Birds

Baird Court

Carnivores

Children's Zoo

World of Birds

Bison Range

Seal Pool

Monkeys

Elephants

Zoo

Reptiles

North America

Gorillas

Penguins

World of Darkness

Bronx Lake

African Plains

Skyfari

South America

Monorail

Wild Asia

N

| 0 | 250yd | 500yd | ½ mile |

| 0 | 250m | 500m | 1km |

59

Throughout the park are specimens no longer found in the wild. In the **Children's Zoo**, young and gentle animals are available for petting and feeding.

New York Botanical Garden ☆
Southern Blvd. (200th St.), Bronx, NY 10460 ☎ *220–8700*
▥ **⃌** ▣ ✳ *Open 10.00–1hr before sunset. Conservatory Tues–Sun. Museum Mon–Fri 9.30–16.00.*

Adjacent to the zoo on its northern border, these 250 acres also straddle the Bronx River, but here the river is narrow and untamed, tumbling through a deep gorge. Its course is bordered by a 40-acre preserve of virgin hemlock – the trees that covered much of the metropolitan region before the Europeans arrived.

Entry can be made opposite the Pelham Parkway gate of the zoo. At the first main pedestrian intersection, detour W into the azalea glen, then retrace the route E. After the bridge, the **Old Lorillard Snuff Mill** becomes visible on the left. The 1840s building is restored and used as a summer snack bar. Continue E and N, pausing along the way for displays of lilac, dogwood, magnolia and rhododendron. Eventually the paths converge on the **Museum**, which mounts changing exhibitions on horticultural and ecological themes and incorporates a herbarium and botanical library. To the SW is the centrepiece of the preserve, the **Conservatory**. A grand rotunda of leaded glass is the focus of a complex of ten connecting greenhouses. The effect, inside and out, is of an enchanted crystal palace of the Victorian era. After years of deterioration, it was in danger of demolition. Reason and philanthropy prevailed in this glorious rejuvenation, and it contains topiary, desert plants and tropical flora.

Obviously the best time to go is Apr–Aug, when the groves and gardens are ablaze with colour, but special events draw visitors at Christmas and Easter.

Brooklyn-Battery Tunnel
Map 2V4 ▥

Master builder Robert Moses intended an overwater span at this site, just S of the *Brooklyn Bridge*, to connect lower Manhattan with the Belt Parkway, which skirts the edge of Long Island on the way to JFK Airport. Despite his clout as the most powerful city planner of his time – from the early 1930s into the 1960s – he bowed to public pressure and settled for a tunnel. At that, it is the longest vehicular tunnel in the United States – nearly 2 miles.

Brooklyn Botanic Garden ☆
1000 Washington Ave. (Eastern Parkway), Brooklyn, NY 11225 ☎ *622–4433. Map* **12***E3* ▣ *Tues, Fri* ▥ *other days* ✗ *Open Apr–Sept Tues–Fri 8.00–18.00, Sat, Sun, public hols 10.00–18.00; Oct–Mar Tues–Fri 8.00–16.30, Sat, Sun, public hols 10.00–16.30. Closed Mon. Subway 2,3,4 to Eastern Parkway–Brooklyn Museum.*

Much smaller than its big brother in the Bronx (see *Bronx Zoo and New York Botanical Garden*) the Brooklyn Botanic Garden is nonetheless worthwhile, especially in concert with a visit to the neighbouring *Brooklyn Museum*. Specialized gardens include one with fragrances for the blind, another exclusively of roses, one of herbs, three authentic Japanese settings supplemented by a superb bonsai display, and an ebullient horticultural tribute to Shakespeare, incorporating 80 plant species mentioned in his plays. The restrained Victorian conservatory was designed by the ubiquitous McKim, Mead & White in 1918, with variously tinted glass panes arching over equatorial fern and fruit trees.

Brooklyn Bridge ▥ ★
Map 3U5 ▣ ▨

Perhaps the most spectacular engineering achievement of its time, the enduring grace of the 1,595ft (486m) span has inspired paeans by painters and poets. John Roebling conceived it in 1857, but construction did not begin until 1869. There was scepticism about its feasibility, the need for a bridge over a river well-served by ferry lines, and the projected expense. In the manner of public projects, those costs routinely multiplied, eventually totalling the then-stunning sum of nearly $16,000,000. Since construction paralleled the reign of one of New York's most corrupt political regimes, undetermined portions of the budgeted funds were diverted to the accounts of the notorious Boss Tweed and his cronies.

Roebling died in the first year of construction, contracting tetanus after his foot was crushed by a docking ferry. His son Washington took over. While rising from an underwater chamber, he suffered an attack of the bends and was permanently disabled. Although confined to a wheelchair, he oversaw the project to its conclusion, employing his wife Emily as a go-between. Thousands of new immigrants, largely Irish and Italian, laboured 14yr on the project. Uncounted numbers died, many of them victims of diseases associated with the nascent technology.

Six days after the opening on May 24, 1883, a rumour that the bridge was collapsing raced through the festive crowd of sightseers. There were 12 fatalities in the ensuing panic. Since then, the 133ft (40m) height of the span has proved tempting to the foolhardy and suicidal. At least 34 jumpers have not survived the fall. Despite early doubts about its stability, there is every reason to believe that the grande dame of New York bridges will be there when today's youngest pedestrians bring their grandchildren. There are incomparable **vistas** ✿ of East River traffic and the lower Manhattan skyline from the elevated walkway.

Brooklyn Heights ▥ ✿
Map 3U6.

In 1646, a handful of Dutch families decided to give official status to their settlement on the bluffs overlooking the juncture of the Hudson and East rivers and the larger village at the toe of Manhattan Island. They called their new home 'Breuckelen'. The establishment of a regular steam ferry service in 1820 transformed the rural community into a suburb. Shipping magnates and wealthy merchants chose to move in, insulated from the traumas of the troubled city and yet in a position to monitor river traffic. The terraces they lived in competed in harbour vistas and luxury of appointments. A substantial number persisted into the 20thC, but by the 1950s the Heights were in decline.

A plan to ram a highway through the neighbourhood was narrowly averted, and the resulting community spirit signalled its renaissance. Now designated an Historic District, it is the most desirable residential enclave in the borough. (See *Walk 8* in *Planning*.)

Brooklyn Museum ☆
*188 Eastern Parkway (Washington Ave.), Brooklyn, NY
11238 ☎ 638–5000. Map 12E3 ▨ ▣ ✻ Open Wed–Sat
10.00–17.00, Sun 12.00–17.00, public hols 13.00–17.00.
Closed Mon, Tues. Subway 2,3,4 to Eastern Parkway –
Brooklyn Museum.*

Although in constant struggle with fiscal uncertainty, this fine
institution is the keystone of the borough's cultural and
recreational complex that includes the adjacent *Brooklyn
Botanic Garden*, *Prospect Park* and zoo, and the Brooklyn
Public Library. The museum must be ranked among the most
important in the city and might have challenged even the
nonpareil *Metropolitan Museum of Art* had the initial plans of
the architectural firm of McKim, Mead & White been carried
out. As it is, the scaled-down scheme that was erected at the
turn of the century is an imposing Neo-Classical pile, flawed
only by a misguided 1930s modernization that removed the
noble exterior staircase. Some compensation for that
desecration is provided by the two 1916 Daniel Chester French
statues that were moved to pedestals outside in 1963.

Our admiration of the antique is not admiration of the old but of
the natural.

Emerson, *Essays, First Series: History*

Inside are five floors of arts and antiquities spanning
centuries and continents from Egypt to Oceania. Exhibits are
grouped essentially along geographical or societal lines. The
first floor is devoted to the **arts and crafts of the primitive** (or at
least pre-colonial) **peoples of the Americas, Africa and the
South Pacific**. Totem poles of the NW tribes loom over cases of
New Guinean ceremonial masks, Columbian ritual urns, Inca
jewellery, Hopi and Zuni dolls, African fetishes and weapons.
Adjacent rooms house a gallery reserved for art shows drawn
from the Brooklyn community, a cafeteria, and a museum shop
that purveys a remarkable array of crafts from around the world
at reasonable prices.

On the second floor are **arts of Asia and Islam**, spotlighting
ceramics, rugs, textiles, paintings, metal and jade secular and
religious objects from India, China, Persia, Japan, Tibet and
Indochina. A separate print room encompasses European and
American graphic arts from the 14thC to the present.

The pride of the museum is the collection of **relics of
Dynastic and Coptic Egypt** on the third floor, with sarcophagi
mingling with alabaster figurines and an ebony sphinx. Of
particular interest are the **Assyrian reliefs ☆** in the Kevorkian
Gallery, just beyond the lift vestibule. The wall sculptures,
some from the Palace of Ashurnasirpal II, depict winged deities
and griffin-headed genies. On the right side of the hall is a case
of ceremonial vessels, partly animal-shaped, followed by one
filled with engraved silver bowls. This corridor leads into an
unexpectedly dramatic inner court ringed with shallow cases of
exquisite objects ranging from Egyptian to Cypriot and Greek:
amulets, amphoras, glass bottles as fragile as paper, beakers,
fragments of textiles, busts of monarchs. Additional rooms are
given to still more jewellery, pottery and funerary pieces.

The fourth floor is devoted to **furniture and decorative
arts**, largely of the 17th and 18thC, but also including the early
Colonial period and some Manhattan Art Deco. The Jan
Martense Schenck House, a Dutch two-room dwelling of New

York c.1675, is reconstructed and fully furnished with authentic pieces. There is also a costume institute.

Just inside the fifth floor entrance is a lush **landscape**☆ by the 19thC American Albert Bierstadt, startlingly overpowering the viewer with its rolling thunderclouds, shafts of light, alpine cascades and snowy peaks. The smaller canvasses of the Hudson River School that follow are pale by comparison, but are momentarily diverting. The first doorway leads into the East Galleries, reserved for **European painting**. After the glories of the first and third floors, these are disappointingly minor works by important artists. The supposed highlight is *Mlle. Fiorre in the Ballet La Source*, a very early (1866) Degas that looks merely half-finished and gives barely a hint of the off-centre composition that was to become his hallmark. Next to it are two minor Corots. The rest of the room holds portraits of modest distinction and some bucolic scenes by Millet. A small room of preliminary studies in pastels and gouache includes an appealing Toulouse-Lautrec, alongside drawings by Manet, Gauguin, Degas and Pissarro. They and their compatriots Renoir, Monet and Cézanne are represented in the last room by larger oils that demand little attention. On the way out of this section, note the 15th and 16thC Italian religious paintings on wood. The rest of the floor is normally used for special exhibitions, often of an Americana theme.

An unusual outdoor court at the rear of the building preserves ornamental fragments scavenged from such lamented buildings as the razed Penn Station. Lectures, films, concerts and gallery talks are regular features in the museum's programme.

Brotherhood Synagogue ⋒
28 Gramercy Park S (3rd Ave.), NY 10003 ☎ *674–5750. Map* **5**Q4 ⊡ ⚍ *No tours Fri, Sat, Jewish hols. Telephone 24hr in advance for appointment.*

From 1859 until 1975, this was a Quaker meeting house, which explains its relief from unessential ornamentation. It is part of the *Gramercy Park* Historic District.

Bryant Park
Ave. of the Americas and 42nd St. Map **5**O4

Most midtown blocks have supported disparate functions over the last 150yr of development, but few as profound as this site. In the early 19thC, it was a potter's field. Two decades later, a fortress-like reservoir was completed, and in 1853, an imitation of London's Crystal Palace was erected on an adjacent strip of land. That was destroyed by fire in 1858, and the scorched earth was designated a park, dedicated to poet and journalist William Cullen Bryant (1794–1878). At the turn of the century, the reservoir was drained and filled and the *New York Public Library* and park extension took its place. Office workers drop by to enjoy the sun and concerts of live and recorded music. Lolling among them are a number of drug dealers of placid mien and largely bogus merchandise. They are easily ignored.

Burlington House
1345 Ave. of the Americas (54th St.), NY 10019. Map **5**N4 ⊡ *Open during business hours.*

The otherwise undistinguished glass tower in midtown is enlivened by two thistledown fountains in the wide plaza fronting 6th Ave. A ground-floor space on the left has housed a procession of long-term exhibitions of catholic inspiration and execution. These have included a slick multi-image treatise on the development of the textile industry and a much-praised environmental representation of New York called *Ruckus Manhattan*. Now it is a monument to another phenomenon, a members-only video cassette 'supermarket' called Cine Club Video. The branch of a French chain, it is alleged to stock as many as 50,000 cassettes.

Carl Schurz Park
Map 7L5.
Schurz was a German-born immigrant who became a US senator. The park in his name is at the eastern end of 86th St., the central artery of the German community known as *Yorkville*. The official residence of the mayor, *Gracie Mansion*, is at the northern edge of the green.

Carnegie Hall
154 W 57th St. (7th Ave.), NY 10019 ☎ 247–7459. Map 4N3.
It was feared that the 1891 hall would be demolished along with the old Metropolitan Opera House after the completion of the *Lincoln Center*. Preservationists scored a too-infrequent victory, however, and funds were raised to renovate the interior. The acoustics are still superb and the concert schedule is full, with artists and groups clamouring for dates.

Castle Clinton National Monument ▥
Battery Park (foot of Broadway), NY 10004 ☎ 344–7220. Map 2V4 ▣ ✗ ✿ Open 9.00–17.00 June–Aug daily, Mar–May, Sept–Dec Mon–Fri. Closed Jan, Feb.
Concern over a possible second conflict with the English prompted initial plans for the battery of 28 cannon on the rocky outcrop 200ft (60m) off the SW tip of Manhattan. The eventual reality of British impressment of crews of American merchant ships lent credence to the fear, and additional fortifications were thrown up. The intention was to discourage hostile ships attempting to enter the East River, in concert with crossfire from a similar installation on nearby Governor's Island (still a military post). Perhaps it worked, for the fort never had a chance to lose a volley.

When the lingering hatreds of the 1812 War faded, the circular sandstone structure was given to New York City. It was transformed into an entertainment centre, hosting concerts and recitals. By the middle of the century, it had been joined with Manhattan, and in 1855 it became an immigrant processing centre. By 1892, that function was assumed by *Ellis Island*, and the fort was converted into a public aquarium, a role it held until 1941. After World War II, it was restored to its original status, and is now a Federal landmark administered by the National Park Service.

Cathedral Church of St John The Divine ▥ † ☆
1047 Amsterdam Ave. (112th St.), NY 10025 ☎ 678–6888 Map 8I3 ▣ ✗ Open 7.00–17.00. Occasionally closed for special events.
Work on the cathedral started in 1892. By the year 2000, they hope to have the two towers completed. That will still leave the transepts and other additions to be undertaken – perhaps somewhere around 2050? Even now, the interior space is

second only to St Peter's in Rome, and the combined floor space of Chartres and Notre Dame (Paris) would fit within the 146 by 601ft (44 by 183m) area. The measured pace of construction is due to the determination to use methods that reach back to the Middle Ages. English master masons instruct American apprentices in the **stonecutting yard** (*open to the public Mon–Fri 8.45–15.45*). Religious and secular works have been donated to the cathedral over the last 100yr and offhandedly stored for future display. A recent inventory revealed the surprising scope of the collection, which includes 13th–16thC tapestries and paintings of the Italian Renaissance. They are on view on a circulating basis in the **Museum** ☆ (▣ *Mon–Sat 11.00–16.00, Sun 12.00–17.00; guided tours Mon–Sat 11.00, 14.00, Sun 12.30.*).

Center for Inter-American Relations
680 Park Ave. (68th St.), NY 10021 ☎ *249–8950. Map **7**M4* ▣ 𝕶 *by appointment. Open Tues–Sun 12.00–18.00. Closed Mon.*

The architectural firm of McKim, Mead & White was responsible for many notable buildings of the late 19th and early 20thC in New York, and a substantial number still exist. Perhaps because the third and most famous partner, Stanford White, died at the hands of a jealous husband in 1906, this 1909 structure is a Neo-Georgian departure from the Italianate preferences of their earlier projects. After a period as home for the Russian Delegation to the UN, one of the many Rockefellers bought it and gave it to the Center. Although arts and crafts of every country and age of the Western Hemisphere are exhibited, the emphasis is on Latin America.

Central Park ★
*Maps **6**&**7**.*

Throughout its history, pragmatic visionaries have tempered the city's headlong rush to squeeze every penny of profit from the limited available land. In 1844, most of Manhattan N of 50th St. was a wasteland, supporting only squatters. Poet William Cullen Bryant prodded City Hall into acquiring 840 acres between what were to become 5th Ave. and 8th Ave. and 59th St. and 110th St. Frederick Law Olmsted and Calvert Vaux submitted the winning landscaping scheme in 1857. Its execution required 20yr, but the results are cherished by every New Yorker – whether cyclist, jogger, stroller, lover, picnicker or baseball player. There are lakes, bridges, ponds, glades, hillocks, meadows, fountains, zoos, boat houses, playgrounds, bandstands, bridle paths, sculptures, terraces, a skating rink and an outdoor theatre for summer Shakespeare. In a real sense, it is New York's greatest single achievement. (See *Walk 6* in *Planning*.)

Central Park Zoo
5th Ave. and 64th St., NY 10021 ☎ *360–8213. Map **7**M4* ▣ *Children's Zoo* ▣ ▆ ✿ *Open 11.00–17.00; Children's Zoo 10.00–16.30.*

Small and always crowded, the zoo is a handy alternative for those without the time or inclination to travel to the far superior *Bronx Zoo and New York Botanical Garden*. It is undergoing needed rejuvenation. Feeding time for the seals (mid-afternoon) is the major draw, but the lions, monkeys, elephants, polar bears, jungle cats and camels are nearly as diverting, even if they often seem dispirited. An elevated cafeteria provides facilities for creature-watching. Stroll N, crossing the Transverse Rd., to reach the separate **Children's Zoo** where farm animals come forward to be fed and scratched behind the ears. (See *Walk 6* in *Planning*.)

Chelsea
Map 4Q3

The genesis of the neighbourhood known as Chelsea is attributed to an unlikely creator. Writer Clement Clark Moore inherited the land and drew up plans for streets and buildings. Many of his blocks of terraced houses remain, albeit often scarred by 20thC so-called improvements, but all too frequently they have been displaced by uninspired residential and industrial buildings. There are signs of an intensifying gentrification process, with antique shops, off-off Broadway experimental theatres, music pubs, art galleries, and nightclubs sufficiently chic to incite uptowners into long taxi rides. The principal landmark is the *Chelsea Hotel*, one of the first luxury apartment houses. Less well known is the **General Theological Seminary**: enter the door at 175 9th Ave. and emerge in an unexpected square of trees and lawns. Boundaries of the district are 14th St. to 23rd St., 7th Ave. to the Hudson River.

Chelsea Hotel ▥
222 W 23rd St. (8th Ave.), NY 10011 ☎ *243–3700. Map 4Q3.*

Constructed in 1884 as one of the first apartment houses, the Chelsea was meant to attract wealthy tenants from a class which until then had nearly always chosen private homes. Inducements were its duplex suites, marble fireplaces, new-fangled lift, generous proportions, and proximity to what was the main theatre and shopping district. In addition, the fireproof construction was so cautiously designed that it exceeds even present-day safety standards.

Unlike the uptown *Dakota Apartments*, completed the same year with similar objectives, the Chelsea slid in reputation as the city rolled northward. In 1905, it was converted to a hotel that has proved irresistible to artists, writers and composers. Thomas Wolfe, Virgil Thompson, O. Henry, Tennessee Williams, Jackson Pollock, and Sarah Bernhardt are but a few of those who lived here. The Bohemian panache they imparted persists, and there are paintings by former and present tenants in the dingy lobby. About half the rooms are available to transients; the rest have permanent tenants.

China House
125 E 65th St. (Park Ave.), NY 10021 ☎ *744–8181. Map 7M4* ▨ *Open Mon–Fri 10.00–17.00, Sat 11.00–17.00, Sun 14.00–17.00.*

Ferocious carved dogs at the entrance, biannual exhibitions of art from the mother country, and cooking and language classes help satisfy (and arouse) the current occidental curiosity about things Chinese. But China House has had a longer life and different sponsorship than might be expected. The parent institute was created in 1926 to aid Chinese-Americans and foster cultural relations with the West. In 1945, a grand East Side house was donated by controversial publisher Henry Luce to serve as headquarters. Luce was co-founder of the Time-Life empire and had been born in China of missionary parents. A full

range of educational and cultural offerings is available to
citizens of Chinese origin and the larger public, including films,
lectures, courses in calligraphy, opera, and vocational training
for newly-arrived immigrants. The twice-yearly art exhibitions
are usually held in spring and late autumn.

Chinatown ☆
Map 2T4.

Traditionally defined as eight square blocks between *The
Bowery*, and Mulberry, Worth, and Canal Sts., Chinatown has
spilled over the boundaries in recent years. From 1882, when a
Federal law specifically excluded Chinese immigrants, until the
1960s, when such clearly racial restrictions were raised, the
population of the community was relatively stable. The core of
the neighbourhood is gratifyingly exotic, the air heavy with
dialects and enticing aromas. Every other restaurant is hung
with golden ducks and even the telephone boxes have pagoda
roofs. (See *Walk 3* in *Planning*.)

Chinese Museum
8 Mott St. (near Park Row), NY 10013 ☎ *964–1542. Map
3S5* 🍴 ♣ *Open Mon–Sat 10.00–18.00. Closed Sun.*

Dominating the hall is a cousin of the fearsome gilded dragon
that snakes through Chinatown on the shoulders of tireless
young men every New Year's Day (after the first full moon in
Jan). But this small and funky repository – its entrance is off an
arcade of bleeping electronic game machines – also houses
printed materials, fireworks, costumes, coins and musical
instruments. Among the less offbeat exhibits are scores of
labelled wax specimens of Chinese foods, which aid
identification of the real thing in nearby restaurant windows.

Chrysler Building 🏛 ☆
405 Lexington Ave. (42nd St.), NY 10017 ☎ *682–3070.
Map 5O4* 👁 *Open Mon–Fri 9.00–17.00. Closed Sat, Sun.*

For a flicker of time after its completion in 1930, this was the
highest structure in the world at 1,048ft (320m), the first to
surpass the Eiffel Tower. But that was a period of intense
speculative competition, and the *Empire State Building* soon
took the title. Over 50yr later, however, the Chrysler is still in
the top ten, and it remains the most satisfying aesthetic result of
the skyscraper mania. Art Deco arches of stainless steel
surmount the tower, flaring in the sun, base for a slender spire
that thrusts 123ft (37m) into the clouds. Abstract
representations of automobile parts inform friezes and other
decorative details, in deference to the first owner's business.
There is no observation floor, but look at the Cubistic
assemblages of grained marble and chrome in the lobby.

Church of the Ascension 🏛 †
36 5th Ave. (10th St.), NY 10003 ☎ *254–8620. Map 2R4.
Open Mon–Sat 12.00–14.00, 17.00–19.00. Closed Sun.*

The first church on lower 5th Ave. (when upper 5th was still
country), this was also the first to be executed in the Gothic
Revival mode then sweeping through Europe. Brownstone was
used for the facing, a material that was to become a favourite of
the well-to-do for their terraced houses. In 1889, McKim,
Mead & White remodelled parts of the interior and the parish
house, hiring Louis Comfort Tiffany for the design of some of
the stained glass.

Church of the Transfiguration

1 E 29th St. (5th Ave.), NY 10016 ☎ *684–6770. Map* **5***P4
Open 8.00–18.00.*

It is said that when an actor asked to be married, he was firmly dispatched to this 'Little Church Around the Corner', an institution presumably not overly concerned about the dubious professions and social status of its parishioners. The church was built around 1850 and has a long association with show folk.

Citicorp Center 🏛 ☆

153 E 53rd St. (Lexington Ave.), NY 10022 ☎ *559–4259.
Map* **5***N4* 🖃 *Open 8.00–24.00.*

Posterity has yet to render its verdict on this building. Its distinctive sloping roof line moves it into the Post-Modernist category of skyscraper design, away from the rectangular glass boxes of the Bauhaus school. The roof was intended to house solar energy collectors, a good intention sacrificed to the gods of cost accounting. Quibbles aside, the 1978 building brought life to a dreary block and accommodated into its design the modest but striking **St Peter's Lutheran Church**. Office floors begin at 127ft (39m), clearing the church steeple and providing a public atrium embracing 22 shops and restaurants. The interior plaza is filled with trees and tables, and live music is often laid on by the management. Co-operating were Hugh Stubbins and Emery Roth & Sons – the latter firm was also partly responsible for such looming local monoliths as the *World Trade Center* and *Pan Am Building*.

City Hall 🏛

City Hall Park (Broadway and Murray St.), NY 10007
☎ *566–5200. Map* **2***T4* 🖃 *Open Mon–Fri 10.00–15.00.
Closed Sat, Sun.*

Both dwarfed and enhanced by the taller buildings that enclose it on three sides, the third and present City Hall (1811) is a Georgian-Federal-Renaissance gem which even the Sun King might have accepted (at least as a summer cottage). (See *Walk 3* in *Planning*.)

Cleopatra's Needle

Central Park. Map **7***L4.*

One of only four obelisks outside Egypt, it was erected in *Central Park* in 1881, behind the *Metropolitan Museum of Art*. The red granite spire is covered with hieroglyphics from the time of Thutmose III (c.1600 BC). Regrettably, the change in climate, plus air pollution, has worn them down.

The Cloisters 🏛 ☆

Fort Tryon Park, NY 10040 ☎ *923–3700 ext 26. Map* **10***B2*
🖼 𝟀 ⌕ *Open Tues–Sat 10.00–16.45, Sun 13.00–16.45.
Closed Mon, Sun (Sept–May). Half-price entry for senior citizens, children. Subway A to 190th St.*

Save The Cloisters for a day when the freneticism of the Big Apple becomes overbearing. This far-uptown unit of the *Metropolitan Museum of Art* is a wondrous oasis in *Fort Tryon Park*, overlooking the Hudson River from the northern heights of the island. On the crest of a hill banked by woodland and meadows, parts of several European monasteries and chapels have been blended in a unified edifice of blissful serenity. The collection was founded by George Grey Barnard, who gathered vast amounts of superb medieval sculpture on his many visits to

The Cloisters Main floor

Gothic Chapel

Early
Gothic Hall

West Terrace

Cuxa

St Guilhem
Cloister

Fuentidueña Chapel

Cloister

Late Gothic Hall

Entrance Hall

Froville
Arcade

Upper driveway

Lower
driveway

N

1 Pontaut Chapter House
2 Nine Heroes Tapestries
3 Unicorn Tapestries
4 Boppard Room
5 Burgos Tapestries

6 Spanish Room
7 Romanesque Hall
8 Langon Chapel
9 Books and
   Reproductions

Bonnefont
Cloister

Glass Gallery

Trie
Cloister

Treasury

Lower driveway

Lower floor

Europe. It was first opened to the public in 1914 and moved to
its present home in 1938, following a donation by the
Rockefeller family.

Main floor (N and W)   Approach is made up a curving
driveway from the bus stop and car park, and entry is past nine
arches from the **15thC Benedictine friary of Froville**. Walk
through the French 12thC archway into the **Romanesque Hall**
and turn right into the **Fuentidueña Chapel**✩ The low black
stone baptismal font just inside is from Belgium, the barrel-
vaulted apse from Segovia, the fresco above the altar from
Catalonia. All are believed to be of the 12thC. On the left is a
16thC painted limestone sculpture from Zamora. The grinning
hyena-like creature was meant to be a lion, and is surmounted
by a headless Christ figure placing a crown on Mary's head.
Return to the Romanesque Hall and turn into the **St Guilhem
Cloister**✩ Perhaps because of the delicacy of the
ornamentation on the ancient pillars, this is the only indoor
cloister. A glass ceiling permits boxed plants to grow in winter.
Paired capitals and columns feature stylized leaves, flowers,
and human figures. No two pairs are the same. As in the other
rooms, a plan on the wall shows which portions are authentic.

69

Return to the Romanesque Hall once more and turn into the **Langon Chapel**. Note the thick oak doors banded with ironwork that serves both decorative and support functions. Much of the stonework is from an 11thC church in Langon, near Bordeaux, and the carved faces of the capital high on the right of the nave are often alleged to be Henry II and Eleanor of Aquitaine. The centrepiece of the chapel is the marble ciborium or tabernacle, a roofed structure on four pillars that shelters an altar and a 12thC Burgundian *Virgin and Child* carved from birch. Leave the chapel through the door on the left and turn sharply right to the **West Terrace**, a belvedere overlooking the usually placid Hudson and the high bluffs on the opposite shore called the Palisades. Apart from the *George Washington Bridge* to the s, there is little to detract from the impression that this was the way the riverscape looked when the first European settlers arrived. Go back inside, turning right at the end of the short corridor.

The **Pontaut Chapter House ☆** is from a Benedictine abbey in Gascony, probably dating from the late 12thC. Because the room is nearly all original, it conveys the strongest sense of place of anywhere in The Cloisters. Ribbed, vaulted ceilings hint at early Gothic influences, but the rounded arches, sombre capitals, and massive walls are clearly Romanesque. Bands of brick alternate with crudely shaped stone, all of which was once covered in plaster. Walk out in the **Cuxa Cloister ☆** in which the monastic mood is usually enhanced by recorded Gregorian chants and other sacred music of the Middle Ages and Renaissance. This is the largest of the cloisters, open to the sky, its four-sided colonnade enclosing a garden. It covers approximately half the area of its original 12thC site, a monastery in the French Pyrénées. Look closely at the capitals of the rose-streaked marble columns, for each is different, depicting simple leaf motifs, lions, complex hunting scenes and mythical animals. Circle the courtyard in this observation, looking for the mermaid capital in the E arcade, the best decorative work in the group.

> But let my due feet never fail
> To walk the studious cloisters pale,
> And love the high embowed roof,
> With antique pillars massy proof
>
> Milton, *Il Penseroso*

Continue past the Chapter House and enter the **Early Gothic Hall** to examine the ecclesiastical figures, then move on to the **Gothic Chapel**. Distinctions from the Romanesque style predominating to this point are evident in the pointed arches and ribbed vaulting, the 14thC stained glass, and the greater delicacy of the stonework, especially at the tops of the window openings. Large effigies and sarcophagi are dotted about. Their origins are French and Catalan, while most of the glass is Austrian. Take the stairs down to the lower floor.

Lower floor In the **Glass Gallery**, pause to study the 15th–16thC stained glass from which it takes its name. At the end is a large section of intricately carved woodwork that once enclosed the staircase of a house in Abbeville, France. Although holy figures are duly depicted, the effect is of secular Gothic exuberance. The room straight ahead houses 37 carved wood panels, again from Abbeville but this time they convey a distinctly religious impression.

Turn left into the **Treasury** ✿ which features exquisite chalices of silver and gold, one from the 4thC. This route leads back past the Abbeville woodwork to a door opening into the **Trie Cloister**. Off the main traffic lanes of the museum, this secluded spot encourages the contemplative frame of mind for which it was intended. Each capital varies from the others, the scenes more literal than those so far encountered, and the slender double pillars are of differently coloured marble. The plants surrounding the fountain are examples of those found in the Unicorn Tapestries (below). Leave by the doorway at the NW corner, walking along the arcade modelled on the cloister of the abbey at **Bonnefont-en-Comminges**. Here, the attraction is not the architecture but the **garden** ✿ that is heady with lemon thyme, marjoram, mace and woodruff. Brick paths separate beds of violets and forget-me-nots, dominated by four quince trees. A low wall affords views of the park to the S, and birdwatchers are often surprised by the variety of species attracted to the garden. When ready, re-enter the Glass Gallery and return upstairs.

Main floor (S and E) From the Gothic Chapel, turn into the **Nine Heroes Tapestries** room. The late 14thC hangings show five of the heroes who featured in this popular theme, among them Alexander the Great, Charlemagne and Julius Caesar. Understandably faded and fragmented, the tapestries provide a foretaste of the splendid 16thC **Unicorn Tapestries** ✿ in the next hall. Scholarly consensus ranks this set of seven superbly executed panels among the finest in existence. That assessment may be restrained, for in concept, detailing and craftsmanship, they are peerless. The remarkable petal-by-leaf renderings of plants and flowers make it possible to identify many of the live specimens seen in the Trie Cloister (above). Beyond such surface delights is the telling of a tale with deep symbolic undercurrents. Christ is seen as a Unicorn, Gabriel as a hunter with a horn, Satan as a snake; pagan beliefs mingle with Christian convictions, fruits and blossoms represent purity, lust, fertility. Baronial German furnishings and a flamboyant French Gothic fireplace suggest the surroundings in which the tapestries were for a long time viewed.

The **Boppard Room** is named after the German town where its six 15thC stained glass panels originated. Go past the late 15thC **Burgos Tapestries**, executed to the glorification of Charles VIII of France, and turn into the **Spanish Room** to see Robert Campin's *Annunciation* triptych (c.1425). The altarpiece is remarkable for the choice of setting: a simple Flemish interior rather than the traditional ecclesiastical or historical environment. The painted Gothic red pine ceiling in this room is also worthy of attention. Leave the museum through the **Late Gothic Hall**, noting the fine 15thC Spanish retable on your way out.

Coliseum   See *New York Coliseum*.

Columbia University 🏛

Broadway (116th St.), NY 10027 ☎ *280–1754. Map 8I2* ☒
Open 24hr. Subway 1 to 116th St. – Columbia University.
Established in 1754 as King's College, and fuelled by over two centuries of alumni bequests and gifts, Columbia is now one of the wealthiest universities in the US. As a member of the prestigious group known as the Ivy League, which includes Harvard, Yale and Princeton, it is also one of the most

distinguished. With the end of the Revolution, 'King's' College became 'Columbia', and after an intermediate move to Madison Ave. and 49th St., settled here at Morningside Heights in 1897. Over the years, the original men's college has joined with a teacher's college and Barnard College for women, and courses now include business administration, law, medicine, dentistry, librarianship, journalism, social work and public health. Founding father Alexander Hamilton graduated from here and Dwight Eisenhower was the university's president after World War II before moving on to higher office.

The original layout of the campus and two of the first buildings were products of McKim, Mead & White. Fortunately, their design was opened up to permit larger pedestrian plazas which in turn lent greater drama to the most prominent building, **Low Library**. Its style is Neo-Classical, with a surmounting dome and a portico with ten columns and coffered ceiling. The elevated site makes the most of the building's monumentality. Halfway up the wide front steps is a statue of *Alma Mater* by Daniel Chester French, best known for his sculptures of Abraham Lincoln. Low Library is essentially an administration building. **Butler Library**, to the s, is the main repository of the university's 5-million volume collection.

The Terrace Restaurant on the top floor is open to the public. Given its auspices, the food and service are quite good, and it affords excellent views of Manhattan.

Coney Island

Brooklyn. Map 12F3. Subway B, D, F, M, N, QB to Stillwell Ave. – Coney Island.

For generations of working-class New Yorkers, Coney Island was Riviera-on-the-Subway, a wide strip of powdery sand that gave surcease from the steaming streets and tenements of the city. It has fallen on hard times, the shattered and burned-out housing inland occupied only by pensioners and the poor, the Steeplechase Park amusement centre a wasteland. Still, the beach has been cleaned up, the boardwalk repaired, the original **Nathan's Famous** grills hundreds of incomparable hot dogs daily, teenagers squeal through rollercoaster dips at Astroland, and families gape at the sharks and dolphins of the *New York Aquarium*. The district is on the Atlantic Ocean in s Brooklyn, along Surf Ave. between W 37th St. and Ocean Parkway.

Cooper-Hewitt Museum ▥ ☆

2 E 91st St. (5th Ave.) ☎ 860–6868. Map 7K4 ▨ Ж Open Tues 10.00–21.00, Wed–Sat 10.00–17.00, Sun 12.00–17.00. Closed Mon.

In this pricey venue at the top of the 5th Ave. 'Museum Mile', even millionaires built their mansions flush with their property boundaries, foregoing lawns and gardens. But in that lamented time before the imposition of income taxes, Scottish-born Andrew Carnegie was more than simply rich. He had just sold his steel company (1901) for over $250 million. When he built this 64-room house in the same year, he left himself a green buffer all around and transplanted mature trees from upstate. Only a friend and business associate like Henry C. Frick could indulge himself in a similar fashion (see the *Frick Collection*).

If pressed, an art historian might describe the Carnegie house as Georgian, but the design was carried out with such an elephantine hand that this label is hardly appropriate. Despite the unfortunate facade, there is a pleasant garden behind the cast-iron fence and a marvellous stained-glass canopy over the entrance. Within are the decorative art acquisitions of Peter Cooper (founder of *Cooper Union*) and his granddaughters Eleanor and Sarah Hewitt. The only New York branch of the Smithsonian Institution, its sub-title is the National Museum of Design. That objective is broadly defined, to incorporate wallpapers, furniture, glassware, metalwork, lace and ceramics, with superb examples of each. The dual strengths of the museum are its textiles and over 30,000 drawings. The drawings include works by Dürer, Rembrandt and Winslow Homer. Fabrics and embroidery come from as far afield as Persia, France, India, Egypt and Italy, and span 14 centuries.

Cooper Union 🏛

Cooper Sq., NY 10003 ☎ *254–6300. Map **2**R4. Open 8.00–22.00.*

Peter Cooper became a millionaire through participation in the key, 19thC industries of railways and ironmaking. In the benevolent if paternalistic manner of his fellows, he founded this college for the training of artists and engineers and built the sombre pile (1859) that still houses part of the institution. The Foundation Building rather resembles a railway station of the time – dark, brooding, ponderous.

Still, Cooper made provision for a free-tuition curriculum for talented persons of any race, sex, creed or economic status at a time when such notions were deemed dangerous to the natural order of things. That policy persists, and has profited tens of thousands of Americans who might not otherwise have had the chance of higher education. The Great Hall within hosted many celebrated speakers of the last century, among them suffragette Susan B. Anthony, abolitionist Henry Ward Beecher, Mark Twain and, in a rare New York appearance, Abraham Lincoln.

Craft Museum   See *American Craft Museum*.

Dakota Apartments 🏛

*1 W 72nd St., NY 10023. Map **6**M3.*

Until 1884, members of New York's establishment would not consider living in anything but a private house. This luxury 10-floor apartment building changed their minds, even though it was so far uptown that wags said it was in Dakota Indian territory. Its capacious rooms, high ceilings, thick-walled quiet, and offbeat Bavarian fortress exterior ensure its continued cachet with celebrities and other privileged folk. *Rosemary's Baby* was filmed here. John Lennon was murdered outside the entrance in 1980.

Downtown Whitney Museum

33 Maiden Lane, NY 10005 ☎ *431–1621. Map* 2U4 ▣ *Open Mon–Wed, Fri, Sat 11.00–18.00, Thurs 11.00–19.30. Closed Sun.*

A child of the uptown *Whitney Museum of American Art*, this branch caters to the mostly non-residential population of the *Financial District*. After a decade of migrations around lower Manhattan, it seems to have found a permanent home here on Federal Reserve Plaza on the concourse level of a 26-storey skyscraper. Rotating shows from the permanent collection and other sources are augmented by art appreciation classes and concerts. This new facility was due to open Jan 1986, and the hours and telephone number may be subject to alteration.

Dyckman House 🏛

*4881 Broadway (204th St.), NY 10543 ☎ 923–8008
(Morris-Jumel Mansion) for information. Map **10**B2 ◻ Open
Tues–Sun 11.00–17.00. Closed Mon. Subway 1 to 217th St.*

The original owner of the property was Jan Dyckman. He came
to New Amsterdam in 1661 and swiftly assembled the
substantial estate he was to pass on to his descendants. For no
recorded tactical reason, the house built here in 1748 was
burned to the ground by British troops near the end of the
Revolutionary War. The existing replacement was erected in
1783, before they left Manhattan. The estate was once thick
with fruit trees and was tilled by tenant farmers well into the
19thC. Parts of the orchard still bloomed past 1900. Brick and
flagstone form portions of the lower sections of the house, with
weatherboarding rising to a low gambrel roof. The effect is
appropriately Dutch Colonial, and some of the furnishings are
authentic not only to the period but to the original family.

Although it is a long subway ride N to the Inwood district, the
tranquil setting and park-like grounds smooth nerve ends
frayed by the clamour of midtown.

East Side ☆

*Map **7**L4.*

From 5th Ave. to the East River and 59th St. to 92nd St., this
chic precinct (also known as Upper East Side) harbours most of
the city's major museums, upscale single people, and
resident millionaires, foreign and domestic. Tree-shaded cross
streets near 5th Ave. are lined with attractive terraced houses,
the owners of which have succeeded in fending off the
blandishments of developers. Commercial interlopers tend to
be low-profile boutiques and art and antique galleries. Near the
river are the luxury enclaves of **Beekman Place** and **Sutton
Place**. Along the avenues, beautiful people swirl in a fickle flow
from this month's bistro to the of-the-minute bar and meet each
other in queues for the latest film. (See *Walk 7* in *Planning*.)

Ellis Island

*New York Harbor, NY 10004 ☎ 732–1236/1286. Map
12D3 ▨ ✗ Open May–Nov 9.30–18.00. Ferry from Battery
Park 9.30, 11.45, 14.00, 16.15 (check first)*

The echoing, gloomy halls must have seemed forbidding to the
12 million immigrants who passed through this bureaucratic
purgatory between 1892–1954. Some were held for weeks and
months before being permitted entry to the tantalizing city in
sight across the bay. Restoration of the island's 30-odd
buildings is underway.

Empire State Building 🏛 ★

*350 5th Ave. (34th St.), NY 10001 ☎ 736–3100. Map **5**P4
▨ ✗ ■ ♦ Open 9.30–24.00. Check visibility notice before
buying tickets.*

From its inception, the Empire State Building attracted
superlatives – in achievement and in tragedy. Now only the
third highest building in the world, after the Sears Building in
Chicago and the downtown *World Trade Center*, it
nevertheless remains the foremost symbol of New York. And it
does, after all, stand 1,472ft (448m) high, including TV mast.
By comparison, the Eiffel Tower is 984ft (300m).

King Kong swatted at biplanes from his perch in the 1931

classic, a plane crashed into the 79th floor in 1945, and at least 17 people have flung themselves to their deaths off parapets and down lift shafts. The distinctive stepped cap was sketched in during one of the later design stages. It was to have been a mooring mast for airships. One attempt to bring that fanciful notion to reality resulted in some celebrated citizens nearly being blown away, and the idea was discarded. Without the rounded cap, the original 86 stories were only 2ft (61cm) higher than the *Chrysler Building*. With it, another 200ft (61m) and a second public observatory were added. Perhaps as remarkable as its height was the fact that the Empire State came in under schedule and under budget.

Twice a month, 6,500 windows must be washed. There are 60 miles of water pipes within the walls and 60,000 tons of structural steel. For reasons best known to the participants, an annual foot race is run *up* the 1,575 steps to the 86th floor. The facing is limestone, fashioned in modified Art Deco. The observatory on the 86th floor is wide open, the one on the 102nd floor enclosed with glass. Go during the day or at night, saving the other time for another of Manhattan's eyries.

Federal Hall National Memorial 🏛

26 Wall St. (Nassau St.), NY 10005 ☎ *264–8711. Map* **2***U4* ⊠ 𝘟 *by appointment. Open Mon–Fri 9.00–17.00. Closed Sat, Sun.*

Paradigm of the early 19thC enthusiasm for the Greeks, Federal Hall is not the building in which Washington took his oath of office in 1789, as is inferred by many. The **statue of George Washington** outside stands where the first President did indeed make those vows, but the building behind was not completed until 1842. It housed government offices from then until 1955, when it was converted to its present use as a museum. The main floor has artefacts of the Revolutionary War period – such as railings from the porch on which Washington repeated the famous words – while the *Downtown Whitney Museum* of contemporary art takes up most of the mezzanine level.

Architects Town & Davis resisted the impulse to slap on sculptured friezes and ornate capitals, opting for fluted Doric columns and an unadorned pediment, all of marble quarried a few miles N of the city. Their only major deviation from their Greek inspiration was the interior rotunda, but the dramatic space works, which is ample justification. All in all, it is a trimlined Parthenon of disciplined stolidity and the finest example of Greek Revival in Manhattan.

Financial District ☆

Map **2***U4.*

Bits and scraps of Little Old New York remain, but the southern end of Manhattan has long shuddered beneath the thrusting monoliths of international commerce and the machinations taking place within. The world eavesdrops on every whisper at the Stock Exchange, and conglomerates eye each other from their steel and concrete eyries.

Not long ago, the restaurants closed in this district in the evenings and at weekends, and Sun afternoons drew only a few strollers down ghostly windswept canyons. Now a trickle of people are moving back to live in rehabilitated warehouses and middle-aged skyscrapers, and visitors come for sun and nautical history to the *South Street Seaport Museum*. (See *Walk 2* in *Planning*.)

Fire Department Museum

278 Spring St. (near Varick St.), NY 10013 ☎691–1303.
Map 2S3 ⬚ 𝄞 ✸ Open Mon–Fri 9.00–16.00, Sat, Sun
9.00–14.00

New York bristles with quirky and beguiling specialized
museums tucked into out-of-the-way corners. They take little
time to explore and often enchant in unexpected ways. This is
one. Three floors of antique firefighting equipment are
currently housed in a 1909 fire station, although a move to
a new location seems likely. A lovingly polished silver-plated
steam engine highlights the collection of hand- and horse-
drawn vehicles that dates back to the early 19thC. This
collection is to be combined with that of the former Firefighting Museum and renamed the **New York Fire House**.

Flatiron Building � ☆

175 5th Ave. (23rd St.), NY 10010. Map 5Q4.

The reasons to visit are its status as the first true skyscraper (a
disputed claim) and its odd triangular shape (dictated by its plot
at the confluence of 5th Ave. and Broadway). In the earliest tall
buildings, made possible by the invention of the electric lift,
metal cages supported floors while masonry facings bore their
own weight. In the decade before the Flatiron, new techniques
allowed riveted steel frames to bear both floors *and* facing. That
sort of steel skeleton was employed here, 286ft (87m) high and
only 6ft (2m) wide at its narrow end. To calm the conservative
citizenry, a rusticated limestone facade imitated a stacked
Italianate palace. Nevertheless, many were convinced that the
building would collapse in the high winds characteristic of the
area. It didn't. You can enter the lobby during business hours,
but there is no compelling reason to do so.

Ford Foundation Building ⬚

320 E 43rd St. (2nd Ave.), NY 10016 ☎ 573–5000. Map
5O5 ⬚ Open Mon–Fri 9.00–17.00. Closed Sat, Sun.

Atriums are in danger of becoming a cliché as pervasive as
sunken plazas in contemporary New York commercial
architecture – a sop to planning boards and environmental
groups dismayed by the loss of landmarks and the addition of
thousands of new commuters straining public services.
Resulting spaces are often bleak and inhuman. The Ford
Foundation presented a gift to the city, however, not a burden,
with this 1967 headquarters. Its interior is enclosed within a
glass shell hung between four granite columns and contains a
third of an acre of mature trees and shrubs. A brook, hushed
and clear, curls through the garden. Passers-by are welcome to
step inside for a moment's respite.

Striking as it is, the exterior is in harmony with the scale of
the block, contributing rather than intruding. The offices
above the greenery are for the staff of the Foundation, which
was created by Henry and Edsel Ford. It is the largest
philanthropic trust in the world, concerning itself with a broad
spectrum of human welfare issues, although best known for its
contributions to education and the arts.

Fort Tryon Park

Map 10C2 ⬚ ✸ ⬚ Subway A to 190th St.

While *The Cloisters* museum is the prime motive for a subway
ride to this pastoral far-north Manhattan sanctuary, also
tendered are hills, woodlands, meadows, a small but fascinating

botanical garden, a children's playground with paddling pool, and staggering Hudson River vistas from the site of the namesake fortification. During the week, only an occasional cyclist or jogger interrupts the solitude.

Fraunces Tavern Museum

54 Pearl St. (Broad St.), NY 10004 ☎ *425–1778. Map 2U4* ☲ *✗ by appointment* ℝ *Open Mon–Fri 10.00–16.00. Closed Sat, Sun.*

Tourist literature routinely implies that this is the tavern where George Washington bade farewell to his troops. It isn't. Rather, it is a 20thC approximation of debatable accuracy, constructed on the site of the original and incorporating parts of the remaining walls. The first building was a three-storey mansion, converted into a tavern in 1762 by Samuel Fraunces. A West Indian, he became steward to Washington when the English took New York in 1776. The General returned on December 4, 1783 for lunch with his officers and delivered the famous address. Downstairs is now a restaurant; upstairs and in adjacent buildings there is a collection of Revolutionary musketry and mementoes and two period rooms.

French Institute

22 E 60th St. (Madison Ave.), NY 10022 ☎ *355–6100. Map 5N4* ☲ *Open Mon–Thurs 10.00–20.00, Fri 10.00–17.30, Sat (Sept–June) 10.00–13.30. Closed Sun.*

In a spectrum of activities to gladden the heart of every Francophile, the institute offers language and cooking classes, recent and venerable films, concerts, recitals, lectures – all relating to the mother country. Students and homesick expatriates can find French magazines and newspapers and perhaps a new friend in the small gallery and library.

Frick Collection ☆

1 E 70th St. (5th Ave.), NY 10021 ☎ *288–0700. Map 7M4* ☲ ☲ *Open Sept–May Tues–Sat 10.00–18.00, Sun 13.00–18.00; closed Mon. June–Aug Wed–Sat 10.00–18.00, Sun 13.00–18.00; closed Mon, Tues, July 1. Children under 10 not admitted, 10–16 only with adult.*

From the 1890s onwards the part of 5th Ave. facing lower Central Park has been a millionaires' row. Now the privileged live in duplex penthouses, for not even the very wealthy can afford to maintain the palatial residences built by their antecedents. Most of those mansions have been demolished, a few converted to institutional use. The Andrew Carnegie residence, for example, is now the *Cooper-Hewitt Museum*. All this makes the Frick Collection even more special, for the house is much the way that it was left by the first and only owner — filled with paintings, furniture, clocks and Persian carpets.

Carnegie and industrialist Henry C. Frick were business associates who parted company over policy disputes. Frick chose to build his house (in 1914) only 20 blocks s of his former friend's 64-room residence. Although bearing allegiance to no particular style, its low roofline and front lawn are a welcome visual break in the prevailing wall of high-rises. And there is no more gracious oasis in the city than the interior court with its splashing fountain and flowering plants. After Frick's death, a harmonious addition doubled the floor space. The house was opened to the public in 1935.

Frick Collection

Entrance is made from E 70th St. The first important room
on your left is the **Boucher Room**, with eight panels
representing the *Arts and Sciences* that Francois Boucher
painted for one of Madame de Pompadour's legendary Rococo
bedrooms. Next is the corner **Dining Room ✩** which is perhaps
the most striking room in the mansion, with its French
furniture and 18thC paintings by Hogarth, Gainsborough and
Reynolds. To the N is the **Fragonard Room ✩** where four
paintings known as *The Progress of Love*, once owned by
Madame du Barry, celebrate the different stages of love. The
other seven panels were also executed by Jean-Honoré
Fragonard, a disciple of Boucher and a favourite at the court of
Louis XV. Furnishings in the room are consistent with the
period. The high point of the **Living Hall** is the El Greco
portrait of *St Jerome* over the fireplace. It is flanked by two
Hans Holbein paintings, and there are also works by Titian and
Bellini. On the centre table is a bronze by Pollaiuolo. Leading
off from this room are the **South Hall**, notable for Vermeer's
Officer and Laughing Girl, and **North Hall**, which has Ingres'
portrait of *La Comtesse d'Hausonville*. The **Library** concentrates
once again on English painting, with a George Romney portrait
of *Lady Hamilton* and a luminous early Turner. Priceless
Chinese vases add to the authentic appeal of this panelled room.
    Largest of the chambers is the **West Gallery ✩** with its
imposing chilliness offset by the splendour of the masterpieces.
They deserve a methodical clockwise examination. (On the
way, turn into the small **Enamel Room** for a look at Limoges
painted enamels of the 15th–17thC.) Among the treasures of
this trove are a trio of Rembrandts, two works by Van Dyck, a
Velazquez, a Goya and an El Greco. Turner was a progenitor of
the Impressionist revolution that followed his death in 1851,
and his vivid cityscape of Dieppe is particularly significant in
this respect.
    Pass through the **Oval Room** with its Whistlers and terra
cotta *Diana* into the **East Gallery** where Goya, Gainsborough
and Van Dyck are featured. Finally, there is the **Garden
Court ✩** with its glass roof and fountain. Chamber music

concerts take place on occasional Suns. Inquire at the entrance desk for detailed information.

Garment Center
Map 4P3.

Neither steel nor automobiles nor their ilk are fabricated in New York so, by default, people in suits conjuring advertising jingles and peddling stocks describe themselves as 'industries'. As that word is commonly understood, however, the primary manufacturing enterprise of the city is clothing. Somewhere between 80,000 and 300,000 citizens are employed in the rag trade, depending upon how a statistician tots up the cutters, shippers, salesmen, suppliers, designers, messengers, models, packers, deliverymen, buyers, union organizers and sewing machine operators. Between breakfast and dinner, all of them seem to pour through the streets of this scruffy district along 7th Ave. between 34th and 40th Sts., dodging handcarts, gulping coffee from paper containers, grabbing lapels, scuttling to appointments, making deals. The fashions they produce often rival the best of Paris and Milan.

General Grant National Memorial ▥
Riverside Drive (122nd St.), NY 10027 ☎ 666–1640. Map 8H2 ⊡ ✗ Open Wed–Sun 9.00–17.00. Closed Oct–May Mon, Tues.

Popularly known as Grant's Tomb, it is no accident that the official designation honours the Civil War service of Ulysses S. Grant rather than his scandal-ridden tenure as the eighteenth President. The mausoleum is fashioned after a 4thC Greek tomb and was financed by private contributions rather than by Congress. After its completion in 1897, both Grant and his wife were interred within, behind impressive bronze doors. A gallery shows photographs and memorabilia from both careers. The Gaudiesque mosaic benches around the plaza outside are more interesting.

George Washington Bridge ▥
Map 10D1 ▨

Dreamers of the 19thC insisted that the broad Hudson River could be spanned, but it took the capitalistic euphoria of the late 1920s to bring together the necessary funds and determination. The bridge was completed in 1931, within months of the *Empire State, Chrysler* and *RCA Buildings* and, like them, was defiant of the economic desolation of the Great Depression. For a time, the 3,500ft (1,067m) between its main towers made it the longest suspension bridge in the world. Budgetary considerations and public opinion fortunately prevented plans to sheath the open steel framework in concrete and granite, as envisioned by architect Cass Gilbert. A second deck for trams and trains was planned by engineer Othmar H. Ammann, but was not added until 1962, when it was given over to general road traffic. There are eight lanes on the upper deck, six below.

Goethe House
1014 5th Ave. (82nd St.), NY 10028 ☎ 744–8310. Map 7L4 ⊡ Open Wed, Fri, Sat 12.00–17.00, Tues, Thurs 11.00–19.00. Closed Sun, Mon.

Films, lectures, art exhibitions and research materials fill this cultural repository, one of dozens sponsored by the Federal Republic of Germany around the world.

Grace Church 🏛 †

802 Broadway (10th St.), NY 10003 ☎ 254–2000. Map 2R4. Open Mon–Fri 9.00–17.00, Sat, Sun for services only.
Although a practising engineer, James Renwick took advantage of the mid-19thC tolerance for professional generalism to design this fine Episcopal church. Its success led to commissions for *St Patrick's Cathedral* and the Smithsonian Institution in Washington, all in the Gothic Revival style then in favour. The wealthy congregation already had a church downtown, but opened a competition in 1843 for a new one closer to their homes. Renwick won, although he was only 25, and construction began in the same year. The marble steeple with its delicate filigrees and curls replaced the wooden original in 1884. There is a lovely **English garden☆** to the N, in front of the rectory, a later Renwick accomplishment. Although the parishioners were largely from fashionable society, propriety was briefly rent when circus promoter P.T. Barnum wangled a wedding of his stellar attraction, Tom Thumb, to a lady midget also in his employment.

A style of Architecture (the Gothic) which, to me at least, is, in comparison with all others, the most beautiful of all, and by far the most in harmony with all the mysteries of religion.
John Keble, *Lectures on Poetry*

Gracie Mansion 🏛

East End Ave. (E 88th St.), NY 10028. Map 7K5 ☎ ⓘ Visit by appointment only Apr–Oct, Wed 10.00–16.00. Write to: Mayor's Office of Special Events, 42 Broadway, New York, NY 10004.
Now the residence of the mayor, the mansion is named after the merchant who built it in 1799. Prominent details are the encompassing veranda and lattice railings at porch and roof levels. It is hard to believe that the house once served as a public lavatory in *Carl Schurz Park*, in which it is still located. The wealth that permitted Archibald Gracie to erect this stately Federalist house evaporated when two of his ships were seized by the French in 1807. His family was forced to sell in 1823, and it went neglected for a century, even though the city purchased it in 1887. Popular Fiorello LaGuardia was the first mayor to move in, during World War II. Tours are difficult to arrange and tourists are fenced off at some distance, so the best way to view it is from the deck of a Circle Line tour boat (see *Addresses and telephone numbers in Basic information*).

Gramercy Park 🏛 ☆

Map 5Q4.
A small community forever battling against the dreary commercial encroachments nibbling at its edges, these few square blocks evoke 19thC residential elegance as no other area in Manhattan can. The focal point is the rectangular park from which the district takes its name. The park is protected by a high fence and only people living in the surrounding houses have keys to the gate. Edwin Booth is represented by a statue inside; by all accounts, he was a better actor than his brother John Wilkes Booth, the assassin of Lincoln. Another president, Theodore Roosevelt, lived nearby. Gramercy Park is part of an official Historic District, a designation awarded to many areas of the five boroughs by the city's Landmarks Preservation

Commission. Although the agency's enforcement powers are tenuous, it has prevented the demolition or defacement of many worthwhile examples of the architectural heritage.

Grand Central Terminal
Park Ave. and 42nd St., NY 10017. Map 5O4 🚇 Ⓡ ☿ *Open 6.00–2.00.*
An attempt to level the terminal to make way for yet another speculative office tower was thwarted in the late 1970s. Grand Central was therefore saved from the fate of Penn Station, over on the West Side. The conservationist effort was worthwhile. Straddling Park Ave., the main facade looks s, towards what was in 1913 the centre of population and commerce. Its Beaux Arts adornment includes a heroic sculpture group comprised of Mercury, Athena and Hercules draped around a clock, but this is masked from street level by the second-storey flyovers that encircle the terminal and join lower and upper Park Ave.

Inside, a vast vaulted space 125ft (38m) wide, and more than twice as long, arcs over rush-hour throngs of 120,000 daily commuters. Despite their headlong rush, not even those who have accumulated 20yr of workday arrivals and departures are unaware of the grandeur of this main concourse. Line paintings depict the celestial constellations against the pale blue ceiling, and light streams through high arched windows. It can still awe, despite the intrusion of an offtrack betting office and the distraction of the giant Kodak picture-of-the-month on the N wall. Take it all in from the new bar inside the Vanderbilt Ave. entrance or wend down to the **Oyster Bar and Restaurant** (see *Restaurants*) between the main and lower levels. Despite the inauspicious location, this is one of the top seafood restaurants in town.

Grant's Tomb   See *General Grant National Memorial.*

Greenacre Park
51st St. (2nd Ave.). Map 5N5.
An admirable trend has private benefactors contributing public 'pocket' parks that bestow touches of grace and greenery in otherwise congested neighbourhoods. This is a somewhat ostentatious example, its open space cluttered up with banks of lights, a slatted pavilion and a semi-sculptural arrangement of rough-hewn sentinels, but it is nevertheless an agreeable retreat from exhaust fumes and noise.

Greenwich Village 🏛 ☆
Map 2R3.
Those who could afford it fled the disease, fires and squalor of the city in the s to build homes in this rural village of the late 18thC. Pastoral serenity was shortlived, for the northward sprawl of the metropolis soon swamped it. The rich moved further uptown, and artists took their places, turning terraced houses into flats and studios. Henry James, Winslow Homer, Edgar Allen Poe and, later, Edna St Vincent Millay and Edward Hopper lived here, and 'The Village' became America's Left Bank. Although present-day rents are beyond the means of most poets and painters, laissez-faire lifestyles pertain and eccentricity remains in evidence. *Washington Square* is the focal point of an area that is usually delineated by Houston St., 14th St., 4th Ave. and the Hudson River. (See *Walk 5* in *Planning.*)

Grey Art Gallery
33 Washington Pl. (Washington Sq. E), NY 10003
☎ 598–7603. Map 2R4 ◻ ✗ by appointment. Open
Sept–June, Tues, Thurs 10.00–18.30, Wed 10.00–20.30,
Fri 10.00-17.00, Sat 13.00–17.00; closed Sun, Mon. Open
July–Aug Mon–Fri 11.00–19.00; closed Sat, Sun.

A foresighted chairman of the New York University art
department spearheaded the effort to collect examples of the
New York School of Abstract Expressionism before popular
acceptance caused their prices to skyrocket. For 20yr, the
collection was stored or parcelled out for display in
administrative offices. This gallery was created to make it
available to the community. That mission has been expanded to
include frequently rotated exhibitions of art and photography
that combine scholarship and inventive juxtaposition. (See
Walk 5 in *Planning*.)

Guggenheim Museum 🏛 ☆
1071 5th Ave. (89th St.), NY 10028 ☎ 860–1313. Map 7K4
◻ ✗ ♿ Open Wed–Sun 11.00–17.00, Tues 11.00–20.00.
Closed Mon.

Curmudgeonly genius Frank Lloyd Wright detested New York
– he suggested that it be razed and begun again – and the
Solomon R. Guggenheim Museum was his only completed
commission in the city. To say that the result was controversial
falls some way short of the truth. Along a boulevard
characterized by conservative apartment houses and Neo-
Classical public buildings, the exterior of the Guggenheim
resembles a flower pot teetering on the edge of a coffee table.
The circular central gallery with its spiral stripe of glass is
smaller at the base than at the top and squats off-centre on a
floating horizontal slab. Wright wanted a marble facing, but the
concrete used instead had an unfortunate yellow cast. Reaction
was predictably divided, even before the 1959 opening.
Scornful perplexity was perhaps the most common response,
not unlike that accorded the non-objective and abstract works
of art displayed inside. By then, however, Wright was unable to
counter-attack as he was dead.

However one feels about the exterior, there can be little
argument over the effectiveness of the interior design, at least in
the core structure. Simple logic insists that the best way to view
a museum's exhibits is to begin at the top and work down, not
exhausting yourself with thoughts of missing rooms and finding
lifts. That's how it is here. Take the lift to the top and slowly
descend along the spiral ramp, past bays of paintings and
sculptures. Illumination comes from the glass dome and
continuous window band, supplemented when necessary by
artificial lighting.

The collections and loan exhibitions tread a line between the
modern art establishment – represented by Picasso, Mondrian,
Braque, Klee, Chagall and Kandinsky – and exponents of the
New York School of Abstract Expressionism and their
successors. Younger experimental artists provide spice. The
adjacent horizontal gallery is given to the Thannhauser
collection of Impressionists and *their* descendants – Manet,
Pissarro, Gauguin, Van Gogh, Cézanne. Once out of the door,
the question persists as to whether the architecture serves to
enhance or overwhelm the art it is intended to set off. Whatever
you decide in the end, it certainly sharpens the experience on a
first visit.

Guinness World Records Exhibit Hall
Empire State Building (350 5th Ave. – 34th St.)
☎ *947–2335. Map* **5***P4* 📷 ✳ *Open 9.30–18.30.*

Trafficking in predictable astonishments presented through
video, film and replicas, the hall is an understandable favourite
with those suffering a surfeit of profundity from other
exhibitions. Compare yourself with lifesize photographs of the
tallest, fattest, fastest humans, all under the rubric of the
famous encyclopaedia of trivia published by the Anglo-Irish
brewer. It's fun, for a quick circuit.

Hall of Fame for Great Americans 🏛
Bronx Community College, 181st St., Bronx, NY 10453
☎ *220–6187. Map* **10***B3* 🅿 *Open 10.00–16.00.*

This neglected national monument was dedicated in 1901,
when the land it stood on was part of the new uptown campus of
New York University. Stanford White designed the first three
buildings for academic use – a domed library flanked by two
classroom buildings devoted to the study of philosophy and
languages. They are above-par representations of his work, but
were built at the crest of a steep incline leading towards the
Harlem River, and their high foundations lacked any visual
interest.

To mask the foundations and simultaneously attract the
prestige coveted by its administration, the university decided to
invent a memorial to Americans who had made substantial
contributions to the arts, sciences, statesmanship and
pedagogy. White conceived a semi-circular Neo-Classical
loggia, with busts of national heroes like Lincoln, Benjamin
Franklin, Edison, Thomas Paine and Alexander Graham Bell.
To be considered for inclusion, candidates must have been dead
for at least 25yr. The offbeat vista takes in northern Manhattan
and *The Cloisters*, as well as a section of the Hudson River and
the New Jersey Palisades on the far shore. The campus is now
Bronx Community College, part of the City University of New
York.

Harlem
Map **8***H3.*

At the turn of the century, Harlem was still a semi-rural district,
shrinking farms alternating with the summer homes of the city
to the s. Blocks of tenements were spreading out from the
main streets, however, and shortly before World War I,
they began to fill with American blacks migrating from the
harshly segregationist South. Their lot improved little, but
despite unspeakable poverty, there existed a number of lively
music halls and nightclubs. During the 1920s and early 1930s,
whites from downtown engaged in the social ritual of dancing to
jazz and drinking bathtub gin at such places as the Cotton Club
(in which blacks worked and entertained but could not be
patrons). Many foreigners still cherish that romantic image,
which is no more real today than that of cowboys pushing cattle
herds through downtown Dallas.

It is necessary to stress, therefore, that Harlem is an
uninviting area, its addicts and desperate unemployed posing a
constant threat to residents and outsiders alike. With admitted
exceptions, it is emblematic of the failures of American society,
of interest primarily to visiting sociologists. That said, there are
isolated streets and institutions that deserve attention even of
casual tourists. Among these are the museums of the *Audubon*

Terrace complex, the *Museo del Barrio*, *Aunt Len's Doll and Toy Museum*, the **Schomburg Center for Research in Black Culture** (*515 Lenox Ave. near 135th St.* ☎ *862–4000*) and the **Studio Museum** (*2033 5th Ave. at 125th St.* ☎ *427–5959*). Architectural restorations of note include the Victorian cottage row of **Sylvan Terrace** near the *Morris-Jumel Mansion* and the 1890s **St Nicholas Historic District**, popularly known as Strivers' Row. The safest way to see these is by chauffeured car, while the most informative is, without doubt, by the Penny Sightseeing Co (☎ *247–2860*), which specializes in tours of Harlem.

The district is bounded, roughly, by 96th St., 165th St., Broadway and the East and Harlem rivers. Spanish Harlem, called El Barrio by its largely Puerto Rican residents, is the subdivision from 5th Ave. to the East River and N to 125th St. Remnants of Italian Harlem are found in the vicinity of the intersection of 116th St. and 2nd Ave.

Hayden Planetarium
Part of the *American Museum of Natural History* complex, the Planetarium features 'cosmic laser concerts', as well as the more usual heavenly explorations.

Hispanic Society of America
Part of the complex known as *Audubon Terrace*, a splendid museum that focuses on the culture and history of the Iberian Peninsula rather than the Spanish and Portuguese colonies of America.

Historical Society
See *New York Historical Society*.

Holland Tunnel
Map 2S2 🚗
The first road tunnel (1927) under the Hudson River, and therefore something of a technological feat, it links Jersey City and Canal St. in Manhattan. The longer, westbound tube is over $1\frac{1}{2}$ miles in length. Even though the air is changed by giant fans every $1\frac{1}{2}$ min, few drivers envy the guards who take it in turns to be stationed inside. The tunnel is named after the chief engineer.

International Center of Photography
1130 5th Ave. (94th St.), NY 10028 ☎ *860–1777. Map 7K4* 🚗 **K** *Open Tues–Fri 12.00–20.00, Sat, Sun 12.00–18.00.*
One of New York's latest museums (1974) is housed in a 1914 Georgian-Federal terraced house, its bricks and shutters made more attractive by contrast with the grandiose mansions that are customary along this stretch of 5th Ave. The expanding collection focuses on 20thC luminaries Ernst Haas, E. Eugene Smith, Henri Cartier-Bresson, Weegee, and Robert Capa, supplemented by special theme and one-person shows twice a year. Lectures, audio-visual presentations, workshops and a book-and-print shop contribute to the generally lively atmosphere.

Jacques Marchais Center of Tibetan Art
Until recently, this was the official designation of the *Tibetan Museum* on Staten Island. Jacques Marchais, the founder, was in fact a female (and American) art dealer, but in the 1940s a male (and French) name was still a business asset.

Japan House Gallery
333 E 47th St. (1st Ave.), NY 10017 ☎ 832–1155. Map 5O5
▨ ✗ by appointment. Open 11.00–17.00, Fri during
exhibitions 11.00–19.30.

The contemplative and ordered *shibui* tradition flourishes in
this otherwise electric neighbourhood, with frequent loan
exhibitions of such delicacies as Noh masks, decorated paper
screens, scrolls, and diverse Shinto and Buddhist objects.
Founded in 1907 to promote understanding between the two
countries, the parent Japan Society has grown even more
relevant with the influx of Japanese businessmen and their
families and attendant adjustment problems. While
symposiums, lectures and counselling programmes are major
features of the society's agenda, the gallery is of greater interest
to tourists. Frequently changed shows focus on everything
from ceremonial swords and kimonos to contemporary
photography and art films.

It was three years before we saw New York again. As the ship
glided up the river, the city burst thunderously upon us in the
early dusk – the white glacier of lower New York swooping
down like a strand of a bridge to rise into uptown New York, a
miracle of foamy light suspended by the stars. A band started to
play on deck, but the majesty of the city made the march trivial
and tinkling. From that moment I knew that New York,
however often I might leave it, was home.

F. Scott Fitzgerald, *My Lost City*

Jewish Museum
1109 5th Ave. (92nd St.), NY 10028 ☎ 860-1888. Map 7K4
▨ ✗ Open Mon–Thurs 12.00–17.00, Sun 11.00–18.00.
Closed Fri, Sat.

Within this conventional 1908 'chateau', with its bland 1963
wing, is an important collection of Judaica of interest to people
of all faiths. Special collections of contemporary painting and
sculpture are mounted on the first floor beyond a vestibule that
reproduces a section of a Persian synagogue, with lighted niches
for Torah containers.

The second floor is devoted to ceremonial objects, both
intricately wrought and stunningly simple: wedding rings,
Torah headpieces and crowns, circumcision instruments,
eight-candle menorahs, prayer-holding mezuzahs, spice boxes,
holiday ritual pieces and amulets.

The third floor is a mixture of folk arts, coins, medals, Torah
arks, and artefacts of the Jewish experience in Colonial
America, and the Middle East. Especially poignant are
reminders of the poverty of Lower East Side immigrants and
the incomprehensible tragedy of the Holocaust.

The fourth floor exhibit, a diorama of Israel executed by
schoolchildren, is unexpectedly charming and enlightening.

Judson Memorial Baptist Church ▥ †
55 Washington Sq. S (Sullivan St.), NY 10012
☎ 477–0351. Map 2R4 Open Mon–Fri 9.00–17.00. Closed
Sat, Sun except for Sun service 11.00; July–Aug closed
Mon.

More than merely supportive of the cultural and political
concerns of its *Greenwich Village* constituency, Judson
initiates. Parishioners and ministers carry forth energetic

programmes in the arts and community affairs. Architects McKim, Mead & White elected a Venetian variation on their customary predilection for the Romanesque, and the 1892 facade continues to brighten the hotchpotch of Washington Sq. South. The adjacent campanile is now part of a *New York University* hall of residence.

Lever House ▥ ☆
390 Park Ave. (53rd St.), NY 10022. Map 5N4.
In its way as difficult to miss as *St Bartholomew's Church* two blocks s, Lever House was in the forefront of the Bauhaus-influenced third phase of skyscraper fever that seized the imagination of developers in the post-World War II years. The builders embraced the new glass-and-steel curtain wall technology, but with important variations. For one, they broke the unvarying high-rise canyon of Park Ave. by the astonishing decision not to use every bit of available air space. The wide side of the unadorned slab tower is turned s, at a right angle to the avenue, permitting air and sun to circulate. For another, the colour is an unusual blue-emerald. In its totality, Lever House is the promise of the International Style that was to be denied by its descendants. Even architects Skidmore, Owings & Merrill infrequently matched their achievement in subsequent efforts.

Liberty Island   See *Statue of Liberty.*

Lincoln Center ▥ ☆
140 W 65th St. (Columbus Ave.), NY 10023 ☎ 877–1800. Map 6M3 ▣ X inexpensive ▦ ℝ ℽ Open 10.00–17.00; theatres various times.
An ambitious conglomeration of six concert halls and theatres, the Lincoln Center for the Performing Arts is the home of the Metropolitan Opera Company, New York Philharmonic Orchestra and New York City Opera and Ballet. It also hosts a variety of visiting ballet and repertory companies, symphony orchestras, and popular and classical musical artists and events. No project of such magnitude, especially one concerned with the arts, could hope to sail from conception to realization without conflict. The Lincoln Center provoked dismay, outrage, and a chain reaction of second-guessing that persists to this day, all on a scale consistent with its monumentality.

It happened that in the post-World War II years, several of the city's premier performing arts organizations were seeking new premises. This need coincided with planners casting about for ways to arrest the decline of various Manhattan neighbourhoods. The new United Nations Headquarters accomplished that on the *East Side*, helping to establish New York as a world capital of statesmanship. It seemed that the proposed Lincoln Center might do the same for the arts. On balance it has, allowing for quibbles over decor and acoustics. Admittedly, the architectural whole is more impressive than its parts, despite the participation of Eero Saarinen and Philip Johnson.

Approach is customarily made from Columbus Ave., up long, low steps into the main plaza. Most impressive at night when the centre fountain and facades are lit, the **New York State Theater** is on the left, **Avery Fisher Hall** on the right, and the rounded arches of the **Metropolitan Opera House** directly ahead. To reach the **Vivian Beaumont Theater**, cut between the Opera House and Avery Fisher Hall. The larger structure to the N is the **Juilliard School**, a prestigious arts college. The Beaumont building incorporates the research library and Museum of the Performing Arts, a branch of the public library system. To the S of the Opera House is a tree-lined park with a bandstand. In warmer months, the pedestrian spaces are enlivened by outdoor cafes, ice-cream kiosks and wandering buskers.

To greater or lesser degree, the buildings reveal classical inspiration informed by modernist sensibilities, austere to romantic in interpretation according to the predilections of their designers. Each enjoys the presence of large-scale artworks by notable painters and sculptors. Avery Fisher Hall, with the New York Philharmonic in residence, has Richard Lippold's *Orpheus and Apollo*; the Opera House, two Marc Chagall murals; the New York State Theater, a Lee Bontecou and a Jasper Johns, among others.

Restaurants are the Allegro Cafe (*12.00–20.00*) and Fountain Cafe (*12.00–24.00*) in Avery Fisher Hall, and the Grand Tier (*open 2hr before performances to ticketholders*) in the Opera House. Guided tours of the Center are approximately 1hr in length (☎ *877–1800 ext 516*). Backstage tours of the Opera House are also available (☎ *582–7500*). Box office telephones are listed by theatre under *Nightlife*.

Lincoln Tunnel
Map 4O1 ▨ *only when crossing W–E.*
The three tubes of the tunnel were completed in 1937, 1945 and 1957, and the one in the middle is the longest at over 1½ miles. They connect the city of Weehawken in New Jersey with W 38th St. in Manhattan, providing an additional Hudson River crossing. Construction of the approaches entailed the demolition of a large slum area.

Little Italy
Map 3S5.
Sicilian and Neapolitan immigrants made this their urban hamlet during the same period (1880–1925) that European Jews were establishing their Lower East Side community on the other side of *The Bowery*. Bounded on the W by Lafayette St., and by Houston St. and Canal St. to the N and S, the neighbourhood is shrinking, but still vibrant. The quarter was always small, for arriving Italians and their children dispersed quickly throughout the five boroughs. But this warren of narrow streets and stunted tenements became symbolic of the Old Country and retains that flavour. Grey-haired women in black clutch string bags as they move from fish shop to bakery while their menfolk play *bocce* (Italian bowls) or sip espresso at coffee houses around the corner. The *Festa di San Gennaro* in Sept booms with brass bands and sizzles with booth after booth of sausage and *calzone*. (See *Walk 3* in *Planning*.)

Lower East Side
Map 3R5.
Although immigrants of every race and nationality have made this shabby tenement district E of *The Bowery* and N of Canal St. their first stopover, its identity is East European Jewish. That image persists, although blacks and Hispanics dominate now. Millions of indigent Slavs, Poles, Russians and Lithuanians poured into these mean streets from 1870 until harsh new laws stemmed the flow in the 1920s. They lived in

five-storey buildings without plumbing, two or three families to an apartment. For decades, the population density surpassed that of Calcutta. The lucky ones were streetcar sellers, the others laboured in the sweatshops of the garment trade. Yiddish was the prevailing tongue, and at one time there were 500 synagogues. A taste of that era – and some remarkable shopping bargains – can be had on Sun along Orchard St. (See *Walk 4* in *Planning*.)

Madison Square Garden
8th Ave. (33rd St.), NY 10001 ☎ *564–4400. Map 4P3* ▨
▣ *Opening times vary according to events scheduled.*
Although the present complex is the fourth version on the third site, only the first two were even in the vicinity of Madison Square. Nor did any of them have plants or flowers in sufficient quantities to justify the 'Garden' label. In all its manifestations, from 1871 to the present, Madison Square Garden has been concerned with sports and popular entertainment. It has a circus, ice shows, hockey, basketball, horse and dog competitions, rodeo, prizefighting, rock concerts, and 48 bowling lanes. For no good reason, the architecturally imposing Penn Station was razed to street level in 1968 to permit the construction of this insipid building. That desecration aside, this is where many major events take place.

Marble Collegiate Church ▥ †
272 5th Ave. (29th St.), NY 10001 ☎ *686–2770. Map 5P4. Open Mon–Fri 9.00–17.00. Closed Sat, Sun except for Sun services.*
An 1854 edifice by Samuel A. Warner, it was commissioned by a congregation of the Dutch Reformed faith, which had its roots in the earliest settlement. The official landmark designation is due as much to age as to architectural worth. Consistent with its time, both Gothic and Romanesque motifs were used in a satisfactory (if not especially striking) blend. One of the pastors is Dr Norman Vincent Peale, author of the Eisenhower-era best-selling guide to the good life, *The Power of Positive Thinking*.

Metropolitan Museum of Art ▥ ★
5th Ave. (82nd St.), NY 10028 ☎ *879–5500 (office), 535–7710 (recorded information), 570–3949 (concerts, lectures). Map 7L4* ▨ *ⵏ on rented tapes* ⓡ ▣ ⵗ ⛟ *entrance on 5th Ave. (80th St.). Open Tues 10.00–20.45, Wed–Sat 10.00–16.45, Sun and hols 11.00–16.45. Closed Mon. Free entry for children under 12 accompanied by adult. Photography without flash permitted, except at special temporary exhibitions.*
Grand in concept and numbing in scope, this is the largest repository of art and antiquities in the Western Hemisphere. There are 18 departments and 248 galleries with well over one million prints, paintings, sculptures, furnishings, costumes, ceramics, musical instruments, armour and reassembled sections of ancient temples and palaces. Barely 25% of the collection is on view at any one time. There are, in addition, three libraries, two auditoriums, an art and book shop, a gift shop, a cafeteria, a restaurant with table service, and a snack shop, and concerts, films and lectures are staged.

It might all be intimidating, were it not for an imaginative administration determined to enhance accessibility. Huge,

Metropolitan Museum of Art

2nd Floor

André Meyer Galleries

American Wing

Astor Court

Closed to the public

1st Floor

Michael C. Rockefeller Wing

Fountain Restaurant and Cafeteria

Great Hall

Garden Court

American Wing

Lehman Pavilion

5th Ave. and 82nd St.

A	European Paintings	**K**	Far Eastern Art
B	Musical Instruments	**L**	Lehman Pavilion
C	20thC Art	**M**	French Period Rooms
D	Drawings and Prints	**N**	English Period Rooms
E	Recent Acquisitions	**O**	European Sculpture and Decorative Arts
F	Sackler Wing		
G	Greek and Roman Art	**P**	Medieval Art
H	Special Exhibition Area	**Q**	Arms and Armour
I	Islamic Art	**R**	Greek, Cypriot and Roman Art
J	Ancient Near Eastern Art	**S**	Egyptian Wing

colourful banners billow from the 5th Ave. facade, touting the two or three special exhibitions always on view. These nearly always tie in with popular enthusiasms of the moment – Chinese costumes, the treasures of Tutankhamen, Viking artefacts – the better to draw infrequent museum-goers who are unfamiliar with the permanent exhibits. Galleries are laid out in an orderly manner, attendants are gracious and often bilingual, there are special programmes for children, and ready access for older or disabled people. There is an air of authority flushed with innovation and a desire to relate past to present. The philosophy works: nearly four million people visit every year.

The building itself is of interest, an amalgamation of the architectural styles dominant at the time of each addition. Its core is the unassuming Ruskinian Gothic structure that was the first home of the museum in 1880. The only major edifice

within the boundaries of Central Park, its front then faced W
into the trees. This exterior is now enclosed by the Lehman
Pavilion. The familiar 5th Ave. facade was completed in 1902,
reorienting the building and dictating its future development.
Best defined as of the Beaux Arts School for its blending of
Roman and Renaissance conceits, it is approached by broad
steps rising from the street. Three massive arches are bracketed
by four pairs of impressive columns with Corinthian capitals.
Resulting niches were intended to house figures representing
the four epochs of human history, but these were never
commissioned. Wings reach N and S to a length of almost three
blocks.

Inside, the Great Hall is the fulfilment of a Piranesi vision,
but without the oppressive gloom that this implies. There are
plants and benches and huge sprays of cut flowers in stone urns.
An information booth in the centre stocks floor plans and
announcements of special events. The Met cannot be absorbed
in one lightning tour. Sit down for a moment and determine
which departments are of greatest appeal.

The curatorial staff is engaged in the later stages of a master
reorganization plan that requires much of the square footage to
be closed to the public for varying periods. The effect is to
make it a trifle easier to decide what to see. Most of the major
attractions remain open to view either in whole or in
part.

The **Egyptian Wing** ☆ is as good a place to start as any, for it
is acknowledged to be one of the major collections of its kind.
Turn right from the main entrance on the first floor, following
the passageway at the N end of the Great Hall. A child's
innocent enthusiasm for the macabre may be stimulated by the
sepulchre of *Lord Chamberlain Per-nedbi* that is first
encountered and by the mummies and sarcophagi displayed in
the corridors leading off to the left and right. **Galleries 13 and
14** are concerned with the Roman and Coptic periods from the
century before Christ until the 7thC AD. There is a superb
jewellery collection ☆ as well as textiles, glass and ceramic
objects of ceremonial and household use. **Gallery 10** is a long
room of meticulous paintings, facsimiles of those found in
temples and burial places. Next are artefacts of the Ptolemaic
period, including numerous funerary figures, sculptures and
reliefs. Papyri from the *Book of the Dead*, a compilation of
medicinal formulas and religious rituals, date from around the
5thC BC.

While the galleries encompassing the 1st to 18th dynasties
are closed, you have to view the next series of rooms in reverse
order – from the 30th to the 19th dynasties. Their delicately-
crafted reliefs, facsimiles of tomb paintings and funerary relics
finally lead up to the **Sackler Wing**. This handsome two-storey
pavilion encloses (and somewhat overwhelms) the **Temple of
Dendur** ☆ A gift of the Egyptian government, it was
painstakingly dismantled, pieces numbered and charted, and
sent here for reassembly. Light through a vast bank of glass in
the N wall bathes the temple and reflects on the water of the
U-shaped pool that frames it. Reorganization continues in
adjacent galleries, currently scheduled for reopening some time
in 1983.

To maintain historical sequence, return to the Great Hall and
cross to **gallery 11**, where a portion of the **Greek, Cypriot and
Roman collection of statuary and ceramics** ☆ is on view.
Many of these pieces were contributed by the first director of

the museum, Luigi Palma di Cesnola, who was responsible for their discovery and excavation. Just beyond is the Fountain Restaurant and Cafeteria (*open Tues 11.00–20.15, Wed–Fri 11.00–16.45, Sat–Sun 12.00–16.15*).

The adjoining **Michael C. Rockefeller Wing**☆ opened in Feb 1982, with 42,000sq. ft (3,900sq. m) of the arts of Africa, Oceania, and pre-Columbian and native America. Among over 1,500 objects on display are Papuan masks of barkcloth and cane, Olmec jade and ceramic figurines, Mayan reliefs, wood carvings of Benin and the Ivory Coast, and Eskimo sculptures. The collection was donated by Nelson A. Rockefeller and named after his son, who disappeared on an anthropological expedition in 1961.

Return again to the Great Hall and go down the corridor to the right of the central staircase. This leads into the section devoted to **medieval art**. After a clockwise circuit of the tapestries and ecclesiastical objects, make your way to the **arms and armor gallery**, which is dominated by a mounted troop of knights and augmented by heraldic banners, crossbows and other armaments.

A door in the W wall leads into the enclosed garden court of the **American Wing**☆ Trees, 19thC statues and a reflecting pool provide a quiet resting place beneath a glass roof. At the N end is the 1824 Greek Revival facade of a former Wall St. bank. Enter the door at the right to view portions of the most extraordinary collection of **American furniture and decorative arts** in existence. Three floors of 18 period rooms and 12 galleries proceed from Colonial times (1630) into the Federal period, ending about 1825. Installations still in progress will carry the story forward to the early 20thC. Splendid Chippendale bureaux and paintings of the **Hudson River School** are joined with comprehensive assortments of silver, pewterware, antique glass, ceramics and textiles. For a chronological view, begin on the third floor of the wing and walk down.

Afterwards, leave the garden court by the doorway at the S corner. Pass through a large **gallery of European sculpture and decorative arts**, covering essentially the same time period as the American Wing. Bear right, then left, through the **English period rooms**. Just beyond is the entrance to the **Lehman Pavilion**, where Robert Lehman's collection of early Italian and 19th and 20thC French art is displayed in modern galleries and sombre period rooms, the latter reconstructed from his house on W 54th St. Among the Italian works are drawings by Leonardo da Vinci and Botticelli. Of the later period, Ingres' *Portrait of the Princess of Broglie* is characteristic of his uncanny aptitude for naturalistic reproduction. The Fauvists, an Expressionist offshoot of Post-Impressionism, are represented by Vlaminck and Derain. A quick circuit of the wing is sufficient. Leave by the door through which you entered, noting in passing the 1880 facade of the original museum building. Turn right into the **French period rooms**, which include a reconstructed 18thC Parisian storefront and boudoir furnishings commissioned by Marie-Antoinette. An adjoining room has additional **European sculpture and decorative arts**. Return to the Great Hall. This is a good interval at which to break off the visit, saving the rest for another day.

On that occasion, mount the central staircase at the W of the Great Hall. Remarkable riches are confronted on the second floor, and the layout does not lend itself to a programmed tour.

Straight ahead are the enormously popular **galleries of European paintings**☆ They commence with large Baroque canvasses of debatable content but undeniable drama. Continuing W, a maze of smaller galleries reveals the gems of the **Dutch collection**. Rembrandt's *Aristotle Contemplating A Bust of Homer*☆ is the work of the artist's mature years, less theatrical than some of his earlier masterpieces. The concern with light remains, but it is a subtle mist, not a blinding shaft through clouds or portal. An oddity was Rembrandt's decision to clothe Aristotle in contemporary dress. The *1660 Self Portrait* ★ is an unsparing examination of his late middle age, the face pallid and corpulent, but with dignity intact. Vermeer was also intrigued by the properties of light, but in a narrow optical sense. The flesh of his *Young Woman with a Water Jug* ★ has the luminosity of an eggshell lighted from within by a candle flame. Any emotional impact is vitiated by the serenity of his subject matter and compositions, but he inspires admiration for his flawless technique.

For powerful imagery, move on to the **Spanish section** and El Greco's *View of Toledo*, his only landscape and one of his greatest works: a big, sombre canvas that conveys an uneasy sense of foreboding through its lowering storm clouds. The portrait of *Juan de Pareja* ★ by Velazquez was acquired in 1970, the most costly single purchase the museum has ever made. Velazquez was perhaps unequalled in his sensitive portrayal of character, and in this painting he focuses all his skill on bringing the humanity of a friend to eternal life.

The connecting **French galleries** include fine examples of Claude and Watteau as well as Poussin's celebrated *Rape of the Sabine Women*.

Complete your tour of the European galleries with a wander through the **English rooms**, where portraits by Reynolds and Gainsborough hang alongside Turner's visionary cityscape, *The Grand Canal*.

To the N of these rooms is an enchanting accumulation of lutes, sitars, gongs, temple bells, nose flutes, sarindas and other exotic **musical instruments**☆ To the S side of the entrance to the European galleries are select examples of **20thC art**, including works by Modigliani, Georgia O'Keeffe, Stuart Davis, Jackson Pollock, and such instantly recognizable paintings as Picasso's portrait of *Gertrude Stein* and Ivan Albright's *Fleeting Time Has Left Me Old*. Return to the top of the central staircase and turn right into a corridor given to **recent acquisitions** and **drawings and prints**.

This empties into the **André Meyer galleries**, an important, recently installed collection of 19thC European art. Turn left into a room of drawings by Degas, Renoir and Manet. In the centre are Degas bronzes of dancers☆ – his favourite subject. Only one piece of Degas sculpture was exhibited in his lifetime, yet here alone are 12. In the second room is the charming miniature oil on wood, *The Dancing Class*, and a dozen more sculptures, all by Degas. The instinctive grace of his dancers is only made more profound by the odd angularity or awkward position, or the implied sheen of sweat brought on by endless repetition of exercises. Further confirmation of his mastery is found in the third room, dominated by a large bronze figure (1922) with a tutu of real muslin.

Bearing right, you enter a large hall filled with heroic sculptures by Rodin and Maillol. Especially arresting is the former's tormented study of *Adam*. The rest of the Meyer galleries are devoted to paintings, a cornucopia of 19thC artistic fecundity. The transition away from both Classicism and Romanticism towards as yet unimagined frontiers is illustrated here in the manifold works of Corot and Courbet. The 'Establishment' these artists competed with is also represented by the polished Neo-Classicism of Ingres. Despite Courbet's own strivings towards greater realism, he is said to have been dismayed by Manet's rejection of principles of perspective. In the 21 canvasses by this younger artist, you can see striking concessions towards the two-dimensionality of the picture-plane. His flat, poster-ish portraits are almost devoid of shadow and simulated depth. Manet is often classified erroneously as an Impressionist, but his real kinship lies with such Post-Impressionists as Cézanne and Van Gogh, both equally well represented here. The scope and complexity of these works–most of them mounted in a large central room that does them full justice – is nothing less than breathtaking.

Eventually, these galleries lead into the **Islamic art collection**, the highlight of which is the **Syrian Nur Ad-Din House**☆ (1707). The wall panels of the room produced here are modelled out of gesso, with ornate floral patterns and inscriptions in Arabic. Adjacent galleries show ceremonial vessels, chess pieces and silk carpets and hangings. Beyond the halls containing **Greek and Roman art** and **Ancient Near Eastern art**, you reach the open balcony square above the Great Hall.

Continuing N past **Far Eastern art**, go through the special exhibition areas until you arrive at the **Astor Court**☆ Yet another recent addition, it is a reconstruction of a Chinese garden of the Ming dynasty (1368–1644), based on an authentic example that still exists in Soochow. It is a pleasantly tranquil spot in which to pause for a while and reflect upon all that has been experienced so far within the walls of this vast treasure house.

Complete your tour by travelling two escalator flights down to the **Costume Institute**☆ Its biannual exhibitions have featured ancient Chinese garments, Parisian haute couture, and theatrical wardrobes.

Also down in the basement is the **Junior Museum**, created to introduce children and teenagers to the mysteries of art and history manifest in the floors above. There are frequent lectures and films intended to be shared with parents, as well as displays drawn from the larger collections.

Recorded cassette tours are available at moderate rentals, covering 21 subjects and galleries, some of them in languages other than English. Lectures, films and concerts range from discussions of painting techniques to cinematic explorations of biblical and aesthetic inter-relationships to recitals by the Juilliard Quartet.

Midtown East
Map 5.

This concentration of corporate headquarters, foreign consulates, publishing houses and advertising firms brings to it streams of business people and diplomats, and shoppers are inexorably drawn towards the fabled luxury emporia of 5th Ave. Coping with this elitist influx are many of Manhattan's most exclusive hotels (Palace, Waldorf-Astoria, Grand Hyatt) and restaurants (Four Seasons, Lutèce, Le Cygne). It's also a residential area, but only for people who needn't concern themselves with the price of a second Mercedes. Penthouses with roof terraces, gardens and even swimming pools perch above the East River, their foliage visible from the streets. Principal sights are *St Patrick's Cathedral*, the *United Nations Headquarters*, *Grand Central Terminal*, and those exemplars of the International Style in architecture, *Lever House* and the *Seagram Building*.

Morris-Jumel Mansion 🏛

Edgecombe Ave. (W 160th St.), NY 10032 ☎ 923–8008. Map 10E3 🖼 ✗ Open Tues – Sun 10.00–16.00. Closed Mon. Subway 1 to 157th St.; AA, B to 163rd St. – Amsterdam Ave.
Given its age (1768), Georgian core, and Federal overlay (1810), the mansion warrants attention for its architecture alone. But great historical figures lived and loved and dined here, and as is only fitting, ghosts are reported to have materialized. Roger Morris was the builder. Although a friend of George Washington, he was a loyal subject of the King and left the country at the outbreak of the Revolution. Both Washington and the British general Henry Clinton made the house their headquarters during the War. After a period of service as a tavern, it was bought by French wine merchant Stephen Jumel for his wife Eliza. They renovated the house in Federal style and filled it with Empire furniture, much of which is still here.

The Jumels laid on lavish parties and banquets, which encouraged New York Society to overlook the rumour that Eliza was the illegitimate child of a prostitute. She reportedly commenced an affair with Aaron Burr before Stephen died in 1832, surprising only in part because the former Vice President was then in his seventies. Scheming Eliza and the brilliantly devious Burr kept house for a while after Stephen's death, but it was not a happy match and he soon moved out. Burr's room is at the top of the stairs, and there is a portrait of Eliza in her 80th year. The ghosts? A Hessian soldier and Eliza herself. Perhaps they are aided by the secret passageways.

Murray Hill ☆

Map 5P4.
A low-key residential quarter with indistinct boundaries, Murray Hill lacks the kind of attractions that capture the attention of developers and tourists. No doubt that suits the residents, who make no effort to grab the spotlight. Following the usual pattern from Colonial farmland to Federalist village to elegant suburb to bypassed backwater, Murray Hill managed to avoid the usually inevitable decay. Compressed by commercial development along the central N – S avenues, it is delineated, roughly, by Park Ave. and 3rd Ave. from 33rd St. to 42nd St. Strips of 19thC terraces and mews such as Sniffen Court (36th St., between Lexington and 3rd Aves.) have been transformed into quietly handsome private apartments and houses. Several good hotels trade tranquillity for the slightly out-of-the-way location and a number of competent restaurants have opened in recent years.

Museo del Barrio

1230 5th Ave. (104th St.), NY 10029 ☎ 831–7272. Map 7J4 🖼 ✗ Open Tues – Fri 10.30–16.30, Sat, Sun 11.00–16.00. Closed Mon.
The vitality of Puerto Rican culture is repeatedly validated by the changing exhibitions of photographs, paintings and crafts in

this gallery of El Barrio (Spanish Harlem). Pre-Columbian figures and works by other contemporary Latin Americans broaden the appeal.

Museum of American Folk Art
125 W 55th St. (6th Ave.), NY 10019 ☎*581–2474. Map **5**N4* 📷 *Open Tues 10.30–20.00, Wed–Sun 10.30–17.30. Closed Mon.*

While waiting to move to much larger permanent digs on w 53rd St. (next to the *Museum of Modern Art*), this charming museum shows frequently changed exhibitions of work produced by unschooled but talented American craftsmen. Works displayed date from Colonial times to the present and include enchanting assortments of weathervanes, carved and painted saints, toys, kitchen implements, quilts and clean-lined furniture that predates Danish Modern by a century.

Museum of American Illustration
128 E 63rd St. (Park Ave.), NY 10021 ☎ *838–2560. Map **7**M4* 📷 *Open Mon–Fri 10.00–17.00. Closed Aug and Sat, Sun.*

Rotating exhibitions of commercial art for books, magazines and print advertising are mounted under the sponsorship of the Society of Illustrators. The permanent collection is augmented by theme shows and the eagerly anticipated annual exhibition of award-winning works.

Museum of the American Indian   Part of the *Audubon Terrace* complex, this has the largest collection of Native American artefacts in the United States.

Museum of Broadcasting
1 E 53rd St. (5th Ave.), NY 10022 ☎ *752–7684. Map **5**N4* 📷 *✗ by appointment ✷ Open Tues, Wed, Fri, Sat 12.00–17.00, Thurs 12.30–19.30. Closed Sun, Mon. Mornings reserved for groups by appointment.*

Over 7,000 recorded radio and television programmes from the 1920s to the present are available for transmission in 23 individual listening/viewing booths. Selected TV shows, changed daily, are presented on giant screens, usually illustrating a sociological, journalistic or dramaturgical point. Although the emphasis is on television, with particular attention to the years prior to the introduction of tape technology around 1960, there are recorded broadcasts by President Warren Harding and Lord Haw Haw as well as a lengthy catalogue of commercials. While it might be wise to inquire about the availability of specific programmes, no advance booking is required.

Museum of the City of New York ☆
5th Ave. (103rd St.), NY 10029 ☎ *534–1672. Map**7**J4* 📷 *✗ ✷ Open Tues–Sat 10.00–17.00, Sun 13.00–17.00. Closed Mon.*

A museum as lively as the city it celebrates, the five floors of this Neo-Georgian building are crammed with historical dioramas, antique playthings, model ships and decorative arts. Take the elevator to the top and work down.

On the fifth floor are two rooms from the first Rockefeller mansion, done up in High Victorian manner and featuring furnishings by English designer Charles Eastlake. On the third floor are the dolls' houses and tiny trams, model farms and penny banks, miniature table settings and hobby horses. On the way out, linger over the Duncan Phyfe furniture, characterized by graceful curves, restrained inlays and stylized swags and lyres. Phyfe worked in Albany, NY and New York City from around 1783–1854 and borrowed from Hepplewhite, Sheraton and French Empire examples to formulate his own style.

The second floor has still more period rooms, ranging from the Colonial to the Theodore Roosevelt era. Model ships and displays trace maritime development from New Amsterdam onwards, and spill over to the first floor. Space is left for a dazzling multimedia presentation that spins through four centuries of local history in barely 20min, employing light, sound, and 24 synchronized projectors. Concerts and walking tours of the city are presented some Suns during warm weather.

Museum of Holography ☆

11 Mercer St. (Canal St.), NY 10013 ☎ *925–0526. Map 2S4* 🖾 ✳ *Open Wed, Fri–Sun 12.00–18.00, Thurs 12.00–21.00. Closed Mon, Tues.*

In its present state, holography may be only the first tentative flicker of a 21stC mass communication technique – film-in-the-round in your living room. Or it might be a technological trick that never develops beyond the level of a sideshow curiosity. At this unique museum, it is treated as an art form. Film is exposed to laser beams and mounted within a plastic cylinder. With illumination, the photographic image appears to be in three dimensions, changing as the observer walks around it. The effect is otherworldly and fascinating. Special exhibitions are mounted on a quarterly basis, with evening lectures.

Museum of Immigration See *American Museum of Immigration*.

Museum of Modern Art ★

11 W 53rd St. (6th Ave.), NY 10019 ☎ *708–8480 (special exhibitions), 708–9490 (films), 708–9500 (other info). Map 5N4* 🖾 𝒴 💷 *Open Mon, Tues, Fri–Sun 11.00–18.00, Thurs 11.00–21.00. Closed Wed.*

Known with ironic affection by its acronym – MOMA – this daring and innovative museum first lobbied for the validity of modern art at a time when that belief was by no means conceded, then in later years assumed the role of arbiter. An artist represented in the collection is among the anointed, assured of at least a sliver of immortality. It is alleged by some that the museum has retreated from the forward edge of the avant-garde, that it has grown conservative and protective of its stature. Evidence can be cited in support of that conclusion but, given the uncertain directions of contemporary art over the last decade or two, caution is understandable. In any event, controversy is the life-blood of an institution like MOMA.

Modern art is here defined as commencing with the Impressionists in the 1880s and, although the history of the many movements that have since evolved favours abstract and non-objective modes, figurative options are also shown. Magic Realist Andrew Wyeth's *Christina's World*, for example, is one of the most popular canvasses on view. The scope of the founders' intentions is demonstrated by the extensive film library and samples of superior design in such otherwise mundane objects as toasters and tableware. An ambitious expansion programme was recently completed, involving the construction of a new West Wing that nearly doubled gallery and storage space. About 30 percent of the permanent collection can now be placed on view.

The book and gift shop is to the right of the main entry hall, the admission booths and information desk are straight ahead. Beyond these, an escalator takes you to two lower levels housing the **Titus Theaters** and the **René d'Harnoncourt Galleries**, which display temporary exhibitions. The glass wall bordering the hall gives access to the outdoor **sculpture garden** ☆ a leafy retreat of pools and fountains dominated at the w end by Rodin's majestic *Balzac* and Gaston Lachaise's equally heroic *Standing Woman*. In counterpoint at the E end are monumental metal sculptures of more recent vintage, including works by Caro, Newman and Oldenburg.

To view the permanent exhibitions inside, return to the main hall. Take the escalator to the second floor and turn left into the first room of the painting and sculpture collection. Approximate chronological order of the development of modern art commences with the Post-Impressionists, represented here by *The Bather* and several smaller works of Cézanne. The next three galleries exhibit the work of Gauguin, Seurat, Redon, Toulouse-Lautrec (*La Goulue at the Moulin Rouge*) and van Gogh (*The Starry Night*). A powerful study of three bathers by Derain dominates the smaller Matisses in the fourth room.

Next are the Cubists, primarily Georges Braque and Pablo Picasso. At the far wall, detour to the left to see Monet's vast angled triptych ☆ and the only slightly smaller flat painting of his famous lily ponds. Retrace your steps and continue straight ahead, bearing right past varied examples of Picasso's Cubist paintings and sculptures, large Léger canvasses and a platform of sculptures by Brancusi. A large Chagall looks as fresh as if it were finished yesterday, however faint its Cubist elements. The Expressionists are highlighted by Wilhelm Lehmbruck's sculptures, *Kneeling Woman* and *Standing Youth*. Two rooms on, the eye must adjust to the linear geometrics and flat rectangles of 14 deceptively simple studies by Piet Mondrian. A large gallery, farther on, is devoted to Matisse; his vibrant tones invest *The Red Studio* with delightful intimacy.

After two rooms of intriguing paintings by Klee, Kandinsky and Modigliani, another large space is devoted to Picasso. These astonishingly inventive sculptures and canvasses show his advance beyond Cubism, as in the celebrated *Girl Before a Mirror* and *Head of a Woman*. His wrenching anti-war mural *Guernica*, installed here for over 40yr, has now been returned to Spain, in deference to the artist's wishes. But there is ample testimony to his genius in the works that remain.

Through the door to the right, a salon of Dadaists includes the once shocking work of the French-born American Marcel Duchamp. Joan Miró is next, his light and witty work classified as Surrealist, but quite unlike the often dark visions of Dali, Magritte and Pavel Tchelitchew that follow.

On the third floor, the American Realists Andrew Wyeth and Edward Hopper are first on view, followed by Abstractionist Stuart Davis. Bear left, then right, through two rooms of the early 1940s Abstract Expressionists, notably Newman, Gorky, Pousette-Dart, Rothko, De Kooning and Motherwell. Also displayed are works by the 'Action Painter' Jackson Pollock, who galvanized the art world towards the end of that decade with his technique of applying paint in balletic swoops and traceries. A hiccup in the chronological layout, Room 6 contains Matisse's canvasses jointly labelled *Swimming Pool*; but they are followed by more Abstract Expressionists.

The next large rooms are concerned with long-term rotating exhibitions of contemporary works that push the boundaries of even these mid-century pioneers. Expect to see assemblages by Robert Rauschenberg, plaster figures by George Segal, Jasper Johns' flag painting, Warhol's and Lichtenstein's Pop icons.

The architecture-and-design collection is displayed on the fourth floor, featuring industrial objects and handcrafted items of the last few decades; for example, bentwood chairs, Art Nouveau glass, office equipment, architect-designed furniture, television sets and even a 1946 Pinin Farina car.

Museum of Natural History　See *American Museum of Natural History*.

New York Aquarium
Boardwalk (W 8th St.), Coney Island, Brooklyn, NY 11224
☎ *266–8500. Map 12F3* 🔁 💷 ✱ *Open 10.00–17.00.*
From 1892 until 1941, the aquarium was in Castle Clinton (see *Castle Clinton National Monument*) in lower Manhattan. That monument was threatened by proposed highway construction, so the fish were transported to this new aquarium at *Coney Island*, on the southern rim of Brooklyn. It is a schizophrenic operation, part amusement centre, part marine science laboratory. That does not diminish its appeal. Predictably, popular exhibits are the sharks, 2-ton beluga whales, performing porpoises, and electric eels that light up bulbs. Some of them are flown to Florida for the winter, so the best time to go is between May and Oct.

New York Botanical Garden　Incorporating a river and specialized gardens and ponds of astonishing diversity, these 250 acres constitute the northern half of the *Bronx Zoo and New York Botanical Garden* complex.

New York Experience
1221 Ave. of the Americas (48th St.), NY 10036
☎ *869–0345. Map 5O4* 🔁 ✱ *Open Mon–Thurs 11.00–19.00, Fri, Sat 11.00–20.00, Sun 12.00–20.00.*
A glossy, fast-paced multiscreen sound-and-light zip through the life and times of the city, and a good way to start off a first visit. Most of the senses are brought into play, dense fog billows over your feet, and the swivel chairs are necessary to keep up with the action. The show takes less than an hour, so expect only a skim over the surface, not any degree of profundity.

New York Historical Society ☆
170 Central Park W (77th St.), NY 10024 ☎ *873–3400. Map 6L3* 🔁 *Open Tues–Fri 11.00–17.00, Sat 10.00–17.00, Sun 13.00–17.00. Closed Mon.*
The name is misleading, for although the orientation is America as viewed from a New York perspective, the net is widely cast. Founded in 1804, the society moved to its present home in 1908. While it lives in the shadow of the *American Museum of Natural History*, just across the street, the five floors of galleries are well worth perusal. In most cities, this would be regarded as a major museum.

There are examples of folk art, period rooms, carriages, drawings and watercolours by John James Audubon, works in silver, Colonial maps and prints, early American toys and carvings, farm and household implements, even fire engines. The fourth floor is devoted primarily to portraits and landscapes, mostly by American painters, the third floor concentrates on such primitive art as weathervanes and cigarstore Indians (large, eye-catching wooden figures used in the 18th and 19thC to advertise the sale of tobacco).

In addition to the research library on the second floor, there is an entrancing collection of **antique toys**☆, mechanical and carved, highlighted by a Noah's Ark crowded with paired beasts. On the ground floor, prints, maps and drawings illustrate the growth of the city from the days of Dutch rule, and in the basement is an array of horsedrawn coaches and carriages.

New York Public Library
5th Ave. (42nd St.), NY 10018 ☎ *790–6161. Map 5O4 X Open Mon–Wed 10.00–21.00, Fri, Sat 10.00–18.00. Closed Thurs, Sun.*

The city-wide library system has over six million volumes and three times as many related materials – much of it in this, the main branch. They are housed in what many regard as *the* paradigm of the Beaux Arts style that was in vogue at the beginning of the 20thC. Certainly its 5th Ave. facade is more subdued than that of the flamboyant *Metropolitan Museum of Art.* Beyond the famous pair of reclining lions (sometimes called Patience and Fortitude), long steps and a terrace lead up to the Roman portico.

The library is for reference, not for lending, but there are frequent exhibitions of books and prints. *Bryant Park* is on the other side of the block.

New York University
Washington Sq., NY 10003 ☎ *598–3127. Map 2R4. Open Mon–Sat 8.00–22.00. Closed Sun.*

With over 44,000 registered students, most of them post-graduate or involved in adult education programmes, New York University claims to be the largest private university in the country. Founded in 1831, its first permanent home was a Gothic Revival pile at the NE corner of *Washington Square* in Greenwich Village (see *Walk 5* in *Planning*). That was replaced by the present unremarkable structure in 1894.

Over the last century, expansion has been unremitting, with a post-graduate School of Business Administration in the *Financial District*, a medical-dental complex on the *East Side*, a respected Institute of Fine Arts on 5th Ave., and a second campus in The Bronx. Fiscal retrenchment in the 1970s forced the sale of the Bronx campus and other smaller units, but the university retains ownership of most of the buildings on the E and S sides of Washington Sq., and these are only the most visible of substantial properties in the area.

The schools of law and medicine are ranked among the best in the nation. Distinguished teachers and graduates have included Samuel Morse, Thomas Wolfe, Jonas Salk, Joseph Heller, Albert Sabin, Lillian Hellman and Edward Koch.

Numismatic Society   See *American Numismatic Society.*

Old Merchant's House
29 E 4th St. (Broadway), NY 10543 ☎ *777–1089. Map 2R4*
🗙 *Open Sun 13.00–16.00, other times by appointment.*
No one seems to be certain, but the house is attributed to
Minard Lafever, pre-eminent architect of the early 19thC. The
design falls between Federal and Greek Revival, and was
completed as a speculation in 1832. Merchant Seabury
Tredwell bought it in 1835. His family lived here until 1933,
and since then it has been restored and preserved by the
Historic Landmark Society. The original furnishings and floor
coverings are still in place, and there is an intriguing secret
passage.

Paley Park
*3 E 53rd St. (5th Ave.). Map 5N4. Open May–Oct Mon–Sat
8.00–19.00, Nov, Dec, Mar, Apr 8.00–18.00. Closed Jan,
Feb and Sun.*
A chunk of valuable midtown real estate was here employed,
not as a multi-storey car park or apartment block, but as an
enclosed 'pocket' park. The combination of trees, tables, chairs
and simulated waterfall was underwritten by the chairman of
the board of the Columbia Broadcasting System and presented
as a gift to the people of New York City. A gift which turned out
to be just what they wanted; it is so popular that there is often a
queue.

Pan Am Building 🏛
200 Park Ave. (45th St.), NY 10017. Map 5O4 👁 ⚲ *Open
6.00–2.00.*
Praise has not been the Pan Am's lot, even before its completion
in 1963. By forming a visual octagonal wall across Park Ave.,
it does almost nothing right. The fact that Bauhaus doyen
Walter Gropius had a hand in it is little compensation. But it is
unavoidable, so enjoy the cocktail lounge at the top, which has
decent views towards Wall Street and the *United Nations
Headquarters*. A fatal accident in 1977 ended its rooftop
heliport function.

Pierpont Morgan Library 🏛
29 E 36th St. (5th Ave.), NY 10016 ☎ *685–0008. Map 5P4*
🗙 *Open Tues–Sat 10.30–17.00, Sun 13.00–17.00. Closed
Aug, Mon, and Sun in Jul.*
One of the quiet pleasures of subdued *Murray Hill*, the library
was constructed for financier J. Pierpont Morgan in 1902 by the
omnipresent firm of McKim, Mead & White. The Neo-
Classical design reflects Pierpont Morgan's passion for the
Italian Renaissance. An unobtrusive 1928 addition was finished
15yr after his death.

Consistent with its name, the building is primarily a
repository of rare books, illuminated manuscripts, and other
documents of the Middle Ages and Renaissance, but there is
also a great deal more that warrants attention: stained glass,
sculpture, enamel- and metal-work, and a number of sombre
Italian and Flemish paintings.

The **West Room**, with its carved, painted ceiling and red
damask curtains, has been kept exactly as it was during
Pierpont Morgan's lifetime.

Planetarium, Hayden   See *American Museum of
Natural History.*

Police Academy Museum
235 E 20th St. (2nd Ave.), NY 10003 ☎ *477–9753. Map 5Q5* ⊡ ❋ *Open Mon–Fri 13.00–17.00. Closed Sat, Sun.*
Not recommended for those of nervous disposition, the museum makes a forthright depiction of crime prevention and punishment in New York. Displays of the improvised weapons of teenage street gangs are mixed with semi-historical lethal artefacts of the gangster era.

Prospect Park
w of Flatbush Ave., Brooklyn. Map 12E3 ❋ *Subway D, M, QB to Prospect Park.*
Frederick Law Olmsted and Calvert Vaux collaborated on this landscape design (1866–74), as they had on the larger *Central Park* in Manhattan. Many think this is the better of the two, with fewer roads and a more imaginative composition of wooded glades, water, and pathways. A small **zoo** established in 1935 along Flatbush Ave. contains elephants, zebras, monkeys and bears (☎ *965–6560; open Apr–Nov 8.00–17.00, Dec–Mar 8.00–16.30*). Nearby is the **Lefferts Homestead**, built in 1783 in the Dutch Colonial style, and fitted out with period furnishings (☎ *as above; open Wed–Sun 13.00–17.00, closed Mon, Tues, second Sat of each month in winter*).

In gentler times, this bucolic setting adjacent to the *Brooklyn Museum* and *Brooklyn Botanic Garden* would constitute a rare urban retreat. Sad to say, it is subject to severe acts of vandalism and lack of funds. Go only during daylight.

Puerto Rican Museum for the Arts   When the
American Geographical Society moved out of town, this collection took its place in the *Audubon Terrace* complex.

Queensboro Bridge
Map 5N5 ⊡
Once it was possible to drive halfway along this bridge over the East River and turn right into an elevator that lowered to **Roosevelt Island** (formerly Welfare Island). For safety and security reasons, that service was ended in the mid-1970s when the island became home to an ambitious new residential community, called Southtown, an attempt to integrate all economic classes in new housing financed by both public and private funds. No cars are allowed and travel to and from the island is now by cable car. The bridge, symbolic of *East Side* glamour, appears in dozens of old movies.

Queens-Midtown Tunnel
Map 5O5 🚗
This two-tube, four-lane East River tunnel is of note only because it is likely to be the one used by arrivals from LaGuardia and JFK airports. It emerges between 36th and 37th Sts. in Manhattan.

RCA Building 🏛 ☆
30 Rockefeller Plaza (5th Ave. and Ave. of the Americas, 49th and 50th Sts.), NY 10017 ☎ *489–2947 (observation roof). Map 5O4* 🚗 ❋ *Open Apr–Oct 10.00–20.45, Nov–Mar 10.30–19.00.*
Centrepiece of the 19-building *Rockefeller Center* development, the RCA stands highest at 850ft (259m) and 70

storeys. Completed in the Depression years, its ground floor murals are in the heroic Social Realist mode. The observation roof proffers panoramic vistas of Manhattan that many natives feel surpass those of taller buildings to the s. (See *Walk 1* in *Planning*.)

Richmondtown Restoration 🏛 ☆
441 Clarke Ave., Staten Island, NY 10306 ☎ *351–9414. Map 12F2* 🖼 *✗ by appointment* ⬛ *✳ Open July–Aug Tues–Sat 10.00–17.00; closed Sun, Mon. Sept–June, Sat 10.00–17.00, Sun 12.00–17.00; closed Mon–Fri. Ferry from Battery Park. Take a taxi or S113 bus from the Staten Island Ferry terminal.*

Eventually this is to be a museum village of over 30 buildings – restored, reconstructed, reassembled, recreated – ranging from the early Colonial period up to the 19thC. The Staten Island Historical Society has been working on this project for 40yr, and while progress is painstakingly slow, the rewards are evident. Several buildings are fully furnished and open to the public, among them a colourful **general store** ☆ and a 1696 elementary school. Costumed artisans give demonstrations in pottery, leatherwork, weaving and printing. The grounds include a mill pond and picnicking is encouraged.

Riverside Church 🏛 †
490 Riverside Dr. (122nd St.), NY 10027 ☎ *222–5900. Map 8I2. Open 8.00–22.00.*

Despite the 74-bell carillon and 20-ton bell at its top (both the largest of their kind anywhere in the world), the 392ft (120m) tower of this inter-denominational church looks vaguely like a Gothic 1930s office building – and is, in part. There is an **observation deck** ☆ which affords a sweeping panorama of the Hudson River from Wall St. to the *George Washington Bridge* (*open Mon–Sat 11.00–15.00, Sun 12.00–16.00* ☎ *749–7000 for times of carillon performances*).

Riverside Park
Map 8 & 10E–F2.

New Yorkers owe an eternal debt to Frederick Law Olmsted and Calvert Vaux, the 19thC landscape architects who created *Central Park*, *Prospect Park* in Brooklyn, and this sylvan strip of trees and hills bordering the Hudson River. It runs from W 72nd St. to W 125th St., banked to the E by a wall of handsome apartment houses and blemished only by the Henry Hudson Parkway, which was built along its length in the 1930s. The **Soldiers and Sailors Monument** (*W 89th St.*) and *General Grant National Memorial* (*W 122nd St.*) are within its boundaries.

Rockefeller Center 🏛 ☆
Map 5O4

John D. Rockefeller Jr. put together the grand scheme for this 22-acre compound of office towers – a 'city within the city'. The heart of the complex is between 5th and 6th Aves. and 49th and 50th Sts. Here are found the sights familiar from tourist literature, most of them completed in the 1930s. Dominating is the *RCA Building*, facing E. While it does not compare in scale or inventiveness with the contemporary *Chrysler Building*, it bears a mantle of restrained elegance. At the NW corner of its base is the Art Deco **Radio City Music Hall**, with a breathtaking vaulted interior in which rock concerts and elaborate revues are staged. To the E, directly in front of the entrance, is a sunken plaza that is an ice-skating rink in winter and outdoor cafe in summer. A gold statue of *Prometheus* floats above. At the approach of Christmas, a tree over 70ft (21m) high is placed behind him. Still further E, banks of plants and flowers take up the centre of a pedestrian precinct that ends at 5th Ave. (See *Walk 1* in *Planning*.)

St Bartholomew's Church 血 † ☆
109 E 50th St. (Park Ave.), NY 10022 ☎ *751–1616. Map* **5**O4 🖭 *Open 8.00–18.00. Closes 15.00 during major hols.*
Providing a welcome antidote to the slab-sided canyon of midtown Park Ave., this pinkish pile of glorious Byzantine-Romanesque excess features Stanford White's **triple portals** (1903)☆ salvaged from an earlier church by James Renwick, located downtown on 24th St. The present church opened in 1919, and the prominent dome was finished in 1930. See it quickly, for the Episcopalian church has financial problems and developers are casting covetous eyes.

St John The Divine   See *Cathedral Church of St John The Divine*.

St Mark's Church-In-The-Bowery 血 †
2nd Ave. (10th St.), NY 10003 ☎ *674–6377. Map* **3**R5. *Parish hall open 9.00–17.00. Main building closed indefinitely for repairs.*
One of the oldest houses of worship in Manhattan, this church was built on farmland in 1799. The basic structure of the building is Federal, with a Greek Revival steeple added in 1828. Dutch Director-General Peter Stuyvesant is buried here, in ground that he once owned. A fire in 1978 destroyed much of the roof and interior of the church, and costly restoration is still underway.

St Patrick's Cathedral 血 † ☆
5th Ave. (51st St.), NY 10022 ☎ *753–2261. Map* **5**N4 🖾 *except by prior approval. Open 7.00–20.00.*
When James Renwick submitted his drawings in 1850, the fashion for Gothic Revival was on the wane. By the time the cathedral was completed in 1888, it must have seemed dated. No matter, for the style returned to favour soon afterwards, and by then St Patrick's was already in the ranks of the timeless. Echoing great cathedrals of Europe (for Renwick formulated his ideas after intense study of European examples), it is part lacy stonework, part soaring caprice, part massive pretence. Authenticity might have demanded flying buttresses, but the site would not accommodate them and they were not required structurally, for the roof was lighter than in the earlier Gothic prototypes.

The siting of the cathedral was to cause consternation in some quarters. At the time, Irish immigration had reached sufficient proportions to be threatening to the Protestant majority. The latter found it distasteful in the extreme to endure such a blatant monument to the Roman faith, especially in the midst of a neighbourhood chosen by the monied classes as refuge from the teeming masses downtown. In time, both groups came to uneasy union in the face of succeeding waves of even less familiar creeds.

St Paul's Chapel 🏛 ✝ ☆
Broadway (Fulton St.), NY 10002 ☎ *285–0874. Map 2U4. Open 8.00–15.45.*

The only existing non-residential building in New York that predates the Revolution (1766), it holds its own against the silvery glass curtain walls of the *World Trade Center*, at least when viewed from street level. Made of Manhattan schist quarried at the site, the exterior facing is brownstone. Apart from the steeple, added in 1794, it is authentic Georgian, inside and out, although the blue and pink paint was perhaps not always so vivid. Architect Thomas McBean is believed to have been a pupil of James Gibbs, who designed St Martin-in-the-Fields in London.

Chandeliers of Waterford crystal dominate the interior and the altar screen (1787) is by Pierre L'Enfant, the Frenchman who later planned Washington DC. George Washington put in frequent appearances during his first presidential term. His pew is marked. The graveyard is a shaded resting place for footsore souls still living, and there are lunchtime concerts of classical music on Mon, Tues and Thurs.

Seagram Building 🏛
375 Park Ave. (52nd St.), NY 10022. Map 5N4.

First came *Lever House*, just across Park Ave., then the Seagram (1958). After them, the glass-and-metal box International Style went downhill, swallowed up in greed and misinterpretation of its deceptive simplicity. (For confirmation of that conclusion, simply look s to the *Pan Am Building*.) The Plaza in front of the Seagram may appear banal but, considering the almost unbelievable cost of midtown property, even this much walking space seems generous. The narrow slab looming above is the colour of well-aged bourbon, consistent with the preoccupation of the client, a prominent distiller. Ludwig Mies van der Rohe was the architect, Philip Johnson his assistant.

Snug Harbor Cultural Center 🏛 ☆
914 Richmond Terrace, Staten Island, NY 10301 ☎ *448–2500. Map 12E2* 🔲 *Entrance to grounds and most exhibitions* 🔳 *Guided tour and some exhibitions and performances. Grounds open 10.00–dusk; exhibitions Wed–Sun 13.00–17.00. Ferry from Battery Park. Take a taxi or S1 bus from the Staten Island Ferry terminal.*

Sailor's Snug Harbor, a wealthy charitable foundation providing shelter for retired merchant seamen, purchased these 80 waterfront acres in 1831. The organizers proceeded to build, in a grand manner that might seem inconsistent with their mission. Their dedication left a trove of over 20 contiguous buildings representative of the Greek Revival, Italianate, Victorian and Beaux Arts modes. One of the architects was Minard Lafever, as prominent in the early 19thC as Stanford White was to be 75yr later.

Now renamed and anointed a National Historic Landmark District, Snug Harbor is still in the process of often tentative conversion to an arts centre. Should all the acquired buildings be utilized eventually for that purpose, it would be an unprecedented complex. As it is, only a few galleries are presently in use, and on a limited schedule. Fiscal concerns and public indifference appear to be frustrating the great plans of the trustees. In the meantime, the complex is a compressed lesson in 19thC architecture.

SoHo 🏛 ☆
Map 2S4.

Whoever coined the name no doubt had the famous London quarter in mind, but the two places have little in common. This 'SoHo' is a contraction of 'SOuth of HOuston St.'. (Incidentally, that street is pronounced 'HOWston', not 'HEWston'.) Less than two decades ago, SoHo was a dreary industrial district with broken concrete pavements piled high with boxes of refuse and pot-holed streets of worn Belgian blocks. Lorries backed into loading bays, rows of sewing and die-cutting machines clattered and thumped behind grimy windows, crates of fabrics and plastics were trundled about by forklifts and bowed backs. At night, everyone left.

It will not be reassuring to learn that this description still applies – but only in part. In the early 1960s, artists of the New York School, no longer content with easel painting in conventional studios, sought ever-larger work space. The problem was cost. They discovered the lofts of what was then called 'The Valley' – five- to ten-floor buildings with vast unpartitioned rooms designed for warehouses, shipping firms and labour-intensive light industries. Marginal businesses were closing up, and artists moved in. This was illegal, according to zoning laws. Yet they doubled their transgression by adding living spaces to their new studios, installing bathrooms and kitchens. Hanging plants and curtains were glimpsed from the streets. Other artists with similar needs – film-makers, dancers, sculptors – followed the leaders.

By 1970, the trickle became a torrent. Since the municipal authorities could no longer ignore the fact that their ordinances were being violated, they simply changed them. Bona fide artists could now live in the converted lofts. SoHo went from cultural work place to artistic community to general free-for-all in just a few years. Bars, restaurants, food and craft shops catering for artists were supplemented by branches of established uptown galleries. Stockbrokers and lawyers bought up the lofts and fitted them out with saunas, billiard tables, luxury bathrooms and eight-track hi-fi equipment. Rents skyrocketed and many artists left. But SoHo remains a vital, passionate community, despite pretentious boutiques and eating places with breathtaking prices.

Saturday is the time to go, for the art-lover's ritual gallery tour and a drink at an engaging pub. (See *Guide to the galleries* in *Culture, history and background*.) Along the way, observe the **cast-iron facades** for which the district is also known. After a brief mid-19thC period during which SoHo was the fashionable centre of town, hotels and stores were displaced by factory buildings. To dress them up, iron cast motifs taken from European palaces were prefabricated in sections and assembled on the site, apparently an American innovation. Entire buildings were erected in four or five months by this method. Although they proved not to be fireproof and the technique was abandoned in the early 20thC, over 200 examples survive. They are notable for their gargoyles, Corinthian columns, and ornamentation and sculptural detail taken from Venetian, Romanesque and French Second Empire examples. Most of them are within an official landmark district created by the city to ensure their preservation.

SoHo is bounded by Houston St., Canal St., Sullivan St. and Broadway. The main street is West Broadway, and the oldest house (1806) is at 107 Spring St.

South Street Seaport Museum 🏛 ☆

16 Fulton St. (South St.), NY 10038 ☎ *766–9020. Map 3U5* 🖼 *✗* 🖺 ✴ ⬌ ⇌ ◁€ *Open 11.00–18.00.*

A living museum-in-progress, the Seaport contributes mightily to the resurrection of lower Manhattan as a place to live and stroll and cherish. Centred around Piers 15 and 16, just s of the Brooklyn Bridge and what remains of the old Fulton Fish Market, it makes nine antique sailing vessels available for viewing. Their masts and spidery rigging stand in arresting contrast to the majestic backdrop of Wall St. skyscrapers. Most are in a seemingly endless process of renovation, but manage to convey a sense of the romantic epoch of early steam and clipper ships that made the city the busiest port in the New World. At the time of writing, only five can be boarded. Prides of the fleet are the four-masted, metal-hulled bark *Peking* and the classic 1885 square-rigger *Wavertree*. Among the others are the 1906 lightship *Ambrose* and an 1893 schooner, the *Lettie G. Howard*. Two- and three-hour cruises of New York harbour can be taken (May–Oct) on the century-old schooner *Pioneer*. Jazz concerts are among the special events held during the warmer months.

Seafarers required land-based support services, and the museum has taken them into account. In association with a private development corporation, it is restoring an 11-block official national historic district adjacent to the piers. Over $5 million has been spent on quayside rows of Greek Revival, Georgian, Federal and Victorian warehouses and ship chandleries. Venerable Schermerhorn Row and Front St. have undergone careful renovation, with much of their interior space given over to retail enterprises. A new three-storey structure was opened in 1983. Dubbed the 'Fulton Market', it is crammed with speciality food shops and pavement cafés.

The Museum Block building on Water St. is partly old, partly new, and contains a variety of shops, exhibition galleries, and a theatre showing a slick multi-screen film about the evolution of the district, entitled *South Street Venture*. Another three-storey pavilion, less pleasing in design, has been erected on an overwater platform N of the piers. Opened in 1985, it too contains 100 shops and restaurants. (See *Walk 2* in *Planning*.)

Staten Island Zoo

613 Broadway (Forrest Ave.), Staten Island, NY 10310 ☎ *442–3100. Map 12E2* 🖼 🖾 *on Wed* ✴ *Open 10.00–16.45. Ferry from Battery Park. Take a taxi or S107 bus from the Staten Island Ferry terminal.*

Specialization can make otherwise modest institutions rival grander establishments blessed with better resources. Although this zoo is of principal interest to residents of Staten Island, its reptile collection rivals any in North America. Typical of this comprehensiveness are specimens of every known type of rattlesnake. There is also an aquarium and a well-regarded collection of birds.

Statue of Liberty ☆

Liberty Island, New York Harbor, NY 10004 ☎ *732–1236. Map 12D3* 🖼 🖺 ✴ *Open 9.00–18.00. Ferry from Battery Park.*

A description of 'Miss Liberty' is as enlightening as one of a telephone. Everyone knows what she looks like, although the first sight of her is undiminished by *déjà vu*. French sculptor Auguste Bartholdi created her out of thin, beaten copper panels, with the engineering counsel of Gustave Eiffel, a man of recognized expertise in such matters. At 151ft (46m), the statue dwarfs that wonder of the ancient world, the Colossus of Rhodes. Extensive renovation has prepared the monument for its official centennial in 1986.

While the cost of the statue itself was underwritten by French contributions, the American public was slow to come up with the requisite matching funds to build the pedestal. It was nearly 20yr from conception to unveiling, in 1885. The statue weighs 225 tons, each eye is 2ft 6in (75cm) wide, and the tip of the up-raised torch is 395ft (120m) above sea level. Inside, a lift carries visitors halfway up and 168 steps lead to the perforated crown. This gives a remarkable view of the bay, from the *Verrazano Narrows Bridge* to the spires of Manhattan. The *American Museum of Immigration* is housed in the points of the star-shaped base.

Temple Emanu-El
5th Ave. (65th St.), NY 10021 ☎ 744–1400. Map 7M4. Open 10.00–17.00, services Sun–Thurs 17.30, Fri 17.15, Sat 10.30. (For services, enter by 5th Ave. door; at other times, by E 65th St. door.)

The largest Reform Jewish synagogue in North America, it can accommodate 2,500 worshippers. Limestone is the primary material, buttressed by steel. Its size is the principal attraction for sightseers, given the ambiguity of its half-Turkish, half-Italianate make-up.

Theater District
Map 4O3.

Depending upon context, Broadway is either the city's longest avenue or a synonym for the theatrical district through which it passes on its diagonal slash through midtown. **Times Square** is essentially the intersection of that famous street and 7th Ave. Within the area bounded by 40th St., 55th St., 6th Ave. and 8th Ave. are many large cinemas and most of the major legitimate theatres. The huge electrified signs and marquees that gave Times Square the sobriquet 'Great White Way' are still there, although they now advertise Japanese cameras as well as coming attractions. Crowds of gawkers, New Jersey teenagers, matinee ladies from the suburbs, French sailors, winos, disco dancers, hustlers, and tourists from everywhere fill the streets. On New Year's Eve, they are wall-to-wall, over 100,000 strong (but watch it on television).

Despite repeated efforts to clean it up, 42nd St. between 7th and 8th Aves. is a sludge of pornographic cinemas, prostitutes, addicts and troublemakers. Avoid it, and the northerly stretch of 8th Ave. it joins, but don't let it deter you from seeing a show on the streets nearby. Restaurants in the area cater for every taste and budget. Few are more than middling-good, most are noisy, but they specialize in pre- and post-show meals.

Theodore Roosevelt Birthplace
28 E 20th St. (5th Ave.), NY 10003 ☎ 260–1616. Map 5Q4 ▨ ⚔ Open Wed–Sun 9.00–17.00. Closed Mon, Tues.

The twenty-sixth President (1901– 09) was born in this house in 1858 and lived here until 1873. The Roosevelts were a large and wealthy family even then, and this Greek Revival house, rebuilt to original specifications, reflects that prosperity. In the five period rooms open to the public, careful attention has been paid to authenticity. The parlour is agleam with crystal chandeliers and gilt-framed mirrors. Plump horsehair sofas and chairs are arranged in inviting groups and fringed satin curtains frame the tall windows. Few oddities here, but an impression of elegant solidity consistent with the time and social class.

Trophies reflect Roosevelt's roles of rancher, big-game hunter, explorer and soldier. Tiger and bear skins cover the floor of one room, and there are branding irons, a stuffed lion, uniforms and cavalry bugles. Yet this complex man – a progressive republican at home, an imperialist abroad – was above all a dedicated public servant. One glass case after another, filled with campaign buttons, public documents, family records and letters, and newspaper cartoons, attests to the energy he applied to that calling. (See also *Gramercy Park*).

Tibetan Museum 🏛

338 Lighthouse Ave., Staten Island, NY 10306
☎ *987–3478. Map* **12F2** 🔳 *𝕏 by appointment. Open Apr–Nov, Sat, Sun 13.00–17.00; closed Mon–Fri. Telephone for Dec–Mar opening times. Ferry from Battery Park. Take a taxi or S113 bus from the Staten Island Ferry terminal. Near Richmondtown Restoration.*

The Staten Island Ferry is worth taking just for the breathtaking views it affords. But if an additional excuse is required, this museum should head the list. Within the relatively accurate replica of a Buddhist temple (1947) are exquisite bronzes, scrolls, painted silks and religious books. Many are Tibetan in origin, but China, Nepal and adjacent regions are also represented. Linger afterwards in the terraced gardens dotted with oriental deities and animal sculptures.

Transfiguration, Church of the   See *Church of the Transfiguration*.

TriBeCa
Map **2T4**.
When the artists who resurrected *SoHo* were forced out by landlords and speculators who saw the profits to be realized in sales to non-artists with regular incomes, many simply moved a few blocks s and w. They called their new homestead TriBeCa, for 'TRIangle BElow CAnal St.'. Inevitably, the SoHo phenomenon is asserting itself, with galleries, bars, restaurants and funky discos. Down here, where streets have names instead of numbers and the straightforward grid of uptown does not apply, the approximate boundaries are West St. to Church St. and Barclay St. to Canal St.

Trinity Church 🏛 †
Broadway (Wall St.), NY 10006 ☎ *285–0872. Map* **2U4** *𝕏 Open 7.00–18.00* 🔳 *Museum open Mon–Fri 10.30–12.00, 12.30–15.30, Sat 10.30–15.30, Sun 12.30–15.30.*

The first Trinity Church was erected here in 1698, entirely of wood. That burned down in 1776, in the first of the two great fires that decimated old New York. The second version was razed in 1839, and the present Gothic Revival manifestation (by Richard Upjohn) went up in 1846. No one has seriously considered washing the outside since, and the red sandstone is now so black it nearly shines. Over the intervening years, additions have included a chapel (1913) and bronze entry doors

(1894) modelled on those of the Baptistry in Florence. A small museum displays photographs and artefacts relating to the history of the church. Pause in the graveyard for a glance at the memorials to statesman Alexander Hamilton and steamboat inventor Robert Fulton.

Ukrainian Museum
203 2nd Ave. (12th St.), NY 10003 ☎ *228–0110. Map* **3***R5* 🚇 *Open Wed–Sun 13.00–17.00. Closed Mon, Tues.*
Embroidery is the speciality – on garments, textiles and ritual panels – but the intricately decorated Easter eggs are equally entrancing. There are two galleries, also featuring folk carvings and metalwork.

Union Square
Map **5***Q4*
In the 1930s, the 3.6-acre park was a vigorous if shabby version of Speakers' Corner in London's Hyde Park. Anarchists, trade unionists, radicals and simple eccentrics mounted soapboxes and endured hecklers. Its decline accelerated after World War II and it eventually became the habitat of drug peddlers and prostitutes. The Parks Department hopes that an increased police presence and a major beautification project completed in 1985 will encourage families and office workers to return. The early signs of increased use are encouraging.

United Nations Headquarters 🏛
1st Ave. (45th St.), NY 10017 ☎ *754–1234. Map* **5***O5* 📷 X 🚇 🍴 *Open 9.00–17.20.*
John D. Rockefeller Jr. donated the East River site and the first three buildings were ready for occupation in 1952. Despite the presence of several significant works of art by Marc Chagall and Barbara Hepworth, the overall visual effect of the complex is somewhat vapid, in the manner of quasi-governmental edifices.

Most offices and rooms are closed to the public, but are of little general interest. The library is open to scholars and journalists. One-hour tours with multilingual guides leave about every 10min from the Main Lobby of the **General Assembly Building**. That is the low structure with the concave roofline to the N of the simple slab of the **Secretariat Building**. The latter is probably the more familiar from photographs.

Tickets to sessions of the General Assembly, the Security Council and certain other meetings can be obtained at the Information Desk shortly beforehand. (*Admission is free, but on a first-come basis; starting times are usually 10.30 and 15.00.*) The opening of the General Assembly, usually Mon of the third week in Sept, is the most intriguing time to go.

Outsiders can lunch at the Delegates' Dining Room on the top floor of the **Conference Building**, which sits astride the FDR Drive at the edge of the river. They are seated in order of arrival; no reservations are accepted. (*Lunch only, Mon–Fri.*) A coffee shop in the public concourse is open daily (*9.30–17.00*). Nearby shops sell souvenirs, books, UN postage stamps, and handicrafts of many nations.

Upper West Side ☆
Map **6***J2.*
Of all the recently resurgent neighbourhoods – *SoHo*, *TriBeCa*, *Chelsea*, Park Slope in Brooklyn – the Upper West

Side most resists easy classification. It is too large, for one thing – from Central Park W to the Hudson River, and from 59th St. to as far N as 120th St., according to some definitions. Secondly, it lacks the handy ethnic, social or cultural identity of other districts. Well-to-do refugees from the more fashionable *East Side* have long lived here, in such still desirable apartment houses as the gabled *Dakota Apartments*. But they understandably chose the narrow strips along *Central Park* and Riverside Drive, and the blocks in the middle were allowed to fester.

Many people mark the renaissance of the Upper West Side from the completion of the *Lincoln Center* (1966) and this event was no doubt influential. Another factor was the escalating rents of Greenwich Village, which drove out writers and other professionals associated with publishing and communications. The newcomers spruced up their apartments, their buildings, even whole blocks. They opened gourmet and book shops and brought new life to those already there. Pubs of sufficient atmosphere attracted customers whose conversation was of royalty contracts and writer's block. Dim, woody bistros featuring allegedly Provençal cuisine proliferated at such a rate that natives refer to one stretch as 'Quiche Alley'. Ratification of the area's new-found panache was the arrival of Eastsiders, who not long ago were insisting that only the imminent demise of a close relative would cause them to cross Central Park.

Diversity continues, with smart boutiques beside seedy but colourful bodegas, working-men's bars adjoining glittery singles' hangouts, upper-crust Bohemians jostling with welfare mothers in corner delis. Important sights and institutions include the *American Museum of Natural History*, the *New York Historical Society*, the *Cathedral Church of St John The Divine*, *Columbia University*, *General Grant National Memorial* and the city's grandest boulevard, Riverside Drive.

Van Cortlandt Mansion and Museum ⋔

Van Cortlandt Park (242nd St. and Broadway), Bronx, NY 10471 ☎ *543–3344. Map 13B4* ▨ ✗ *Open Tues–Sat 10.00–16.45, Sun 12.00–16.45. Closed Mon. Subway 1 to 242nd St. – Van Cortlandt Park.*

George Washington spent a lot of time in and around New York, usually with British troops hot on his heels. This country house (1748) with its deceptively modest stone exterior served as one of his headquarters, as did the *Morris-Jumel Mansion* in Manhattan. It has elements of the Dutch Colonial style, but is essentially Georgian. Note the carved faces in the window keystones. Unlike most of the city's historic houses, it remains in a preserved rural setting, although the nearby meadows are now playing fields. Nine rooms are open to the public, including a cellar kitchen with a Dutch oven, and a parlour with a spinet and excellent Chippendale pieces. Note the Delftware and English china, crewelwork, cooking implements, doll's house and unusual cupboard bed.

Verrazano Narrows Bridge

Map 12E2–3 ▨ *only when crossing w–E.*

When opened in 1964, it became the longest suspension bridge in the world, a position it held until 1981 when overtaken by the Humber Bridge in Britain. Two decks and 12 lanes link Staten Island and points w with the Belt Parkway in Brooklyn. Giovanni da Verrazano was an Italian explorer in French employment, who is believed to have been the first European to sail into the bay. The New York Marathon starts at the w end of the bridge on the last Sun in Oct.

Villard Houses (Palace Hotel) ▥

451 Madison Ave. (51st St.), NY 10022. Map 5N4.
This U-shaped Italian Renaissance palace, commissioned by German-born financier Henry Villard, was a departure for the firm of McKim, Mead & White. As the most popular architects of the late 19thC, they had dabbled in most revivalist styles except this one. In effect, these are six connected brownstone houses unified by a Roman aesthetic. After changes in ownership that included the Random House publishing firm and the Roman Catholic Archdiocese of New York, they were purchased by Harry Helmsley. He intended to tear them down, but was prevailed upon to restore them instead and erect his Palace Hotel to the E. The houses were incorporated into the overall design and became part of the hotel. The cost was substantial, but the result is a triumph of enlightened development.

Washington Square ▥

Map 2R4.
Now it is the heart of *Greenwich Village* – playground, meeting place, open-air venue for street musicians, *de facto* campus of *New York University*. Over the centuries, it has been hunting preserve, potter's field, public execution place, military parade ground. Brick Greek Revival terraced houses of the 1830s survive along the N side. Stanford White's **Washington Arch** (1892) marks the s end of 5th Ave., while Philip Johnson's **Bobst Library** dominates the SE corner. (See *Walk 5* in *Planning*.)

Waterside Houses ▥

FDR Drive (25th and 30th St.), NY 10016. Map 5P5.
These arresting brown monoliths repudiated the notion that subsidized public housing was inevitably banal while simultaneously proving a harbinger of the Post-Modernist reaction to glass Bauhaus boxes. Completed in 1974, the four towers at the shore of the East River have bevelled, faceted corners and channelled planes, massed with pleasing irregularity.

Whitney Museum of American Art ▥ ☆

Madison Ave. (75th St.), NY 10021 ☎ 570–3676 (general information), 288–9601 (film information). Map 7M4 ▣ Tues 17.00–20.00 and at all times for senior citizens and students ▣ at all other times ☾ Open Tues 11.30–20.00, Wed–Sat 11.00–18.00, Sun 12.00–18.00. Closed Mon.
Depending upon whose interests are promoted – or ignored – the show called the Whitney Biennial is predictably cited as presumptuous, bland, stunning, inept and seminal. The ambitious survey of contemporary American art rarely fails to outrage or dismay the creative community, which may be fairly taken as evidence that the museum is doing something right. As befits the basic premise, the exhibition ranges from such luminaries as James Rosenquist and Wayne Thiebaud to fresh unheralded talents, from the arrestingly experimental to polyresin sculpture so life-like it all but breathes. There are, in addition, avant-garde films, slide and video presentations of

'site works' by conceptual artists, and dance programmes and events that push conventions beyond their limits. The Biennial is normally held from late Jan to mid-Apr.

At other times, works of particular schools and trends are grouped for varying lengths of time. They are supplemented by rotated selections from the permanent collection. Virtually every major American talent of the last 50yr is represented, with an ample showing of their predecessors in the first 30yr of this century. Among the later artists are Willem de Kooning, Louise Nevelson, David Smith, Andy Warhol and Hans Hofmann; the earlier ones include Stuart Davis, Edward Hopper, George Bellows and Reginald Marsh. But the strength of the Whitney lies in its refusal to settle back and wait for artists to establish themselves. The trustees take chances, from acquiring kapok-and-vinyl 'soft' sculptures to rooms of randomly-tuned radios to heaps of fabric and timber. In the process, they make curious choices, but their nerve is refreshing.

All this came about through the energy and commitment of Gertrude Vanderbilt Whitney, a sculptress who happened to be rich. She began by expanding her studio in *Greenwich Village* into exhibition space and purchasing the work of unacknowledged young artists. Periodic moves to larger premises led from 8th St. to 54th St. to the present location. As is often true of New York museums, the Whitney building (1966) is as provocative as the creations it houses. Marcel Breuer met the requirements of his clients with the sort of unconventional solution for which he was noted. The building is sheer on three sides, but the facade rises in three cantilevered tiers from the moated patio below street level, the top floor looming over the pavement and the suspended bridge connecting pavement with lobby. The granite sheathing is pierced by assymetrically placed trapezoidal windows. Interior walls are in part raw concrete bearing the impressions of the grains of the forming planks. A new wing is planned.

Some 50 Alexander Calder mobiles and stabiles are positioned around the courtyard and inside the tall plate glass of the basement floor.

A small airy cafeteria edged with potted trees serves lunch, snacks and cocktails (*Wed–Sat 11.30–16.30, Sun 12.00–17.00, Tues 11.30–19.30 including dinner*).

Woolworth Building 🏛 ☆
233 Broadway (Barclay St.), NY 10007. Map 2T4 📞 *Open Mon–Fri 9.00–17.00. Closed Sat, Sun.*

Although best known as the consulting architect for the *George Washington Bridge*, Cass Gilbert was a favourite of tycoons and Federal bureaucrats, largely on account of his unabashed enthusiasm for the Neo-Classicism in vogue during the 50yr bracketing the turn of the century. His 1907 Beaux Arts **US Customs House** (next to *Bowling Green*) bows only to the *Metropolitan Museum of Art* in effusive grandeur. It is said that he drew inspiration for that design from the Paris Opera House, and there is little question that the British Houses of Parliament played a role in his Woolworth commission. Replete with Gothic traceries and gargoyles carved primarily from terra cotta, a blend of modern technology and stylistic nostalgia that so often fails, this 'Cathedral of Commerce' is one of the most successful of the first generation of skyscrapers.

From its completion in 1913 until the opening of the *Chrysler Building* in 1930, Woolworth's monument to himself and his

empire of nickel-and-dime stores was the tallest in the world.
The observation floor has long been closed to the public, but
you can step into the lobby to admire the terra cotta and marble
walls, bronze ornamentation, and vaulted ceiling.

World Trade Center ▥ ☆

Church St. (Liberty St.), NY 10007 ☎ *466–7377. Map **2**U4*
▨ Ⓡ ▣ ❋ *Open 9.30–21.30.*

Long before their completion in 1974, the twin towers of the
World Trade Center encountered censure, on both aesthetic
and environmental grounds. They were visually banal,
displaced a thriving market district of little charm but much
vitality, threw the lower Manhattan skyline out of balance, and
placed unnecessary strain on public transport and services.
Those complaints are now irrelevant. Rentable space was
leased, shops and restaurants were installed, and there are no
more stunning vistas in the urban world. At 1,350ft (411m) they
are eight storeys taller than the *Empire State Building*, but
were surmounted within months by the Sears Building in
Chicago.

The **observation decks** are in 2 World Trade Center.
There is an **enclosed deck**☆ on the 107th floor, and an open
rooftop promenade on the 110th. The latter is not for the
vertiginous, nor is it open in blustery or otherwise inclement
weather. On a clear day, you can see 75 to 100 miles. Most of the
40 shops and 22 restaurants are at ground level or below, but the
Windows on the World restaurant in 1 World Trade Center
takes advantage of the views from the 107th floor. The Vista
International Hotel between the towers opened in early 1981,
the first important downtown hotel in over a century.

Yeshiva University ▥

187th St. (Amsterdam Ave.), NY 10033 ☎ *960–5400. Map*
***10**C3. Subway 1 to 181 or 191 Sts.*

The largest and oldest Jewish university in the Western
Hemisphere, it began in 1886 as a seminary called Yeshiva Eitz
Chaim. Now a fully-fledged university with over 7,000 students
engaged in both undergraduate and post-graduate studies, it
maintains reverence for its origins while drawing wide respect
for its courses in medicine and the mathematical sciences. The
main building is a Moorish-Byzantine extravaganza of tiles,
cupolas, minarets, domes and arches, completed in 1928.

Yeshiva University Museum ☆

Yeshiva University Library, 2520 Amsterdam Ave., NY
10033 ☎ *960–5390* ▨ *Open Tues–Thurs 11.00–17.00,*
Sun 12.00–18.00. Closed Mon, Fri, Sat.

A rich collection focuses on the Jewish experience through
photography, religious objects, paintings, and scale models of
ten famous synagogues of the ancient world.

Yorkville

*Map **7**L5.*

Germans were among the earliest large immigrant groups of the
19thC. Many of them settled in this Upper East Side district
centring on 86th St., but they were speedily assimilated and had
largely dispersed by the 1930s. Traces of their occupation
remain, with a *bierstube* or two, several bakery-coffee houses,
and some dark-panelled restaurants specializing in
wienerschnitzel and *sauerbraten*. Prodigals return for the
Steuben Day parade in mid-Sept.

Where to stay

An unprecedented surge in hotel construction and renovation signalled the emergence of the city from the miasma of the 1970s. Harry Helmsley, a pragmatic visionary with the financial clout to realize his fantasies, burst into the local consciousness with the purchase or erection of no fewer than six hotels. The Marriott chain is introducing the **Marquis**, the first major hotel on Times Square in over 20yr. And Hilton International created the **Vista International** in the *Financial District*, curiously deprived of transient lodgings.

These thousands of new rooms are all of the grand and super-de-luxe category, however, and there's the rub. Budget accommodations are invariably mean and soulless, and there are few enough even of those. Nothing is available that might be compared in cost and homeliness to family-run Italian *pensioni* or British bed-and-breakfast houses. The best that can be expected in this category is a reasonably clean room with minimal amenities: no more than a private shower, daily sheet changes and a TV set, and none of those are certain. At the other end of the scale, full baths, ankle-deep carpets, and meticulous housekeeping are the rule, and such additional touches as refrigerators, fresh-cut flowers, closed-circuit movies, and mints at bedside are common. Even in these up-market establishments, however, 24hr room service is increasingly hard to find.

Whatever their classification, a majority of the worthiest choices are found in midtown Manhattan, in an area bounded by 3rd Ave. and 7th Ave. from 38th St. to 60th St. There is a scattering through the Upper *East Side*, a handful w of Times Sq. and a half-dozen motels near the airports. Rates are moderated somewhat by location, season, and duration of stay. To make up for the absence of businessmen, for example, hotels devise weekend package plans to attract suburbanites and tourists with such extras as theatre tickets or brunches and up to 40% off standard room rates. Availability of discounts fluctuates with occupancy levels, obviously, and finding a room at any price can be a chore between Apr and Oct, especially at short notice. On those occasions, it is wise to enquire at hotels outside the immediate midtown area, particularly those in the *Gramercy Park* and *Murray Hill* districts. Ideally, reservations should be made at least a month in advance.

Children under 14 often may stay in their parents' room at little or no extra charge. Ask when booking. Several hotels have swimming pools and other recreational facilities to keep teenagers occupied, and lists of babysitters are customarily available. Dogs and other pets are usually prohibited or discouraged. Garage parking is rarely free and most levy an in-and-out charge when cars are used.

An 8¼% city sales tax is added to room bills, but the most unpleasant surprise at checkout time might be the hefty surcharge added for telephone calls. Not all hotels do this, but it is a good idea to inquire on arrival. Tipping is expected, and is not especially complicated. The bellman expects to be tipped according to the number of bags carried, and to get something extra if they are heavy. A doorman expects something small for merely opening a car door, and more if he devotes some time to hailing a taxi. Add 15% to the bill for room service waiters.

When hotels, restaurants and clubs are described elsewhere, they are shown in individual entries in **bold** type.

Hotels classified by area

Lower Manhattan (*below 14th St.*)
The River Hotel ▥
Vista International ▥ ▦

Gramercy Park/Murray Hill (*E 14th St.–E 42nd St.*)
Bedford ▥
Doral Park Avenue ▥ ❀
Doral Tuscany ▥ ❀
Gramercy Park ▥
Kitano ▥
Morgan's ▥
Sheraton-Russell ▥

Lower West Side (*W 14th St.–W 42nd St.*)
New York Penta ▥

Midtown East (*E 42nd St.–E 59th St.*)
Berkshire Place ▥
Beverley ▥ ❀
Doral Inn ▥ ❀
Grand Hyatt ▥ ▦
Halloran House ▥
Harley ▥
Inter-Continental ▥
Lexington ▥
Lombardy ▥
Middletowne ▥ ❀
Palace ▥ ▦ ▦
Plaza ▥ ▦
Roosevelt ▥
St. Regis-Sheraton ▥ ▦
Sherry-Netherland ▥ ▦
Summit ▥
Swissôtel Drake ▥
United Nations Plaza ▥ ▦

Waldorf-Astoria ▥ ▦

Midtown West (*W 42nd St.– W 59th St.*)
Algonquin ▥
Barbizon Plaza ▥
Best Western Skyline ▥ ❀
Dorset ▥
Essex House ▥ ▦
Holiday Inn-Coliseum ▥ ❀
Howard Johnson's ▥ ❀
Milford Plaza ▥
New York Hilton ▥
Omni Park Central ▥
Park Lane ▥ ▦
Parker Meridien ▥ ▦
Ramada Inn-Midtown ▥ ❀
Ritz-Carlton ▥
St Moritz ▥
Salisbury ▥ ❀
Sheraton Centre ▥
Sheraton City Squire ▥
Warwick ▥
Windsor ▥
Wyndham ▥ ❀

Upper East Side (*E 60th St.– E 95th St.*)
American Stanhope ▥
Carlyle ▥ ▦
Lowell ▥
Mayfair Regent ▥ ▦
Pierre ▥ ▦
Plaza Athénée ▥ ▦
Regency ▥ ▦
Westbury ▥

Upper West Side (*W 60th St.–W 96th St.*)
Mayflower ▥ ❀

Algonquin
59 W 44th St. (near 5th Ave.), NY 10036 ☎ *840–6800. Map* **5** *O4*
☎ 200 ▭ 200 ▤ ▨ ⇌ AE CB
Ⓟ CD VISA

Location: Near Grand Central Terminal. Dorothy Parker, George Kaufman, Robert Benchley and others traded japes and aphorisms around the famous Round Table here. That is history. But this turn-of-the-century hotel is still the clubby choice of many literary and theatre folk. But be sure to check your room before accepting it, because some are dated or even shabby. The lobby, crowded with sofas, wing chairs and ill-matched tables, has the feel of a well-used country inn. Afternoon tea and cocktails can be taken there. The checkout time of 15.00 is unusually generous.
‡ □ ▱

American Stanhope
995 5th Ave. (81st St.), NY 10028 ☎ *288–5800 Cable HOPESTAND. Map* **7** *L4* ▥

☎ 600 ▭ 600 ▤ ▨ ⇌ AE CB
Ⓟ CD VISA

Location: Opposite Metropolitan Museum of Art. With a gracious style that reflects its Upper East Side environs, this medium-size stopping-place boasts commodious lodgings, blessed serenity, a limousine shuttle to midtown and, during warm months, an engaging sidewalk cafe. It's ideally located if you intend to spend time along museum row from the *Frick Collection* to the *Cooper-Hewitt Museum.* Weekend discount packages include breakfast and museum passes.
▭ ‡ □ ▱ ▣

Barbizon Plaza
106 Central Park S (6th Ave.), NY 10019 ☎ *247–7000* ▧ *424442. Cable: BARBPLAZA. Map* **5** *N4* ▥ ☎ 805 ▭ 805 ▤ ▨ ⇌
CB CD VISA

Location: Midtown, near shops and theatres. The lobby manages to be both glittery and dowdy at the same time and the rooms are often gloomy. But the hotel enjoys a fine central location, an unintimidating if rather sedate disco called the **Library**, and the moderate Inn on the Park restaurant. Owned by the Best Western motel chain, it offers family and weekend discounts.

♨ □ ☞ ✇ ☕ ☂ ♈ ◉

Bedford
118 E 40th St. (near 5th Ave.), NY 10016 ☎*697–4800. Map 5O4* ▥▥
☎ *135* ▭ *135* ▤▤ ⇌ AE CB ⊕
CB VISA

Location: Near Grand Central Terminal and UN. Frequent visitors often prefer the relative tranquillity of Murray Hill to the thumping heart of midtown. Prices are usually lower, hotels smaller, package tours fewer, and there are bonuses in facilities and personal attention to compensate for the few extra blocks of distance. The Bedford offers family rates and kitchenettes with every room, and a family can stay for the price of a single in more glamorous locations.

⌂ ♨ □ ☞ ✇ ☂

Berkshire Place
21 E 52nd St. (Madison Ave.), NY 10022 ☎*753–5800. Map 5N4* ▥▥
☎ *420* ▭ *420* ▤▤ ⇌ AE CB
⊕ ◉ VISA

Location: Near Rockefeller Center, St Patrick's Cathedral. Formerly a no-nonsense executive stopover, but now spruced up under new ownership and aggressively promoted with advertising and generous weekend packages. Suburban couples escaping the kids find themselves treated to breakfast in bed, chocolates at bedside and bowls of fresh flowers, all at almost half the price of the same rooms Mon–Thurs. Harmonious tints of green, peach and beige accompany tasteful seating arrangements and decorative accessories. The handsome lobby soothes with print fabrics, potted palms and ivy, amidst which you can take an above-par afternoon tea. Added to these allurements are the best 5th Ave. shops, just outside the door.

♨ ♿ □ ☞ ✇ ☂

Best Western Skyline ❀
725 10th Ave. (near 49th St.), NY 10019 ☎*586–3400. Map 4O2* ▥▮
☎ *230* ▭ *230* ▤▤ ⇌ AE CB
⊕ ◉ VISA

Location: w of Times Sq. Theatre District. On the one hand, this motel allows easy entrance and exit from the city by car; prices are reasonable, especially for family groups, and there is an indoor swimming pool. On the other, it is at some distance from major attractions and in a barren setting of parking lots and marginal commercial enterprises. If it were better situated, its upper-middle level of accommodation would make it difficult to rival.

♨ □ ☞ ✇ ≋ ☂

Beverley ❀
125 E 50th St. (Lexington Ave.), NY 10022 ☎*753–2700. Map 5O4* ▥▮ ☎ *200* ▭ *200* ▤▤ ▣ ⇌ AE
CB ⊕ ◉ VISA

Location: Midtown East, near Grand Central Terminal. Moderate cost and a midtown situation usually suggest shabbiness, but the Beverley is well above that category. The cramped reception area does not calm suspicions and the corridors are gloomy, but many rooms have serving pantries and terraces and all are recently decorated in soothing tones. Room waiters are on call past midnight. There is a 24hr chemist on the premises.

♨ □ ☞ ✇ ☂ ☕ ♈

Carlyle ▥▥
35 E 76th St. (Madison Ave.), NY 10021 ☎*744–1600. Map 7L4* ▥▥
☎ *500* ▭ *500* ▣ ⇌ AE CB ⊕
⊕ ◉ VISA

Location: Upper East Side, one block from the Whitney Museum. Many hotels pretend to offer continental standards of hospitality, but here the grand traditions of Europe really are emulated. Over-sized rooms pamper with bathroom phones and custom toiletries. Most have serving pantries and well-stocked refrigerators. There is 24hr room service, and the cashier exchanges foreign currency until 24.00. Pets are permitted at an extra charge, and dog walkers are on hand. Afternoon tea is an event, as is an hour spent with stylish singer-pianist Bobby Short or the great jazz musician George Shearing in the Cafe Carlyle. Limousines stand ready to shuttle guests to midtown shops and theatres. A few steps away, in Madison Ave., is a large concentration of dealers in rare antiques and works of art, where browsers are generally welcome.

⌂ ♨ □ ☞ ☂ ♈ ⅄ ♫

Doral Inn ♣
*541 Lexington Ave. (49th St.),
NY 10022* ☎ *755–1200*
Ⓣ *236641. Map 5O4* ▮▮▮ ♨ *700*
🛏 *700* ▦ ⧈ ⌓ AE CB ⊕ ⓒ VISA
Open all year.

*Location: Midtown East, near
United Nations and Grand Central
Terminal.* Big brother to the
Doral Park Avenue, it is neither
an inn nor as appealing as its
sibling. Like so many of the city's
commercial hotels, it is clean,
brisk, bustling and largely
unremarkable. The airline crew
and salesmen who frequent it can
squeeze in some racquetball and a
sauna between flights. The suites
on the top two floors have terraces,
kitchens and bars, but at a stiff
increase in price.
‡ □ ◩ ⚲ ≛ ⵀ

Doral Park Avenue ♣
*70 Park Ave. (38th St.), NY
10016* ☎ *687–7050. Cable:
DORALPARK NY. Map 5O4* ▮▮▮
♨ *200* 🛏 *200* ▦ ⧈ AE CB ⊕
ⓒ VISA

*Location: Near Grand Central
Terminal.* Murray Hill doesn't
have the gloss and hum of the
midtown core around Rockefeller
Center, but that is its virtue. This
serene stopping-place, small by
Big Apple standards, makes the
most of its setting. Reasonable
needs are skilfully met, without
fuss or show, although the
restaurant and room service close
down before 22.00. All bedrooms
have refrigerators; some have
serving pantries. There is a
sidewalk cafe in summer, and most
central office buildings and tourist
sights are within walking distance.
⌂ ‡ □ ◩ ≛ ⵀ

Doral Tuscany ♣
*120 E 39th St. (near Park Ave.),
NY 10016* ☎ *686–1600*
Ⓣ *640243. Cable: TUSCOTEL.
Map 5P4* ▮▮▮ ♨ *143* 🛏 *143* ▦
⧈ ⌓ AE CB ⊕ ⓒ VISA

*Location: Near Grand Central
Terminal and United Nations.*
Perhaps the best dollar-for-dollar
value in its class, it charms in many
small details – at the entrance, a
large thermometer-barometer; on
the desk, an arrangement of
flowers; in the bedroom, a serving
pantry with refrigerator; in the
bathroom, a telephone and three-
nozzle massaging showerhead; in
the closet, an electric shoe-
polisher; outside the window,
another thermometer. It is quieter
by many decibels than its larger
cousins deeper in the midtown
district, yet is only a few blocks
farther from the action. The
capable staff treats guests with an
avuncularity that is at once
amusing and reassuring.
Conventioneers and tour groups
are never in evidence. The hotel is
also less likely to be booked up at
short notice, and checkout time is a
civilized 14.00.
‡ □ ◩

Dorset
*30 W 54th St. (near 6th Ave.), NY
10019* ☎ *247–7300. Cable:
DORSETOTEL. Map 4N3* ▮▮▮ ♨
400 🛏 *400* ▦ ⧈ *nearby* ⌓ AE
CB ⊕

*Location: Near Rockefeller Center,
Museum of Modern Art, and 5th
Av. shops.* The fact that over half
its rooms are under permanent
lease is testimony to the
desirability of this underpublicized
hostelry. The panelled lobby is a
welcoming retreat from the
midtown bustle, the front desk
staff uncommonly amiable.
Personalities from the nearby ABC
television network headquarters
frequent the streetside bar-cafe at
lunchtime. Some rooms have
pantries and balconies. There is no
charge for children under 14
sharing their parents' rooms. A
complimentary *New York Times*
arrives with breakfast.
⌂ ‡ □ ◩ ⵀ

Essex House ▥
*160 Central Park S (near 6th
Ave.), NY 10019* ☎ *247–0300*
Ⓣ *125205. Map 5N4* ▮▮▮ ♨ *810*
🛏 *810* ▦ ⧈ AE CB ⊕ ⓒ VISA

*Location: On Central Park, near
Lincoln Center and shopping areas.*
Although it aspires to rank with
the cream of Manhattan hotels, the
Essex House falls short.
Participants in large conferences
and formal dinners mill about the
panelled and chandeliered lobby at
all hours. And the King's Wharf
restaurant is out of place in this
precinct. That said, however, the
hotel nevertheless qualifies as a
strong runner-up to the best. Its
location is excellent, the staff speak
18 languages, the bedrooms are
spacious. There are scales in the
bathrooms for weight-watchers;
and when the maid turns down the
bed at night she leaves a chocolate
mint. Bills can be paid in foreign
currency.
‡ □ ◩ ≛

Gramercy Park
2 Lexington Ave. (21st St.), NY 10010 ☎*475–4320. Map 5Q4* ◫▥
🕿 500 ⊟ 500 ⊞ ⇌ AE CB ◉
◉◉ VISA

Location: Near Gramercy Park, away from main traffic arteries.
The relatively quiet situation is the primary attraction for its predominantly European clientele, which has included second-string rock groups and film actors. There are other reasons too; among them access to the attractive private park a half-block away, the clusters of historic houses within range of a morning stroll, and non-confiscatory tariffs. Apart from the unfortunate colour schemes in many of the rooms, there is an amiable warmth that finds its glamour in its guests rather than in its fixtures.

▱ ‡ ▢ ◪ ☧

Grand Hyatt ▥
42nd St. and Park Ave., NY 10017 ☎*883–1234. Map 5O4* ◫
🕿 1,407 ⊟ 1,407 ⊞ ⇌ AE CB ◉
◉◉ VISA

Location: Next to Grand Central Terminal. A leader in the city's hotel boom, this 1980 addition to the Hyatt holdings also takes a giant share of the credit for the continuing rehabilitation of E 42nd St. The effect of the place is sleek, showy, and quintessentially New York, although by the standards of others in the chain, this Hyatt is downright sedate. Nevertheless, there is drama in abundance in its exuberant architecture. The effect of the four-storey atrium is horizontal rather than vertical, one side knuckling out over the street. There is a tiered waterfall beneath a vast spidery wire sculpture, rows of greenery, great columns cloaked in brass and steel. All rooms have colour and cable TV, there is a health club with sauna, squash and tennis, and Trumpet's is one of the city's better hotel restaurants.

‡ ও ▢ ◪ ∿ ☧ ▾

Halloran House
525 Lexington Ave. (near 48th St.) NY 10017 ☎*755–4000*
📞*668844. Map 5O4* ◫ 🕿 650
⊟ 650 ⊞ ⇌ AE CB ◉ ◉◉ VISA

Location: Midtown East, near Grand Central Terminal and United Nations. Livelier than most of the rather anonymous commercial hotels that stretch Lexington Ave., Halloran House offers a health club, swimming pool, two restaurants and a bar named after the owner – Biff's Place – that swings to jazz or pop from 17.00 until whenever. The bedrooms satisfy basic needs, with the welcome addition of small personal safes in the closets.

‡ ও ▢ ◪ ∿ ⇌ ☧ ▾

Harley
212 E 42nd St. (3rd Ave.) NY 10017 ☎*888–1624. Map 5O5* ◫
🕿 793 ⊟ 793 ⊞ ⌂ ⇌ AE CB
◉ ◉◉ VISA

Location: Near Grand Central Terminal and United Nations. One of the chain assembled or built by Harry Helmsley, the Harley is geared to the expense account crowd, and on the assumption that travelling executives have little time for ceremony, it is forthright rather than frisky, though all comforts are provided. Multi-lingual stenographers are available. Breakfast trays arrive with the *Wall Street Journal.* Rooms are crisply conservative. When business people go home for the weekend, sharply discounted rates draw the suburbanites for museum-hopping and Broadway shows.

‡ ও ▢ ◪ ∿ ⇌ ☧

Holiday Inn-Coliseum ✿
440 W 57th St. (9th Ave.), NY 10019 ☎*581–8100. Map 4N3* ◫
🕿 600 ⊟ 600 ⊞ ⌂ ⇌ AE CB
◉ ◉◉ VISA

Location: Midtown West, near Columbus Circle. A conventional motel representative of the mother chain, it dosen't mean to surprise, and succeeds. The immediate neighbourhood is grim but unthreatening, with the Lincoln Center, major theatres and Central Park all within walking distance. Businessmen and families on tight budgets find it satisfactory, and children enjoy the rooftop swimming pool.

‡ ▢ ◪ ⇌ ☧ ▾

Inter-Continental
111 E 48th St. (Lexington Ave.), NY 10017 ☎*755–5900*
📞*7105816535. Cable: BARCLOTEL. Map 5O4* ◫ 🕿
777 ⊟ 777 ⊞ ⌂ ⇌ AE CB ◉
◉◉ VISA

Location: Near Grand Central Terminal and United Nations. Several changes in management, the last three treading on each other's heels, have not altered the

courtly European flavour. An aviary with live songbirds is still the lobby trademark. The spacious public areas and halls suggest bedrooms of larger dimensions. Thick walls and double windows ensure quiet, while TV, AM-FM radio, free closed-circuit movies, and 24hr room service remove the need to brave the streets for food and diversion. The Theater District is only a few blocks w and several celebrated restaurants are even closer. Within the building is the oldest chemist in New York, **Caswell Massey**, featuring soaps and hairbrushes that have their origins in Colonial times.
🖂 ‡ & ☐ ☞ 🐾 ⋐

Howard Johnson's ✿
851 8th Ave. (near 51st St.), NY 10019 ☎*581—4100* ⓣ*147183. Map 4N3* ▥ ☏ *300* ☐ *300* ▦ 🖂 ⥱ AE CB ⓘ ⓒ VISA
Location: w of the midtown Theater District. One of a trio of relatively new midtown motels, it shares the virtues and the liabilities of the others – ready access by car, walking distance from the major theatres and moderate tariffs; but charmless rooms and a bleak neighbourhood.
‡ ☐ ☞ 🐾

Kitano
66 Park Ave. (38th St.), NY 10016 ☎*685—0022* ⓣ*424429. Cable: AMEKITANO. Map 5O4* ▥ ☏ *91* ☐ *91* ▦ 🖂 ⥱ AE CB ⓘ ⓒ VISA
Location: Near Grand Central Terminal. The Japanese-owned and operated Kitano offers an intriguing blend of Colonial American order and *shibui* serenity. About half the bedrooms are done up in chintz, the others with oriental understatement. There are several authentic *tatami* suites featuring hot tubs and bedrolls. Avoid the cheapest rooms, for they are excessively small. More efficient than sybaritic, the hotel provides no room service and the noon checkout is early.
🖂 ‡ ☐ ☞

Lexington
511 Lexington Ave. (E 48th St.), NY 10017 ☎*755—6963. Map 5O4* ▥ ☏ *800* ☐ *800* ▦ 🖂 ⥱ AE ⓘ ⓒ VISA
Location: Near Grand Central Terminal and United Nations. The immediate neighbourhood is noisy

and commercial and the hotel itself is an ageing edifice of no distinction. But the management keeps the average-sized bedrooms perked up, endlessly painting, papering and upgrading. Services are comparable to those of more expensive competitors, except for the languid check-in. Chateau Madrid is the long-running restaurant-nightclub with a pronounced Latin flavour on the ground floor, its performances tangy enough for adults, tame enough for kids.
‡ ☐ ☞ 🐾 🚢 ⋐

Lombardy
111 E 56th St. (near Park Ave.), NY 10022 ☎*753—8600. Map 5N4* ▥ ☏ *160* ☐ *160* ▦ ⥱
Location: near smart shops and Rockefeller Center. This is a 'co-op' hotel, meaning that the individual rooms and suites are privately managed. Its virtue is that the uniformity of most hotel lodgings is evident only in the floor plans. Rooms are decorated according to the tastes of their owners. Given the Park Ave. location, the standards and resources of those owners are high, and this is reflected in the furnishings, fabrics and accessories. Serving pantries with refrigerators are the rule, and in keeping with the European ambience a continental breakfast is included in the remarkably reasonable rate. The clubbily masculine bar on ground level is so traditional it requires coats and ties. As hotel restaurants go, the Lombardy Laurent is high calibre.
🖂 ‡ ☐ ☞ 🐾 ⅄

The Lowell
28 E 63rd St. (near Madison Ave.), NY 10021 ☎*838—1400* ⓣ*275750. Map 7M4* ▥ ☏ *60* ☐ *60* ▦ 🖂 ⥱ AE CB ⓒ VISA
Location: Residential street near Central Park Zoo. The first thing you notice about The Lowell is its rose-and-cream tiled Art Deco exterior, a mild visual shock on this sedate block. Erected as an exclusive residential hotel in the late 1920s, it had gone through several ownerships and marked decline until its recent facelift. There is much to distinguish the hotel from its midtown rivals. In an energy-conscious city of sealed glass and steam heat, all of the casement windows open and 34 of the units have woodburning fireplaces. There are real books on

the shelves, and live plants, cut flowers, twice-daily maid service and two bathrobes in every bathroom. None of the rooms is exactly alike, although a crisp European contemporary look sets the tone. A charming Tea Room is hidden away on the second floor, serving breakfast, lunch and afternoon tea. The Post House restaurant is separately operated.

🖂 ‡ ☐ ◿ ⚲

Mayfair Regent 🏨
610 Park Ave. (65th St.), NY 10021 ☎*288–0800* 🖬*236257. Map 5M4* ⫼⫼⫼ ☎~ *500* 🛏 *500* ▦ 🖭 ⥱ ⟨AE⟩ ⟨CB⟩ ⟨◉⟩ ⟨◐⟩ ⟨VISA⟩

Location: Upper East Side, in art and antiques country. The Mayfair Regent earns a respect approaching reverence. In part, that assessment reflects the personal attention that is only possible when the number of guests is carefully limited. No one seems to know exactly how many rooms there are, for most are privately owned, but the total available to transients is probably no more than 125 at any one time. Most of them are suites, sumptuously appointed. The presence on the premises of the redoubtable **Le Cirque** restaurant lends stature, although it is independently operated. Ceilings soar, carpets cover ankles, wood and metal surfaces glow. There are even working fire-places in some suites. Smooth functioning is assured by a succession of managers from the likes of London's Connaught and Venice's Gritti Palace. High tea in the lounge offers cucumber sandwich slivers and brews of loose leaves kept warm with a cosy.

🖂 ‡ ☐ ◿

Mayflower
Central Park W (61st St.), NY 10023 ☎*265–0060. Map 4N3* ⫼⫼⫼ ☎~ *400* 🛏 *400* ▦ 🖭 ⥱ ⟨AE⟩ ⟨CB⟩ ⟨◉⟩ ⟨◐⟩ ⟨VISA⟩

Location: Near Lincoln Center and New York Coliseum. The otherwise resurgent Upper West Side is woefully short of decent hotels. By default, top slot goes to the Mayflower. Although it is not in the same league as the East Side leaders, recent refurbishment of already spacious rooms makes it a reliable choice. The parkside Conservatory restaurant has live entertainment and an above-par Sunday brunch. Suites with

pantries cost no more than a standard double at many expensive crosstown competitors.

🖂 ‡ ☐ ◿ ♫

Middletowne ♣
148 E 48th St. (near Lexington Ave.), NY 10017 ☎*755–3000. Map 5O4* ⫼⫼ ☎~ *192* 🛏 *192* ▦ 🖭 ⥱ ⟨AE⟩ ⟨CB⟩ ⟨◉⟩ ⟨◐⟩ ⟨VISA⟩

Location: Midtown East, near Grand Central Terminal. Visitors settling in for a week or more sometimes wish it were possible to trim the overheads implicit in full hotel services in exchange for more home-like quarters. They can do precisely that here, trading waiters and elaborate lobbies for comfortable rooms that are all equipped with full kitchens, including stoves, refrigerators and, if desired, silverware and crockery. Some suites have fire-places and/ or terraces. Rates might be negotiable for longer stays. There is neither bar nor restaurant, but both are abundant in this neighbourhood.

🖂 ‡ ☐ ◿ ⚟

Milford Plaza
270 W 45th St. (8th Ave.), NY 10036 ☎*869–3600* 🖬*147193. Cable: MILPAZNY. Map 4O3* ⫼⫼ ☎~ *1,310* 🛏 *1,310* ▦ 🚗 ⥱ ⟨AE⟩ ⟨CB⟩ ⟨◉⟩ ⟨◐⟩ ⟨VISA⟩

Location: Heart of the Theater District. This used to be the Royal Manhattan, a commercial hotel of little distinction. It is no more sumptuous under its new name and management, nor is the neighbourhood less seedy, the rooms less cramped. They are cheerier, however, newly furnished and equipped with television and radios. Security arrangements are reassuring. For those who feel that a New York holiday means seeing a different show each night, there is no more convenient situation, and the reasonable rates leave enough dollars for an extra matinee.

‡ ☐ ◿ ⚐

Morgan's
237 Madison Ave. (near 37th St.), NY 10016 ☎*686–0300* 🖬*288908. Map 5P4* ⫼⫼ ☎~ *154* 🛏 *154* ▦ 🚗 ⥱ ⟨AE⟩ ⟨CB⟩ ⟨◉⟩ ⟨◐⟩ ⟨VISA⟩

Location: Busy avenue near Morgan Library and the Empire State Building. Call it a 'boutique hotel'. The owners do, and they know whereof they speak. Two of the principals were responsible for the original **Studio 54** and the brand-new **Palladium** mega-disco (see *Nightlife*). It is zippy, youthful, and trendy enough to draw Mick Jagger, Billy Joel, Andy Warhol and executives of the fashion and design industries. To highlight this in-the-know status, there is no identifying sign outside and never will be. Guests are whisked into rooms of almost Oriental simplicity decked in chic black, white and grey tones. Built-in storage walls are of grey-stained bird's-eye maple, the low beds covered with pinstriped duvets. There are refrigerators, and this may be the only hotel in the country with AM-FM audio cassette decks as well. (The hotel stocks over 100 videotapes.) The fresh-faced staff provide twice-daily housekeeping and 24hr room service. For a special treat, consider the duplex penthouse suite with a dramatic view of the Empire State Building.

🛗 □ 🖼 ☕ Ψ

New York Hilton
1335 6th Ave. (53rd St.), NY 10019 ☎*586–7000* 📞*238492. Cable: NYHILTH. Map* 5N4 🏦 📞 *2,131* 💳 *2,131* 🖥 🚗 🏛 🚳 AE CB 🔾 🆔 VISA

Location: Midtown, at Rockefeller Center. Big, brassy and bustling, this vertical town within the city makes it unnecessary to brave the weather. Everything is here, from shops to secretarial services to a week's worth of bars and restaurants and live entertainment. Of the many types of room, only the claustrophobic singles are to be avoided. Comforting features include close-circuit films and heated bathroom floors. Half-day rates are available for lie-downs and wash-ups between shopping excursions and theatre matinees.

🛗 🛗 □ 🖼 ☕ Ψ 🎵

Omni Park Central
870 7th Ave. (56th St.), NY 10019 ☎*247–8000. Map* 4N3 🏦 📞 *1,295* 💳 *1,295* 🖥 🚳 AE CB 🔾 🆔 VISA

Location: Midtown, near Carnegie Hall, Theater District. Under new management, this former Sheraton hotel has been revamped with an eye-catching post-modern lobby, an ambitious brasserie-style dining room and new furnishings and fresh paint from top to bottom. The preferred rooms and suites are on the 'Omni Classic' upper floors, which enjoy such perquisites as free copies of the *New York Times* delivered to the door and arrays of complementary toiletries in the baths. Carnegie Hall is across the street and the theatre district only a few blocks away.

🛗 🛗 □ 🖼 ☕ Ψ

New York Penta
7th Av. (33rd St.), NY 10001 ☎*736–5000. Map* 4P3 🏦 📞 *1,700* 💳 *1,700* 🖥 🚗 🏛 🚳 AE CB 🔾 🆔 VISA

Location: Across the street from Penn Station. Large, anonymous, unremarkable, this giant looks in all significant ways like an ageing version of dated modernity. Look upon it as an alternative to more luxurious stops, perhaps when they are full or when business or pleasure requires ready access to Penn Station, *Madison Square Garden* or the *Garment Center.* Tariffs are moderate, by local standards, and the rooms comfortable enough.

🛗 □ 🖼 ☕ Ψ

Palace 🏨 🏛
455 Madison Ave. (50th St.), NY 10022 ☎*888–7000. Map* 5N4 🏦 📞 *773* 💳 *773* 🖥 🚗 🏛 🚳 AE CB 🆔 VISA

Location: Midtown, near shopping. Preservation of worthwhile buildings has a chequered history in New York. More often than not, commerce has triumphed over heritage. Not so the Palace. Bent upon erecting a princely flagship for his ever-growing real estate empire, Harry Helmsley was persuaded not only to spare the proud Villard Houses from demolition, but to restore them to their 1886 opulence. His efforts were rewarded by a fat dossier of enthusiastic press notices and bookings that stretch months in advance. The Franco-Italianate interiors were lovingly scrubbed and mended, revealing marble inlays, Tiffany glass, frescoes, rich panelling, gold-leaf ceilings, and intricately carved wood friezes. In the adjoining modern tower, guest rooms are unusually spacious and continue the theme with huge Baroque headboards, soft velvets, and stately Louis XV reproductions. With all this visual pampering, service sometimes falters by comparison, but not for lack of trying. The concierge, for example, can arrange for translators of nearly 40 languages. There aren't five other hotels in town that can match this experience.

♦ & ▢ ⌂ ✎ ▲ ▼

Park Lane 🏨

36 Central Park S (near 5th Ave.), NY 10019 ☎371–4000
📺668613. Map **5N4** ▮▮▮▮ ⌘ 640
🛏 640 ▦ ▭ ⇌ AE CB ⓟ
ⓓ VISA

Location: Across from Central Park, near shops and Lincoln Center. Much is made of the fact that Harry Helmsley, owner of half a dozen New York hotels, chose to live in this one. The in-house management sets high standards, for though this modern high-rise cannot achieve the grace of the older luxury hotels, it certainly tries. Lavish applications of brocade and suede dress the corridors and public rooms. There is a concierge to secure theatre tickets and limousines. Try afternoon tea in the Park Room and you won't be disappointed. The higher the room on the park side of the hotel, the better the views.

♦ & ▢ ⌂ ✎ ◁≪ Ⓡ ▼

Parker Meridien 🏨

118 W 57th St. (6th Ave.), NY 10019 ☎245–5000. Map **4N3** ⌘ 600 🛏 600 ▦ ▭ ⇌ AE CB ⓟ ⓓ VISA

Location: Near Central Park, Rockefeller Center and Carnegie Hall. Air France is the parent company, and the Gallic touch is evident, although not as pervasive as its advertisements insist. Aubusson tapestries adorn the walls, a multilingual concierge attends to arrangements for booking theatre tickets and limousines, and the bars and restaurants smack of the Champs-Élysées. The jogging track, the squash and racquetball courts, and the whirlpool and sauna cater to the fitness mania of the contemporary international business-person; the 100 lavishly appointed 'executive apartments' also offer luxury. Breakfast in bed includes croissants and is usually accompanied by a copy of the *International Herald Tribune*. All rooms have stocked mini-bars and closed-circuit movies. The Parker Meridien offers weekend package plans, and corporate discounts are also available.

♦ & ▢ ⌂ ≈ ▲ ▼

Pierre 🏨

5th Ave. and 61st St., NY 10021 ☎838–8000📺127426. Map **5N4** ▮▮▮▮ ⌘ 700 🛏 700 ▦ ▭ ⇌ AE CB ⓓ ⓟ VISA

Location: Across from Central Park, near museums and shops. Monarchs and presidents select the Pierre. Long limousines line the kerb outside and studiedly inconspicuous men stand about whispering into micro-transmitters. There isn't a safer address in town. Marble baths and floral-painted basins are happy touches, as are magnifying shaving mirrors and electrically operated window drapes. The staff members make notes of preferences in flowers and other idiosyncrasies and try to remember names. Barely half the rooms are available to temporary visitors, but they are given no hint of second-class status. Book as far in advance as possible.

⌂ ♦ & ▢ ⌂ ✎ ◁≪ ▲

Plaza 🏨

5th Ave. and 59th St., NY 10019 ☎759–3000📺236938. Cable: PLAZA NEW YORK. Map **5N4** ▮▮▮▮ ⌘ 900 🛏 900 ▦ ▭ ⇌ AE CB ⓟ ⓓ VISA

Location: Corner of 5th Ave. and Central Park. Seemingly endless renovations are nearly finished in this long-time favourite of celebrities. Brass window and door frames gleam, carpeting is new, statuary and capitals sparkle. Viennese strings accompany tea in the Palm Court, and there is music for dancing in the Edwardian Room. Hallways and rooms are lavishly proportioned. Many rooms overlook Central Park; many have refrigerators, radios, alarm clocks and antique furnishings.

♦ ▢ ⌂ ✎ ◁≪ ▲ ▼ ♫♪

Plaza Athénée 🏨

37 E 64th St. (near Madison Ave.), NY 10021 ☎734–9100
📺697–2900. Map **5M4** ▮▮▮▮ ⌘ 160 🛏 160 ▦ ▭ ▭ ⇌ AE CB ⓟ ⓓ VISA

Location: Upper East Side block, near bistros, shopping and Central Park. Of the several new hotels opened since 1984, only this one can be accorded the grand-luxe stature of such venerable luminaries as the **Carlyle** and the **Pierre**. Literally no expense has been spared to transform what was the lacklustre Hotel Alrae into a paragon of the Continental standard of superb innkeeping. The aged, tiered structure was stripped to the shell and rebuilt, from plumbing and wiring to the lavish use of Brazilian mahogany in the public rooms and padded silk wallcoverings in the spacious suites. The overhaul cost $50 million, and operating expenses are as dazzling a testament to intent – the monthly florist bill is said to total $100,000. Only the sourest curmudgeon can find serious fault. Consider this roster of amenities, by no means complete: cable TV with remote control; newspaper delivered each morning; every message delivered by phone, at the desk *and* to the guest's room; room safes; bathroom scales; bathrobes; blissful tranquillity; superb dining in a glamorous setting. For those who can afford to stay in the same hotel as Joan Collins, Michael Caine and Clint Eastwood, there are few better choices this side of the Atlantic.

⌂ ‡ □ ▱ ⍦

Ramada Inn-Midtown 🏨
790 8th Ave. (near 48th St.), NY 10019 ☎*581–7000* ⓋO*147182. Map 4O3* ▥ ☙ *365* ▱ *365* ▤
▱ ⍰ AE ⍰ ☁ ⍰ VISA

Location: Midtown, Theater District. Parents appreciate the relatively modest family rates and their children like the swimming pool, a rare facility in the city. Inside, fair value is given, with crisp decor and exemplary maintenance. Outside, deeply tawdry 8th Ave. gives pause even to hardened New Yorkers.

‡ □ ▱ ⍩ ♟

Regency 🏨
Park Ave. and 61st St., NY 10021 ☎*759–4100* ⓋO*147180. Map 5N4*
▥ ☙ *500* ▱ *500* ▤ ▱ AE
☁ ⍰ ⍰ VISA

Location: Upper East Side, amidst exclusive shops and galleries. Moneyed Europeans and their counterparts in the American elite choose the Regency at least partly for its low profile. The key-note of the style is Louis XVI, naturally updated by such niceties as bathroom telephones and scales. The rooms luxuriate in extravagant applications of marble and brocade, and an alert staff if ready to satisfy the merest whim. Book far in advance.

⌂ ‡ ♿ □ ▱ ⍩ ♟ ♪

Ritz-Carlton
112 Central Park S (near 6th Ave.), NY 10019 ☎*757–1900. Map 5N4* ☙ *300* ▱ *300* ▤
▱ ⍰ AE ☁ ⍰ ⍰ VISA

Location: On Central Park, near Lincoln Center. After extensive renovation and a grander name to mark the transformation, the former Navarro has taken a long step up into the rarefield rank of top Manhattan hostelries. It has been compared to London's Connaught, and although that is a bit of a stretch, certainly a visiting Briton will feel at home. Hunting prints, chintz, leather wing chairs, four-poster beds, and antique pine and carved mahogany give it the feeling of an up-market English country inn. And the chef in the ground-floor Jockey Club restaurant once worked in the kitchens at Blenheim Palace. Service is both solicitous and proper throughout the hotel and all expected conveniences are provided. Ask for a high room with a view of Central Park, just across the street.

⌂ ‡ □ ▱ ⍨ ⍦

The River Hotel
180 Christopher St., NY 10014 ☎*206–1020. Map 2R3* ▥ ☙ *48*
▤ *48* ▤ ▱ ⍪ ▱ ⍰ ⍰ VISA

Location: In w Greenwich Village overlooking the Hudson River. The beginnings of a desirable trend are heralded here. In living memory in Manhattan, there has been not a single facsimile of the Florentine *pensione* nor the London bed-and-breakfast. Now there is, but with a decidedly New York kick. In what might be the swiftest check-in around, guests are greeted by a deskman in a tuxedo and spirited off to rooms with platform beds, large original canvases of the New Expressionist mode, and walls and fabric in this year's colours. The accommodation – even in the suites – is admittedly compact, but the clientele inclines toward executives of the creative trades, and they don't spend their free or working hours in hotel rooms. They like being within easy distance of the *Garment Center*, *SoHo* and *TriBeCa*. The stunning penthouse bar and restaurant glitter and buzz with those of like mind. The street-level bar is essentially gay, reflecting the majority preference of this part of Greenwich Village.

‡ □ ▱ ⍦ ⍦

Roosevelt
*45th St. and Madison Ave., NY
10017* ☎*661–9600* 📠*645629.
Cable: THE ROOSEVELT NYC.
Map 5* ☐**4** ▦ ☎⌑ *1,050* ▭ *1,050.*
🔲 ▭ ⟷ *AE* *CB* ⊕ ⊙ *VISA*

*Location: Grand Central Terminal
area:* Given its size, no-nonsense
atmosphere, and midtown
situation, the Roosevelt identity is
that of a businessman's stopover.
Its public rooms and most of the
bedchambers have been primped
up in recent years, and telex and
photocopying machines are made
available to visiting workaholics.
Consistent with their guests'
occupations and early rising
habits, the house restaurants and
services tend to close down by
23.00. Sturdily comfortable it is,
glamorous it is not.
‡ ☐ ▭ ☀ ☇ Y

St Moritz
*50 Central Park S (6th Ave.), NY
10019* ☎*755–5800* 📠*668840.
Map 5* ☐**4** ▦ ☎⌑ *800* ▭ *800* 🔲
▭ ⟷ *AE* *CB* ⊕ ⊙ *VISA*

*Location: Overlooking Central
park, near theatres and shopping.*
Decades of advertisements in *The
New Yorker* magazine proclaimed
in the 'Biggest Little Hotel' in
town, but most citizens know it for
its sidewalk cafe. Rooms are
compact, and those high in front
seem larger by virtue of the
expansive views of the park. The
entry to the street-level
Rumplemayers restaurant is,
improbably, lined with stuffed
animals; ice-cream concoctions are
the big item. Harry's Bar doesn't
match its namesake in Venice, but
is an amiable retreat in which to
pass pre-dinner hours. Book
ahead.
⌂ ‡ ☐ ▭ ⧗ ≪ ☀ Y

St Regis-Sheraton 🛏
2 E 55th St. (5th Ave.), NY 10022
☎*753–4500. Map 5* ☐**4** ▦ ☎⌑
520 ▭ *520* 🔲 ▭ ⟷ *AE* *CB* ⊕
⊙ *VISA*

*Location: Midtown, near
Rockefeller Center.* Unlike most of
its contemporaries of the turn of
the century – decayed, demolished
or converted to other uses – the
1904 St Regis has not only
prevailed but taken on added lustre
at the grand-luxe pinnacle. Even
back then, it cost financier John
Jacob Astor nearly six million
dollars to build and furnish what
was to be the tallest hotel in the
city. In opulent detail, it rivalled

the **Waldorf-Astoria**, its
principal competitor for the
carriage trade. Astor went down
with the *Titanic*, but the St Regis
rolls on. She carries her age well,
from the buffed brass doorman's
booth at the entrance to
commodious bedchambers,
intricately carved mouldings and a
Maxfield Parrish mural in the
King Cole Room. The
aristocracy still stays here,
including now the princes of film
and pop music. Book in advance.
⌂ ‡ ☐ ▭ ☀ Y ♨

Salisbury ♣
*123 W 57th St. (near 6th Ave.),
NY 10019* ☎*246–1300*
📠*668366. Map 5* ☐**4** ▦ ☎⌑ *320*
▭ *320* 🔲 ▭ ⟷ *AE* *CB* ⊕ ⊙ *VISA*

*Location: Across from Carnegie
Hall.* A family of four can have a
suite here for the cost of a double
in one of the posh hotels nearby.
More than half the rooms have
kitchenettes, most have at least a
refrigerator, so there can be
economies in eating out. Major
shopping streets, the Lincoln
Center, theatres and Rockefeller
Center are all within blocks. Even
conceding its lack of elegance or of
such facilities as bars, the
Salisbury is good value.
⌂ ‡ ☐ ▭ ⧗ ☀

Sheraton Centre
*8117th Ave. (52nd St.), NY
10019* ☎*581–1000. Map 4* ☐**3** ▦
☎⌑ *1,842* ▭ *1,842* 🔲 ▭ ⟷ *AE*
CB ⊕ ⊙ *VISA*

*Location: Near Rockefeller Center
and Theater District.* When it
opened as the Americana, the jibe
was that it was 'a little far from the
beach', implying its style was more
to Miami than New York. This
was not unfair, but things have
improved somewhat under the
Sheraton aegis. Tranquillity
cannot be claimed an asset, yet the
rooms are comfortable, if
uninspired, the in-room movies
are diverting, and every midtown
tourist attraction is within walking
distance.

Major upgrading was reserved
for the luxury section known as the
Sheraton Towers, which has a
separate reception area on the 46th
floor with its own express elevator
and lobby bar-restaurant. The
rooms are not usually larger than
those below, but come with extra
touches – electric blankets and
shoe-polishers, nightly turndown
service, bathrobes and

complimentary continental breakfasts. Rates are about 20% higher.

Sheraton City Squire
790 7th Ave. (near 51st St.), NY 10019 ☎581–3300 ⊕421130. *Map 4N3* 📶 720 🛏 720 ▦
Location: N edge of Times Sq. Theater District. Of all Manhattan's motels, this achieves the happiest compromise between cost and convenience. Parking is available, lodgings are routinely comfortable, there is a swimming pool and its situation is as touristically central for tourists as it could possibly be.

Sheraton-Russell
45 Park Ave. (37th St.), NY 10016 ☎685–7676 ⊕421308. *Map 5P4* 📶 175 🛏 175 ▦
Location: Murray Hill, s of Grand Central Terminal. The oak-lined lobby and its library set the cultivated tone. Fire-places in some rooms and the prevailing calm of corridors and public spaces buttress that impression. Similar rooms and accoutrements a few blocks to the N cost 20% more, simply because they are somewhat closer to the freneticism of midtown.

Sherry-Netherland
751 5th Ave. (59th St.), NY 10022 ☎355–2800. *Map 5N4* 📶 372 🛏 372 ▦
Location: SE corner of Central Park. Less than a third of the Sherry-Netherland's space is available to short-term visitors, the rest being on permanent lease, and the management understandably feels no compulsion to sell itself to travellers. The fact that they accept no credit cards is emblematic. Residents of the upper-floor suites expect tranquillity and unobtrusive attendance to their needs. The rooms that are available lean to handsome evocations of 19thC European styles, but are equipped with refrigerators and the usual gadgets. The location couldn't be better – at the foot of 'Museum Mile' and at the top of the 5th Ave. shopping district, with the park directly across the street.

Summit
569 Lexington Ave. (51st St.), NY 10022 ☎752–7000 ⊕147181. *Map 5N4* 📶 770 🛏 770 ▦
Location: Near midtown shopping and United Nations. All the comforts are to be found in this large hotel of the international breed – once inside, you might be in any of its counterparts in Lisbon, London or Rio, right down to the concierge. There are few surprises, good or bad. Refrigerators, bathroom telephones, in-room films and radios are standard. A new health club has been added. For additional indulgences, ask for a room on the ESP (Extra Special Patron) plan – expect a surcharge.

Swisôtel Drake
440 Park Ave. (56th St.), NY 10022 ☎421–0900. *Map 5N4* 📶 650 🛏 650 ▦
Location: Midtown East. During extensive recent renovation, the lobby was expanded to ease former crowding around the reception area and the lifts. Upstairs, the rooms off the twisting halls reveal luxury touches – hideaway refrigerators, AM-FM radios, digital clocks, same-day laundry service, first-run films, four-poster beds (in some rooms), and serving pantries (in the suites). The prime East Side venue is the best asset.

United Nations Plaza
1 United Nations Plaza (44th St.), NY 10017 ☎355–3400 ⊕128603. *Cable: UNPLAZATEL. Map 5O5* 📶 289 🛏 289 ▦
Location: Near United Nations Headquarters. The hotel's 'International Style' of architecture is appropriate to its ownership by the eponymous world organization. The ground floor Grill dazzles with alcoved, faceted mirrors. Guest rooms begin on the 27th floor. The views are arresting, and they can also be enjoyed from the huge indoor swimming pool. On the 39th floor is a tennis court, exericise room and sauna. Felicitous touches include made-to-order breakfast doughnuts, baskets of fruit on arrival, jogging maps, and limousine service to Wall St.

Vista International 🏨
3 World Trade Center, NY 10048
☎938–9100 📞661130
VISTANY. Map *2U3* ▮▮▮ 🛏 825
▭▭825▤▤ ▭ ⫴⫴ 𝐀𝐄 CB ⊙ ⊙ VISA
Location: At base of World Trade Center. Apart from filling a glaring need (since 1836 no one had built a major hotel in lower Manhattan), the Vista has enhanced a neighbourhood. Its dining-rooms are several cuts above those in most of its competitors, and add such weekend features as a sumptuous seafood buffet and a 'Country and Western Fair' with barbecued ribs, *chorizo* and live music. Rooms are conventionally comfortable, with such amenities as alarm clocks, AM-FM radios and closed-circuit movies. 'Vista Club' rooms on the 20th and 21st floors enjoy complimentary breakfasts with morning newspapers, a private lounge with free drinks and hors d'oeuvres, and a special concierge. All guests have access to the jogging track, racquetball courts, sauna and swimming pool on the top floor. Several discount weekend packages heap the extras still further and include: free bicycles and ferry tickets, tours of SoHo and the 'Heritage' trail, theatre tickets and limousine service to midtown.
🏠 ‡ ♿ ▢ 🖼 ⫴⫴ ⇄ 🛎 ♨ ▾ 𝄞

Waldorf-Astoria 🏨
301 Park Ave. (49th St.), NY 10022 ☎355–3000 📞666747.
Map *5O4* ▮▮▮ 🛏 1,400 ▭ 1,400
▤▤ ▭ ⫴⫴ 𝐀𝐄 CB ⊙ ⊙ VISA
Location: Midtown East, near Grand Central Terminal. The original Waldorf, a name long synonymous with luxury, gave way to the Empire State Building. This replacement threw open its doors in 1931, but it is really too large to measure up on all counts to the reputation of the original. Nevertheless, all the amenities you might expect are in place, and the rooms and suites of the 'Towers' section are superior or equal to comparable accommodations elsewhere. The lower floors are crowded with a remarkable variety of shops, restaurants and bars, among them the famous Peacock Alley, a kind of indoor sidewalk-cafe. There are several top restaurants within walking distance of the hotel, although every meal for a week could be taken within the building without repetition.
‡ ♿ ▢ 🖼 ⫴⫴ 🛎 ▾

Warwick
65 W 54th St. (6th Ave.), NY 10019 ☎247–2700 📞147179.
Map *5N4* ▮▮▮ 🛏 500 ▭ 500 ▤▤
▭ ⫴⫴ 𝐀𝐄 CB ⊙ ⊙ VISA
Location: Midtown, near TV network headquarters and Museum of Modern Art. Overshadowed by the mammoth **New York Hilton** across the street, this medium-sized hotel attracts a clientele of communications executives and TV luminaries. It surpasses its assertive neighbour in dignity and reassuringly traditional refinements. Recent refurbishment didn't stop with the lobby; spacious bedrooms were primped and refitted, too. Some have serving pantries or refrigerators. An exercise room is available, as are closed-circuit films.
‡ ▢ 🖼 ⫴⫴ 🛎 ▾

Westbury 🏨
15 E 69th St. (Madison Ave.), NY 10021 ☎535–2000 📞125388.
Map *7M4* ▮▮▮ 🛏 325 ▭ 325 ▤▤
▭ ⫴⫴ 𝐀𝐄 CB ⊙ ⊙ VISA
Location: Upper East Side, amidst smart boutiques and art galleries. The Trust House Forte chain does not always impress in Europe, but its incursions here are of the highest order – particularly evidenced by the Westbury. Converted from a 1920s apartment house, this fashionable and luxurious retreat endeavours to retain a residential quality – that is, if one is accustomed to crystal chandeliers, sprays of dewy-fresh flowers and 17thC tapestries in the vestibule. Most bedrooms do not stint in space or detail, although some baths are rather on the dainty side. The streetside Polo Lounge has considerable *éclat*.
🏠 ‡ ♿ ▢ 🖼 ⫴⫴ 🛎

Wyndham ✿
42 W 58th St. (near 5th Ave.), NY 10019 ☎753–3500. Map *5N4* ▮▮▮
🛏 202 ▭ 202 ▤▤ ▭ ⫴⫴ 𝐀𝐄 CB
⊙ ⊙ VISA
Location: near corner of Central Park and 5th Ave. The owner-managers live on the premises and cater to theatre folk settling in for long runs on Broadway. No two rooms are alike, and suites on the higher floors feature some interesting antique furnishings. There is a reasonable bar and the restaurant is good but you will have to make do without room service.
🏠 ‡ ▢ 🖼 ▾

Where to eat

In New York, eating is a basic need elevated to an event, a debating issue, an investment opportunity, conversation topic, even reason for existence. There are 28,000 eating places in the five boroughs, over half of them in Manhattan alone.

Ask Americans who have spent time away from home what they most missed and it will likely be that mythic two-inch-thick slab of steak seared a charred mahogany ouside, rosy-pink within, captured juices flowing at the stroke of the knife. Seafood is nearly as popular, and the ultimate fantasy dish might well be lobster and beef, unfortunately described on the menus of indifferent eateries as 'surf and turf'. If anything can be accurately labelled as American food, this is it: beef and seafood, simply prepared, in hefty portions. These twin yearnings are easily satisfied in New York, at tariffs ranging from the almost reasonable to the heartstopping.

But this type of cooking is essentially straightforward, and novelty and wonderment must be sought elsewhere. In this city of immigrants, that has never been a problem. Exponents of every major cuisine fostered on the inhabited continents compete for attention. The classic modes are purveyed in abundance: French, inevitably, with admirable representations of the *nouvelle* and *haute* cuisines, but also Russian, Czech, Polish, Swiss, German and Hungarian; Chinese, of course, in most of its variations, but also Korean, Indian, Japanese, Thai, Filipino, Indonesian and Pakistani: Italian, in all its manifestations, but also Greek, Portuguese, Spanish and Armenian; Mexican, but also Brazilian, Cuban and West Indian. In all, more than 30 national gastronomies are represented, supplemented by such hybrids and subspecies as Kosher Chinese, Soul, Puerto Rican, Polynesian, Jewish and Cuban Cantonese. And there is the catch-all 'continental' category, harbouring all manner of predilections, but usually with a Gallic rallying point.

Until recently, distinctive regional American styles such as Creole-Cajun and Tex-Mex were under-represented and largely ignored here. That has changed, with a vengeance. Louisiana blackened redfish and ribs barbecued over embers of mesquite wood are found in every neighbourhood that aspires to chic. French *nouvelle* techniques are being applied to purely domestic products in combinations that are by turns revelatory and bizarre. The result is called 'New American' or 'California Cuisine'. And wherever Californians go, expect such perversely inventive concoctions as sweetbreads with strawberries, and deep-filled designer pizzas topped with asparagus, salmon and avocado.

Happily for the gourmand, ethnic groups cling more tenaciously to their food preferences than to their creeds and ikons, though they have had to adapt available ingredients to the recipes of their former homelands. Availability and quality of produce, along with dietetic need, have always influenced culinary invention, and it is best to approach the restaurants of New York with an understanding of this gustatorial heterogeneity. Chunks of Maine lobster and Long Island littleneck clams may be substituted for the cuttlefish and sheep innards in the *paella* of Valencia, but it will be no less tasty for that. American caviar does not yet match the lofty Caspian standard, but it is half the price, and vastly superior to the inky lumpfish roe masquerading in the supermarkets. A few transplanted chef-

127

proprietors still air-freight Dover sole and Brittany turbot, out of chauvinistic myopia or simple snobbery, but their bay scallops and bass were harvested within 100 miles. And while Americans have little interest in larks and pigeons, unlike the French, the local duckling and quail are unsurpassed.

These efforts to duplicate the fare once set before them by parents and mentors inevitably attract audiences from the larger community. The evolution is unending, and it has brought New York the widest selection of good to superior restaurants in its history. Although restaurants of French, Italian and Chinese cuisine dominate every listing of the city's top-drawer establishments, no matter how immutably classic they pretend to be, they too continue to change and diversify. Sauces are lighter, vegetables are lifted from the pot while their flavour remains, ingredients retain their separate identities. Even the once stodgy Cantonese, Neapolitan, and Provençal kitchens have aired out mouldering recipe books and applied new techniques.

None of this is to assert that every meal is sublime. As everywhere, mediocrity and ineptitude prevail. Bringing together the elements that comprise an agreeable dining experience proves elusive. Several of the prettiest restaurants feature grumpy personnel and truly appalling food. On the other hand, above-average viands are often set before customers in garish or dreary quarters so cramped it is difficult to raise a fork.

The selection that follows is but a wisp of a hint of available choices. As far as possible, it reflects a consensus of the best restaurants in the city – numerous others of all prices and styles can be found throughout New York, and for a guide to the most likely locations see *Area planners* in *Planning*. Although the price range is necessarily skewed toward the high end, there are many suggestions of places where wholesome and/or exotic meals may be sampled at what are, for New York, budget levels. A number of newer restaurants are included that appear to have sufficient strength to beat the odds. The usual caveats still apply: even the hardiest performers stumble, through changes in management, departures of key personnel, last-minute substitutions and shortages, or simple off days. Loyalists will continue to exchange blows over the relative virtues of **Christ Cella** and **The Palm**, **Lutèce** and **Le Grenouille**, all recommended here. No amount of arbitration will resolve the disputes, and anyway they're fun.

What to expect

In the luxury category – achieved or pretended – four discernible strata of staff are nearly always present. The *maître* (or *maîtress*) *d'hôtel* greets customers in calibrated degrees of warmth or *hauteur* at the entrance to the dining area. He (or she) checks reservations, assigns seating, and often escorts guests to their tables. The captain then takes over. Assigned responsibility for a specific section of the room, he brings menus, advises on unlisted specials, points out specialities of the house. He might never return, concentrating on directing his minions. Or he might take orders for cocktails and meals, supervise or perform tableside preparations, even pour water and fill wine glasses. Waiters are the work-horses, identified by less formal attire. Depending upon the organizational structure, they may absorb some or all of the captain's duties, as well as bringing food, drinks, and wine. The busboy, younger and in still another costume, often an apprentice, clears dishes, replenishes bread baskets and empties ashtrays.

One other post is rapidly disappearing – that of the *sommelier* or wine steward. Where he exists, his sole function is to aid in selection of bottles, to open them and to pour. Those who find the tasting ritual silly or intimidating might think of it as a harmless ceremony, no more meaningful than a man opening a door for a woman. Others will appreciate the *sommelier*'s knowledge of his cellar and willingness to discuss alternatives.

New York waiters – and New Yorkers in general – have an undeserved reputation for churlishness. Service can be lackadaisical, and individuals are sometimes sullen or arrogant, but in roughly the same proportion as in any large city. More frequently, complaints are of benign ineptitude, for there is a shortage of formally trained employees. The slack is taken up by recent arrivals to the city, by students and the legions of young actors, dancers and artists drawn to the area every year. As often as not, their spriteliness compensates for their lack of experience, especially in those trendy bistros in which food is less than the main event.

Foreign visitors find agreeable surprises as well as lapses. Year-round availability of usually seasonal commodities often delights, as with oysters in non-'R' months and fresh fruit in Feb. This convenience is expensive, however, and winter tomatoes can be as hard as croquet balls and April apples often taste like potatoes. The prodigious portions of food can dismay – for instance, prime rib hanging over the rim of the plate, leaving little room for the heap of cottage fries. Travellers accustomed to spicy-hot seasonings may be disappointed by the mildness of Indian and Mexican dishes, but insistence on authentically fiery food usually produces results.

Cocktails, wines and other drinks

Although many Europeans regard it as a barbarism, the custom of a pre-dinner cocktail or two persists. If trying one for the first time, be forewarned that they are large and potent. The best-known is the Martini, which is two to three ounces of gin or vodka with a splash of dry vermouth, usually taken over ice. Garnished with pickled onions rather than the conventional green olive or strip of lemon peel, it becomes a Gibson. Some people still order a Manhattan, a sweetish mix of two ounces of rye whiskey with red vermouth swirled with bitters and topped with a cherry. Combinations and variations are endless. Even at a conservative count, there are no fewer than 1,000 recognized cocktails and related concoctions. Some are favoured for particular meals or foods – the Bloody Mary for brunch and the Margarita before Mexican or Latin meals. But in recent years, a glass of white wine, perhaps with a dash of cassis (kir), or soda water (spritzer), or mineral water with lime is increasingly preferred to the harder spirits, and such dark liquors as bourbon and scotch have suffered declines in sales. The practices of smoking cigarettes and drinking cocktails throughout a meal are still seen, but are regarded as gauche, at least in more sophisticated places. While still wines are appropriate for most cuisines, beer is thought satisfactory for Middle-European, Chinese, Mexican and Indian meals.

New Yorkers were long reluctant to embrace the wines of California. This attitude was part pretension and part pragmatism. Sea ports tend to face across the water rather than inland, and European bottlings were substantially cheaper than the Cabernets and Zinfandels of the West. Currency fluctuations changed that, and blind tastings in Paris and elsewhere proved that the vintages of the Gironde and Napa valleys bore separate but equal virtues. The French and Italians still dominate the city's wine cards, but the California challenge mounts as more labels of the select wineries are introduced. Labels to look for are Robert Mondavi, Sterling, Heitz Cellars, David Bruce, Stag's Leap, Charles Krug, Beaulieu, Burgess, Caymus and Mayacammas, among many, many others. Popular-priced wines are blends of several varieties of grapes and typically carry names suggestive of type – 'Chablis', 'Burgundy', 'Chianti' – or such fanciful appellations as 'Emerald Dry' or 'Rhine Garten'. The better pressings are comprised primarily (at least 51% or more) of a single varietal grape and bear that name, without adornment. Some are familiar to European wine buffs, others are native strains or hybrids. Among the prominent reds are Cabernet Sauvignon, Petite Sirah, Pinot Noir and Zinfandel; favoured whites are Chardonnay, Chenin Blanc, Johannisberg Riesling and Sauvignon Blanc. While weather is a factor in California wines, its influence is less pronounced than in Europe. Estimable red vintages of recent years are those of 1968, 1970, 1974 and 1977. Least successful were the years 1971, 1972 and 1973. Whites have stayed on a fairly even keel. Few pre-1970 bottles are available.

New York State is a distant second in production, accounting for only 10% of domestic consumption. Its Finger Lakes and Hudson Valley vineyards are best known for sparkling wines, but a number of vintners create worthy blends of offbeat varietals. Try Konstantin Frank, Benmarl and Bully Hill.

Beers are served at glacial temperatures and imported brands are sold everywhere, in greatest profusion at pub-style restaurants. Tap water is excellent.

Restaurants classified by area

Lower Manhattan (*below Canal St.*)
Bridge Cafe, The
Hee Seung Fong
El Internacional
Odeon
Phoenix Garden
Say Eng Look
Thailand
Windows On The World

SoHo/Greenwich Village (*Canal St.–14th St.*)
Chanterelle
Coach House, The
Greene Street
Jane Street Seafood Cafe
One Fifth
Mulino, Il
Rincón de España, El
Sabor
SoHo Charcuterie
Spring Street Restaurant
Trattoria da Alfredo
Vanessa

Chelsea (*W 14th St.–W 23rd St*)
Ballroom, The

Gramercy Park/Murray Hill (*E 14th St.–E 42nd St.*)
Louisiana, La
Parador, El
Salta in Bocca

Midtown East (*E 42nd St.–E 59th St.*)
Box Tree
Chantilly, Le
Christ Cella
Cygne, Le
Four Seasons
Girafe
Gloucester House
Grenouille, La
Hatsuhana
Lutèce
Oyster Bar and Restaurant
Palm, The
Quilted Giraffe, The
Sichuan Pavilion
Sparks
Takesushi

Midtown West (*W 42nd St.–W 59th St.*)
Arirang House
Barbetta

Cabana Carioca ▯▯ ✿
Carolina ▯▯▯
Darbár ▯▯ ✿
Orsini's ▯▯▯▯
Raga ▯▯ ✿
Russian Tea Room, The ▯▯▯
Sardi's ▯▯▯
Shezan ▯▯▯ ✿
21 Club ▯▯▯▯
Un Deux Trois ▯▯▯▯

Upper East Side (*E 60th St.–E 96th St.*)

An American Place ▯▯▯▯ △
Cafe Lavandou ▯▯▯▯ △
Chez Pascal ▯▯▯ △
Cirque, Le ▯▯▯▯ △
Claude's ▯▯▯▯ △
Contrapunto ▯□ ✿
Côte Basque, La ▯▯▯ △
DeMarco ▯▯▯▯
Elaine's ▯▯▯

Hoexter's Cafe ▯▯▯
Maxwell's Plum ▯▯▯
Monello, Il ▯▯▯
Mortimer's ▯▯▯
Parioli Romanissimo ▯▯▯▯
Relais, Le ▯▯ △
Uzie's ▯▯▯
Veau d'Or, Le ▯▯▯
Vienna '79 ▯▯▯ △

Upper West Side (*W 60th St.–W 96th St.*) △

Café des Artistes ▯▯□
Cafe Luxembourg ▯▯▯▯
Caravelle, La ▯▯▯ △
Ginger Man, The ▯▯□
Shun Lee West ▯▯□
Tavern On The Green ▯▯▯

Brooklyn
Gage and Tollner ▯▯□ ▥
River Cafe ▯▯▯▯

Restaurants classified by type of cuisine

American
An American Place ▯▯▯▯ △
Bridge Cafe, The ▯□ ✿ ✿
Carolina ▯▯□
Christ Cella ▯▯▯▯
Gage and Tollner ▯▯□ ▥
Ginger Man, The ▯▯□
Gloucester House ▯▯▯
Hoexter's Cafe ▯▯▯
Jane Street Seafood Cafe ▯▯□
Louisiana, La ▯▯□
Oyster Bar and Restaurant ▯▯□
Palm, The ▯▯▯▯
Sparks ▯▯▯
Vanessa ▯▯▯ △

Chinese
Hee Seung Fong □ ✿
Phoenix Garden □ ✿ ✿
Say Eng Look □ ✿
Shun Lee West ▯▯□
Sichuan Pavilion ▯▯□

Continental/International
Box Tree ▯▯▯▯ △
Café des Artistes ▯▯□
Cafe Luxembourg ▯▯▯▯
Claude's ▯▯▯▯ △
Coach House, The ▯▯▯
Elaine's ▯▯▯
Four Seasons ▯▯▯▯
Greene Street ▯▯□
Maxwell's Plum ▯▯▯
Mortimer's ▯▯▯
One Fifth ▯▯▯▯
River Cafe ▯▯▯▯
SoHo Charcuterie ▯▯▯▯
Spring Street Restaurant ▯□
Tavern On The Green ▯▯▯
21 Club ▯▯▯▯
Windows On The World ▯▯□ ▯▯▯ ▯▯▯

Cuban
Sabor ▯□ ✿

French
Cafe Lavandou ▯▯▯▯ △
Caravelle, La ▯▯▯ △
Chanterelle ▯▯▯▯
Chantilly, Le ▯▯▯ △

Chez Pascal ▯▯▯ △
Cirque, Le ▯▯▯▯ △
Côte Basque, La ▯▯▯ △
Cygne, Le ▯▯▯ △
Grenouille, La ▯▯▯ △
Lutèce ▯▯▯ △
Odeon ▯▯▯
Quilted Giraffe, The ▯▯▯▯ △
Relais, Le ▯▯□
Un Deux Trois ▯▯▯▯
Veau d'Or, Le ▯▯▯

German/Austrian
Vienna '79 ▯▯▯ △

Indian
Darbár ▯▯ ✿
Raga ▯▯ ✿
Shezan ▯▯▯ ✿

Italian
Barbetta ▯▯▯▯
Contrapunto □ ✿
DeMarco ▯▯▯▯
Girafe ▯▯▯ △
Monello, Il ▯▯▯
Mulino, Il ▯▯▯
Orsini's ▯▯▯▯
Parioli Romanissimo ▯▯▯▯
Salta in Bocca ▯▯□ ✿
Sardi's ▯▯▯
Trattoria da Alfredo ▯□
Uzie's ▯▯▯

Japanese
Hatsuhana ▯▯□
Takesushi ▯▯□

Korean
Arirang House ▯▯□

Latin American
Cabana Carioca ▯□ ✿
Parador, El ▯▯□

Russian
Russian Tea Room, The ▯▯▯

Spanish
Ballroom, The ▯▯▯ △
Internacional, El ▯□ ✿
Rincón de España, El ▯▯□

Thai
Thailand ▯□

131

Restaurants

An American Place ⌂
*969 Lexington Ave. (near 70th),
NY 10021* ☎*517–7660. Map
7M4* ▦ ▦ ▦ ▣ ☿ AE CB ◉ ⬤
VISA *Open Mon–Sat 17.45–22.45.
Closed Sun.*

Chauvinism – that of myopic
Gallic food nabobs on one side and
bumptious US-bred chefs on the
other – has inspired a rash of
hybrid 'New American' eating
places such as this. What they
purvey are *nouvelle* techniques
applied to devoutly native
products and regional cuisines.
What the paying customers get is
novelty, snippets of education, and
not a little defensive pretension.
Strangers step down into this
smallish, placid room unaware that
they are about to part with a
sizeable sheaf of their travel
dollars. It is done up in restful
beige and tans, the wall fabric
spotted with aimless squiggles
intended, no doubt, to suggest a
Navajo motif. The waiters are
pleasant, the menu clear, the
preparations always tidy if
sometimes uninspired. Here the
initiate can discover duck *foie gras*,
Louisiana crawfish, Dungeness
crab, free-range chicken and
California caviar. All are
domestically raised or gathered,
and quite good. Star-spangled
Americanism fades only after
dessert, with espresso coffee. This
is a competent middle-level
restaurant with regal prices.

Arirang House
*28 W 56th St. (near 5th Ave.), NY
10020* ☎*581–9698. Map 5N4* ▦▯
▯▭ ▦ AE CB ◉ ⬤ ▣ *Open
Mon–Sat 12.00–14.30,
17.00–22.30 (23.00 Sat).*

Korean cuisine hovers, as might be
expected, between Chinese and
Japanese, but carves out its own
identity. Blisteringly hot sauces are
mostly optional – dips rather than
intrinsic to the dish. The
waitresses have been
described as butterflies, and they
are undeniably enchanting in their
han pok ensembles. Tables are
close. Try a ginseng cocktail
before, *jung jong* (rice wine)
during, and plum wine after.

The Ballroom ⌂
*253 W 28th St. (off 8th Ave.), NY
10001* ☎*244–3005. Map 4P3* ▦▯
▭▭ ▦ ☿ ♫ ♥ (sometimes).
Open Tues–Sat 16.00–2.00.
Closed Sun, Mon.*

Spanish cuisine has received short

shrift in the city. Granted, it is not
among the world's greats – French,
Italian, Chinese – but it has
deserved better than the pallid
paellas and limp *gazpachos* that
New Yorkers came to accept as
representative. That was changed
by the emergence of chef Felipe
Rojas-Lombardi as a force on the
local culinary scene. He started
with a fresh look at *tapas* – the tasty
snacks Spaniards take before in
lieu of meals. They are laid out
along the handsome bar: platters of
marinated sliced sow ears, chunks
of rabbit, fist-sized quail, scallop
seviche, fried squid rings. The
display changes by night and
season. Two or three dishes
constitute a light meal, but the full
dinner is not to be shunned, and
you are offered *tapas* as appetizers.
The young venturesome
customers snaffle up these goodies
as they absorb the live flamenco
guitar. To keep them happy, the
management lay on a cabaret in a
separate room. Once settled in,
there's hardly a reason to leave,
unless it be the highish prices.

Barbetta
*321 W 46th St. (near 8th Ave.),
NY 10036* ☎*246–9171. Map
403* ▦▦ ▭ ▦ ▦ AE CB ◉ ⬤
VISA *Open Mon–Sat 12.00–14.00,
17.00–23.00.*

The entry rooms have the look of
Tuscan *palazzi*, hinting of an
ancient patina buffed and scoured
and buffed again. Beyond the large
main room, a summer garden
beckons, with a pool and stone
cherubim beneath shimmering
ornamental trees. The food usually
does justice to the surroundings,
but concentrate on the pasta and
veal. There are pre-theatre
dinners, and patrons may return
after the show for their desserts.

Box Tree ⌂
*242 E 50th St. (near 2nd Ave.),
NY 10022* ☎*758–8320. Map
5N5* ▦▦ ▦ ▦ *Open Mon–Fri
12.00–14.00, 18.30–22.30,
Sat–Sun 18.30–22.30.*

An eatery of such *haute* aspirations
and *très haute* prices inevitably
draws mixed responses. Most
patrons find the meticulous
assemblage of antiques and
reproductions very pretty,
brightened as it is by tiny wall
sconces and Tiffany chandeliers,
pewter objects and floral displays.
Others feel it verges on the
precious, a conviction reinforced

by the theatrical demeanour of waiters and such gestures as the rose that introduces the bill. For them, the snug arrangement of eight tables is not cosy, but crowded. Few quibble over the food, however, for it rarely disappoints. Witness the triumphant *vacherin*, a wizardry marrying hazelnut meringue, raspberries and froth of cream. Bookings must be made weeks in advance; there are two seatings nightly. Wine is the only liquor.

The Bridge Cafe 🍂 ♣
16½ Dover St. (Water St.), NY 10038 ☎227–3344. Map **3T5** ▯▯
▭▯ ▿ Open daily 12.00–15.00, 18.00–24.00, late lunch Sat, Sun, to 16.00.
Wavy floors, a stamped tin ceiling, and a well-used bar-counter attest to the age of this venerable seamen's watering hole. It is believed that the core structure went up in 1801, though there have inevitably been remodellings. Since the recapture of the cafe from disintegration a few years ago, an imaginative menu at uncommonly fair tariffs has drawn a growing clientele of politicians from the nearby Civic Center and aware New Yorkers from the burgeoning lower Manhattan and Brooklyn communities. The owner's boast is that there is no freezer on the premises. Everything is at its freshest – fish, vegetables, fowl. The blackboard of the day's fare changes daily, according to market availability. Among the seasonal staples the chili, calamari, tortellini and omelettes are remarkable. Wines are priced at only slightly above retail, and there are several imported beers on tap. Mulled cider and Irish coffee with real whipped cream are sufficient reason to stop by after a chilly day at the nearby South Street Seaport Museum. They accept neither reservations nor credit cards.

Cabana Carioca ♣
123 W 45th St. (near 6th Ave.), NY 10036 ☎581–8088. Map **504** ▯▯ ▭▯ ▙ ▿ ▣ ▣ VISA Open daily 12.00–23.00.
When the tariffs of the city's best-known restaurants seem too dizzying, consider the ethnic restaurants. The Cabana Carioca, serving Brazilian food, is in a midtown block handy for the Broadway theatres but

constituting a veritable Little Rio. Brazilian food has not caught the attention of the larger populace, so a full dinner for two here is still very reasonable. The street entrance and flight of stairs to the Cabana Carioca do not look promising, but press on. Success has bred a sleeker downstairs room and an annex a few doors w. Try to arrive on Wed or Sat, when the national dish, *feijoada*, is on hand. Otherwise, venture into the mysteries of the stew the Portuguese call *cozido* or take the safer route of shrimp *paulista*. The best soup is *caldo verde*. Desserts are the bland Latin norm.

Café des Artistes
1 W 67th St. (Central Park W), NY 10023 ☎877–3500. Map **4M3** ▯▯ ▭▯ ▣ AE CB ▣ ▣ VISA Open Mon–Sat 12.00–15.00, 18.00–22.30, Sun 11.00–15.00, 17.00–21.00. Closed Christmas, Jan 1.
George Lang has transformed this long dreary dining-room into one of the liveliest bistros on the West Side. Praise for the rejuvenation lies more with the menu than the decor, if only because the decor needed less effort – with touch-ups, a nostalgic 1920s glow was wrested from the former dowdiness. Murals by Howard Chandler Christy featuring chastely voluptuous nudes are set off by banks of plants and ornate mirrors. Vaguely familiar faces lean over hurricane lamps and snowy napery. The already ambitious *carte* is supplemented by up to a score of daily specials in all categories. Standards are gazpacho with unexpected chunks of shrimp, oysters in two or three guises, duckling more tender than crispy. Not every dish is memorable, but at these reasonable prices grousing is inappropriate.

Cafe Lavandou ⌂
134 E 61st St. (near Park Ave.), NY 10021 ☎838–7987. Map **5N4** ▥▥ ▭▯ AE Open Mon–Sat 12.00–15.00, 18.00–22.00.
A wave of intimate, sprightly French restaurants broke upon these shores in the mid-1970s. They were owned and operated by dedicated young careerists who had no wish to be cogs in conglomerate feeding stations. Chefs of their tender years could be expected to make mistakes, often in capitalization and

administration, but a number of them rode out the rough waters and prospered. Jean Jacques Rachou, for example, created Cafe Lavandou and went on to revive **La Côte Basque**. It has been argued that his first baby has suffered slightly in the process, but if so, it is barely perceptible. A gracious establishment it remains, unforbiddingly elegant, a place to acquire insight into the mysteries of the French kitchen without any sense of rigorous instruction.

Cafe Luxembourg
200 W 70th St. (near Amsterdam Ave.), NY 10023 ☎*873–7411. Map 6M2* ▥▥▥ ▭ ▰▰ ▤▤ ☿ 🄰🄴 🄲🄳 🆅🅸🆂🅰 *Open Mon–Fri 17.30–1.30, Sat, Sun 18.00–1.30.*

This, the younger sibling of TriBeCa's **Odeon**, replicates the jovial blend of funk and culinary professionalism that made that estimable bistro such a solid success. It might be the ultimate Upper West Side restaurant, serving as it does a community with a happily confused identity of high-minded art, New Wave frivolity, traditional bohemianism and simple urban striving. The Deco-Moderne setting of marble and mirrors, jazzy window treatments and colourful tiles is filled from late afternoon to early morning with an ecumenical spectrum of social types: elderly neighbourhood couples, flamboyant singles, young executives and conceptual artists. They come for food that observes fashion and stimulates all the appropriate senses, but doesn't demand the sham reverence of those places that imagine a sole *meunière* to be the equivalent of a Bach sonata. Daily appetizer, entrée and wine specials supplement the set menu. Of particular value is the nightly *prix fixe* dinner served between 17.30–18.30, about half the price of a regular meal.

La Caravelle △
33 W 55th St. (near 5th Ave.), NY 10019 ☎*586–4252. Map 5N4* ▥▥▥ ▭ ▰▰ 🄰🄴 🄲🄱 🄲🄳 🆅🅸🆂🅰 *Open Mon–Sat 12.00–14.30, 18.00–22.30. Closed Sun, Aug.*

Perhaps a shade too traditional to be awarded a place at the very tip of the gastronomic pyramid, La Caravelle is perceived to be slipping from that pinnacle. Still, for those not inclined to expend

their treasure on cuisines *nouvelle* and *minceur*, it is among the happiest of choices for the commemoration of events. There is almost always a celebrity or two to lend credence to the selection, although they are of the established, rather than chic, stripe. Stab a finger at the menu – there will be few disappointments, and several delights.

Carolina
355 W 46th St. (8th Ave.), NY 10036 ☎*245–0058. Map 4O3* ▥▥▥ ▭ ▤▤ ☿ 🄲🄳 🆅🅸🆂🅰 *Open Mon–Fri 12.00–15.00, 18.00–24.00, Sat, Sun 11.30–15.30 (breakfast) 15.30–20.00 (dinner).*

Mislabelling is a not-infrequent by-product of New York's current enthusiasm for domestic regional cuisines. The states of North and South Carolina may be in the SE, but this 'Carolina' features the cooking of the SW. No matter. Most of what comes out of the open kitchen tastes just fine, be it grilled salmon or swordfish steak, or racks of barbecued ribs slow-cooked over mesquite coals. This is simple, tangy fare that sets the nostrils flaring even before it arrives at the table. To start, there is corn chowder or hot smoked sweet sausage with roasted peppers. To follow, bourbon baked ham with black cherry sauce or meltingly tender beef brisket. The snug back room, beyond the kitchen, is visually opened with wrap-around mirrors and a pyramidal skylight, but the tables in front are less crowded. It is a welcome addition to the theatre district's lacklustre 'restaurant row'.

Chanterelle
89 Grand St. (Greene St.), NY 10013 ☎*966–6960. Map 2S4* ▥▥▥ ▭ 🄰🄴 🄲🄳 *Open Tues–Sat 18.30–23.00. Closed Sun, Mon, July.*

Anti-establishmentarians develop their own rituals, uniforms and convictions. For a while, it seemed that every bar and restaurant in the new Bohemia of SoHo was to be a garage or loft stripped to bare brick walls, hung with green industrial lamps and filled with potted ferns. Chanterelle has only its lofty space in common with its neighbours. It is of a spare serenity, with brass chandeliers above, grey carpeting below and antiseptic white everywhere else. The young chef–

owner pursues his trade with not a trace of frivolity, which may be counted among his few failings. His productions demonstrate respect for *nouvelle cuisine*, but none of the extremes to which some of his colleagues have gone. Furthermore, measured growth is evident. If the meal taken there last year was good, the one tonight will be better. The menu changes constantly. Book ahead.

Le Chantilly ⌂
106 E 57th St. (near Park Ave.), NY 10022 ☎*751–2931. Map 5N4* ▥ ☐ ▱ ▱ AE ◑ VISA *Open Mon–Sat 12.00–14.30, 18.00–22.30.*

Although a relative newcomer (1978), Le Chantilly is a seamless facsimile of the second generation of grand luxe restaurants that trod the heels of Le Pavillon and **La Côte Basque** in the early 1960s. All the design elements are *comme il faut* – banquettes, conical glass chandeliers, closely spaced tables, flowers in brandy snifters, mirrored walls, an indifferent mural of the eponymous Loire chateau, and even a celebrity row along the entry corridor. But the fact that Le Chantilly is interchangeable with a dozen others of the classical Gallic family (sub-species Manhattan) hardly demeans it. All is thoroughgoing professionalism – formal and intolerant of novelty or unsettling surprises. Ties and jackets and advance bookings are required.

Chez Pascal ⌂
151 E 82nd St. (near 3rd Ave.), NY 10028 ☎*294–1334. Map 5L5* ▥ ☐ ▱ AE ◑ VISA *Open Mon–Sat 18.30–23.00.*

There are people who have no need to agonize over which Manhattan restaurant to select for the big splash. They simply rotate – **Lutèce** on Tues, **La Grenouille** on Wed, **La Côte Basque** on Thurs and Chez Pascal on Fri. At least they *look* like the same crowd – immaculately coiffed, bespoke suits, Halston frocks, tasteful flares of gold at wrist and throat. The space doesn't permit grandeur, just burnished wood, mellowed brick and grey upholstery. Tables are relatively large, set with balloon goblets that permit the proper savouring of a Chateau Lafite. It will take a wine of that calibre to do justice to the food. Mediocrity is not permitted.

Christ Cella
160 E 46th St. (7th Ave.), NY 10017 ☎*697–2479. Map 4O3* ▥ ☐ ▱ AE CB ◑ *Open Mon–Fri 12.00–22.30, Sat 17.00–22.45. Closed Sun, hols.*

Call it 'Krisella' or 'Kreechella'. Either way, it is a place for people who like their food simple – and are willing to pay for it. The two floors of this 1926 landmark steakhouse are assertively plain, with bare floors, indifferent seascapes on the walls, uncushioned chairs and waiters in aprons. There isn't even a written menu, but the recited selections do not tax the memory. Basic appetizers are shrimp or crabmeat cocktails, Caesar salad; entrées are roast beef, sirloin steak, veal or lamb chops, broiled fish, scallops; desserts are cheesecake, ice-cream. Obviously, people who prefer drama or elegance or intricacy of preparation should go elsewhere. Those who have business to conduct, without distraction, find Christ Cella suits their purposes exactly. Men have to wear jackets and ties.

Le Cirque ⌂
58 E 65th St. (near Madison Ave.), NY 10021 ☎*794–9292. Map 5M4* ▥ ☐ ▱ AE CB ◑ *Open Mon–Sat 12.00–15.00, 18.00–22.30.*

Nancy and Ronald Reagan dine here when in the city, and, however one might feel about their ideology, their taste in restaurants (on this evidence) cannot be faulted. The First Lady reportedly lunches on *pasta primavera* – vegetables tossed with noodles, butter and cream – a concoction not listed on the menu but available whenever the appropriate ingredients are on hand. The pâtés are notable, as are *carpaccio* (marinated uncooked beef), game birds, *quenelles de brochet* with two sauces, and pastries. If the dishes named seem schizophrenic, there is the handy explanation that the owner is Italian, the chef French and the pastry-chef German. Yet that combination is nirvana for those gourmets who admire the specialities of all three countries. Should there be disappointments, they will be in the occasional imperiousness of the restaurant's senior staff and in the often excessively high noise levels of the dining-room.

Restaurants

Claude's ⌂
*205 E 81st St. (near 3rd Ave.), NY
10028* ☎*472–0487. Map 5 L5* ▮▮▮
▢ AE CB ◐ ⓔ VISA *Open
Mon–Sat 18.00–22.30.*

In New York there are a number of
restaurants that are set up
primarily with the convenience of
the chef-owner in mind. These
places frequently attract a
masochistic clientele willing to
suffer at the altar of gastronomy
under the strict supervision of the
resident guru. Should you wish to
dine at Claude's, for example, you
must be a party of four and must
tender advance notice of 48hr.
Permission to ingest its delicacies
is granted during only 4½hr of each
24, excluding Sun. Large sums of
currency are given in return. The
trouble is, Claude's is nearly as
good as it thinks it is, and the faithful bridle at any suggestion that it
falls short of perfection.

The Coach House
*110 Waverly Pl. (near Washington
Sq. W), NY 10011* ☎*777–0303.
Map 2 R4* ▮▮▮ ▢ AE CB ◐ ⓔ
VISA *Open Tues–Sun 17.30–22.30.
Closed Mon, Aug.*

Having been long and consistently
ranked among the best in the city
(or state, or country), The Coach
House has faded from that stature,
but still warrants attention. The
food served is essentially
American. It has certain
international accents, to be sure,
but the staples are prime ribs of
beef, baby lobster tails, lump
crabmeat and chicken pie.
Reservations are essential.

Contrapunto ♣
*1009 3rd Ave. (corner of 60th
St.), NY 10022* ☎*751–8616.
Map 5 N5* ▢ ▢ ▤ ▾ AE ⓒ VISA
*Open Mon–Sat 12.00–24.00.
Closed Sun.*

The minimalist quasi-Milanese
setting is on the second floor
overlooking lively Third Avenue,
above another bar-restaurant of
little distinction. Track lighting,
wooden chairs, a pleasingly perky
espresso machine, and glass tops
over white tablecloths are the
extent of the decor. Concentrate on
the food. It is fetchingly fresh
pasta, dressed rather than sauced.
Mushrooms of the season are
grilled, peppered, sprinkled with
minced garlic and parsley, drizzled
with oil – a delicious starter.
Bresaola e parmigiano (dried beef

with oil and cheese) is good, too.
All manner of pasta types are
tossed with sweet pepper slivers,
or with tomato and Pecorino
cheese, or with exotic *funghi*, or
with Ricotta, grated nutmeg and
chopped chives. Italian-style
gelati are made right here, in such
surprising flavours as praline,
grapefruit and white chocolate.
Chocolate fudge cake is a boggler.

La Côte Basque ⌂
*5 E 55th St. (near 5th Ave.), NY
10022* ☎*688–6525. Map 5 N4* ▮▮▮
▢ ▬ AE *Open Mon–Sat
12.00–15.00, 18.00–23.00.*

Henri Soulé is credited both with
the introduction of serious *haute
cuisine* to New York and with its
propagation, by nurturing the
ambitions of the talented young
chefs in his employ. Soulé clones
sprouted on every fashionable
block. Some persist, more than
20yr later. His own fabled
restaurants went into decline or
closed. That seemed the ultimate
fate, until recently, of La Côte
Basque, but miraculously it has
been resuscitated, its theatrical
spaces primped and its
performances both in the kitchen
and out front restored to their
former integrity. The original
Lamotte murals of the Basque
coast and harbours are still there,
models to be emulated by the
proprietors of otherwise equally
ambitious places who consistently
choose vapid pastel depictions of
chateaux and meadows. Reception
is gracious, the staff once again
informative and anticipatory. The
fixed-price lunch is 30% cheaper
than dinner.

Le Cygne ⌂
*55 E 54th St. (Madison Ave.), NY
10022* ☎*759–5941. Map 5 N4* ▮▮▮
▢ ▬ ▭ AE ◐ ⓔ VISA *Open
Mon–Fri 12.00–15.00,
18.00–23.00, Sat 18.00–23.00.
Closed Sun, Aug.*

You may very well have your best
meal in New York at 'The Swan'.
The host treats with equal favour
patrons old and new, celebrities
and unknowns, and he harbours no
lofty notions of his station. He
makes menu suggestions, clears
dishes, and fills glasses with grace
and warmth. The new facility
(next door to the original) is cool
greys and slate blue, severely
modernist outside and faintly
nautical (as in QEII) within. The
upstairs room is as soothing as the

main floor, a touch less frenetic at peak hours. Bouquets of flowers are everywhere. Fixed-price lunches and dinners are not inexpensive, and with supplemental charges and injudicious wine selection, dinner for two can rocket into the stratosphere. . . . and higher.

Darbár ♧
44 W 56th St. (5th Ave.), NY 10020 ☎*432–7227. Map 5N4* ◨
◻ ▬ ▦ ▼ ⟨AE⟩ ⟨CB⟩ ⟨◐⟩ ⟨◑⟩ ⟨VISA⟩
Open 12.00–15.00, 17.30–23.00.
Of late there is competition to produce the most elegant Indian eatery. Leader of the moment is Darbár, a tranquil oasis that shuts off the clamour of one of the city's best-known restaurant rows. Its welcoming bar fronts two floors of velvety russet walls hung with tasteful silk weavings, relief panels of beaten metal, artfully framed mirrors and a splendid carpet in muted tints that hangs down from the top floor. Tables downstairs are separated by carved wood screens; the resulting private mood is enhanced by subdued lighting and quiet taped sitar music. Everyone likes the fried onion appetizer *bhajia*, with good reason, although the cool salad of chick peas, potato chunks and onions is as delightful with its tamarind dressing. The several tandoori dishes retain more moisture than is typical of that form of clay-oven cooking, but the kitchen is seen to greater advantage in other specialities. Among these: beef and lamb *vindaloo*, the vegetable-and-cheese *shahi sabz korma* and *jheenga masala* (shrimp tossed with onion and pepper nuggets and a complex spice mixture). Weekend brunches and weekday luncheon buffets are popular and, as these things go, bargains. This is the place to save for those days when everything else seems closed.

DeMarco
1422 3rd Ave. (82nd St.), NY 10028 ☎*744–2819. Map 7L5* ◨
◻ ▦ ▼ ⓘ *(Sun brunch)* ⟨AE⟩ ⟨CB⟩
⟨◐⟩ *Open Mon–Sat 18.00–23.30, Sun 12.00–15.00, 17.00–22.00.*
With a single plate of admittedly good pasta going for the price of a full meal for two in Chinatown, DeMarco obviously appeals to a somewhat restricted number of diners. In the main, these are the over-35 businesspeople and celebrants of special events who

enjoy sharing space with the likes of Robert Redford and Michael York. They are given a warm welcome into a long, high room of rather bleak mien, its severity softened by flowers, a copse of cast-iron columns, and quiet landscape paintings executed by the owner. Not-quite-classic Northern Italian recipes dominate the menu, the components arranged with a *nuova cocina* eye. From antipasti to sweets, all is at least tasty and, at its occasional best, out of this world. As proof, try the deep-fried mozzarella with tomato sauce and the Italianate bouillabaisse, *'umido di pesce'*.

Elaine's
1703 2nd Ave. (near E 88th St.), NY 10028 ☎*534–8114. Map 7K5*
◨ ◻ ⟨AE⟩ *Open Mon–Fri 12.00–15.00, 18.00–2.00, Sat–Sun 18.00–2.00.*
Luminaries of the literary world and, by mutual attraction, also from show business and politics make this saloon-restaurant their own. The proprietress takes care of them, saving their favourite tables and shooing away *paparazzi* and gawpers. There is no reason to believe they come for the mainly Italian food, for it is only adequate, and may account for the fact that no one shows up before 22.00.

Four Seasons
99 E 52nd St. (Park Ave.), NY 10022 ☎*754–9494. Map 5N4* ◨
◻ ▬ ▬ ⟨AE⟩ ⟨CB⟩ ⟨◐⟩ ⟨◑⟩ ⟨VISA⟩ *Open Mon–Sat 12.00–15.00, 17.00–23.30.*
Lunch is the main event here, and the Grill Room is the arena. Publishers soothe brand-name authors and their agents in a daily ritual in which every change of table or occupant is duly charted. The dinner *locus* shifts to the Pool Room, with its floral bounty and marble-bound pool. It is a vaulted space three storeys high at the base of the Seagram Building. Some find it visually chilly, but the tables are comfortably spaced, and much of the artwork is rotated four times a year, as are menu selections. The food, usually of the highest calibre, is almost worth the prices. The scope is broad enough to qualify for the catch-all 'continental' label, with chocolate cake the preferred topper. The superior cellar highlights American vintages. Fixed-price pre-theatre dinners are a way to sample at lower cost.

Restaurants

Gage and Tollner ▥

*372 Fulton St. (near Borough
Hall), Brooklyn, NY 11201
☎875–5181. Map 3V7* ▥ ⌂ AE
CB ◉ ⊙ VISA *Open Mon–Fri
11.30–21.00, Sat 16.00–23.00.*

This is an officially designated
landmark, handy for Brooklyn
Heights. The gaslit Gay Nineties
atmosphere is authentic, because it
opened in 1879. It hasn't changed
much since, and some of the staff
look as if they might also have been
around as long. They wear
emblems attesting to their years of
employment. A seafood restaurant
in a port city oddly lacking in this
respect, the bisques and soles and
snappers are all good, in some
cases surpassing so. Mutton
chops are also available, and the
fried chicken is good.

The Ginger Man

*51 W 64th St. (near Broadway),
NY 10023 ☎399–2358. Map
6M3* ▥ ⌂ AE CB ◉ ⊙ VISA
*Open Mon–Sat 11.30–16.00,
17.00–24.00, Sun 11.30–22.00.*

Sustenance, not wonderment, is
the function of the hamburgers
and full dinners in this turn-of-
the-century tavern-restaurant
directly across Broadway from the
Lincoln Center. The patrons, after
all, are either anticipating or
savouring the ballet or opera or
concert they will attend or have
just attended. In that frame of
mind, a profound culinary
experience would be wasted, even
if it were available. Serviceability
is therefore the keynote and
simplicity the greater virtue.
Choose from the menu
accordingly. From 18.00–20.00
and 22.00 until closing it is
jammed, from the glass-enclosed
sidewalk room all the way to the
back. On weekends there is live
jazz.

Girafe ⌂

*208 E 58th St. (3rd Ave.), NY
10022☎752–3054. Map 5N5* ▥
⌂ AE ◉ ⊙ VISA *Open Mon–Fri
12.00–15.00, 17.30–1.30, Sat
17.30–1.30. Closed Sun, hols,
first three weeks in July.*

Despite the name and the pictures
of African beasts, this is a
prototypical northern Italian
eatery in the Upper East Side
style. Costly it is, but very good,
too. Regulars seem to prefer the
close proximity of the ground
floor, where sculptured hair and
black suits predominate. Strangers

are led up the spiral staircase to the
more spacious second-floor room,
where they are no less skilfully
attended, by captains who take
their responsibilities seriously.
Off-menu specials are suggested
and preparations are carefully
described. The soups and antipasti
are unremarkable, but the half-
portions of pasta are an excellent
starter choice. If it is autumn (the
white truffle season), and money is
no object, they will grate a shower
of the precious pungent fungus
over the top. Various pasta dishes
to start with and main courses of
veal, poultry and fish are fresh and
copious.

Gloucester House

*37 E 50th St. (between Madison
and Park), NY 10022
☎755–7394. Map 5O4* ▥ ▬ ▦
AE CB ◉ ⊙ VISA *Open Mon–Fri
12.00–15.00, 17.30–23.00, Sat,
Sun 12.00–23.00.*

Be prepared: this has the loftiest
tariffs of any fish house in town.
Men must wear coats and ties at all
times. And there is no longer
anything even remotely
fashionable about it. After all, it
has been here for over half a
century. Accordingly, it
approaches institutional stature, a
haven for old money and corporate
expense accounts, where the decor
need only be unobtrusive and the
food devoid of superfluous
trappings. Still, the crustaceans
and swimmers are as morning-
fresh and precisely cooked as any
to be found in these parts. Cost is
apparently irrelevant to most of the
regular patrons. For the price of
the perfectly cooked lobster, you
could buy four of your own at the
market. Desserts are as good as
everything else. Service is
avuncular.

Greene Street

*101 Greene St. (near Prince St.),
NY 10012☎925–2415. Map 2S4*
▥ ⌂ ♉ ♫ ◉ VISA *Open
Sat–Sun 12.00–15.00, daily
18.00–24.00.*

This dazzling new eatery functions
as an all-inclusive drinking-
dining-entertainment centre. The
interior expands beyond the SoHo
standard with walls of brick and
groves of greenery within a
towering cube of space modified
by balconies and staircases. The
young, courteous and uniformly
attractive waiters are capable of
reeling off numbingly long lists of

daily specials. *Nouvelle* departures from classical French assumptions are the inclination of the dedicated executive chef, with deviations towards larger portions and slightly richer sauces. Most preparations are well above par and prices are surprisingly fair. It is easy to start with cocktails in the busy front bar and stay past midnight. Piano or chamber music usually accompanies dinner (allowing for the latest enthusiasm of the owner) and there is jazz most nights at 23.00 (for which there is a cover charge and a two-drink minimum for non-diners). It is essential to make a reservation in advance.

La Grenouille ⌂
3 E 52nd St. (near 5th Ave.), NY 10022 ☎ *752–1495. Map 5N4* ▥
▢ ▦ ▱ AE ◑ *Open Mon–Sat 12.00–15.00, 18.00–23.00.*

The leadership in classical French cookery in New York is held by a bare handful of restaurants, whose relative position is a subject warmly debated by those who can afford frequent comparisons. **Lutèce** is surely one, La Grenouille another. La Grenouille has infelicities, to be sure. One *maître d'* is a relic from the Prussian school of hospitality, although it must be conceded that certain customers tend to demand their rights more vociferously than is necessary in a place like this, simply to show they will not be intimidated. Divert your attention from the lot of them by scanning the array of appetizers and pastries set by the entrance. This table underscores the primary reason you have come, and when you are ushered into the main dining-room with its tiny lamps and bowls and vases and pots of variegated blooms, momentary irritations at the door peel away. Ask questions, even if they reveal ignorance. Preparations and options will be patiently explained by captains who apparently have unlimited time just for you. They always seem to know when to go away, too. Choose from the menu without fear, for the simplest dishes are likely to surpass the best versions previously enjoyed, and the complicated ones are those you will recall 5yr hence. The list to follow is hopelessly inadequate to the task. Book as far in advance as possible and it is advisable to avoid weekends.

Hatsuhana
17 E 48th St. (5th Ave.), NY 10017 ☎ *335–3345. Map 5O4* ▥
▢ AE CB ◑ CD *Open Mon–Fri 12.00–14.30, 17.30–21.30, Sat 17.00–21.30.*

The idea of ingesting raw fish is daunting, even for those to whom oysters on the half-shell are routine. Make the first attempt here: it is authentic, the close quarters make it easy to strike up a conversation, dieters can save calories, the cost is low, and a full meal is light enough to precede 2hr in a theatre seat. Young Japanese adroitly slice quivering fresh tuna and shrimp, wrap them in sheets of kelp, top with salmon eggs, arrange them artistically on lacquered trays of vinegared rice, all within inches of the diners at the two long narrow pine counters. Most customers eat at the *sushisashimi* bars where they can see their food prepared, but there are tables, too.

Hee Seung Fung ♣
46 Bowery (near Elizabeth St.), NY 10013 ☎ *374–1319. Map 3S5* ▢ ▦ ▤ *Open 7.30–2.00.*

There are three branches of 'HSF', but this is the original. Although full meals are served after 17.00, the source of its success is Hong Kong-style *dim-sum*. These are tasty morsels in appetizer portions, of apparently limitless variety. The division of labour is clear: waiters bring drinks (for which you pay immediately) and the bill. In between, waitresses trundle endlessly by with trolleys loaded with dumplings, sliced fowl, shrimp rolls and assorted exotica. You choose what appeals. Be selective, for something better is just behind. When the place is crowded, strangers may be seated at your table. They don't remain strangers long, and if they are Chinese-Americans, they can be of help in identifying the contents of dishes. Dinners are truly remarkable bargains. If in a large party, order the Chinese-language special. It has nine courses for the price of an indifferent French meal for one uptown.

Hoexter's Cafe
1442 3rd Ave. (83rd St.), NY 10028 ☎ *472–9322. Map 7I5* ▥
▢ ▤ ▾ ◑ AE CB ◑ CD VISA *Open Mon–Fri 18.00–24.00, Sat, Sun 12.00–16.00.*

Despite a modest fine-tuning

process that included a slight name change ('Cafe' replaced 'Market'), strikingly attractive people still fill the large front bar room and the rear dining area. Even the waiters are handsome, as well as facile at their trade. They serve from a simplified menu that leans to batter-fried shrimps, classy hamburgers, black bean soup and six versions of California-style 'gourmet' pizza. Food after all is just a diversion to these hordes of seekers and strivers. There is dancing in the later hours. Wear your tailored silks.

El Internacional ✿
219 W Broadway (near White St.), NY 10013 ☎*226–8131. Map 2T4* ▯▯ ▭ ⊕ ▦ ▾ ▣
Open Mon–Sat 12.00–1.00, Sun 17.00–1.00.

Boy George and his ilk would feel very much at home here. Super-kitsch reigns, with colours and motifs that don't clash, so much as cry out. There are shades of violet and pink, some sprayed with glitter, tiles, a fish-less aquarium and purple carpeting. Allegedly a gangster favourite when it was 'Teddy's', that name can still be discerned on the facade. The service staff fulfils its decorative obligations. Many are in spiky punk hairdos, a single earring hanging to the shoulder, with crimson eyelashes, fuchsia vests, velvet hats. And those are the men. Don't be dismayed. It is a fun *TriBeCa* experience, and the biggest reason is not the trappings but the food. This is an authentic Spanish *tapas* restaurant. Trays of these nibbles are set out along the marble-topped bar: grilled sardines, marinated mushrooms, *chorizo* sausage, the thick egg-and-potato omelet called a *tortilla*. Three or four dishes make a meal, although conventional dinners are also served. As the night wears on, the place becomes ever more convivial and crowded.

Jane Street Seafood Cafe
31 8th Ave. (Jane St.), NY 10014 ☎*243–9237. Map 2R3* ▯▯ ▭ ▾ ▣ ▣ ▣ *Open Tues–Thurs 18.00–23.00, Fri–Sat 18.00–24.00, Sun 18.00–22.00.*

This is a hint of spare and salty New England in the NW corner of Greenwich Village. The ceiling is low and of moulded tin, the walls exposed brick, tables are bare wood and there is even a fire-place

– with a fire, when weather dictates. Wear your most comfortable clothes, bring your own wine and settle in to a meal composed of produce fresh from the market. Everyone raves about the bread, the coleslaw, the chowder, but those are merely starters. Little that follows will disappoint. As no advance reservations are accepted, there will be a wait. The bar in front is convivial.

La Louisiana
132 Lexington Ave. (near 29th St.), NY 10016 ☎*686–3959. Map 5P4* ▯▯ ▭ *Open Mon–Sat 18.00–23.00.*

Cooking of the American South is too often dismissed as merely fried chicken and grits (a cereal substance unworthy of description). Yet in the hands of able practitioners of appropriate heritage, it is the most distinctive of the American regional cuisines. Unfortunately, it is infrequently represented this far N, and less still in a form likely to draw converts. The advent of this charming little spot therefore filled a gap in New York's otherwise comprehensive culinary library. Only a quick flight to New Orleans could surpass its renditions of a cooking that can best be described as Soul-Cajun-Creole. To a substantial degree, it is the creation of poor people compelled to make the best of ingredients once shunned by the middle and upper classes – vegetable greens, leftover organs and extremities of pigs, shellfish free for the gathering. What those years of deprivation has wrought is wondrous, and while purists will quibble, La Louisiana is the place to learn about it.

Lutèce ⌂
249 E 50th St. (near 2nd Ave.), NY 10022 ☎*752–2225. Map 5O5* ▯▯▯ ▭ ▱ ▣ ▣ ⊕ *Open 12.00–15.00, 18.00–23.00. Closed Sun, Mon lunchtime, Aug.*

Lutèce is the standard against which any American restaurant that presumes to purvey *haute cuisine* must be measured. Hardly half a dozen establishments in New York approach its mark, and probably not that many in the rest of the country. While to dine here is an event and very nearly an honour – reservations must be secured at least two weeks in advance – no one is made to feel less than an eagerly anticipated guest. Rank, class, prominence and frequency of visit have no discernible bearing on treatment at the hands of the staff. That is the way it should always be, of course – especially at these prices – but too rarely is. The captains contrive to be attentive but not unctuous, friendly but not familiar, helpful but never patronizing, and their young minions carry through without a clatter or pretence. This exquisite balance, which carries from reception to appetizer to entree to coffee, is orchestrated by chef-proprietor Andre Soltner and his wife, who functions as *maîtresse d'*. Mr Soltner has been here more than 20yr, and is perhaps the only man in America that the great chefs of France acknowledge as their equal. He emerges from the cramped narrow kitchen periodically, circulating among his patrons, his whites so unsoiled as to suggest that he now administers rather than stirs – but the dishes that follow his appearances are still as good. Human endeavour can only aspire to perfection, however, and there are quibbles. The famous Garden Room might be a hangar for a scaled-down Zeppelin, its vaulted severity softened by white lattice-work and ferns in brass pots. And the Soltners persist in an untranslated menu with prices noted only in the copy handed to the presumed host, ignoring the fact that the woman might be the one who is paying. Those grumps aside, simply stab at the card. Everything on it is a speciality. The cellar is a library of the great vintages of Bordeaux and Burgundy, usually at breathtaking prices. A secondary list of serviceable wines offers rational substitutes.

Maxwell's Plum
1181 1st Ave. (64th St.), NY 10021 ☎*628–2100. Map* **7M5** **||||** ⌂ ▢ ♈ ♈ AE CB ⑩ VISA *Open daily 11.30–1.30.*

From its inception, astonishment was expressed that a high-volume restaurant of such multipurpose exuberance could actually produce dishes deserving serious attention. That reputation declined with kitchen changes and the perception that it was just another hangout for an especially rapacious singles crowd. A conspicuous effort to alter that image was undertaken in 1982. The large U-shaped bar was

cut in half and the area set aside for (relatively) formal dining was expanded. At the front, a glass-enclosed cafe still offers burger-and-chili cookery and views of the passing East Side scene. The ceiling and upper walls bristle with scores of plaster animal heads. More serious eating is done at the back, beneath panels of glorious stained glass. An attempt is made to forge a version of upper-middle-brow cuisine. Often it succeeds, as with beef, pasta and game. As often, it falls short, usually in pursuit of novelty. But joyous flamboyance is all too rarely encountered, and many can forgive the Plum its trespasses.

Il Monello
1460 2nd Ave. (near 76th St.), NY 10021 ☎*535–9310. Map* **7L5** **||||** ⌂ AE CB ⑩ ⑩ VISA *Open Mon–Sat 12.00–15.00, 17.00–24.00.*

This sort of Upper East Side Italian eatery tends to attract men in black silk suits, faintly silvery white-on-white shirts, diamond rings and sculptured hair. They probably have nothing to do with the profession you imagine, and in this case they have chosen an Upper East Side Italian eatery that also serves commendable food – a rare species. Try to ignore the heavy-handed decor and concentrate on mussels, clams, fish stews, veal and ambrosial tortellini. Try to ignore the captains, too, functionaries who are impatient with your lack of knowledge of what is, and what is not, available in the kitchen.

Mortimer's
1057 Lexington Ave. (75th St.), NY 10021 ☎*861–2481. Map* **7L4** **||||** ⌂ ♈ AE ⑩ ⑩ VISA *Open Mon–Sat 18.00–2.30, Sun 18.00–24.00.*

The ingredients of success cannot be isolated, otherwise everyone would do it. What wizardry transforms a restaurant with OK food at middling-high prices in unremarkable surroundings into a white-hot centre of attention for trendsetters and their eager followers? Probably even the owners of Mortimer's don't know. They are simply grateful, and no doubt utter small prayers that they don't unwittingly jar the composition out of balance. To witness the phenomenon at flood stage, drop in after 23.00 – always assuming that the lemmings have not pressed on to still another *boîte*. A parade of costumed lovelies and their attendants fill the arenas of a big bar and a modest dining-room. If they choose to eat, it is from a fairly direct continental menu, mostly in English, featuring such fashionable items as *gravlax* and *paillard of chicken*. Considering the floor show, prices are reasonable.

Il Mulino

86 W 3rd St. (Bleecker St.), NY 10012 ☎*673–3783. Map 2R4* ▮▮▮ ⬜ ▤ ☲ ⌖ AE *Open Mon–Fri 12.00–14.30, 17.00–23.00, Sat 17.00–23.00. Closed Sun.*

Italian restaurants in the Village used to mean checkered tablecloths, melted candles in old Chianti bottles and watery sauces on overdone spaghetti. Il Mulino is a good deal more ambitious, and its efforts have paid off. Limousines and expensive foreign sedans line drab W 3rd St. on weekend nights and often reservations for Sat evening must be made three weeks in advance. Except for those nights, the welcome is gracious and service is deft and knowledgeable. A dish of nibbles arrives with cocktails and the menu. Have the prosciutto with ripe figs and the soft-shell crabs when they're available. Otherwise, you won't go wrong with any of the various pasta offerings, the fish or shellfish. The value received is greater than at most of the posh Italian eateries of the Upper East Side, and at no sacrifice in ambience. Go for lunch to avoid the crowds.

Odeon

145 W Broadway (Thomas St.), NY 10013 ☎*233–0507. Map 2T4* ▮▮▮ ⬜ AE ☲ VISA *Open Sun–Fri 12.00–15.00, 19.00–2.30, Sat 19.00–2.30.*

This is an 'Art Moderne' cafeteria of World War II vintage left pretty much as it was, with a speckled-marble floor and chrome-tubular chairs with leatherette upholstery. Tapes of Betty Hutton and the Andrew Sisters are background music and the staff wear pencil-thin ties and wraparound aprons in imitation of an era none of them remember. Some customers show up in New Wave green cropped hair or pleated pegged trousers or jackets with Joan Crawford shoulders. Most, however, are simply jeans and tweed sorts of the

TriBeCa-SoHo art community. They come for semi-*nouvelle cuisine* concoctions of leeks and truffles and lobster out-of-the-shell with *crème fraîche*. Most of the food is imaginative and some of it splendid. Full dinners are served until 24.30, light suppers until 2.30, and the clientele grows more entertainingly bizarre as the night wears on.

One Fifth

15th Ave. (8th St.), NY 10003 ☎*260–3434. Map 2R4* ⬜ ⌖ ♪ AE CB ☲ ⌖ VISA *Open Mon–Fri 12.00–15.00, 18.00–24.30, Sat–Sun 12.00–16.00, 18.00–24.30.*

As the name suggests, One Fifth is at the base of 5th Ave., a half-block from Washington Square Park. Salvaged artefacts from a ship called the *Caronia* set the nautical tone. The clam and oyster bar at the front, the live duo that plays at night, and the wine list are the best reasons to go. Weekend brunch is popular.

Orsini's

41 W 56th St. (near 5th Ave.), NY 10019 ☎*757–1698. Map 5N4* ▮▮▮ ⬜ ▤ AE ☲ ⌖ VISA *Open Mon–Sat 12.00–15.00, 17.30–1.00. Closed Sat lunch in summer and Sun.*

The chi-chi crowd has a warm spot in its heart for Orsini's, but no longer besieges it, so there is room for mortals possessed merely of discretionary income. Romantics head for the dim downstairs room, but for lunch and being seen, the airy upstairs chamber is preferred. Clients unknown to the management are treated as well as glamorous old friends. The kitchen is competent, and tableside preparations are brisk, not showy. Midnight supper is popular.

Oyster Bar and Restaurant

Grand Central Terminal (42nd St. and Vanderbilt Ave.), NY 10017 ☎*532–3888. Map 5O4* ▮▮▮ ⬜ ☲ ☲ ⌖ *Open Mon–Fri 11.30–24.00. Closed Sat, Sun.*

Reclaimed from oblivion a few years back, this venerable (1913) fish-house is better than ever. The cavernous vaulted space is sheathed in beige tiles, its high arches echoed by pinlight traceries. When seasons and shipments overlap, the menu is crammed with more than 120 items, changed daily according to availability. The day's catch can include such rarities as *loup de mer*, shark, sea urchin, sand dab and ray. Five to ten types of oyster are usually on hand, along with chowders, pan roasts, stews, lobsters and crabs. Lake sturgeon, salmon and trout are smoked on the premises. Everything is super-fresh, and the simplest preparations are best. Service is speedy, without flourishes. There is an unexcellent list of California white wines. Since they do not close between lunch and dinner, unhurried pre-theatre meals are possible.

The Palm
837 2nd Ave. (near E 45th St.), NY 10017 ☎ *687–2953. Map 5O5* ▢▢ AE CB ⊙ ⊙ VISA *Open Mon–Fri 12.00–22.45, Sat 17.00–23.00.*

Steak is the reason for The Palm, and for its annexe across the street, Palm Too. Admirers of precisely seared slabs of unadorned prime cow flesh are a manly lot, it would appear, impatient with the fancy rituals of those swishy French places. Beef is what they want, and they get it, along with loaves of hashed brown potatoes, preceded by shrimp and followed by cheesecake, all in stupefying portions. Sawdust is on the floor, faded cartoons line the walls and ceiling, and women are mostly decoration, preferably silent. The bored waiter recites the menu, for none is written, and there isn't all that much to remember. Those inclined to stoking up in such places insist that this is one of the three best steakhouses in New York and are willing to pay for the privilege. Reservations for lunch, none for dinner.

El Parador
325 E 34th St. (near 1st Ave.), NY 10016 ☎ *679–6812. Map 5P5* ▢▢ ▢ *Open Mon–Sat 17.00–23.00.*

Of all the world's cuisines, Mexican seems the least amenable to transplantation. At least this is true on the evidence of New York's proponents of that not-always-fiery cookery. None of them do more than approximate, and enthusiasts must take what they can get. Settle in over a margarita – tequila and lime juice with a salted glass rim – while perusing the menu. *Seviche* (a marinated raw fish cocktail) is the best starter, but

from there you are on your own. The decor simulates Old Mexico rather more engagingly than most of the competition and lights are kept low, so those who associate *guacamole* and *tostadas* with romance will be content. Expect a wait as you can't book in advance.

Parioli Romanissimo
1466 1st Ave. (near 76th St.), NY 10021 ☎ *288–2391. Map 7L5* ▮▮▮▮ ▢▢ AE CB ⊙ *Open Tues–Sat 18.00–23.00.*

No satisfactory explanation is advanced for the practice – primarily of Chinese and Italian restaurants – of not listing on the menu dishes nonetheless nearly always available. They do that here, but the food, hidden or not, is so good and the ambience so seamlessly amiable that quibbling is small-minded. Be certain to book ahead, for they cannot serve more than 50 or 60 at a time. Among your fellow diners are certain to be an actor or two, a fashion designer, a recognizable power broker. They come here to eat, not to ogle their peers, which is a refreshing change to other celebrity hang-outs. Although the starters and main courses are estimable, you can do worse than to hand the menu unread back to the captain and inquire about delights they might be concealing in the kitchen tonight. He will not be evasive, and if he mentions game, have it.

Phoenix Garden ⬛ ❀
46 Bowery (near Elizabeth St.), NY 10013 ☎ *962–8934. Map 3S5* ▢▢ ▢ ■ ▤ *Open Tues–Sun 11.30–22.30. Closed Mon.*

Fans of Chinese food have been infatuated in recent years with the fiery Hunan and Szechuan cuisines, with a parallel contempt for that of Canton. This is understandable, if only for all the preceding decades of insipid *won ton* and *chow mein*. Yet, properly done, Cantonese cooking is subtle, varied and most decidely worthy of attention. In this regard the Phoenix Garden might just be the leader in all New York. The owners haven't made it easy. The room couldn't be plainer nor the exterior less beguiling – a dingy, littered alley drilled through a commercial block. The adventure is abundantly rewarded, nevertheless. Unlike many Chinatown eateries, staff recommendations can be trusted. These might be 'pepper and salty shrimp', 'steam flounder' or 'fried stuffed bean curd', all far tastier than they sound. Leave selections in the waiter's hands. You won't regret it. They aren't licensed, so pick up beer at the store across the way.

The Quilted Giraffe ⌂
955 2nd Ave. (near 50th St.), NY 10022 ☎*753–5355. Map 5O5* ▐▐▐▐
🖵 🍽 ▦ AE CB ⓓ ⓒⓓ VISA *Open Mon–Fri 18.00–22.00. Closed Sat, Sun.*

Jaded? Weary of snails in their shells, salmon in pastry envelopes, sole sprinkled with almond slivers, and similar conventionalities? Owner-chef Wine (his real name) fabricates antidotes. . . . or scares timid venturers back to the traditionalists. Innovation is primary, provender is from the top of the bin, and almost everything emerges from the kitchen raw, quickly warmed, or barely seared. Combinations can be outrageous – shellfish and raspberries, ravioli stuffed with chocolate – and perversely bland. But most of it works, the reward for experimentation.

Raga ✿
57 W 48th St. (near 5th Ave.), NY 10036 ☎*757–3450. Map 5O4* ▐▐▐
🖵 🍽 ▦ AE CB ⓓ ⓒⓓ VISA *Open Mon–Fri 12.00–15.00, 17.00–23.00, Sat–Sun 17.00–23.00.*

The Indian restaurant that deviates from the stereotype is no longer a novelty in the city. But Raga achieves a blend of formality and engaging exotica that is less chilly than others of the genre while preserving an unpatronizing authenticity in its dishes. There is tandoori, if you must, although the popularity of simple broiled chicken is a puzzlement in the presence of eggplant, *bhurta*, *nargisi kofta* and *jingha chat*. Many nights, there is live flute or sitar music.

Le Relais
712 Madison Ave. (64th St.), NY 10021 ☎*751–5108. Map 7M4* ▐▐▐ 🖵 🍽 🚗 AE *Open daily 12.00–15.00, 17.30–23.00.*

London pubs and Rive Gauche bistros are institutions that resist transplantation. Perhaps it is the alien language, the customers, the ambient sound. Nevertheless, this immensely popular cafe evokes half-remembered afternoons in the shadow of the Sorbonne, with hints of Gauloises in the air. Inside are velvet banquettes, walls crowded with framed mirrors and etchings, gaggles of East Siders seated haunch to denimed haunch, and aproned waiters who remain calm and cogent despite the clamour. The short menu is adjusted to seasonal availabilities, but might include sorrel soup, bass cloaked in seaweed, tender soft-shelled crabs and rosy-centred lamb.

El Rincón de España
226 Thompson St. (near Bleecker St.), NY 10012 ☎*475–9891. Map 2R4* ▐▐▐ 🖵 🍽 ⓓ ⓒⓓ VISA *Open daily, 18.00–24.00.*

Some restaurants flare like meteors and burn out as quickly; others quietly appear and hum along at an unwavering tempo, immune to fashion. Spanish food does not dazzle, and that might be another reason for the longevity of El Rincón de España. Lost in the seedy flash of the most abused quarter of Greenwich Village, its *paellas* and shellfish concoctions have attracted a steady patronage for decades. Prominent flavourings are garlic and that most costly of spices, saffron. Aficionados are advised that the northwestern region of Galicia is the primary influence, a fact as relevant as the distinction between Bologna and Naples in Italian cookery. Shun the sangria and overlook the vulgar decorative approximations of a Torremolinos tourist trap. Usually, there is a guitar player.

River Cafe
1 Water St., Brooklyn, NY 10001 ☎*522–5200. Map 3T6* ▐▐▐ 🖵 ⌁ 🚗 🍽 ⓓ AE CB ⓓ ⓒⓓ *Open daily 12.00–14.30, 18.30–23.30.*

The breathtaking views of the Manhattan skyline from this remodelled barge beneath the Brooklyn Bridge more than compensate for occasional lapses in the cooking – and these deficiencies are infrequent, the result of daring rather than indifference. The culinary mix is one part classic Gallic conceit, one part chauvinistic produce. Ingredients are Key West shrimp, Smithfield ham, California snails, New Jersey pheasants – resolutely American – but the twin sauces, aspics and terrines cry out their

Old World origins. Furnishings here are agreeable – bamboo, bentwood and the requisite portholes – but the decor is the vista, which reaches from the Statue of Liberty to the Empire State Building. The best time to be there is at dusk, when interior illumination is kept low. A piano is played, and tables are set out on the terrace in summer. Sunday brunch is popular, and reservations are always essential.

The Russian Tea Room
150 W 57th St. (near 7th Ave.), NY 10019 ☎265–0947. Map 4N3 ▥▭▯ ▦ AE CB ◐ ◑ ◓ VISA *Open Sun–Fri 11.30–1.00. Sat 11.30–2.00.*

Restaurants where celebrities gather are notorious for indifferent food, but here is an exception. A number of eccentricities endear the Tea Room to Princess Grace of Monaco, Woody Allen, Jackie O, the Aga Khan, Diana Rigg, Rudolf Nureyev, Liza Minnelli, Joseph Heller and Max von Sydow (to drop the names of some regular customers). There is the fact that it really does serve superb Russian food, a cuisine not in great favour in these parts. Also Christmas decorations wreathe the light fixtures – all year. And none of the many clocks have the same time. Perhaps most of all, as violinist Isaac Stern said, it is "a private-professional club where the public is allowed". Non-celebrated folk with the wherewithal to afford attendance are *not*, however, permitted to approach the stars, which helps assure their frequent return. While gazing upon each other, they dip into the borscht, dine on salmon *kulebiaka* or *shashlik* or *luli kebab*, and rhapsodize over the finest grades of caviar. Surely the Tea Room will sail majestically into the next century, its slogan intact – 'Slightly to the left of Carnegie Hall'.

Sabor ☛
20 Cornelia St. (near Bleecker St.), NY 10014 ☎243–9579. Map 2R3 ▯▭ ▦ AE ◐ VISA *Open daily 18.00–23.00.*

Cuban food is direct and unassuming, a blending of dishes from the Iberian homeland with the ingredients and tang of the Caribbean. There isn't a better place in the city to make its acquaintance than Sabor. The setting is a narrow former storefront on a tatty side street in the Village, the principal decorative element of which is a 19thC stamped tin ceiling. Start with a birdbath-sized Margarita, made with fresh lime. Move on to plump, tender mussels dressed in a saffron-tomato sauce or to *escabeche* (a cool firm piece of fish hidden beneath a blanket of crisp pickled vegetables). *Pollo con comino* is boneless baked chicken breast marinated in lime juice, cumin and garlic, accompanied by strips of onion and sweet pepper. Don't be put off by the implications of *ropa vieja* – 'old clothes' – for this Cuban classic is in fact shredded beef tossed in a piquant sauce of tomato, cloves and cinnamon. There isn't an ounce of pretension or a mis-step in taste from entrance to departure.

Salta in Bocca ☛
179 Madison Ave. (near 33rd St.), NY 10016 ☎684–1757. Map 5P4 ▥▯ ▭ AE ◐ ◑ VISA *Open Mon–Sat 12.00–15.00, 17.00–22.30.*

It is an inexplicable truism that the most sublime of dishes in northern Italian restaurants are often not listed on the menu. Patrons must ask, or hope, that the captain will volunteer the information. At Salta in Bocca, the tasteful cornmeal known as *polenta* falls into this secretive category. It arrives with a variety of garnishes, all tasty. The Italians are the only Europeans who regard maize to be edible in any form, but that is to the profit of Bolognese and Manhattanites. Pasta dishes can be shared as an appetizer, and the management doesn't mind if a couple does the same with mussels or clams. This reasonableness is carried through to the prices. Although Salta in Bocca rivals the best in town, the final accounting is within the grasp of almost any budget. Simply ignore the dreadful paintings and arrive for dinner, not lunch.

Sardi's
234 W 44th St. (near Broadway), NY 10036 ☎221–8440. Map 4O3 ▥▭▯ ▦ AE CB ◐ ◑ ◓ VISA *Open daily, 11.30–24.30.*

Food is nearly an irrelevance in a place that achieved the status of a theatrical institution decades ago. Probably it is a trick of memory, or youthful naivety, but the *fettucine* and 'devilled roast beef bones' seemed pretty good back then. But who cares? This is a repository of showbiz caricatures – hundreds of them – and was the meeting place of table-hopping stars and gossip columnists in the heyday of Helen Hayes, the Lunts and Walter Winchell. Celebrities still drop in after their curtain calls and enjoy patters of applause from the other diners even if their current plays were demolished by the critics. Identifying the persons depicted in those drawings that line the walls also distracts attention from the plate.

Say Eng Look ♥

5 E Broadway (near Chatham Sq.), NY 10012 ☎732–0796. Map 3T5 ☐ ☐ ▦ AE CB VISA Open Mon–Thurs, Sun 11.00–22.00; Fri, Sat 11.00–23.00.

In Chinatown, decor comes in two versions: bleakly illuminated plastic or unspeakably garish plastic. Try to ignore the appalling crimson and black fittings here and concentrate on the food. The visual sacrifice is then rendered immaterial. Fill yourself to bursting on fried fish with seaweed, spicy carp, stewed pork in bean curd sheet. Little is likely to disappoint. Avoid Fri and Sat when queues of eager eaters snake out of the door and into the street. At these gratifyingly low prices, such popularity is understandable.

Shezan ♥

8 W 58th St. (5th Ave.), NY 10019 ☎371–1414. Map 5N4 ▮▮▮ ☐ AE CB VISA Open Mon–Fri 12.00–14.30, 18.00–23.00, Sat 18.00–23.00.

The sub-street setting might have been gloomy, but the management chose soft grey wall carpeting, reflective ceilings and diffused illumination that expanded space and muffled noise. Those who wish them can request authentically fiery seasonings for the Pakistani-northern Indian food; otherwise, Occidentals will be brought dishes that do not sear the roof of the mouth. Given the slightest encouragement, the captains dispense continuous avuncular advice about selections and preparations – not always correct, but often amusing. A request to split individual choices among the patrons at a table is always honoured – a good idea for

the uninitiated. Napkins are spread upon laps, crumbs are brushed away, plates are hot.

Shun Lee West

43 W 65th St. (near Broadway), NY 10023 ☎595–8895. Map 6M3 ▮▮▮ ☐ AE Open daily 12.00–15.00, 17.00–24.00.

The newest in a chain that introduced high style in Chinese restaurants – **Shun Lee Dynasty**, Shun Lee Palace – this one serves Lincoln Center. It is a happy diversion from, and improvement upon, the quiche-and-burger emporia that dominate the neighbourhood. One might even go there simply to eat, rather than to fuel up for a session of Puccini or Bach. The decor is essentially what was left behind by an unlamented French *boîte* – sedate, just a bit frayed, but preferable to the pervasive plastics of Chinatown. The proprietors introduced New Yorkers to the spicy Szechuan and Hunan cuisines, and the chili oil is shaken with a generous hand, if requested. An agreeable notion is the after-concert *dim sum* supper (from 22.00), when a full meal might rest too heavily in the stomach.

Sichuan Pavilion

322 E 44th St. (near 2nd Ave.), NY 10017 ☎986–3775. Map 5O5 ▮▮▮ ☐ AE CB ✦ ◎ VISA Open daily 12.00–23.00.

Authenticity is overrated, as can be attested by anyone who has braved some of the cherished peasant stews of the Mediterranean. Yet the infatuation with Sichuan (*née Szechuan*) preparations doubtless produced travesties, and who could complain of the importation of ten chefs from the People's Republic to bring enlightenment? Many of the recipes presented are unique to this restaurant. One could only wish that the management had also brought over an authentic decorator as well.

SoHo Charcuterie

195 Spring St. (Sullivan St.), NY 10012 ☎226–3545. Map 2S4 ▮▮▮▮ ☐ AE ✦ ◎ VISA Open Mon–Wed 12.00–15.00, 18.00–23.00, Thurs–Fri 12.00–15.30, 18.00–23.30, Sat 11.00–16.00, 18.00–23.30, Sun 11.00–16.30. Closed July (two weeks), Aug.

At the front is a Frenchified

delicatessen, deep in sausages and imported smoked salmon and imaginatively shaped breads. In the back, self-consciously stringent decor prevails, a meld of high-tech and bentwood and bare polished floors. The fabrications brought to the table slide from the extravagantly simplistic (strips of raw red beef) to compilations of divers ingredients in which colour, shape, line and texture are paramount. Some of each work, but at prices that rival those of uptown eateries in which dash and discipline are in more predictable balance. Under the circumstances, weekend brunch is the best bet.

Sparks

210 E 46th St. (near 3rd Ave.), NY 10017 ☎*687–4855. Map 5 O5* ▨▨▨
▭ ▬ AE CB ⊕ ⊙ VISA *Open Mon–Fri 12.00–23.00, Sat 18.00–23.30.*

Despite its aggressive advertising to the contrary, Sparks doesn't quite measure up to the steakhouses of glossier reputation. On one important count, however, it surpasses all of them. Indeed, few restaurants of any category can match its inventory of fine wines. European wine buffs can here test the remarkable vintages of California, from Robert Mondavi and Sterling, to Mirassou and dozens of other estimable products. There are French, Spanish and Italian bottles, too. Between sips, stick to the simplest of beef preparations.

Spring Street Restaurant

149 Spring St. (near W Broadway), NY 10012 ☎*966–0290. Map 2 S4* ▨▨ ▭ AE ⊕ ⊙ VISA *Open daily 11.30–4.00.*

SoHo has a number of pub-restaurants of this bubbling, lively sort, in which it is possible to drop in for a beer and stay until the small hours. Its predominantly young clients don't dress up to come here: mountaineer-casual is the mode, but pressed and polished, for this is an important meeting place. Perhaps because they are young and have other things on their minds, they don't seem to object to the lack of delicacy in the food preparation. They might have a point: what appears from the clangorous kitchen is usually satisfying, sometimes imaginative and – in a city where dinner can empty pockets fast – relatively cheap.

Takesushi

71 Vanderbilt Ave. (near 46th St.), NY 10017 ☎*867–5120. Map 5 O4* ▨▨ ▭ ▬ ▾ AE CB ⊕ ⊙ VISA *Open Mon–Fri 12.00–14.30, 17.30–22.00, Sat 17.00–22.00. Closed Sun.*

Sushi and *sashimi* – raw fish with and without rice – are sufficiently commonplace now to draw distinctions between their purveyors. Many *sushi* chefs pursue their craft with a *ninja's* fierce solemnity. That can be off-putting, especially for a neophyte diner who would like a little advice along with the dazzling knifemanship. Friendliness is a hallmark of this branch of a growing family-owned chain, from the barman in the bamboo-and-slate vestibule to the kimonoed waitresses and the chefs themselves. While their command of the English language runs from not bad to unintelligible, they go out of their way to gently instruct on the niceties of this specialized sort of eating. They might urge that you begin with the unadorned buttery-soft 'fatty tuna', or that you stir a little horseradish in your dish of soy sauce, or that the yellowtail rolled with rice in seaweed sheets is best eaten with the fingers, not chopsticks. It results in a far more gratifying evening of culinary theatre than at those places where the eating of uncooked fish is regarded as a mystic ritual.

Tavern On The Green

Central Park W (67th St.), NY 10023 ☎*873–3200. Map 6 M3* ▨▨▨ ▭ ▬ AE CB ⊕ ⊙ VISA *Open Mon–Fri 12.00–16.00, 17.30–1.00, Sat 11.00–1.00, Sun 10.00–1.00.*

Tavern On The Green is something that must be mentioned simply because it is there and everybody knows about it. Once a barn for the sheep that wandered in the adjacent meadow, it has been a restaurant for much of this century. Successive managements have consistently fallen short in matching the dining experience to the promise of the building and the park surroundings. The latest to try is a Mr Leroy, of the flamboyant East Side **Maxwell's Plum**, an apostle of the 'eat-with-the-eyes' theory of restaurateurship. It is virtually provocative, crammed with carved plaster, etched mirrors and brass, crystal and copper ornamentation in copious profusion. It is also noisy, disorganized, and pretentiously cute. The food can be good, but it is impossible to predict which dishes at what hours. The service is erratic.

Thailand
106 Bayard St. (Mulberry St.), NY 10013 ☎*349–3132. Map 2T4* ▨ ▭ ▨ *Open Tues–Sun 11.00–23.00.*

It might seem sacrilegious to venture into Thai food while in Chinatown, for a year of uninterrupted consumption would not exhaust the Szechuan, Mandarin, Cantonese and Hunan cuisines to be sampled in its perhaps 200 restaurants. But this admittedly seedy little place across from Columbus Park deserves consideration, and its prices are as low as any in the neighbourhood. The menu is bewilderingly comprehensive, with nearly 100 listed items. A party of four can take advantage of the variety.

Trattoria da Alfredo
90 Bank St. (Hudson St.), NY 10014 ☎*929–4400. Map 2R3* ▨ ▭ *Open Wed–Mon 12.00–14.00, 18.00–22.00. Closed Tues and for three to four weeks in June/July.*

There are several good reasons why it is necessary to make reservations a week or more in advance for Trattoria da Alfredo. It can seat no more than 32 people at a time, has a loyal following, eschews fussiness in preparation, sends forth some of the best pasta dishes in town, and is so inexpensive that the management finds it necessary to impose a minimum tariff at dinner. Part of the explanation for this last uncommon circumstance is that they serve no wines or spirits. You bring your own, thereby saving the 100–150% mark-up imposed by fully licensed restaurants.

21 (Twenty-one) Club
21 W 52nd St. (near 5th Ave.), NY 10019 ☎*582–7200. Map 5N4* ▥ ▭ ▨ ▨ ▨ ▨ *Open Mon–Sat 12.00–24.00. Closed Sat in summer and Sun.*

Once a Prohibition-era speakeasy, '21' went on to become a sanctuary for the power elite. Celebrities are on view, but the carefully tonsured and garbed regulars that frequent the place are more often senior

partners in important law firms, executives of multi-national corporations, or the men who decide who will be permitted to run for political office. It is not a club in the sense that the general public is excluded, but strangers are granted no more than distant courtesy.

Un Deux Trois (One Two Three)
123 W 44th St. (near Times Sq.), NY 10020 ☎*354–4148. Map 4O3* ▨ ▭ ▨ ▨ *Open Mon–Fri 11.30–14.30, 17.30–23.30. Sat–Sun 18.00–23.30*

Its allegiance to the brasserie archetype is not slavish, but with purple handwritten menus, paper tablecloths and hearty rather than delicate victuals, the point is made. At lunch, its clients run to executive sorts, but at nightfall, a disco-theatre crowd prone to spiky hair and violet cheek bones mingles with specimens of the Concorde Set. Selections from the regular *carte* are preferable to the daily specials.

Uzie's
1444 3rd Ave. (82nd St.), NY 10028 ☎*744–8020. Map 7L5* ▨ ▭ ▨ ▨ ▨ ▨ ▨ *Open Sat–Sun 12.00–16.00, Mon–Fri 18.00–24.00.*

With the same ownership and kitchen and basic menu as **Hoexter's Cafe**, it draws the same upscale clientele and is really quite good, if less than memorable. Service is often inconsistent. Weekend brunches are special.

Vanessa ⌂
289 Bleecker St. (7th Ave.), NY 11014 ☎*243–4225. Map 2R4* ▨ ▭ ▤ ▨ ▨ ▨ ▨ ▨ *Open daily 18.00–24.00.*

Elegance is not to be expected in artily iconoclastic Greenwich Village. But here is an exception. The handsome space is painted a creamy plum, with glints of brass, and floors and fixtures of bare oak. The staff, in pink shirts and white aprons, appears to be comprised of young careerists rather than the usual theatrical hopefuls. They bring staples of the New American tradition – free-range poultry, gulf shrimp, duck *foie gras* – but in less slavishly nationalistic renditions than others of the breed. The debt to older Continental culinary conceits is not disguised, and taste and presentation take precedence over bogus 'authenticity'.

Appetizers and desserts are best. Comforting touches abound, with taped classical and jazz on the sound system and flowers and cloth towels in the restrooms. While not cheap, prices are markedly lower than at similar uptown enterprises of lesser accomplishment. Business suits dominate.

Le Veau d'Or
*129 E 60th St. (near Park Ave.),
NY 10022* ☎ *838–8133. Map
5N4* 📶 🖵 AE *Open Mon–Sat
12.00–14.30, 18.00–22.15.*

If there has ever been a moment when this place was not packed with ravenous humanity, it has escaped the memory of its habitués. Staff and patrons are a congenial lot though, patient with each other in the presentation and consumption of consistently good food. Something more than a bistro but less than a *temple de cuisine*, it manifests none of the frequent hyper-trendiness of the former nor the often plodding solemnity of the latter. Walls are chock-a-block with travel posters, Parisian street signs, inconsequential paintings and objects of vague or specific Gallic origin. Seating is fairly comfortable, although it is necessary to guard against dipping your elbow in your neighbour's *vichyssoise*. Go in an attitude of cheerful anticipation and you will be rewarded.

Vienna '79 ⌂
*35 E 60th St. (near Park Ave.), NY
10021* ☎ *758–1051. Map 5N4* 📶
🖵 ━ AE CB ◉ ◉ VISA *Open daily
17.30–23.30. Closed last week of
Aug, first week of Sept, also Sun
June–Sept.*

One influential critic rated this among the best restaurants in town, another deemed it merely adequate. Reality lies somewhere between. The room is on the small side, and despite acoustic ceiling tiles and carpeting, somewhat noisy. But the colours are warm greys, mirrors along one wall expand space, and flowers in painted ceramic pots brighten the tables. The hosts are amiable professionals with impressive credentials who have chosen to purvey Austro-Germanic dishes of a lightness not usually associated with that form of cookery. *Nouvelle cuisine* it isn't, but neither is it leaden. Sauces are

reduced, not artificially thickened. Provender is snappingly fresh and treated gently. Every ingredient of every dish is arranged with an almost oriental regard for complementary hues and textures. Constituent parts are rarely less than satisfactory, and frequently sublime. Austrian wines are the best buys from a superior cellar.

Windows On The World
1 World Trade Center, NY 10048
☎ *928–1111. Map 2U4. Three
restaurants, all* 🖵 ▬ ━ AE CB
◉ ◉ VISA

The Cellar in the Sky 📶 *Open
Mon–Sat 19.30 (one seating).*
The Hors d'Oeuvrerie 📶 ♫
*Open Mon–Fri 15.00–1.00, Sat
12.00–1.00, Sun 12.00–15.00,
16.00–24.00.*
The Restaurant 📶 ◁€ *Open
Mon–Fri 17.00–22.00, Sat
12.00–15.00, Sun 12.00–19.30.*

There are three distinct eating places under the **Windows On The World** umbrella, all of them in the N tower on the 107th floor. Getting past the demigod at the reception desk of **The Restaurant** can be a chore, but persevere, for it justifies the temporary aggravation. Surely there is no more stunning vista anywhere – sparkling spires, bands of winking sapphires, silvered waters and webs of bridges. All is made available to view from tiered tables in a muted spaceship environment. As is usual in rooftop restaurants, perfection on the plate proves elusive. The simplest offerings are the safest – terrines, liver ragoût, rack of lamb, roast duckling. The premise of **The Hors d'Oeuvrerie** is to make entire meals of appetizers, a gimmick that was overdue. The starter dishes of different countries – Chinese *dim sum*, Spanish *tapas* – are featured on a rotating monthly basis. Jazz performers are on duty from 16.30 until closing. Reservations are unnecessary. **The Cellar in the Sky** has no views, but attempts to compensate with ambitious seven-course meals enhanced by five different wines. They have only a single sitting each evening for a maximum of 36 diners. Reservations are essential for **The Cellar** and **The Restaurant**, often two or more weeks in advance. Avoid the hectic Sunday buffet and brunch. Wines available at the complex are often superb, and reasonably priced.

Nightlife

On the evidence of what is available, it might be inferred that half the population of New York never sees the light of day. Following cocktails and dinner, there can be opera, ballet, a symphony concert, a Broadway musical. After that, they can choose the late show at a cabaret or supper club, or drop in at a disco or jazz loft. Many places stay open until 4.00, and most revellers find that enough. But the hardy and knowledgeable move on to after-hours bars, essentially illegal and with the lifespan of a fruit fly, but thriving. Finally, perhaps, they decompress with croissants or bagels at a 24hr Art Deco diner.

The rest of us, however, must make choices – but before we do, some considerations. Apart from on opening nights, theatres impose no dress codes. Many restaurants, nightclubs and discos do, however, if only to prohibit denim clothing. That being the case, it is advisable to plan an evening with an eye on compatible districts and events. For instance, don your dressiest outfit and combine a deluxe restaurant with the trendiest of discos or cabarets, all on the East Side. For an evening in SoHo-Greenwich Village, jeans and a sweater will do for a pub crawl, dinner, and a jazz or rock club. Something in between is suitable for opera or ballet at the Lincoln Center, a post-theatre supper and intimate conversation at a piano bar, all on the West Side.

Liquor laws are liberal. Establishments servicing alcoholic beverages are required to close between 4.00 and 8.00 (4.00 and 12.00 on Sun), although most do not open before 11.00 and lock up whenever business is slow. Anyone of 21 and over can purchase liquor, although some bars and clubs set a higher age limit and require two items of positive identification.

Bars and clubs offering live entertainment often fix a 'cover' charge that is, in effect, an admission fee; and the range can be considerable, depending on the standard or elaborateness of the show. In discos it tends to rise with the chicness of the place. It might be collected at the door or simply added to the bill. Typically, in such places, there is also a 'minimum' charge for consumption of beverages and/or food, per person.

Fine food and music are rarely found in combination. Getting something to eat – a hamburger, a bowl of chili – is nearly always possible, but in general expect no more than alleviation of hunger pangs. Exceptions are such establishments as **The Ballroom** in Chelsea, which serves excellent food and lays on cabaret and dancing, and **Greene Street**, where the owner is determined to create an all-inclusive dining-and-entertainment complex (for these two see *Restaurants*).

To learn who is appearing where, consult the entertainment listings of the Fri and Sun editions of *The New York Times*, the weekly magazines *New York* and *The New Yorker*, and, for more off-beat diversions, the weekly newspaper *The Village Voice*. Even then, call ahead for bookings and to inquire about last-minute changes in hours and performers.

There has been no attempt here to locate sexually-oriented clubs, theatres, massage parlours or cinemas. They soon make themselves apparent, and in any case are too ephemeral for print. It is sufficient to note that all predilections are accommodated. For guidance, check *The Village Voice* and that tasteful journal, *Screw*. Prostitution is illegal, although that does not dissuade its practitioners. While street-walkers are flamboyantly visible around Times Sq., their sisters who work hotel bars are cautious and less readily identifiable.

Ballet

Surely no other city enjoys ballet in such abundance and variety. In addition to a dozen or more locally-based companies, the troupes of other cities and nations are regular visitors. There are four principal venues.

Brooklyn Academy of Music
30 Lafayette Ave. (downtown Brooklyn), NY 11217 ☎*636–4100. Map 12D2.*
Known for the biennial seasons of the Pennsylvania Dance Company, among others.

City Center
131 W 55th St., NY 10019 ☎*246–8989. Map 4N3.*
The Joffrey Ballet, the Alvin Ailey Dance Theater, and the Paul Taylor Dance Company.

Metropolitan Opera House
Lincoln Center, NY 10023 ☎*580–9830. Map 6M3.*
Host for the American Ballet Theater, of which Mikhail Baryshnikov is the artistic director.

New York State Theater
Lincoln Center, NY 10023 ☎*870–5570. Map 6M3.*
Home of the New York City Ballet.

Bars

Passing the night in a bar (or several) is a common diversion and, except when it becomes an addiction, not as decadent as it sounds. Certainly there are hundreds of bars devoted to nothing more elevating than the diligent consumption of alcohol. But the owners know that success lies in distractions. These may be no more than the preservation of antique trappings – stamped tin ceiling, potbellied stove, stained-glass window – but can escalate into exciting meals, collections of imported beers and wines, live music and entertainments of every description, or disco dancing. Alternatively, it may be simply a matter of creating the kind of environment that attracts crowds of likeminded seekers-after-companionship. The roster that follows merely indicates the possibilities. Unless otherwise noted, all bars are open seven days a week, usually from 11.00 or noon until at least 2.00, and serve food.

Fake Tiffany lamps and dark-stained plywood too often substitute for atmosphere in American bars, along with inept imitations of that untransplantable institution, the British pub. Exceptions exist, however. **Fanelli's** (*94 Prince St. in SoHo* ☎*226–9412, closed Sat, Sun*) predates the Civil War, and looks it. Neighbourhood working men share it with the recent artistic immigrants. **McSorley's Old Ale House** (*15 E 7th St.* ☎*473–8800*) is even older, and did not miss a working day during the 13yr experiment called Prohibition. About a decade ago, they grudgingly allowed women inside the door. There still isn't a sign to mark **Chumley's** (*86 Bedford St. in Greenwich Village* ☎*243–9729*), and it retains the Bohemian aura of Edna St Vincent Millay and Eugene O'Neill. Yellowing book jackets of former clients line the walls, and there is a working fireplace in winter. Good 'burgers, too. O. Henry was a regular patron of **Pete's Tavern** (*129 E 18th St.* ☎*473–7676*), which opened in 1864. They have sidewalk tables for warm weather dining, with mostly Italian food. **McFeely's** (*656 W 23rd St.* ☎*929–4432*) breathes its Victorian origins and adds a fairly ambitious fare supplemented by live piano. The venerable **P.J. Clarke's** (*915 3rd Ave. at 55th St.* ☎*759–1650*) remains dark and cobwebby in the corners, with sawdust beneath the feet, an archetypal Irish saloon; but the clientele wears three-piece suits now, and chatters of media campaigns and TV audience shares. **Charlie's** (*263 W 45th St.* ☎*354–2911*) mirrors Clarke's, but with less obviously upmarket custom. **The White Horse Tavern** (*W Hudson St. and 11th St.* ☎*243–9260*) was established in Greenwich Village in 1880. Dylan Thomas, Norman Mailer, poet Delmore Schwartz and Brendan Behan gathered there. British pub grub – shepherd's pie, steak and mushroom pie – is on the menu of the 1868 **Landmark Tavern** (*626 11th Ave. at 46th St.* ☎*757–8595*). Drop in after the theatre, but before 24.00, or for Sunday brunch.

Bars with shorter histories but as much atmosphere include:
Blue Mill Tavern   50 Commerce St. (in Greenwich Village) ☎243–7114. A former Prohibition speakeasy
Broome Street Bar   363 W Broadway (in SoHo) ☎925–2086
Harvey's Chelsea   108 W 18th St. ☎243–5644. Tavern restaurant
The Lion's Head   59 Christopher St. (in Greenwich Village) ☎929–0670
Molly Malone's   287 3rd Ave. (in Gramercy Park) ☎725–8375

Wine bars, in which the titular tipple is the only one available, are receiving increased acceptance. Among them are the appropriately designated **Claret's** (*33 E 60th St.* ☎*758–1051*), the **Wine Bar** (*422 W Broadway, in SoHo* ☎*431–4790*), and **Tastings** (*144 W 55th St.* ☎*757–1160*).

Desperate loneliness pervades hotel bars, and the occupants seem to exude their disinclination to venture more than 100ft from their bedrooms. Among the dozen exceptions, so engaging that even New Yorkers stop in, are **Bemelman's Bar** in the plush **Carlyle** (*Madison Ave. and 76th St.* ☎*744–1600*). Jazz piano is the backdrop, and the justification for the cover charge. The **Blue Bar** at the **Algonquin Hotel** (*59 W 44th St. near 5th Ave.* ☎*840–6800*) is a snuggery that burbles with talk of book packages and theatrical contretemps. Bankers' pinstripes dominate at the handsome **Oak Room** of the **Plaza** (*5th Ave. and 59th St.* ☎*759–3000*) where the principal diversion is eavesdropping on the collision of egos.

The hope of human contact, of conversation, however brief, is a primary motive for bar-hopping. When it became clear that increasing numbers of unmarried people were choosing to retain that status, the 'singles bar' became an explicit entity. Few unencumbered folk admit to visiting such places, which leaves open the question of why they flourish nevertheless. And, of course, they fall into categories, subject to unpredictable change and fashion. Most are for practising heterosexuals, but some are for those of minority persuasions. Allegiances shift, but for the majority interest try:
Boodles   1478 1st Ave. (near 77th St.) ☎628–0900
Friday's   1152 1st Ave. at 63rd St. ☎832–8512
Grass   1445 1st Ave. at 75th St. ☎737–3328
The Greenery   1340 1st Ave. (near 72nd St.) ☎570–0060
Jim McMullen's   1341 3rd Ave. at 77th St. ☎861–4700

It will be noted that these are all within an extended crawl of each other, which is, of course, what most habitués (or habituées) plan. Other places of a similar kind will be encountered along the way.

Cabarets and supper clubs

Gorgeous chorines (as chorus-girls were known), over-plumed and under-dressed, once descended sweeping silvery staircases to the strains of Cole Porter, attended by top-hatted tap-dancing young men. Those days are gone, except in Las Vegas, but leaner versions persist, with contemporary variations. Expect cover charges and indifferent food at unjustified prices.

Amazonas
*492 Broome St. (near W
Broadway), NY 10013*
☎966–3371. Map 2S4 ☰♫❤
Æ CB ◉ Open Mon–Thurs, Sun
18.30–23.30, Fri, Sat 17.30–1.30.
Here is a supper club with an
ingredient usually missing at such
establishments: good food. It is
Brazilian, with a superb seafood
stew called *mariscada* heading the
list. Peruse the menu over a
caipirinha, the potent national
cocktail that blends sugar-cane
brandy and lime juice. More or less
continuous live renditions of the
infectious salsa beat keep diners
moving in their seats.

Café Versailles
*151 E 50th St. (between
Lexington and 3rd), NY 10022*
☎753–3471. Map 5O4 ☰♫
CB ◉ ◉ VISA Open Tues–Sun
17.00–4.00. Closed Sun, Mon.
This is as close as New York comes
to the traditional revues of such
fabled Parisian nightclubs as the
Lido and Moulin Rouge. The
energetic cast of female
impersonators, comics and comely
showgirls zips through its paces so
deftly that the viewer hardly
notices that the entire endeavour
seems a trifle worn and dated in our
jaded age. There is no cover charge
if you eat dinner, and there is live
music before and between shows.

Chateau Madrid
*Lexington Ave. and 48th St., NY
10017* ☎752–8080. Map 5O4 ♫
♫❤▨ Æ CB ◉ ◉ VISA Open
*Tues–Sun 18.00–2.30. Closed
Mon.*
In one of the last refuges of the
showgirl revue, five to eight
shapely women strut and preen
through their routines with
admirable enthusiasm. While they
are no doubt immune to the
common cold, their scanty
costumes are not so much erotic as
mildly naughty. Children will see
nothing that they haven't already
seen on afternoon television.
Authentic flamenco dancing and
guitar playing are performed in the
adjacent Flamenco Suite. To avoid
the cover charge, have dinner
before the first show.

Chippendales
*1110 1st Ave. (61st St.), NY
10021* ☎935–6060. Map 5N5 Æ
Open Wed–Sat 20.00–4.00.
It's only fair: at this 'Ladies Only'
show, girls get to ogle muscular
young waiters without shirts and
equally blessed colleagues who
take off nearly all their clothes to a
disco beat. The male strippers
have their set routine – cowboy,
motorcycle copper, Zorro,
whatever – just like their female
counterparts. The more daring
members of the squealing audience
stuff dollar notes into the
G-strings of the dancers in
expectation of a kiss and an overt
squeeze of glistening flesh. Alien
males are permitted to enter after
22.30.

Copacabana
*10 E 60th St. (5th Ave.), NY
10022* ☎755–6010. Map 5N4 ◉
♫♫❤ Æ CB ◉ ◉ VISA Open
*Thurs 17.00–21.00, Fri, Sat
22.00–5.00. Closed Sun–Wed.*
Hollywood and Las Vegas
performers have appeared here,
but this isn't the 'Copa' of the
1940s and 1950s. That it still
exists, even in this truncated form,
is surprising. A dance band plays
upstairs, recorded contemporary
sounds downstairs (Fri, Sat only).

Freddy's Supper Club
*308 E 49th St. (near 2nd Ave.),
NY 10017* ☎888–1633. Map
5O5 ☰ Æ ◉ VISA Open Mon–Sat
18.00–2.00. Closed Sun.
Pop singers and comedians are the
usual attractions, but Freddy's is
best known as the frequent
showcase of impressionist Charles
Pierce. He stars in a revue of his
own creation in which he plays all
the major roles. It is essentially a
parade of uncanny simulations of
famous film stars and other
performers, all female. There are
two shows on Fri and Sat, only one
the other nights.

153

Ibis
151 E 50th St. (near Lexington Ave.), NY 10022 ☎734–3884. Map 5O4 ♪ ♫ AE CB ⊕ ⊙ VISA Open 18.00–2.30.

Long an apostle of the splashy floor show with barely draped chorus girls and forgettable blaring music, Ibis now features singing stars of the second magnitude, Eartha Kitt and Della Reese among them. Two shows every night except Mon, with cover and minimum charges. Upstairs, a small room is given over to the ripples and bangles of belly-dancers.

King Cole Room
In the St Regis-Sheraton Hotel, 5th Ave. and 55th St., NY 10022 ☎753–4500. Map 5N4 ♪ ♫ ⚞ AE CB ⊕ ⊙ VISA Open 18.00–4.00.

The revues, featuring experienced professionals, are generally built around the music of such legendary composers as Jerome Kern or George Gershwin (no show on Sun). Food is not memorable, but the Maxfield Parrish mural is.

Les Mouches
*559 W 26th St. (11th Ave.), NY 10001 ☎695–5190. Map 4P2 ●
♪ ♫ ✦ AE CB ⊕ ⊙ VISA Open 20.00–4.00. Closed Sun, Mon, Tues.*

Slick cabaret acts are the staple, put together to showcase mostly female singers from the Broadway and pop worlds. These are presented in the dining area, separate from the disco. It isn't cheap to see the show, but it's a good way to cap an exploration of the resurgent Chelsea district.

Rainbow Grill
*30 Rockefeller Plaza (RCA Building), NY 10017
☎757–8970. Map 5O4 ♪ ♫ ♪ ♫
⚞ ✦ AE CB ⊕ ⊙ VISA Open 19.00–2.30. Closed Sun.*

Kicks is the name of the long-running revue, with a Francophile accent. Splendid views from the 65th floor. Across the hall is the Art Deco splendour of the Rainbow Room with live music for dancing.

The Red Parrot
*617 W 57th St. (11th Ave.), NY 10019 ☎247–1530. Map 4N2 ♪
♪ ♫ Open 20.00–4.00. Closed Mon, Tues.*

Those who have bemoaned the near death of big band music since rock and roll now take heart with the substantial popularity of this immense new club in the shadow of the West Side Highway. The orchestra plays for dancing far into the night, choosing from a repertoire from swing to country.

Sounds of Brazil
*204 Varick St. (near Houston St.), NY 10014 ☎243–4940. Map 2S3
⚟ ♪ ♫ AE VISA Open Wed–Sun 18.00–4.00. Closed Mon, Tues.*

Familiarly known as 'S.O.B.', this colourful and persistently lively club is known more for its Latin American and African dance music than for the merely serviceable Brazilian food. It is frequented by a buoyant cosmopolitan crowd that is not even distracted by the offhanded decor, largely comprised of masks and hanging gourds. Dinner is served from 19.00, and the admission charge is lower if you eat there. Fri and Sat are the big nights.

Cinema
Films are of profound conern to many New Yorkers, often to the point of reverence. In strongmindedly rejecting the foolishness of the notorious Cannes event, for example, the **New York Film Festival** (*Alice Tully Hall, Lincoln Center, mid-Sept to early Oct*) overcompensates on the side of solemnity. No prizes are awarded, no starlets drop their bras, and few outsiders notice that anything happened. Worthwhile films are introduced, nonetheless, some of which go on to limited release. 'Art' films – usually foreign-made and of limited domestic appeal – are showcased by managers who no doubt pray for the occasional hit. A few of these do happen. All are sub-titled.

Theatres specializing in such films include:

Art   36 E 8th St. (near University Pl.) ☎473–7014
Cinema Studio   Broadway (66th St.) ☎877–4040
Cinema 3   59th St. (near 5th Ave.) ☎752–5959

Film Forum   57 Watts St. (near Greenwich St.) ☎431–1590
D. W. Griffith   235 E 59th St. (near 2nd Ave.), ☎759–4630
Lincoln Plaza   Broadway (near 63rd St.) ☎757–2280
Little Carnegie   146 W 57th St. (7th Ave.) ☎246–5123
Little Theatre   425 Lafayette St. (near 4th St.) ☎598–7171
Paris   4 W 58th St. (near 5th Ave.) ☎688–2013
68th St. Playhouse   3rd Ave. (68th St.) ☎734–0302

In addition, several cinemas specialize in revivals, often in 'festival' or retrospective form. They can be high-minded or high camp, composed of films, foreign or domestic, and anything from one to 50yr old.

Such cinemas include:
Bleecker St. Cinema   144 Bleecker St. (LaGuardia Pl.)
☎674–2560
Carnegie Hall Cinema   7th Ave. (57th St.) ☎757–2131
Cinema Village   33 E 12th St. (near University Pl.)
☎924–3363
8th St. Playhouse   52 W 8th St. (near 6th Ave.) ☎674–6515
Hollywood Twin Cinema   8th Ave. (47th St.) ☎246–0717
Regency   Broadway (67th St.) ☎724–3700
Thalia   Broadway (95th St.) ☎222–3370
Theatre   80 St. Marks Pl. (near 1st Ave.) ☎254–7400

Several museums have regular film programmes, the most comprehensive being at the **Museum of Modern Art** (*11 W 53rd St. (6th Ave.) ☎956–7070*).

Classical music

Avery Fisher Hall (*Lincoln Center ☎874–2424*) is home for the New York Philharmonic. Chamber orchestras, string quartets and instrumentalists are heard at **Alice Tully Hall** (*Lincoln Center ☎362–1911*). The National Orchestra of New York uses **Carnegie Hall** (*57th St. and 7th Ave. ☎247–7459*), while groups and individual artists use the attached **Carnegie Recital Hall** (*performances continue during extensive renovation*).

Other venues are:
Brooklyn Academy of Music   30 Lafayette Ave., Brooklyn
☎636–4100
Merkin Concert Hall   129 W 67th St. ☎362–8719
Town Hall   123 W 43rd St. ☎840–2824

Comedy

As an alternative to cabaret or a show, try stand-up comedy. Its most typical manifestation is in the form of showcase clubs, in which parades of would-be comics are given opportunities to test their material before live audiences. Should you attend, don't sit near the stage unless you are prepared to be the object of the performers' jibes. Non-Americans and even non-New Yorkers are apt to find many references obscure.

Caroline's
332 8th Ave. (26th St.), NY 10001 ☎924–3499. Map 4P3 [AE]
[CD] [VISA] *Open Tues–Sun 20.00–4.00. Closed Mon.*
Selectivity is the rule here, for most of the performers in the spotlight have garnered at least a measure of journalistic or television attention. They are given time to develop their material, with less pressure from queues of novice comedians standing anxiously about for their turns. The surroundings are not as barren either, with mirrors and neon sculptures brightening the walls. Expect high prices.

Catch a Rising Star
1487 1st Ave. (78th St.), NY 10028 ☎794–1906. Map 7L5 [♪]
[♪] [AE] [CD] *Open 20.00–3.00.*
Continuous streams of singers and

comedians, all unpaid, but so anxious to perform that they queue every week for auditions. Two masters of ceremonies keep the pace brisk. Much of the humour is ethnic, very local in origin, and often mystifying to outlanders.

Comic Strip
1568 2nd Ave. (near 81st St.), NY 10028 ☎*861–9386. Map 7L5* 🔊 🄰🄴 🄲🄱 🔘 🄲🄲 🆅🄸🅂🄰 *Open 18.00–3.00.*
One of the newer comedy showcases, with most of the qualities of the others. The emphasis is on fledgling comics, but with some singers. More misses than hits, but that's the nature of the game. Shows begin between 20.30 and 21.30.

Dangerfield's
1118 1st Ave. (near 61st St.), NY 10021 ☎*593–1650. Map 5N5* 🔊 🄰🄴 🔘 🆅🄸🅂🄰 *Open 20.00–3.00.*
Stand-up comic Rodney Dangerfield grew weary of life on the nightclub circuit and so opened his own place, where he now holds forth two or three times a night. When he is away on television, able comedians fill in. On Sun at 21.30, the stage is given to aspiring talents, some of them funny.

Good Times
449 3rd Ave. (31st St.), NY 10016 ☎*686–4250. Map 5P4* 🔊 🔊 🄰🄴 🄲🄲 🆅🄸🅂🄰 *Open 10.30–2.00.*

This is one of several showcase clubs where young comedians, singers, ventriloquists and others can try out their material on a live audience and pray that a producer will be sitting there and be impressed. A few of them make it. Arrive early as performances start around 21.30.

Improvisation
358 W 44th St. (near 9th Ave.), NY 10036 ☎*765–8268. Map 403* 🔊 🔊 *Open 20.00–3.00.*
The first of the showcase clubs, and therefore able to boast the longest list of alumni who went on to successful careers as comics and singers. The by-play between performers and hecklers can get vicious at times and it is painful to watch obvious failure. But people crowd in to hear the ones who have true promise.

Monkey Bar
In Elysee Hotel, 60 E 54th St. (near Park Ave.), NY 10022 ☎*753–1066. Map 5N4* 🔊 🔊 🄰🄴 🄲🄱 🔘 🄲🄲 🆅🄸🅂🄰 *Open 17.30–3.00. Closed Sun.*
Most hotel rooms traffic in soporific piano music, but the maverick **Elysee** has long chosen to present comedians, sometimes stand-up, sometimes in revue. They can be risqué, but not unusually so. There are few breaks, so the laughs are always frequent.

Country and western
New Yorkers, who prefer to think of themselves as worldly, were the last to adopt this otherwise blatant American genre. Responding some years back to a fad fuelled by such films as *Urban Cowboy*, they took to wearing snakeskin boots and pearl-button shirts, and supporting radio stations and clubs that specialized in the heartfelt plaints of Waylon Jennings and Willie Nelson. That burning fixation has faded to a flicker, but a few places carry on for hardcore enthusiasts. Foot-stompin' and bootin' by transplanted Texans from Houston and Brooklyn sets the walls atremble from 22.00 at **City Limits** (*125 7th Ave. S* ☎*243–2242*). **Cottonwood Cafe** (*415 Bleecker St.* ☎*924–6271*) is a little ol' chunk of Texas plonked down in Greenwich Village, but is so friendly and relaxed that even native New Yorkers fit right in. Distinctions blur at **Eagle Tavern** (*355 W 14th St.* ☎*924–0275*), for they mix bluegrass, country and Irish folk music on different nights. **Lone Star Cafe** (*5th Ave. and 13th St.* ☎*242–1664*) bills itself as "the biggest and best honky-tonk north of Abilene", and is the most popular country and western bar in New York. Second only to the Lone Star Cafe in the allegiance of local aficionados is **O'Lunney's** (*915 2nd Ave.* ☎*751–5470*). See also *Pop/folk/rock*.

Discos

Discotheques nearly disappeared after their 1960s heyday, then came back with a vengeance in the mid-1970s. Some are cavernous spaces ablaze with multi-million-dollar special effects that would do credit to *Star Wars*, others are simply cafes that shove aside a few tables after the dishes are cleared away. Most are expensive, with cover and minimum charges and stiff prices for drinks. The few membership-only clubs are not measurably better than those open to the general public, so none are listed here.

Adam's Apple
1117 1st Ave. (54th St.), NY 10022 ☎*371–8650. Map 5N5* ●
♥ AE CB ● ● VISA *Open 16.00–4.00.*
One of the survivors, this one has been around since the 1960s. There is a bar downstairs, dance floors upstairs, populated by young singles.

Area
157 Hudson St. (S of Canal St.), NY 10014 ☎*226–8423. Map 2T4* ● ♥ *Open Wed–Sat 20.00–4.00. Closed Sun–Tues.*

In competition with the **Palladium**, **Limelight** and **Visage** for the status of club-of-the-moment, the management chooses to redecorate the entire place every six weeks. The themes are usually aspects of conventional middle-class ideology or their institutions, and they are not held in a favourable light. The already frenetic atmosphere is thrown into audio-visual overload by jugglers, mimes, freaks and an entirely unpredictable cast of paid and unpaid performers. Being famous or rich or well-connected or severely strange are requisites for entrance. On many nights, even a combination of all four might not get you in through the door.

Library
Barbizon Plaza Hotel, 106 Central Park S (6th Ave.), NY 10019 ☎*247–7000. Map 5N4* ♥ AE *Open 16.30–3.00 (Sat, Sun 21.00–3.00).*
Perhaps it persists because it doesn't strive to be chic. As discos go, it is almost cosy, with shelves of real books on the walls. Men should wear jackets. The crowd mixed locals and out-of-towners.

Limelight
47 W 20th St. (5th Ave.), NY 10011 ☎*807–7850. Map 5Q4* ● ♥ AE *Open 20.00–4.00.*
At the instant of writing, this is the hottest disco in town. Tomorrow,

who knows? Ecclesiastical eyebrows bobbed at the opening, for the Limelight was once the Gothic Church of the Holy Communion. A confessional booth is the ticket office, stained-glass windows are intact and seating is in side chapels and on upholstered pews. Candles and lasers provide illumination. Androgynous models, flamboyant gays, S & M leathers and three-piece suits circulate around celebrities instantly recognizable by their first names.

Palladium
123 E 14th St. (between 3rd and 4th Ave.), NY 10003 ☎*473–7171. Map 5Q4* ● ♥ CB ● ● VISA *Open Wed–Sun 22.00–5.00. Closed Mon, Tues.*
The creators of the first **Studio 54** are back. As before their brief absence, they have set the night ablaze with another monument to frivolity, a seven-floor phantasmagoria that has attracted the largely positive attention of no less a presence than the architecture critic of *The New York Times*. Elements of the rococo theatre this once was are augmented with towering sculptural dividers, vast post-modern murals and clusters of TV monitors bouncing with the impressionistic imaginings of experimental video artists. Naturally, every member of – or aspirant to – the international glitterati presses through these doors. Even with over 100,000 square feet of space inside, admission cannot be assured. Those who make it are wise to nurse their drinks.

Regine's
502 Park Ave. (49th St.), NY 10022 ☎*826–0990. Map 5O4* ● ♥ AE CB ● ● VISA *Open 18.00–4.00. Closed Sun.*
The local branch of the flamboyant Parisienne's international chain. Pretty people and surroundings,

but outrageous prices. Dinner is served until 24.00, but don't go to eat, and nurse your drinks.

Roseland
239 W 52nd St. (near Broadway), NY.10019 ☎247–0200. *Map 4N3* ⊙ ◻ ⍩ *AE VISA Open Wed, Fri 18.00–2.00, Thurs, Sat, Sun 14.30–2.00.*
Over 60yr old and resisting repeated threats to its existence, this grand old ballroom carries on with two orchestras playing 1930s swing and 1940s Latin American rhythms until 23.00 each night. Then it switches to disco. All ages waltz or samba with each other or with professionals. Huge buffet-style restaurant.

Studio 54
254 W 54th St. (Broadway), NY 10019 ☎489–7667. *Map 4N3* ♪ ⊙ ⍩ *AE* ⊙ ⊙ *VISA Open Tues–Sun 22.00–4.00. Closed Mon.*
This is the one, world-famous and once packed with superstars and jetsetters. Now in its second incarnation, the paparazzi and celebrities are gone, leaving an odd mix of bizarros and suburbanites. The mob scenes at the entrance are markedly less frenetic than they once were, so unknowns are usually ushered through after a ritualistic pretence of exclusivity. They find vast spaces and an amusing light show.

Wednesday's
210 E 86th St. (near 3rd Ave.), NY 10028 ☎535–8500. *Map 7L5* ⊙ ♫ ♪ ⍩ *AE CB* ⊙ ⊙ *VISA Open 20.00–4.00, also Sun 12.00–17.00. Closed Mon.*
One of the first to exploit the emergence of a large class of unmarrieds subsequently described as 'swingles', this is an underground simulation of a stylized European village. Dance in its 'street', eat a hamburger or a full meal, listen to live jazz, and watch various other amusements.

Jazz

American's most exportable art form may have been born in New Orleans and journeyed up the Mississippi to Kansas City and Chicago, but the ultimate destination was New York. Jazz musicians were not – *are* not – certain of recognition until they appeared and were accepted here. One of their number was credited with the invention of that celebrated nickname for the metropolis: "I made it, brother, "I'm going to the Big Apple."

Jazz flourished and grew in New York from World War I into the 1950s. It hung on in the face of the onslaught of Elvis, The Beatles and their progeny. Now it is back, more vital than ever, and in all its permutations – Dixieland, swing, fusion, mainstream, bop, progressive, and wildly experimental. It is performed in old-line clubs on the scene for a half-century and in fifth-floor 'lofts' no more settled than Bedouins. Concerts are also mounted in the halls of colleges and churches all over town. Call the **Jazzline** – ☎718–465–7500 – for a daily recorded announcement. Here are 12 of the 50 possibilities.

Angry Squire
216 7th Ave. (23rd St.), NY 10011 ☎242–9066. *Map 4Q3* ♪ *Open 12.00–2.00 (Fri, Sat 12.00–4.00).*
Another pub-tavern contributing to the Chelsea renaissance, with fittingly British cookery that is at least as authentic as American hamburgers in London. The music is mainstream and hard bop.

Bradley's
70 University Pl. (11th St.), NY 10003 ☎228–6440. *Map 2R4* ♪ *AE* ⊙ *Open 11.30–15.00, 18.30–4.00.*

Din, smoky, bubbling with conversation. The 'burgers are good and the progressive mainstream duos and trios at the end of the long bar even better. They tune up twice nightly, somewhere around 22.00 and 24.00. If on a jazz pub crawl, **The Cookery** is just s on University Pl.

Eddie Condon's
144 W 54th St. (ner 6th Ave.), NY 10010 ☎265–8277. *Map 4N3* ⍩ ♪ *AE* ⊙ ⊙ *Open 20.30–2.00. Closed Sun.*
Even middle-aged enthusiasts of Dixieland jazz can't remember

when their music wasn't presented at some version of Condon's somewhere in the city. Far from reverential, this environment is noisy, crowded, and more consistent with jazz origins than the hushed halls in which the music is often heard. **Jimmy Ryan's** is a few doors down the street.

Fat Tuesday's
190 3rd Ave. (17th St.), NY 10003 ☎*533–7902. Map 5Q4* ♀ 🎵 *AE* *CD* *VISA* *Open 20.00–3.00. Closed Sun.*
Once upon a time, this was Joe King's Rathskeller, a magnet for generations of collegians. The main floor hasn't changed, in spirit. Singles mingle, 'burgers are munched, pitchers of beer are quaffed. Downstairs is a separate place. Jazz prevails, largely of the progressive mainstream variety. There is a hefty cover charge, and the minimum is best consumed in liquid form. Sets are usually at 21.00, 23.00 and, at weekends, 1.00.

Jazzmania Society
40 W 27th St. (near 6th Ave.), NY 10001 ☎*532–7666. Map 5P4* 🎵 ♥ *Open 20.00–2.00. Closed Mon.*
This fourth-floor space in a nearly deserted neighbourhood is the latest home for large bands of progressive bent. Couches on a raised platform overlook the stand, and there is more elbow room than normally associated with jazz clubs. The kitchen produces passable quiches and salads. There is an entrance fee and a minimum tariff. There is sometimes dancing.

Jimmy Ryan's
154 W 54th St. (near 6th Ave.), NY 10010 ☎*664–9700. Map 4N3* ♀ 🎵 *AE* *VISA* *Open 20.00–3.00. Closed Sun, Mon.*
Don't expect solicitous treatment. Just push up to the bar and bathe in Dixieland as pure as it gets in these parts. This qualifies as a landmark of the genre. But no food, no cover, no minimum and no warmth.

Lush Life
Corner Bleecker and Thompson Sts., NY 10012 ☎*228–3788. Map 2R4* 🍴 ♀ 🎵 *AE* *CD* *VISA* *Open 18.00–4.00.*
First-rate duos, trios and quartets perform everything from swing to unclassifiable modern music, with

progressive mainstream dominating. They play three sets nightly, the first at 20.30 Sun–Thurs, 21.00 Fri and Sat. The room is acoustically excellent – not always the case at the city's jazz spots. The food available is of no more than middling interest.

Michael's Pub
211 E 55th St. (near 3rd Ave.), NY 10022 ☎*758–2272. Map 5N5* ♀ *In a dim, woody chain of rooms* that suggests some fleeting exposure to the British pub, the music is by such able practitioners as Marian McPartland and George Shearing. On Mon, it shifts to Dixie, and Woody Allen is known to sit in at clarinet when he's in the mood. Music is from 21.30.

Sweet Basil
88 7th Ave. (Bleecker St.), NY 10014 ☎*242–1785. Map 2R3* ♀ 🎵 *AE* *CD* *VISA* *Open 12.00–3.00.*
Mainstream jazz in an attractive brick-and-wood setting, with such artists as Clark Terry and Chris Conner. Music starts at 22.00, or show up for Sun afternoon sessions and avoid the cover charge.

Village Gate
160 Bleecker St. (Thompson St.), NY 10012 ☎*475–5120. Map 2R4* ♀ 🎵 🍷 *Open Tues–Sat 18.00–2.00. Closed Sun, Mon.*
Stability is not a characteristic of jazz emporia, but the 'Gate' grooves on, now in its third decade. Performers range from good to unsurpassed, their preferences from be-bop to fusion to salsa. They're housed in a large, comfortable, noisy room. Music starts from 22.00. The multi-level complex also puts on comedy acts, revues, theatre, chamber music and anything else that might engage the management's interest.

Village Vanguard
178 7th Ave. (near 11th St.), NY 10011 ☎*255–4037. Map 2R3* ♀ 🎵 *Open 20.00–2.00.*
Landmark cellar club approaching its 50th anniversary. Mainstream jazz, mostly, starting 22.00.

West Boondock
114 10th Ave. (17th St.), NY 10011 ☎*929–9645. Map 4Q2* ♀ 🎵 *AE* *CB* *CD* *CD* *VISA* *Open 18.00–2.00.*
Deserted windswept streets and shuttered meat-packing houses

glower on all sides – not a gracious setting. But the interior is warm and friendly, and the southern soul food authentic. All that is a backdrop for some of the best mainstream jazz in town.

Opera

Full-scale productions are mounted during extended seasons of the Metropolitan Opera Company and the New York City Opera at the **Metropolitan Opera House** (*Lincoln Center* ☎580–9830) and the **New York State Theater** (*Lincoln Center* ☎870–5570).

Gilbert and Sullivan fans support a year-long season at the **Light Opera of Manhattan** (*334 E 74th St.* ☎861–2288).

Singing principals of these and other companies perform in concerts in other venues around the city, including:

Brooklyn Academy of Music   30 Lafayette Ave. (downtown Brooklyn) ☎636–4100
Carnegie Hall   57th St. and 7th Ave. ☎247–7459
Kaufman Concert Hall   1395 Lexington Ave. ☎427–4410
Town Hall   123 W 43rd St. ☎840–2824

Amateurs and young professionals form the companies of the **Amato Opera Theater** (*319 Bowery* ☎228–8200) and the **Bel Canto Opera** (*220 E 76th St.* ☎535–5231).

Pop/folk/rock

Some of these clubs have survived decades of changing fashions, but most opened yesterday and will close tomorrow. Always call ahead to learn of scheduled acts, prices, dress codes and present policies. See also *Country and western*.

The Bitter End
149 Bleecker St. (near La Guardia Pl.), NY 10012 ☎673–7030. *Map 2R4* 🎵 🎵 💟 *Open 15.00–4.00 (Sat, Sun 15.00–3.00).*
Since the 1960s, when it showcased Bob Dylan and Joni Mitchell, this has been one of the most influential rooms in New York. It is still snug and plain, but with an unusually good sound system and acoustics. Genres represented run from folk to jazz to rock and their sub-species. Shows are usually at 21.00 and 24.00, but call ahead.

Bottom Line
15 W 4th St. (near Washington Sq.), NY 10003 ☎228–7880. *Map 2R4* 🎵 🎵 *Open 20.00–2.00.*
Queues form days in advance for tickets to the celebrated acts, more likely to appear here than anywhere else in the city. One-night stands are the rule for a catholic schedule of top performers leavened with groups the management judges to be on the way up. Any musical persuasion might show up – bluegrass, New Wave, folk, blues, jazz, pop.

Cafe Carlyle
Madison Ave. and 76th St., NY 10021 ☎744–1600. *Map 7L4* ═
🎵 AE CB ◉ CD VISA *Open Tues–Sat 18.00–2.00.*
Bobby Short is at the piano and in full silky voice about half the weeks of the year. An eternal favourite of the older strata of local society and the Establishment, his métier is the show tunes of Cole Porter, Rogers and Hart, and George Gershwin. His renditions of songs obscure and celebrated are as smooth as hot butter on glass. You will pay dearly to hear them.

CBGB & OMFUG
315 Bowery (Bleecker St.), NY 10012 ☎982–4052. *Map 2R4* ⅄
🎵 *Open 21.00–4.00.*
Once the home of imported British punk, this grungy but unintimidating ex-garage now promotes less nihilistic New Wave rockers. For those under 30, a visit now qualifies as a nostalgia trip.

Folk City
130 W 3rd St. (near 6th Ave.), NY 10012 ☎254–8449. *Map 2R4* 🎵
Open 20.00–3.00.
The interior was never very appealing to the eye, even 20yr ago when it was at the heart of the

1960s folk music movement, exemplified by appearances by Joan Baez and Bob Dylan. It perseveres, nonetheless, with a mixed bag of blues shouters, comics, and New Wave bands of highly elastic aptitude.

The Ritz
119 E 11th St. (Park Ave. S), NY 10003 ☎ *228–8888. Map 2R4* 🎵 🎤 *Open 20.00–4.00.*

One of the new strain of big rock palaces that care how they look as well as sound. This Art Deco lounge is the place for ageing rock fans (i.e. the over 30s) who don't want to be the oldest people in the room. Attractions are up-and-coming New Wave bands and reggae groups. Shows don't start until midnight.

Sweetwater's
170 Amsterdam Ave. (68th St.), NY 10023 ☎ *873–4100. Map 6M2* 🎵 🍴 AE 💳 💳 VISA *Open Tues–Sat 20.00–2.00. Closed Sun, Mon.*

This can be just the right place for winding down after a cultural stint at *Lincoln Center*. The usual format is a singer backed by a small instrumental group. The thrust toward a glossy mix of pop, rock and soul. Two shows nightly.

Tramps
125 E 15th St. (near Irving Pl.), NY 10003 ☎ *777–5077. Map 5Q4* 🎵 🎤 AE 💳 💳 VISA *Open 20.00–4.00.*

Blues in all its variations is the staple, although experimental jazz features from time to time. Comfortable tavern atmosphere.

Theatre

Broadway, the avenue, long ago gave its name to Broadway, the theatre district. Few of the approximately 40 theatres actually front on to that thoroughfare, however. Rather, they cluster around Times Sq., the intersection of Broadway and 7th Ave. Here are the lavish musicals, popular intimate comedies and, against heavy odds, occasional serious dramas.

Economics mitigated against experimentation, so that role was traditionally assumed by what came to be known as 'Off-Broadway' – smaller houses with lower overheads and greater daring. Many of these are found in and near Greenwich Village, but they are also located throughout Manhattan. In recent years they have grown somewhat more wary, in effect serving as a pre-Broadway tryout circuit, although few productions manage the long step into the big time. Alternative theatre, often raw and wildly avant-garde, is known as 'Off-Off-Broadway'. These productions – happenings – are mounted in garages, churches, lofts, backrooms of restaurants, galleries, anywhere.

Good seats at a hit musical are extremely expensive; and seats are not cheap even at the back of the auditorium. There are ways to reduce the bite, however. Productions nearing the end of their runs issue 'twofer' passes to shops and hotels: take these to the box office of the appropriate theatre and receive two tickets for the price of one. Or, visit the **TKTS** booth at the N end of Times Sq. after 15.00 on the day you wish to attend. Last-minute cancellations and unsold seats are made available at substantial discounts, although not for all plays, of course.

Many theatres sell tickets through **Chargit** (☎ *944–9300 and have a major credit card ready*), a service which takes the card number, adds a small service charge, and advises the box-office to have the tickets ready for you at a specified time. Some theatres will do this directly. There are also dozens of **Ticketron** outlets throughout the city and suburbs at which tickets can be purchased for most Broadway and Off-Broadway productions (and concerts and sports events, too). Ticket brokers and hotel concierges can handle requests, but ensure that their handling fee will not exceed the going rate.

Shopping

All the world's goods pour into Manhattan. There is no material need, and few of the psychic kind, that is not supplied by its shops and stores. Many objects and services are offered at heart-stopping prices, but more often at costs equal to or below those of the countries of origin. Peruvian folk art to Japanese video recorders, Belgian lace to Colombian emeralds, Florentine leather to Chinese porcelain – if it isn't here, somewhere, it probably isn't worth having. Those who shop as a form of recreation cannot exhaust the possibilities for diversion. Those who regard it as a chore can, with prior research, march into a single shop and emerge minutes later with the precise product required.

At this centre of the nation's garment industry, clothing is available in bewildering profusion. Milanese and Parisian couture are represented, of course, often in salons devoted exclusively to the work of a single house. Native designers challenge them on every front, especially in sportswear and ready-to-wear. Part of the success of Calvin Klein, Bill Blass, Geoffrey Beene, Halston, Ralph Lauren and Anne Klein is attributable to their willingness to design for broader markets. While custom tailoring is still available, careful sizing in both men's and women's ready-to-wear garments largely eliminates the need. The better shirts, for example, are calibrated in both neck and sleeve size, and dresses are proportioned to body type – petite, junior, misses, women's – as well as size.

Photographic and home electronic equipment is consistently sold below list price. High volume permits this and heavy competition requires it. Many camera dealers bypass the US distributors, for example, to purchase directly from Japanese manufacturers, thereby eliminating intermediate price rises. With over 90% of the nation's publishers quartered here, discounting of new books is widespread, all languages are represented, and rare and out-of-print volumes are quickly located. Specialization reigns, as with shops that concentrate exclusively on Marxism, homosexuality, feminism, travel or detective novels. Jewellery and unset gems, musical instruments, kitchenware and fashion accessories are of the highest quality and at accessible prices.

The picture is not entirely blue sky and clear sailing, of course. Objects of substantial age, such as antiques or oriental carpets, are available in quantity, but are invariably overpriced. Be wary, too, of stores that proclaim in foot-high letters that they are going out of business: some of them have had those signs up for years. Check labels and identifications carefully, especially of watches and electronic equipment. Unknown brands aren't worth the risk, and some are made to look like products of reputable companies, right down to names with only one letter changed. Street vendors peddle scarves, umbrellas, belts, almost anything portable. Their prices are low, but remember that they move about and might not be at the same site tomorrow.

Weekday mornings are the best times to shop, lunch hours and Sat the worst. The only days on which virtually everything is closed are Thanksgiving (last Thurs in Nov), Christmas and New Year's Day. Other holidays are used as an excuse for sales. Although Sun is still usually a day off, many large stores now open on Sun afternoon. As a rule, midtown shops are open from 9.30 or 10.00 until 18.00, Mon–Sat, with late closing 20.00 or

21.00, on Thurs eve. Elsewhere, the hours reflect the religious convictions or lifestyles of the communities. In Bohemian Greenwich Village and SoHo, doors may not open until 12.00, but close as late as 24.00. Jewish-owned businesses of the Lower East Side are closed Fri afternoons and Sat, but open Sun. In the nine-to-five world of the Wall St. area, many shops close Sat as well as Sun.

Sales personnel, being New Yorkers, can be brusque or helpful, irritable or patient. For no obvious reason, assistants in camera stores and luxury clothing emporia are testy and/or indifferent in undue proportions. Generally, however, encounters will be pleasant and informative. While department stores are logical first stops in the quest of two or more unrelated items, they are frequently under-staffed and the wait can be long at the payment and wrapping counter. Items of a more specific or unusual nature are more easily found in smaller shops. Their owners, fearing crime, often keep their doors locked, buzzing them open only after making snap judgements of potential clients. On that subject, incidentally, take care never to leave a handbag or wallet on a counter while signing a sales slip or examining goods. They can be snatched in a twinkling.

Credit cards are widely accepted, even in the smallest shops, although a minimum purchase price might be stipulated. Travellers cheques are *not* regarded as simply another form of money. Supplementary identification is often required, and cheques drawn in another currency are invariably refused. Personal cheques from out-of-town banks are not welcomed, but individual managers can sometimes be persuaded to take them, with two or more types of identification, if the customer appears trustworthy.

While diversity prevails – a florist next to a hardware store next to a travel agency – certain streets and neighbourhoods have taken on distinct commercial identities, with regard to either cost or similarity of merchandise. Even casual window-shoppers gravitate to the stretch of 5th Ave. from about 47th St. to 57th St., a half-mile of world-famous clothiers, jewellers, booksellers and purveyors of superior luggage and shoes. The same distinction applies along 57th St., especially between 1st Ave. and 5th Ave. Antique hunters and art lovers will want to explore Madison Ave., from 57th St. to 80th. Tucked between the galleries are scores of boutiques trafficking in leather goods, pet supplies, lingerie, materials for needlework, and clothing geared to expectant mothers, debutantes, urban cowboys and country squires.

Before settling on **Tiffany's** or **Cartier**, stroll both sides of 47th St. between 5th Ave. and 6th Ave. for a boggling pageant of jewellery and precious stones of every description and price. For art galleries, see *Guide to the galleries* in *Culture, history and background*. For discount designer and mass clothing, make the excursion to Orchard St. (see *Walk 4* in *Planning*). For photographic equipment, head for 34th St. near Herald Sq. or for Lexington Ave. between 42nd St. and 52nd St. Crafts and offbeat articles of clothing are apparent on a gallery tour of SoHo and along the blocks of W 4th St. and Greenwich Ave., just W of 7th Ave. in Greenwich Village. The compilation that follows in the next few pages does no more than sketch the highlights.

Shops are open normal hours (9.30 or 10.00 to 18.00) unless otherwise stated.

Shopping

Antiques

If rarity and distinction are your criteria and cost is not, there are dozens of exclusive dealers along 57th St., Madison Ave. and the adjoining blocks. For 17th–19thC porcelain, look at:

Antique Porcelain Company   48 E 57th St. (near Park Ave.)
☎758–2363

Robert E. Mann   1050 2nd Ave. (near 56th St.) ☎838–4301

Sarah Potter Conover   17 E 64th St. ☎861–0515

James Robinson   12 E 57th St. (near 5th Ave.) ☎752–6166

Fine European furniture of the same period can be viewed at:

French & Co.   17 E 65th St. (near 5th Ave.) ☎535–3330

Old Versailles   152 E 52nd St. (near Lexington Ave.)
☎753–4479

Gene Tyson   19 E 69th St. (near 5th Ave.) ☎744–5785

Overseas visitors may be more interested in early American furnishings, quilts, funky tat and folk arts. Among shops focusing on these are:

American Hurrah   316 E 70th St. (near 2nd Ave.)
☎535–1930

Bashful Bear   95 E 10th St. (near 3rd Ave.) ☎533–1465

Equator   459 Broome St. (in SoHo) ☎925–5905

Inglenook Antiques   529 Hudson St. (in Greenwich Village)
☎675–0890

Poor Richard's Antiques   369 2nd Ave. (near 23rd St.)
☎677–6064

Somethin' Else   182 9th Ave. (in Chelsea) ☎924–0006

Spirit of America   269 W 4th St. (in Greenwich Village)
☎255–3255

The multi-floored antique galleries of London and Paris have their counterparts here, too. While rewards for the diligent do not qualify as bargains, there can be good buys, somewhat below the stratospheric price ranges of the shops already mentioned. Dealers in silver, enamel, crystal, music boxes, vintage clothing, china, paperweights, brassware and every category of bric-a-brac lease space at:

Manhattan Art and Antiques Center   1050 2nd Ave. (56th St.)
☎355–4400 (85 stalls)

New York Antique and Flea Market   145 E 23rd St. (near Lexington Ave.) ☎777–9609 (20 shops)

SoHo Canal Flea Market   369 Canal St. (near W. Broadway)
☎266–8724 (45 stalls)

Auction houses

Auctions are a source of enlightenment and entertainment even for those who have no intention of bidding. For a recorded announcement of the week's sales at these and other auction houses ☎977–2579.

Christie's
504 Park Ave. (near 59th St.), NY 10022 ☎546–1000. Map **5N4**.
Closest in stature to **Sotheby Parke Bernet**, Christie's is also a British house and nearly as comprehensive in its offerings.

Sotheby Parke Bernet
1334 York Ave. (72nd St.), NY 10021 ☎472–3400. Map **7M5**.
This result of a merger of British and American firms continues to hold centre stage. They deal in snuff boxes, folk arts, antiquities, oriental carpets, Impressionist paintings, toys, Judaica, Art Nouveau – everything.

164

Beauty salons and hairdressers
Once the exclusive province of women, both skin-care centres and hairstylists now cater for men as well. The former retain their markedly feminine decor and emphasis, despite the fact that as much as 40% of their clientele is male. Hairdressers are increasingly uni-sexual (one might say multi-sexual) in character.

Facial treatments typically take an hour to an hour and a half. Inevitably, there are soft-sell efforts by attendants to sign you up for repeat sessions and costly cleansers, creams and lotions. Advance booking is essential. Among the salons that serve both men and women are:

Gabriel   15 Park Ave. (35th St.) ☎683−1639
Anne Keane   16 W 57th St. (near 5th Ave.) ☎586−2803
Georgette Klinger   501 Madison Ave. (52nd St.) ☎838−3200
Klisar   18 E 53rd St. (near 5th Ave.) ☎838−4422
Lea Schorr   527 Madison Ave. (54th St.) ☎486−9670
Christine Valmy   767 5th Ave. (58th St.) ☎752−0303

For shampoo, cut and blow-dry, try the following hairstylists. Appointments are not always required, but call ahead for hours and rates.

Bob Bent   204 Waverly Pl. (near 10th St.) ☎255−6473
Michael Kazan   16 E 55th St. (near 5th Ave.) ☎688−1400
Kenneth   19 E 54th St. (near 5th Ave.) ☎752−1800
Larry Mathews   536 Madison Ave. (near 54th St.)
☎246−6100
Vidal Sassoon   767 5th Ave. (near 58th St.) ☎535−9200

Books and records

Barnes and Noble
600 5th Ave. (near 48th St.), NY 10017 ☎765−0590. Map 5O4 AE CD VISA Open also Sun 12.00−17.00.
One of a chain, this outlet concentrates on recent books at a discount. The selection is limited, but there are many bargains.

B. Dalton Bookseller
666 5th Ave. (52nd St.), NY 10019 ☎247−1740. Map 5N4 AE CD VISA
The substantial stocks include thousands of titles on every imaginable subject.

Doubleday
724 5th Ave. (57th St.), NY 10019 ☎397−0550. Map 5N4 AE CB ⊕ CD VISA Open until midnight.
Large three-level store. Every category is covered, with a marked emphasis on the performing arts. The shop sells records, too.

Sam Goody
666 3rd Ave. (near E 43rd St.), NY 10017 ☎986−8480. Map 5O4 AE ⊕ CD VISA Open also Sun 12.00−17.00.
Records and tapes in all categories,

and at a discount. Audio equipment, musical instruments and sheet music are also on sale. Another branch at 235 W 49th St.

King Karol
126 W 42nd St. (near Broadway), NY 10036 ☎354−6880. Map 403 AE CD VISA Open also Sun 11.00−20.00.
With a comprehensive stock of old and new records in all categories; what they have not got they can quickly obtain.

Murder Ink
271 W 87th St. (near West End Ave.), NY 10024 ☎362−8905. Map 6K2 CD VISA
Bookshop dealing exclusively in crime mysteries.

New York Bound Bookshop
43 W 54th St. (near 5th Ave.), NY 10019 ☎245−8106. Map 5N4.
Although it specializes in rare and out-of-print books about New York, what attracts clients to this shop is its axonometric maps of midtown Manhattan, on which buildings are reproduced right down to the stairs and construction cranes.

Rizzoli
712 5th Ave. (near 56th St.), NY 10019 ☎ *397–3700. Map **5**N4*
AE ⊕ ⓒ VISA

The New York outlet of the prestigious Italian publisher, with books in several European languages and classical background music in keeping with its studied elegance.

Scribner's
597 5th Ave. (near 48th St.), NY 10017 ☎ *486–4070. Map **5**O4*
AE ⓒ VISA

A retail subsidiary of the publishers of Hemingway and Fitzgerald, in a handsome space with a balcony and high ceiling. In front, the hardbacks concentrate on art history and bestsellers. There is a paperback gallery in the rear.

Strand
828 Broadway (12th St.), NY 10003 ☎ *473–1452 Map **2**R4 Open also Sun 11.00–17.00* AE ⓒ VISA

Shelf after shelf of mostly used books in a gratifying clutter that ensnares book lovers for hours. Reviewers sell off their advance copies here at discounts.

Cameras and photographic equipment

Sales and discounts are the rule in this enormously competitive field. Check the full-page ads in the Sun *New York Times* before setting out. Profit margins are slashed to the bone, which makes some floor managers irritable when you inquire if they will match the lower price for the same lens or projector at a store down the street. Ask anyway. When making a purchase, be certain it is handed over in a sealed factory carton. Most shops below are open seven days a week, and take major credit cards.

Camera World
104 W 32nd St. (near 6th Ave.), NY 10001 ☎ *563–8770. Map **5**P4.*
Nearly as well-stocked as **Willoughby's**, and holding frequent sales. It makes a point of carrying electrical products in foreign voltages.

Grand Central Cameras
420 Lexington Ave. (near 44th St.), NY 10017 ☎ *986–2270. Map **5**O4.*
The personnel have proved consistently helpful and the prices are good.

Hirsch Photo
699 3rd Ave. at 44th St., NY 10017 ☎ *557–1150. Map **5**O4.*
Prides itself on its attentiveness to individual needs.

Willoughby's
Main branch at 110 W 32nd St. (near 7th Ave.), NY 10001 ☎ *564–1600. Map **4**P3.*
The largest of the photographic stores. Willoughby's accept trade-ins and members of staff speak several languages.

Chemists

Despite their fanciful European imitations, not all American drug-stores resemble supermarkets. Most concentrate on the sale of cosmetics, perfumes, toiletries, assorted sickroom and surgical devices and, of course, prescription and non-prescription drugs. Be sure to bring along your doctor's prescription. Foreign visitors should also bear in mind the fact that certain drugs they can buy without prescription at home require one here. Two of the oldest pharmacies in New York are **Caswell-Massey** (established 1752) and **Bigelow Pharmacy** (established 1838). The **Duane Reade** chain, with locations all over town, is noted for its discounts.

Bigelow Pharmacy
414 6th Ave. (near 8th St.), NY 10011 ☎ *533–2700. Map **2**R4.*
Still in its original quarters, and open every day.

Caswell-Massey
518 Lexington Ave. (near 48th St.), NY 10017 ☎ *755–2254. Map 5O4. Closed Sun.*
Caswell-Massey blended soaps and colognes for George Washington and Sarah Bernhardt, and its products make good souvenirs.

Kaufman Pharmacy
Lexington Ave. and 50th St., NY 10022 ☎ *755–2266. Map 5O4.*
Open 24hr a day, seven days a week.

Clothing and shoes for men

Barney's
7th Ave. and 17th St., NY 10011 ☎ *929–9000. Map 4Q3* 💲 *AE* 💳 *VISA*

Within the memory of most of its customers, Barney's was an out-of-the-way discount house that drew them to inconvenient Chelsea with promises of bargains. Those low-priced days are gone, but now men of every shape, height and girth come for the unrivalled range of garments in all sizes and fashions. They have installed a coffee shop in which to consider whether the Wall St., Rue de Rivoli or Via Condotti look is for you.

Brooks Brothers
346 Madison Ave. (44th St.), NY 10017 ☎ *682–8800. Map 5O4* *AE*

In an aberrant world, there is Brooks. Tradition cleaves to its stately spaces. This is the 165yr-old home of the natural-shoulder suit preferred by American business leaders and those who aspire to succeed them. Their classic detailing is altered in deference to current fashion only by quarter-inches, and the trenchcoat purchased in 1959 is much the same as the one bought yesterday.

Custom Shop
555 Lexington Ave. (50th St.), NY 10022 ☎ *759–7480. Map 5O4* *AE* 💲 💳 *VISA*

Men of proportions that don't quite fit off-the-shelf shirts – thick neck, short arms; thin neck, long arms – can stop here for made-to-measure cottons and cotton blends that cost little more than average, depending on fabric and collar style. There is a minimum order of four, however. Buy your ties somewhere else.

Dunhill Tailors
65 E 57th St. (near Park Ave.), NY 10022 ☎ *355–0050. Map 5N4* *AE* 💲 *VISA*

They also sell ready-made suits, but their reputation is for custom tailoring in English cuts and fabrics. That Cary Grant has been a steady client should be sufficient recommendation. Expect to pay handsomely for a suit that will last decades.

The Gap
145 E 42nd St. (near 3rd Ave.), NY 10017 ☎ *286–9490. Map 5O4* 💲 *VISA Open also Sun 12.00–18.00.*

This and seven other branches throughout Manhattan purvey jeans in every style, colour and size – but from reputable manufacturers, not overpriced and shoddy, bootleg products – also some tops and related sportswear.

Merns Mart
525 Madison Ave. (near 54th St.), NY 10022 ☎ *371–9175. Map 5N4* 💲 *VISA Closed Sat, Sun.*

Discounts of 25%–50% on American and European menswear of middle quality, with some surprising buys (and some regrettable errors) to be found among racks of shirts, slacks, jeans, sports jackets and suits. They also offer shoes, belts and a selection of women's clothes.

Paul Stuart
Madison Ave. and 45th St., NY 10017 ☎ *682–0320. Map 5O4* *AE* 💲 💳 *VISA*

For the British-American or mid-Atlantic look, Paul Stuart has suits and sports jackets in a subdued palette of checks, herringbones, flannels and twills. The arm-holes are higher than those of the equally traditional **Brooks Brothers**, the shoulders are squared, the waists ever-so-slightly more suppressed. Most are of natural fibres, but there are some blends. Shirts come in an unusually broad range of sizes. There is a small women's department. The prices are middling to high.

Shopping

A. Sulka
*711 5th Ave. (55th St.), NY
10022* ☎ *980–5200. Map 5N4*
AE ◆ CB VISA

Made-to-measure silk shirts are the
ultimate luxury in this exclusive
shop, but there are also suits, coats
and accessories of comparably high
standard. Monogrammed
handkerchiefs make an affordable
gift, custom cashmere bathrobes
do not.

Sym's
*45 Park Pl. (near Church St.), NY
10007* ☎ *791–1199. Map 2T4.*

One of the more prominent
discount men's stores by virtue of
its insistent TV advertising, Sym's
takes a centre path in fashion and
delivers good value. The labels are
left in the garments so the customer
can have an idea of their origins,
and the original list price is
followed on the tag with the Sym's
price. Those willing to examine
carefully three floors of racks and
counters can emerge with twice as
much clothing as the same
expenditure would obtain
midtown, and that is the
temptation.

Victory Shirt Company
*345 Madison Ave. (near 45th
St.), NY 10017* ☎ *687–6375.
Map 5O4* AE ◆ CB VISA

A boon to the odd-sized man or
woman who doesn't care to pay for
custom tailoring. Victory makes
100% cotton shirts of made-to-
measure quality at ready-made
prices. Some sweaters and ties are
available, all in natural fibres.
Monograms and alterations are
extra. There are two more
branches at 10 Maiden Lane and 96
Orchard St.

Clothing and shoes for women

Betsey, Bunky and Nini
*746 Madison Ave. (near 65th
St.), NY 10021* ☎ *744–6716.
Map 7M4* AE CB VISA

With a name like that, one expects
something adorable, and gets it,
with peachy tones, flower-
stencilled walls and rather more
ruffles and flounces than are
absolutely necessary. Individual
separates are sleek and well-
constructed, however, with
examples both from the house
designer and from others. All are
expensive.

Boutique Valentino
*677 5th Ave. (near 53rd St.),
NY 10022* ☎ *421–7550. Map 5N4*
AE ◆ CB VISA

The nearly legendary Valentino
permits us to gaze on his trend-
anticipating lines of dresses,
sweaters and separates, and to
marvel at fabrics and sartorial
details that can be had only at very
high prices.

Fiorucci
*125 E 59th St. (near Park Ave.),
NY 10022* ☎ *751–5638. Map
5N4* AE CB VISA

Have an espresso while
contemplating startling,
imaginative and often popularly
priced clothes that bear no
allegiance to any fashion schools.
Everyone calls it 'fun'; and
certainly no-one who walks out in
one of these zingy tops or slacks
will lack attention.

Gucci
*685 5th Ave. (54th St.), NY
10022* ☎ *826–2600. Map 5N4*
AE CB VISA

Despite the not-unwarranted
reputation of the sales staff for
sullenness, flocks of moneyed
patrons storm these four floors
daily (not Sun). They are men and
women who admire fine Italian
craftsmanship in leather goods –
shoes, belts, handbags and luggage
– and don't mind wearing someone
else's initials – the famed double G.

Halston
*813 Madison Ave. (68th St.), NY
10022* ☎ *744–9033. Map 7M4*
AE CB VISA

Halston, arguably America's high
fashion doyen, and certainly the
designer closest in sensibility to the
Paris houses, lets nothing in the
way of clothes and accessories
escape his attention. Resort wear to
evening dress, gloves to perfumes –
all are supplanted four or five times
a year with fresh ideas.

Charles Jourdan
*700 5th Ave. (55th St.), NY
10022* ☎ *541–8440. Map 5N4*
AE ◆ CB VISA

Imported French shoes of
frolicsome panache – wispy
sandals, and shoes in frothy hues,
lighter than air but remarkably
long-lived. There are men's shoes,
too, but they are much more
traditional. They are all expensive, of
course.

Emilio Pucci
24 E 64th St. (near Madison Ave.), NY 10021 ☎ *752–8957. Map 7M4* AE ⊕ ⊙ VISA
'Signatured' blouses, scarves, bags, etc., in sprightly tints; also perfumes.

Saint Laurent Rive Gauche
855 Madison Ave. (near 70th St.), NY 10021 ☎ *988–3821. Map 7M4* AE ⊕ ⊙ VISA
From the striking front to the metal-and-leather interior, this boutique sizzles with the products of the restless mind of the celebrated French designer. Shirts, trousers, suits, belts are at the leading edge of fashion. One pays dearly to participate.

Yves St Tropez
4 W 57th St. (near 5th Ave.), NY 10019 ☎ *759–3784. Map 5N4* AE ⊙ VISA
Ethereal *crêpe de chine*, buttery-soft

cottons, silks that feel like baby's skin, furs tinted pearl and rose – all the ingredients of the wardrobe for a jet-setting weekend beneath this year's Alp. Prices are rarefied to match.

Unique Clothing Warehouse
718 Broadway (Washington Pl.), NY 10003 ☎ *674–1767. Map 2R4* AE ⊙ *Open additionally on Sun 12.00–17.45.*
As an antidote to the jasmine and musk air of the 5th Ave. boutiques, or simply because it's Sunday, drop down to Greenwich Village. This repository of rugged working man's apparel and military uniforms was the first, it is said, to recognize the inherent chic of such things. A few years later, the Parisian and Milanese couturiers were turning out their own versions for the Côte d'Azur. The prices are good, but the quality is variable so choose very carefully.

Department stores

B. Altman & Co
5th Ave. and 34th St., NY 10016 ☎ *679–7800. Map 5P4* AE *Open Thurs until 20.00.*
Perhaps it hasn't the cachet of other stores further N along 5th Ave., but this long-established emporium (founded in 1865) manages to display similar goods at slightly less inflated prices. As a bonus, the staff are as courteous and as helpful as any in the city. Go there primarily for home furnishings and clothing.

Henri Bendel
10 W 57th St. (near 5th Ave.), NY 10019 ☎ *247–1100. Map 5N4* AE ⊙ VISA
While it avoids the flashy, Bendel's is at the forefront of fashion trends, at least among department stores. A step inside the door and a peek at size labels reveals that the cautious and/or amply proportioned shopper would best spend time elsewhere. Clothes boutiques take up the first floor, but there are five more floors above in which to consider stationery, table linens, shoes, cosmetics, household ware.

Bergdorf Goodman
754 5th Ave. (57th St.), NY 10022 ☎ *752–0303. Map 5N4* AE *Open Thurs until 20.00.*
On what is perhaps the most glamorous corner in New York,

Bergdorf's follows through with unrivalled service and products. Furs, lingerie, fragrances, linens are of the highest order. To a degree, the store is shelter to the glossy boutiques of Givenchy, Halston, Saint Laurent and their like. Men who can afford the tariffs are drawn to the Turnbull & Asser counter for shirts.

Bloomingdale's
1000 3rd Ave. (59th St.), NY 10022 ☎ *355–5900. Map 5N5* AE *Open Mon, Thurs until 21.00.*
Multitudes of New Yorkers and suburbanites slavishly follow the dictates of the great guru Bloomingdale, denying all the while that their sitting rooms are replicas of those in the store, that they dress like the models in the Sat newspaper ads, that the food they eat imitates the delights of the gourmet shops on the ground floor. They need not be defensive, for they could hardly find a better model to follow. In the evening and on Sat they are as likely to drop in just to meet people similarly afflicted as to buy anything.

Gimbel's
Broadway and 33rd St., NY 10001 ☎ *564–3300. Map 5P4* AE ⊙ VISA *Open Mon, Thurs, Fri until 20.30, Sun 12.00–17.00.*
The traditional rival to **Macy's**,

across Herald Sq., Gimbel's has fallen behind in recent years. Product lines and prices are still competitive, but the shop lacks the perkiness of its competitor, which is forever seeking ways to keep its name before the public. There is another branch (*86th St. in the Upper East Side*) which partially succeeds in closing the gap between the two rivals.

Lord & Taylor
424 5th Ave. (39th St.), NY 10016 ☎ *391–3344. Map 5O4* Ⓐ Ⓔ *Open Thurs until 20.00.*
Whether you want a cashmere sweater or a chair, curtain fabric or a crystal bowl, buy it here and it will remain a classic until its natural demise. That might be later than your own, for Lord & Taylor has been around well over a century, and it has no intention of alienating coming generations. Known mainly for sportswear, it also employs interior decorators to advise on renovations both modest and ambitious. Decisions can be made in comfort over soup and salad in one of the store's three cafes.

Macy's
Broadway and 34th St., NY 10001 ☎ *695–4400. Map 5P4* Ⓐ Ⓔ *Open Mon, Thurs, Fri until 20.30, Sun 12.00–17.00.*
In recent years, Macy's has moved to occupy the area between the bland middle ground and the snappy upper-middle ground represented by **Bloomingdale's**. Most welcome innovations are the repository of kitchenware and gourmet foods called The Cellar, and an uncanny reproduction of the trendy Irish saloon, **P. J. Clarke's**. The largest store in the world (so they claim) has something for everyone, from antiques to puppet shows.

Saks Fifth Avenue
611 5th Ave. (50th St.), NY 10022 ☎ *753–4000. Map 5O4* Ⓐ Ⓔ Ⓓ *Open Thurs until 20.30.*
Scrupulously choreographed and relentlessly edited, Saks contrives to retain its conservative image without descending into dowdiness. Clothes are its strength, from sports to formal wear, as delineated by Bill Blass, Oscar de la Renta and the like.

Food and kitchenware

New Yorkers have always been interested in food and cooking, if only to reproduce the cuisines of their homelands. The recent enthusiasm for gourmet cookery has intensified that concern, and these shops are booming. Try to avoid Sat.

Balducci's
422 6th Ave. (near 9th St.), NY 10011 ☎ *673–2600. Map 2R4* Ⓐ Ⓔ *Open daily 7.00–20.30.*
Enter Balducci's immediately after a large meal, or your eyes will grow round as billiard balls and you will be seized with a compulsion to sweep up chunks of everything in sight. You will be in competition with milling throngs anxious to get their hands on the very same cheeses, pastries, choice vegetables, thick slabs of prime meats, ringlets of homemade sausages, smoked fishes, or lobsters. Absolute freshness of produce and ingredients in cooked or baked products is the norm. It is always busy.

Bridge Kitchenware
214 E 52nd St. (near 2nd Ave.), NY 10022 ☎ *688–4220. Map 5N5* Ⓓ Ⓥ
The shelves are packed with quality utensils for the serious cook. Pick through stainless carbon knives by several manufacturers, food processors, graters, coffee grinders, bowls of steel and ceramic, copper moulds, crystal. The prices are neither exorbitant nor low, they are simply fair.

Caviarteria
29 E 60th St. (near Madison Ave.), NY 10022 ☎ *759–7410. Map 5N4* Ⓐ Ⓔ Ⓓ Ⓥ *Open also Sun 9.00–18.00 except July, Aug.*
Unprepossessing inside and out, this small shop is easy to dismiss. But the distractedly helpful proprietor deals in the essentials of a calculated seduction or a dinner designed to impress. His caviar is Iranian, Russian and American. The last is a Californian experiment that appears to be succeeding, and at half the price of the imports. He also stocks smoked salmon, cheeses and related delicacies, and enjoys a large mail order trade.

Dean & DeLuca
121 Prince St. (SoHo), NY
10012 ☎ *254–7774. Map 2S4.*
Open also Sun 10.00–18.00.
Expensive, yes, but not
unconscionably so, and the mark-
up is justified merely by the aroma
encountered at the front door:
coffee, freshly baked bread,
cheeses, fresh produce all
contribute. At the squared counter
in the centre are baskets of exotic
mushrooms, pâtés and terrines.
Along one wall, an extraordinary
selection of herbs; on the other,
honeys and jams. And at the back,
racks of kitchen utensils, including
whisks and cast-iron pans and
oven-usable stoneware. At
Christmas, the management brings
in fresh-killed rabbits, game birds
and haunches of venison.

E.A.T.
869 Madison Ave. (72nd St.),
NY 10021 ☎ *772–1586. Map*
7M4 AE *Open also Sun*
9.00–17.00.
This newer, larger branch is in a
Gothic townhouse and the decor
complements the architecture with
chequered marble floors and
ornamental balustrades.

Prepared dishes and baked goods
are made on the premises, from
sourdough to pâtés to stuffed
breast of chicken. Teas, jams,
salmon and cheeses are imported.
Visit the original store (*1064
Madison Ave.*), or there is an
E.A.T. enclave in the **Henri
Bendel's** department store.

Zabar's
2245 Broadway (near 80th St.),
NY 10024 ☎ *787–2000. Map*
6L2 AE ⊙ ⊙ VISA *Open*
Mon–Thurs 8.00–19.30, Fri until
22.00, Sat until 24.00, Sun until
19.00.
Balducci's and Zabar's are
perennial contenders for the throne
of gourmet shops, but Zabar's may
have pulled ahead by virtue of its
recent second-floor expansion for
kitchenware. Absolute kitchen
essentials – fish poachers and duck
presses – take their place among
food mills and copper pots. On the
ground floor, cheese, coffee,
caviar, smoked fish, prepared
terrines and entrees, pumpernickel
bread, ice-cream, coffee cake,
chopped liver, herring, and all
manner of intoxicating sights and
aromas battle for attention.

Jewellery

From the waiting limousines to the understated window
displays and the hushed, almost ecclesiastical interiors,
Cartier, **Harry Winston**, **Tiffany & Co.** and **Van Cleef &
Arpels**, the Titans of the retail trade in gold, gems, silver and
watches, breathe an ever-tasteful opulence. Dress for the
occasion. All of them have a well-crafted trinket or two at
modest cost for recipients back home who are impressed by the
name on the gift box.

Department store marketing techniques are used by
Fortunoff, and its stock is supplemented with fine jewellery
and watches, antique silver and flatware. There are four floors
and prices are reasonable, as these things go.

While all these shops are within a few steps of each other, true
comparison shopping is best undertaken along 47th St.,
between 5th Ave. and 6th Ave. Every imaginable sort of
jewellery is on hand in shoulder-to-shoulder (and floor-upon-
floor) shops that sell nothing else. Start at the **International
Jewelers Exchange**, with its dealers installed in 84 cubicles,
then work w along 47th St., crossing to the opposite side and
returning E. Prices are often negotiable, so it's best to delay
purchase until several trays of the desired object have been
examined.

Cartier   5th Ave. and 52nd St. ☎753–0111
Fortunoff   681 5th Ave. (near 54th St.) ☎758–6660
International Jewelers Exchange   5th Ave. and 47th St.
☎ 869–8600
Tiffany & Co.   5th Ave. and 57th St. ☎755–8000
Van Cleef & Arpels   5th Ave. and 57th St. ☎644–9500
Harry Winston   718 5th Ave. (near 56th St.) ☎245–2000

Museum shops

Cultural curiosity and the acquisitive impulse are handily combined in the gift and bookshops of all the major museums and most of the smaller ones. While selections naturally reflect the concerns of the museums in which they are located – seafaring motifs at the *South Street Seaport Museum*, folk art at the *Brooklyn Museum* – they interpret their missions with broad strokes. Given their auspices, trashy merchandise rarely slips on to the shelves. For the same reason, expect fair prices but no bargains. See *Sights and places of interest* for addresses and telephone numbers.

Predictably, the shop of the *Metropolitan Museum of Art* is largest, with excellent reproductions of many items in the collections as well as art books and illustrated catalogues. The *Museum of the American Indian* has handcrafted 'squash-blossom' necklaces, silver belt buckles, 'concha' belts, and Navajo rugs. Reproductions of Egyptian jewellery and authentic Latin American ceramics and dolls are the speciality of the *Brooklyn Museum*. Books and posters dominate at the *Museum of Modern Art* shop, but its design collection inspires exquisite glassware, pottery, flatware, cigarette lighters, garden shears and clocks. At the *Jewish Museum*, even Gentiles are drawn to the brass candlesticks and *menorahs*, *mezuzah* boxes, and the jewellery. Finally, there are quilts and crafts, antique and contemporary, at the *Museum of American Folk Art*.

Sports and camping equipment

Athlete's Foot
16 W 57th St. (near 5th Ave.), NY 10022 ☎ 586–1936. Map 5N4.
Runners stop here, or at one of its six branches, for its full line of footwear and warm-up suits.

Herman's
Midtown branches at 135 W 42nd St. (near Times Sq.), NY 10036 ☎ 730–7400. Map 4O3. And 845 2nd Ave. (near E 51st St.), NY 10022 ☎ 688–4603. Map 5N5.
One of the largest general sporting goods stores.

Hudson's
3rd Ave. and 13th St., NY 10003 ☎ 473–7321. Map 2R4.
For camping and outdoor equipment.

Paragon
867 Broadway (near E 18th St.), NY 10003 ☎ 255–8036. Map 5Q4.
Large stock of general sporting goods.

Spiegels
Nassau St. and Ann St., NY 10005 ☎ 227–8400. Map 2U4.
For all sports goods in lower Manhattan.

Toys

It is tempting to begin and end with **F.A.O. Schwarz**, but there are other shops too. All of them will wrap and ship.

Childcraft Center
150 E 58th St. (Lexington Ave.), NY 10022 ☎ 753–3196. Map 5N4.
Focuses on sturdy educational toys.

Penny Whistle
1281 Madison Ave. (near 91st St.), NY 10028 ☎ 369–3868. Map 7K4.
Young patrons are actually encouraged to play with the dolls and games.

F.A.O. Schwarz
5th Ave. and 58th St., NY 10022 ☎ *644–9400. Map 5N4.*
A wonderland of fantasies even for the most cynical adult, it qualifies as a
not-to-be-missed sight of the same order as the Empire State Building.
Imagine 10ft-high stuffed giraffes, storybook villages complete with
dogs and street lamps, child-sized cars that really work, marionettes,
electric trains and, of course, a vast selection of dolls, books and games
. . . . three floors of them.

Westside Toy Center
2305 Broadway (near 83rd St.), NY 10024 ☎ *877–2060. Map 6L2.*
Another leading toyshop.

Wines and spirits

Equidistant from the vineyards of France and California, New
York samples the vintages of Old World and New. Special sales
are frequent, sometimes of wine from unexpected countries –
Lebanon, Chile, Yugoslavia. Their advantage is price, of
course. Choices can be bewildering, but the sales people at the
following shops are helpful, and their wares are exemplary for
price and/or variety.

All are closed Sun and none accept credit cards. Most make
deliveries.

Astor Wines & Spirits 12 Astor Pl. (near Lafayette St.)
☎ 674–7500
Cork & Bottle 1158 1st Ave. (near 63rd St.) ☎ 838–5300
Embassy Liquors 796 Lexington Ave. (near 61st St.)
☎ 838–6551
Morrell & Co. 307 E 3rd St. (near 2nd Ave.) ☎ 688–9370
Sherry-Lehmann 679 Madison Ave. (near E 61st St.)
☎ 838–7500
Sokolin 178 Madison Ave. (near 34th St.) ☎ 532–5893

Clothing sizes
When shops give clothing sizes in inches or centimetres, use
the following conversion scale to determine the correct size

12 in	16	20	24	28	32	36	40	44	48
30 cm	40	50	60	70	80	90	100	110	120

When standardized codes are used, although these may be found
to vary considerably, the following provides a useful guide.

Women's clothing sizes

UK/US sizes	8/6	10/8	12/10	14/12	16/14	18/16
Bust in/cm	31/80	32/81	34/86	36/91	38/97	40/102
Hips in/cm	33/85	34/86	36/91	38/97	40/102	42/107

Men's clothing sizes

European code (suits)	44	46	48	50	52	54	56
Chest in/cm	34/86	36/91	38/97	40/102	42/107	44/112	46/117
Collar in/cm	13½/34	14/36	14½/37	15/38	15½/39	16/41	16½/42
Waist in/cm	28/71	30/76	32/81	34/86	36/91	38/97	40/102
Inside leg in/cm	28/71	29/74	30/76	31/79	32/81	33/84	34/86

Men's and women's shoe sizes

UK/US sizes	3½	4/5½	5/6½	6/7½	7/8½	8/9½	9/10½	10/11½	11/12½
European	36	37	38	39	40	41	42	43	44

Biographies

One of the most cosmopolitan of cities, New York has a history rich in memorable characters – among them the following are a representative selection.

Allen, Woody (born 1935)

The writer-actor-comedian-satirist-director is said to get the bends whenever he ventures beyond the city limits of New York. Nevertheless, by his own account, a Brooklyn childhood and an aborted career at New York University gave him little joy but much material for his *New Yorker* magazine essays and his recent films *Annie Hall* and *Manhattan*.

Beecher, Henry Ward (1813–87)

A minister, lecturer, author and firebrand abolitionist, he was also the older brother of Harriet Beecher Stowe, who wrote *Uncle Tom's Cabin*. His pulpit was the Plymouth Church on Orange St. in Brooklyn Heights.

Booth, Edwin (1833–93)

Often cited as the first important American actor, Booth made his permanent home in New York. His career was blighted after his brother, John Wilkes, killed Abraham Lincoln.

Bryant, William Cullen (1794–1878)

Best known as a poet, Bryant made his living as a reform-minded editor of the *Evening Post* (1826–78). He is credited with prodding the city into the development of Central Park.

Burr, Aaron (1756–1836)

In a chequered political career that saw him lose as many elections as he won, Burr's highest post was Vice-President to Thomas Jefferson. The image of Burr as an amoral schemer gained strength from his shooting of Alexander Hamilton in a duel and from the plan, attributed to him, to establish an independent republic in the southwest. He was tried for treason and acquitted, but never re-entered public life.

Fulton, Robert (1765–1815)

Talented and energetic, Fulton's curiosity led him to careers in painting, gunsmithing, civil engineering and the invention of ambitious mechanical devices. Although he was not the creator of the steamboat, as is widely believed, his *Clermont* (1807) was the first profitable version.

Greeley, Horace (1811–72)

After his arrival in New York at the age of 21, Greeley worked as a printer, editor and newspaper columnist. He founded *The New Yorker* (1834) and the *Tribune* (1841) and edited them, in various combinations, for over 30yr. Although initially considered a conservative, he advocated women's suffrage, abolition of slavery, labour unions and experiments in communal living, all daring stands at that time.

Hamilton, Alexander (1755–1804)

Born out of wedlock in the West Indies, Hamilton came to New York to study at King's College in 1773. His anonymous writings on behalf of the Revolutionary cause drew much attention, as did his service on the battlefield and as General Washington's aide. An influential delegate to the Continental Congress at 25, he was one of the leading proponents of the Constitution drafted by Jefferson. Undeniably brilliant, he nevertheless made many enemies. One of them, **Aaron Burr**, mortally wounded him in a duel in 1804.

Henry, O. (1862–1910)

The pen name of William S. Porter, a short-story writer noted for his tight plots and surprise endings, exemplified in *Gift of the*

Magi. He began writing in prison, to which he was sentenced for embezzlement. Most of his literary production was in the last 10yr of his life, spent in New York.

Hopper, Edward (1882–1973)
Born in a small town on the Hudson River, Hopper moved in young adulthood to Greenwich Village. The muted, melancholy cityscapes of this Realist painter began to gain favour in the 1920s, although they ran against Modernist trends. In later years, his studio was at 3 Washington Sq. North.

Irving, Washington (1783–1859)
Diplomat, biographer, satirist and author – of *Rip Van Winkle* and *The Legend of Sleepy Hollow* among other tales – Irving was born in New York. His estate in nearby Tarrytown is open to the public.

Koch, Edward (born 1924)
Child of immigrant parents, Koch narrowly won election as mayor of New York in 1977; and despite, or because of, his propensity for speaking his mind, he soon established himself as the most popular mayor since LaGuardia. In 1981, as the candidate of both the Democrat and Republican parties, he was returned to office by an overwhelming vote.

LaGuardia, Fiorello Henry (1882–1947)
Probably the most beloved mayor in the city's history – serving from 1935–45 for an unprecedented three terms – the 'Little Flower' gave lustre and colour to an office celebrated for both the flamboyance and corruptibility of its incumbents.

Millay, Edna St Vincent (1892–1950)
The popular lyric poet was a leader of the Greenwich Village Bohemian group that founded the Provincetown Players.

Minuit, Peter (1580–1638).
The famous $24 purchase of Manhattan was negotiated by Minuit, who was then appointed Director General (1626–31) of the new colony by the Dutch West India Company.

Morgan, John Pierpont (1837–1913)
Beginning with the fortune accumulated by his father, J. P. used it as seed money to build a financial empire that is said to have exceeded even that of the first Rockefeller. Along the way, he bought out industrialists Andrew Carnegie and Henry Frick. All of them spent their declining years in New York and engaged in good works.

Morse, Samuel F. B. (1791–1872)
While a member of the arts faculty at New York University, Morse perfected his telegraph device and the code to be used with it. A demonstration was given at Castle Clinton in 1842. Morse was also a pioneer in the development of photography.

Olmsted, Frederick Law (1822–1903)
Travel writer and landscape architect, Olmsted designed Central Park, Prospect Park (Brooklyn) and Riverside Park, all in collaboration with Calvert Vaux.

O'Neill, Eugene (1888–1953)
The work of the playwright who fashioned *The Iceman Cometh* and *Mourning Becomes Electra* is the standard against which all American dramatists must be measured. One of his finest plays, *Long Day's Journey into Night*, was discovered among his papers after his death. O'Neill was awarded the Nobel Prize in 1936.

Parker, Dorothy (1893–1967)
Renowned for the razor-sharp wit she directed as readily at herself as at others, Parker employed that gift in verse, plays, films, essays and short stories. Much of her work appeared in *The New Yorker* magazine.

Biographies

Perelman, S. J. *(1904–79)*
Brooklyn-born Perelman wrote for *The New Yorker* magazine
from 1934 almost until his death. Essentially a humorist and
satirist, his interests focused on the inanities of advertising and
Hollywood. He also wrote film scripts and plays in the 1930s
and 1940s, often in association with such luminaries as the Marx
Brothers, Ogden Nash and George S. Kaufman. His affection
for the elaborate pun was legendary, apparent in such book
titles as *The Road to Miltown*, or *Under the Spreading Atrophy*.

Poe, Edgar Allen *(1809–49)*
Impoverished for most of his adult life, having alienated his
wealthy foster father through repeated alcoholism and
gambling, Poe moved to New York with his child bride in 1844.
Their cottage in the Fordham section of The Bronx is now a
museum. He finally achieved recognition for his poetry with
The Raven, which led to fame for such mystery stories as *The
Gold Bug*, and *The Murders in the Rue Morgue*.

Pollock, Jackson *(1912–56)*
Although contemporaries were working in similar directions,
the seminal work of this innovative artist heralded the explosion
of post-War creativity now known as the New York School.
Inspired by Picasso and impatient with the academic
techniques he mastered in his early years, he applied paint to
vast canvasses by splashing, dribbling, thrusting and pouring in
a method later labelled 'action painting'.

Porter, Cole *(1893–1964)*
The enduring sophistication of Porter's lyrics is remarkable. He
penned both words and music of over 400 songs, for such stage
musicals as *Can-Can*, *Silk Stockings* and *Kiss Me, Kate*.

Pulitzer, Joseph *(1847–1911)*
Hungarian-born Pulitzer emigrated to the USA in 1864 and
became a journalist, editor and publisher in short order. He
bought the *New York World* in 1883 and in competition with
William Randolph Hearst permitted it to plummet to the nadir
of 'yellow journalism'. After the Spanish-American War
(1898), his newspapers altered course to become relatively
dignified. His will bequeathed money for the establishment of
the Columbia University School of Journalism. Annual prizes
for journalistic excellence are given in his name.

Rauschenberg, Robert *(born 1925)*
Rauschenberg first attracted attention with an exhibition of
entirely black canvasses, but then moved on to 'combine-
paintings' – assemblages of pigment, collage and such three-
dimensional objects as stuffed goats and rubber tyres. Born in
Texas, he is nonetheless an exemplar of the New York School.

Rockefeller, John D. Jr. *(1874–1960)*
The son of the incalculably wealthy oil magnate and financier
was granted control of his father's interests at the age of 37. To a
large extent, this involved philanthropic activities, many of
which benefited New York. Among the projects he inspired or
helped underwrite were Riverside Church, the Cloisters of the
Metropolitan Museum of Art and the Rockefeller Center.

Rockefeller, Nelson Alrich *(1908–79)*
After able participation in both Democrat and Republican
federal administrations during World War II and after, Nelson
defeated W. Averell Harriman for the governorship of the State
of New York in 1958. His subsequent bids for the Republican
presidential nomination were unsuccessful, but he was
re-elected governor three times and was appointed Vice-
President for the brief term of Gerald Ford (1974–77). He

made substantial contributions to New York's cultural and educational institutions, as did his siblings.

Roosevelt, Theodore (1858–1919)
The 28th and youngest President passed the first 15yr of his extraordinarily active life at 28 E 20th St., near Gramercy Park. Hunter and environmentalist, rancher and author, statesman and chauvinist, peacemaker and militarist, explorer and politician, he pursued these contradictory interests vigorously until his death.

Runyon, Damon (1884–1946)
Born in Manhattan (the one in the state of Kansas), this popular journalist came to New York, where he quickly mastered the patois of the criminal fringe and transferred that knowledge to a long string of evocative and humorous short stories, which provided the basis of the musical *Guys and Dolls*.

Ruth, George Hermon (1895–1948)
A near-legendary athlete, 'Babe' Ruth played for the New York Yankees professional baseball team from 1920–35. Most of his pitching and batting records went unchallenged for decades, and some still stand.

Stuyvesant, Peter (1610–72)
A harshly autocratic man intolerant of religious and political dissent, this Director General of New Amsterdam held power from 1647–64. In 1664 he surrendered the colony to an English naval force and retired to his farm, near the present Lower East Side.

Tweed, William Marcy (1823–78)
The undisputed leader of Tammany Hall, which controlled the city and state Democrat Party, 'Boss' Tweed ruled the city from 1857 until the early 1870s. He died in prison, having defrauded taxpayers and contractors of unaccounted millions in bribes, kickbacks and related schemes.

Warhol, Andy
No-one is certain when he was born (about 1930), or where (probably Philadelphia), but there is no question of his primacy in the Pop Art movement of the 1960s. Through repeated prints of commonplace objects – cows, soup tins, movie stars – he endeavoured to elevate the mundane and overexposed into subjects worthy of serious consideration. He went on to found a 'factory' that produced films of elusive intent, a magazine of celebrity interviews and autobiographical books that celebrate banality.

White, Stanford (1853–1906)
As the most celebrated partner of the architectural firm of McKim, Mead & White, he probably received more credit than his due for their collective achievements. Many of their buildings have been lost, but a rich heritage remains. These include Washington Arch, the Villard Houses, the portico of St Bartholomew's Church, three buildings at Columbia University and three more at the former Bronx campus of New York University, in all of which White had a hand.

Whitman, Walt (1819–92)
The innovative free verse of *Leaves of Grass* drew mostly negative reaction on its first appearance in 1855, but many 20thC scholars regard Whitman as America's finest poet.

Wolfe, Thomas Clayton (1900–38)
The haunted author of *Look Homeward, Angel* and *You Can't Go Home Again* joined the English faculty at New York University in 1924 and spent most of the last years of his life in the city.

New York for children

From boat trips to children's zoos, New York is a city packed
with interest for children. The following are the most accessible
suggestions.

Boat trips

Circle Line (*Pier 83, w 43rd St.* ☎ *563–3200*). Three-hour
trips around Manhattan Island may be a trifle long for the very
young, but there are few dull moments for everyone else.
Cruises depart at least ten times a day, weather and demand
permitting, during Apr–Nov from 9.45–17.30. Half-price for
children under 12.

Ellis Island Ferry (*Battery Park, Lower Manhattan*
☎ *269–5755*). Ferries to the famous old immigrant processing
centre leave daily during May–Nov at 9.30, 11.45, 14.00 and
16.15. The fare includes a 1hr guided tour of the poignant
national monument.

Staten Island Ferry (*Battery Park, Lower Manhattan*
☎ *248–8097*). The double-decker ferry leaves Whitehall St.
pier every 20–30min. It passes the Statue of Liberty and
provides unparalleled views of bridges, harbour traffic and an
imposing skyline.

Statue of Liberty Ferry (*Battery Park, Lower Manhattan*
☎ *269–5755*). Spectacular views from the crown of the famous
lady and the ride from the city are included in the fare. Keep in
mind the long walk up from the base.

Children's theatre

Courtyard Playhouse (*39 Grove St. (near 7th Ave. S)*
☎ *765–9540*). Productions such as *Flash Gordon Saves the
Universe* and *Wilbur the Christmas Mouse* are representative of
the fare offered by the **Little People's Theater Company**,
usually on Sat and Sun at 11.00 and 15.00. Admission is
inexpensive, but reservations are essential.

First All Children's Theater (*37 W 65th St. (near Central Park
W)* ☎ *873–6400*). Musical productions with casts of children
are usually held during Oct–May on Sat and Sun only, but
there are more frequent performances during school vacations.
Telephone for details and reservations.

Hartly House Theater (*413 W 46th St. (near 9th Ave.)*
☎ *246–9885*). The **On Stage, Children!** company mounts four
plays a year, including such classics as *Androcles and the Lion*.
Shows during Sept–May at 13.00 and 15.30 on Sat.
Inexpensive, but reservations are necessary.

Jan Hus Playhouse (*351 E 74th St. (near 2nd Ave.)*
☎ *772–9180*). Plays and musicals are presented on an irregular
schedule, sometimes two in an afternoon. Inexpensive.

Magic Towne House (*1026 3rd Ave. (near 60th St.)*
☎ *752–1165*). Magic shows are leavened with laughs and cute
animals, and 'assistants' are recruited from the audience.
Reservations are required, and no adults are allowed without
children. Shows are on Sat and Sun at 13.00, 14.30 and 16.00.

New Media Repertory Company (*203 E 88th St. (near 3rd
Ave.)* ☎ *860–8679*). Unpredictable entertainments performed
by the **Children's Improvisational Company** on Sat at 15.30
during the school year. Inexpensive.

13th Street Repertory Company (*50 W 13th St. (near 5th Ave.)*
☎ *675–6677*). Plays with music, based upon children's stories
on Sat at 15.00, Sun at 13.00. Call in advance to confirm times.

Truck and Warehouse Theater (*79 E 4th St. (near 2nd Ave.)* ☎ *254–5060*). A long-running rock 'n' roll musical fantasy called *Captain Boogie and the Kids from Mars* is performed during Oct–June on Sat and Sun at 15.30.

Christmas decorations

The luxury shops and large department stores are ablaze with holiday lights and window-dressing from late Nov to late Dec, and midtown 5th Ave. is a spectacle of dizzying amplitude. The centrepiece is the 70ft tree with myriad winking lights looming above the skating rink at the foot of the **RCA Building**. The **Channel Gardens** that lead into Rockefeller Center from 5th Ave. are transformed by stylized novas and silvery angels. Shop windows and interior displays of invariable delight are those of **B. Altman & Co.** (*34th St.*), **Lord & Taylor** (*38th St.*), **Saks Fifth Avenue** (*50th St.*), and **F.A.O. Schwarz** (*58th St.*).

Elsewhere in Manhattan, a Christmas tree is framed within Washington Arch in **Greenwich Village**, wreaths encircle the necks of the lions outside the **42nd St. Library**, an elaborate tableau of castles and elves fills the lobby of the **Museum of the City of New York** and a tree in the Medieval Hall of the **Metropolitan Museum of Art** emphasizes the spiritual origins of the holiday, supplemented by a panorama of 200 18thC figures gathered about the birthplace of the Christ child.

Comedy and revue

Several nightclubs set aside afternoon sessions for children. But inevitably some clubs change policy and others close, so telephone for schedules and prices.

The **Comic Strip** (*1568 2nd Ave. (near 81st St.)* ☎ *861–9386, Sat 17.00, Sun 17.30*) spotlights professional stage youngsters appearing in current TV and stage shows. Similar showcases are arranged by **Something Different** (*1488 1st Ave. (near 78th St.)* ☎ *570–6666, Sat 19.00, Sun 15.00, 17.30*), and by **Improvisation** (*358 W 44th St. (near 9th Ave.)* ☎ *765–8268, Sun 14.30*). In TriBeCa, the **Ones** disco (*111 Hudson St. (near N Moore St.)* ☎ *925–0011*) turns over the floor to pre-teenagers on Sun (*13.00–17.00*).

Concerts for young people

The American Symphony Orchestra and the New York Philharmonic give irregularly scheduled concerts of classical music directed at ages 6–16. Most are performed in the autumn and winter at **Carnegie Hall** (☎ *247–7459*) or **Avery Fisher Hall** (☎ *874–2424*). Check newspapers for full details.

Events and entertainments

Big Apple Circus. This is New York's very own one-ring circus in a tent, modelled after the intimate European troupes that have no other equivalent in the US. Clowns cavort, aerialists execute the fabled triple somersault, elephants dance, jugglers and acrobats twirl and tumble, all to the delightful cacophony of a tiny band. Prices are variable but low for this not-for-profit enterprise; operation is most likely in summer and the Christmas season. A frequent site is Damrosch Park in the **Lincoln Center**, but it moves through all the boroughs.
Citicorp Center (*Lexington Ave. and 53rd St.* ☎ *559–4259*). The atrium has free entertainment most days, but Sat afternoon is for children, with music, magic, jugglers and puppets.
Gimbels Department Store (*Broadway and 33rd St.*

☎ *564–3300*). The famous store underwrites free shows for
children on Sun at 13.30.

July 4th (Independence Day) festivities. An awesome
fireworks display is put on by Macy's Department Store, set off
from barges in the Hudson River and best seen from **Riverside
Park** (*from 80th St. to 100th St.*). Be there by 21.00. The 'Old
New York' celebrations take place at **Battery Park** in lower
Manhattan, with street performers and suitable ceremonies
from 12.00 to dusk.

Storytelling in Central Park. At the **Hans Christian Andersen
Memorial** (*near 5th Ave. and 72nd St.*) stories are read to
children, some of whom sit in the bronze lap of the master,
during May–Sept on Wed and Sat at 11.00.

Hotels

Various discounts and incentives help keep costs within reason
when children are in tow. At least a dozen hotels permit
children under 12 (or 14, or even 17) to stay with their parents
for free. Most will roll in an extra bed or cot at an additional
but not excessive charge, making a substantial saving over the
alternatives of a suite or separate rooms.

Reception desks or concierges normally have lists of
babysitters available for hire.

Swimming pools are an important feature for children, and
the following Manhattan hotels and motels have them: **Best
Western Skyline** (indoor), **Halloran House**, **Harley**, **Holiday
Inn-Coliseum**, **Parker Meridien**, **Ramada Inn-Midtown**,
Sheraton City Squire (indoor), **United Nations Plaza**
(indoor), and **Vista International**. See *Hotels* for addresses and
telephone numbers.

Museums and exhibitions

Brooklyn Children's Museum (*145 Brooklyn Ave. (between
Eastern Parkway and Atlantic Ave.*) ☎ *735–4432, open Mon,
Wed–Fri 13.00–17.00, Sat, Sun 10.00–17.00* ⊡). The oldest
(1899) children's museum in the US is in a new building.
Exhibits cover basic technologies, social and natural history.
Handling and participation are encouraged. Several levels
support water-wheels, ladders, a windmill, a steam engine,
hydraulic devices, plants, animals, and thousands of other
objects and displays.

Junior Museum of the Metropolitan Museum of Art (*5th Ave.
and 82nd St.* ☎ *879–5500, ext 351, open Tues 10.00–20.45,
Wed–Sat 10.00–16.45, Sun and hols 11.00–16.45*). Somehow
it manages to be intellectually accessible to children under 12
without patronizing them. Exhibits, from the permanent
collections and outside sources, introduce the arts and inspire a
thirst for further exposure in the galleries upstairs. There is also
a lively programme of workshop demonstrations, films, and
gallery tours.

Manhattan Laboratory Museum (*314 W 54th St. (near 8th
Ave.)* ☎ *752–7684, open Tues–Fri 11.00–17.00, Sat
12.00–17.00* ▨). Despite the name, this modest new museum
does not concentrate solely on science. Rather, it emphasizes
hands-on participation by children in games, displays and
workshops concerned with natural history, conservation,
culture and society.

In addition to these three, many of the city's museums have
presentations and programmes of interest for children. For

addresses and opening times, and fuller details, see the
entries for individual museums in *Sights and places of
interest*.

American Museum of Natural History. The reassembled
dinosaur skeletons and dioramas of mounted animals and birds
in simulated habitats are long-time favourites, but they seem
bland beside the vivid and detailed depictions of the peoples
and cultures of Asia, Central America and Africa. Several
rooms are set aside for schoolchildren to rouse their curiosity
about the larger concerns of the museum through participatory
exhibitions, games, performers, films, story hours and guided
tours. The **Hayden Planetarium** is part of the facility, and on
Sat during the school year (Oct–June) mounts a 'Young
People's Sky Show' which includes realistic overhead
projections of galaxies and constellations accompanied by
music and narration.

Aunt Len's Doll and Toy Museum. Hundreds of antique toys,
dolls and miniature houses crowd every inch of space in this
refreshingly informal museum. Visits by appointment only.

Brooklyn Museum. After-school programmes on Wed–Sat
introduce youngsters aged 6–12 to various parts of the
collections through talks and demonstrations that do not abuse
attention spans.

Fire Department Museum. Antique equipment and
firefighting memorabilia housed in an old firehouse provide a
break in a walking tour of Lower Manhattan.

Guinness World Records Exhibit Hall. Excess fascinates, and
this set of tableaux of the longest, highest, shortest, fattest,
oldest, youngest and most bizarre creations of man and nature
never fails to grab attention.

Metropolitan Museum of Art. Apart from the **Junior Museum**
on the basement level, the most alluring items in the many
collections seem to be the Egyptian tombs and mummies and
the medieval arms and armour; older children are drawn to the
special shows of the **Costume Institute**. The recorded cassette
tours are attractive.

Museum of Broadcasting. Children can enjoy tapes and
kinescopes of radio and TV shows of the 'olden times'. Adults
are usually as intrigued, but some might wish to wait in Paley
Park, next door.

Museum of the City of New York. Puppet shows on Sat during
Nov–Apr are the incentive to join in various 'please touch'
demonstrations of objects related to the history of the area.

Museum of Holography. Ghostly three-dimensional images
produced by laser technology represent a glimpse of the 21stC.

New York Experience. This multi-media extravaganza is short
and slick enough to give an impression of the city without a
single stifled yawn.

New York Historical Society. A scale-model of a Noah's Ark
populated by 300 animals dominates the collection of vintage
toys and dolls on the 2nd floor.

Richmondtown Restoration (Staten Island). Costumed
guides and craftsmen bring history to life in this re-created
village with demonstrations of weaving, wool-spinning, basket-
making, leatherwork, and cooperage.

South Street Seaport Museum. The authentic tall ships of this
open-air museum are diverting for all ages, and special events
include folk singers and a theatre designed for children.
Youngsters can take part in lectures and browse in shops
concerned with toys, ship models and games of nautical bent.

181

Observation decks

Empire State Building (*350 5th Ave. (34th St.)* ☎ *736–3100*). There are two decks, on the 86th and 102nd floors, open daily at 9.30–24.00, except Christmas and New Year's Day. Children under 12 half-price.

RCA Building (*30 Rockefeller Plaza (between 49th St. and 50th St.)* ☎ *489–2947*). Not quite as high as the others, its wrap-around vistas and midtown location give a better sense of the New York topography. The 70th floor deck is open daily during Apr–Oct at 10.00–20.45, and during Nov–Mar at 10.30–19.00. Children under 12 half-price.

World Trade Center (*2 World Trade Center, Lower Manhattan* ☎ *466–7377*). An enclosed deck is on the 107th floor, with an open deck on the 110th. On a clear day, it is easy to imagine that you can see the curvature of the earth. Open daily at 9.30–21.30. Children 6–12 about half-price, under 6 free.

Closer to sea-level (and free) are the pedestrian walkways of the **Brooklyn Bridge** and the **George Washington Bridge**, as well as the **Brooklyn Heights** esplanade.

In addition, there are several restaurants with sky-high venues. As long as one does not inspect the bill and/or what appears on the plate too critically, the following can be pleasant: **Act One** (*1 Times Sq.*), **Copter Club** (*Pam Am Building*), **Rainbow Room** (*RCA Building*), **The Terrace** (*Butler Hall, Columbia University*), **3 Mitchell Place** (*49th St. and 1st Ave.*), **Top of the Sixes** (*666 5th Ave.*), **Windows on the World** (*1 World Trade Center*).

Parades

For youngsters, the big one is the **Macy's Thanksgiving Day Parade** on the last Thurs in Nov, with its huge floating balloons of comic book heroes and the Muppets. The longest and most eagerly anticipated is the **St Patrick's Day Parade** on Mar 17, but that has become rowdy in recent years with roving bands of intoxicated teenagers. Most months have a parade of some kind in some part of the city, but 5th Ave. has several events in autumn. See *Calendar of events* in *Planning*.

Playgrounds

Numerous conventional playgrounds dot New York. But the ones suggested below are described as adventure playgrounds, with stacked wooden blocks, rope nets, sections of concrete tubes, and comparable combinations of shapes and materials intended to be transformed into whatever can be inspired in a child's imagination.

Central Park   Central Park West and 68th St.; Central Park West, near 85th St.; 5th Ave. and 85th St.; 5th Ave. and 71st St.
Gramercy Park   2nd Ave. and 19th St.
Greenwich Village   Washington Square Park, between 5th Ave. and University Pl.; Abingdon Square Park at Hudson St. and Bleecker St.
Upper East Side   1st Ave. near 67th St.; East End Ave. and 84th St.
Upper West Side   W 45th St. near 10th Ave.; W 90th St. near Columbus Ave.

Puppets and marionettes

First Moravian Church (*154 Lexington Ave. at 30th St.* ☎ *254–9074*). Participatory puppet shows every weekend on Sat at 14.00. Admission is inexpensive, but book in advance.

Greenwich House Music School (*46 Barrow St. at 7th Ave. S*
☎ *924–4589*). Puppet shows staged each weekend on Sat and
Sun at 15.30. A modest admission fee is charged, but book
ahead.
Museum of the City of New York (*1220 5th Ave. at 103rd St.*
☎ *534–1672*). Shows conducted during Nov–Apr on Sat at
13.30. Inexpensive.
New York Stageworks (*15 W 18th St. at 5th Ave.*
☎ *691–9106*). The **Nicolo Marionettes** perform at weekends
during Sept–May on Sat at 13.00, Sun at 13.00 and 15.00.
Inexpensive, but book in advance.
Origami Center (*31 Union Sq. W at E 16th St.* ☎ *255–0469*).
Weekend performances of **Alice May's Puppets** during
Nov–May on Sun at 14.00. Inexpensive, but reservations are
necessary.
F.A.O. Schwarz (*5th Ave. and 58th St.* ☎ *644–9400*). The
famous toy store has free puppet shows from Mon–Fri at 14.30.
South Street Seaport Museum (*16 Fulton St. at South St.*
☎ *766–9020*). Shipboard puppet shows and related
entertainments on Sun at 14.00.
Swedish Cottage Marionette Theater (*81st St. and Central
Park West* ☎ *988–9093*). Performances on Sat and Sun
afternoons, but call ahead for times. Inexpensive entry;
reservations required.

Restaurants

Apart from their prohibitive cost, the shrines of *haute cuisine* set
children to squirming and are unlikely to have available the
simple fare they prefer. There are many moderately-priced
restaurants catering for families, however, with special
children's menus, high-chairs, and speedy service. The
following tend to be large and rather touristy, but they go to
considerable lengths to amuse young patrons.
Benihana (*47 W 56th St.* ☎ *581–0930*). Diners sit in
groups of six or eight around a horseshoe counter that encloses a
sizzling grill. A cook in *toque blanche* arrives and, with a showy
clatter, swoops over piles of shrimp, zucchini and beef, slicing,
flipping, sautéing, serving. It may not be Japanese, but it is
theatrical.
The Cattleman (*5 E 45th St.* ☎ *661–1200*). A crowded, gaudy
Hollywood version of a Wild West saloon, the cuts of beef are
large if tenderized, and there is a horsedrawn stagecoach for
rides around the block. Lady magicians and singers circulate
among diners.
Gaylord (*50 E 58th St.* ☎ *759–1710*). The chef at the tandoori
oven is fun to watch and they'll keep the seasonings mild for
young palates, but the big treat is a palm reader.
Mamma Leone's (*239 W 48th St.* ☎ *586–5151*). Plates are
heaped high, the walls and ceilings of the cavernous rooms are
encrusted with Neapolitan kitsch, fiddle players stroll, flash
bulbs pop. Boredom is not permitted.

Sports

See also *Sports and activities.*
Bicycling
Bicycles can be rented from many shops, by the hour, day or
week, and the **Loeb Boathouse** (*in Central Park, nere E 72nd
St.* ☎ *288–7707*).
Horse riding
The **Claremont Riding Academy** (*175 W 89th St.*

☎ *724–5100*) rents horses by the hour and offers classes for children in its indoor ring. Trails for more experienced riders are in Central Park.

Ice-skating

The rink at the base of the **RCA Building** is open to all, despite the style of many of its skaters. Less exhibitionistic youngsters may prefer the **Wollman Memorial Rink** (*in Central Park, near 5th Ave. at 64th St., open approximately late Oct to late Mar*). Admission fees are modest but vary. Skates can be rented at all indoor rinks.

Model boats

Miniature boats both humble and elaborate, radio-controlled or sail-powered, are seen nearly every day of the year on the **Conservatory Pond** (*in Central Park, near 5th Ave. and 72nd St.*).

Rowboats

The **Loeb Boathouse** (*in Central Park, near E 72nd St.* ☎ *288–7707*) has rowboats for hire by the hour to persons over 16yr.

Swimming

Many hotels open their pools to non-residents; otherwise there are several beaches near the city. These alternatives are preferable to the municipal pools.

Television shows

A number of game shows and variety specials originate in New York. Tickets are free, and sources are:

American Broadcasting Company   1330 6th Ave. ☎ 581–7777
Columbia Broadcasting System   51 W 52nd St. ☎ 581–4321
National Broadcasting Company   30 Rockefeller Plaza, ☎ 664–3055
New York Convention and Visitors Bureau   2 Columbus Circle, ☎ 397–8222

Children between the ages of 6 and 18 must be accompanied by adults.

Zoos and aquarium

For addresses and opening times, see individual entries in *Sights and places of interest.*

Bronx Zoo. The new Children's Zoo, within the larger park, has gentle animals for petting and camels and pony carts for riding, and is open Apr–Oct. Kids also enjoy the monorail that circles the 'Wild Asia' preserve, the aerial tram that glides over the recreated 'African Plains', and the tractor train that tours the entire park.

Central Park Zoo. Next to the 64th St. entrance is a merry-go-round, and inside are pony rides. The hub is the seal pool. To the N is the Children's Zoo on a triangle of land on 5th Ave. between 65th St. and 66th St. Open seven days a week, all year round. Renovation is underway.

New York Aquarium. From May–Oct, there are performances by dolphins, whales, and sea-lions. Most winter in Florida, but there are still indoor tanks featuring fish that resemble floating flowers and others, even stranger, that inspire shudders.

Prospect Park Zoo. This compact zoo also features pony rides and a section of small farm animals set aside for children.

Staten Island Zoo. The comprehensive reptile collection is the big attraction, supplemented by a children's zoo and pony rides. Admission free on Wed.

Sports and activities

The following guide to sport and leisure in and around New York offers ideas for spectators and participants.

Spectator sports
Arenas and stadiums
Baker Field (*W 218th St. and Broadway* ☎ *567–7423*). American football as played by Columbia University, one of the members of the 'Ivy League' of prestigious colleges; Sept–Nov.
Byrne Arena (*Meadowlands Sports Complex, E Rutherford, NJ* ☎ *(201) 935–8222*). Since its opening in 1981, this facility has been the venue for the professional basketball Nets and college teams, as well as rock concerts, circuses, and other events. Get there by coach from Port Authority Bus Terminal on 8th Ave.
Giants Stadium (*Meadowlands Sports Complex, E Rutherford, NJ* ☎ *(201) 935–8222*). Crowds fill the superb arena on Sun afternoons from late Aug to early Dec to watch professional American football by the venerable Giants; tickets are nearly impossible to obtain. The experiment in professional soccer appears to have failed, but there might be exhibition games here.
Madison Square Garden (*8th Ave. and 33rd St.* ☎ *564–4400*). This is the home of New York Rangers ice hockey (Oct–Apr), Knicks basketball (Oct–Apr), college basketball (Nov–Apr) and indoor soccer with the Arrows (Nov–Mar). Boxing and wrestling matches and such special events as the circus, the Ice Capades, dog and horse shows, and rock concerts are also held here at various times of year.
Nassau Coliseum (*Uniondale, Long Island* ☎ *(516) 794–9100*). Special musical and entertainment events are presented, as are the ice hockey games of the successful Islanders.
National Tennis Center (*Flushing Meadows-Corona Park, Queens* ☎ *592–9300*). These courts are the site of the annual US Open Championships in early Sept.
Shea Stadium (*126th St. and Roosevelt Ave., Queens*). The professional baseball Mets play here from Apr–Sept (☎ *672–3000*); the football Jets from Sept–Dec (☎ *421–6600*).
Yankee Stadium (*River Ave. and W 161st St., The Bronx* ☎ *293–6000*). Frequent champions and one of the oldest teams in professional baseball, the Yankees perform here Apr–Sept.

Racetracks
Aqueduct (*108th St. and Rockaway Blvd., Queens* ☎ *641–4700*). The 'Big A' features thoroughbred flat racing from Jan–May, Oct–Dec. It can be reached by subway. For routes and fares ☎ *330–1234*.
Belmont Park (*Elmont, Long Island* ☎ *641–4700*). Thoroughbred racing from May–July, Sept–Oct. The Long Island Railroad, departing from Penn Station, has special trains and fare-admission packages ☎ *739–4200* for information.
Meadowlands (*Meadowlands Sports Complex, E Rutherford, NJ* ☎ *(201) 935–8500*). Most of the grandstands are enclosed at this new track, permitting comfortable viewing of thoroughbreds from Sept–Dec, and of trotters from Jan–Aug. Races are in the evening, and can be watched from the full-service dining-room called Pegasus.
Roosevelt Raceway (*Westbury, Long Island* ☎ *(516) 222–2000*). Evening trotters go through their paces from Jan–Mar, June–Aug, Oct–Dec. Package fares on the

185

Long Island Railroad from Penn Station include coach transfers and track admission.

Yonkers Raceway (*Yonkers, NY* ☎ *968–4200*). Easily accessible off the Gov. Thomas E Dewey Thruway, just N of The Bronx. The track is devoted to trotting races from Mar–Apr, June–July, Sept–Oct and Dec. Special coaches leave from Port Authority Bus Terminal on 8th Ave.

Participant sports
Baseball
The national game can be played on diamond-shaped fields all over New York. Many are reserved at various times by amateur and semi-professional leagues, but 'pick-up' teams come together for a few innings whenever a sufficient number of enthusiasts gather. Contact the **Heckscher Ballfields** (*Central Park, E of Central Park W at about 64th St.*), or ☎ 397–3100 for the location of the nearest field.

Basketball
There are courts within a few blocks of nearly every address in Manhattan. These are usually occupied by local youngsters or ageing executives who take the game very seriously ☎ 397–3100 for the closest court. Branches of the **YMCA** (*215 W 23rd St.* ☎ *741–9220; 224 E 47th St.* ☎ *755–2410; and 5 W 63rd St.* ☎ *787–4400*) have gymnasiums, but a membership card from a hometown 'Y' is usually required.

Bicycling
Shops in most neighbourhoods rent bicycles by the hour, day, or week – consult the telephone directory 'Yellow Pages' under *Bicycles*. City streets are intimidating for any but unflappable native cyclists, so consider Central Park on weekends, when roads in it are closed to cars. The **72nd St. Boathouse in Central Park** (☎ *288–7707*) has bicycles for hire.

Boating and sailing
Rowing boats are available at the **72nd St. Boathouse in Central Park** (☎ *288–7707*). Sailing instruction is offered by the **New York Sailing School** (*City Island, The Bronx* ☎ *864–4472*), and the **Offshore Sailing School** (*at 820 2nd Ave.* ☎ *986–4570*).

Bowling
All the boroughs have bowling emporia, although they are least obvious in Manhattan. **Madison Square Garden Bowling Center** (*7th Ave. and W 31st St.* ☎ *563–8160, open 9.00–1.00*), with 48 lanes, also has instructors.

Cricket
While it is not a sport that fires the imagination of the local citizenry, immigrants from the British West Indies keep the imperial heritage alive on pitches in **Flushing Meadows-Corona Park** (*in Queens* ☎ *520–5311*), and in **Van Cortlandt Park** (*W 250th St. and Broadway* ☎ *822–4711*).

Diving
Instruction in SCUBA is given by the **Aqua-Lung School of New York** (*1089 2nd Ave.* ☎ *582–2800*), **Atlantis II** (*498 6th Ave.* ☎ *924–7556*), and **Scuba Plus** (*201 E 34th St.* ☎ *689–0035*), all in Manhattan. They also arrange diving trips

throughout the area for qualified divers. There are a number of intriguing wrecks in offshore waters.

Fishing

Anglers over 16 must obtain a licence to use the fresh water lakes and rivers of New York City and State, but these are readily available for a small fee at many sporting goods shops. Anyone can fish in salt water without a permit. Lakes within **Central Park**, **Prospect Park** (*Brooklyn*), and **Van Cortlandt Park** (*The Bronx*) contain such gullible species as catfish, bluegills and carp. Charters and party boats (on which each passenger pays a fare) are available at **City Island** (*The Bronx*) and **Sheepshead Bay** (*Brooklyn*).

Football (soccer)

Enthusiasts might be invited to join a game in **Central Park** (*at W 81st St.* ☎ *397–3110*), or in **Van Cortlandt Park** (*The Bronx* ☎ *822–4599*).

Golf

While there are no golf courses in Manhattan, the outlying boroughs have 13 owned and operated by New York City. Expect to wait for a tee-off. For information:

The Bronx ☎ 822–4711
Brooklyn ☎ 965–6511
Queens ☎ 520–5311
Staten Island ☎ 422–7640

Handball

For the location of the nearest city-owned court in Manhattan ☎ 397–3100.

Horse riding

Instruction and hire-by-the-hour are available at:
Claremont Riding Academy 175 W 89th St. ☎ 724–5100
Clove Lake Stables 1025 Clove Rd. in Staten Island ☎ 448–1414
Van Cortlandt Park Stables Broadway and W 254th St. in The Bronx ☎ 549–6200
  The trails for the **Claremont** wind through Central Park, and it has an indoor ring as well.

Ice-skating

The rink at the base of the **RCA Building** in the Rockefeller Center has a constant crowd of spectators and so is used primarily by skilled and/or exhibitionistic skaters. Central Park has two outdoor rinks: **Lasker** (*near 110th St.*) and **Wollman** (*near the Zoo*). All are open Nov–Apr.
  The **Sky Rink** (*450 W 33rd St.* ☎ *695–6555*) is large, indoors and on the 16th floor. Open all year, it has disco skating on Fri and Sat nights.
  Skating is also permitted on natural lakes and ponds when there is safe ice cover, but it is wise to stick to the artificial rinks.

Racquetball

So popular it threatens to eclipse tennis, racquetball is normally available only at membership clubs. But some are open to the public, at least on an occasional basis. Among these are:
Gramercy Tennis & Racquetball Club 708 6th Ave. ☎ 691–0110

Sports and activities

Grand Central Racquetball Club   25 Vanderbilt Ave.
☎883–0994
Manhattan Plaza Racquet Club   45 W 45th St. ☎ 594–0554
Manhattan Squash & Racquetball Club   41 W 42nd St.
☎869–8969
Racquetball Fifth Avenue   25 W 39th St. ☎944–0144
   Usually they are open seven days a week, 7.00–24.00.
Equipment is sold and rented at each, and credit cards are
accepted. Reserve courts well in advance. Hotels that have
courts include the **Parker Meridien** and the **Vista
International**.

Roller-skating

Skates can be rented at many shops, among them:
Dream Wheels   295 Mercer St. ☎677–0005
New York Skate   113 W 10th St. ☎929–0630
Skate Connection   349 W 14th St. ☎243–6343
Sportiva Sporthaus   145 E 47th St. ☎421–7466
US Roller World   160 5th Ave. ☎691–2680
   Indoor rinks in Manhattan include:
Metropolis Roller Skate Club   241 W 55th St. ☎586–4649
Riverroll Rollerskating   312 E 23rd St. ☎673–0950
Roxy Roller Rink   515 W 18th St. ☎675–8300
   Most of these have disco nights.

Running

New York runners are a hardy breed, seen on every street, at all
hours, in any weather. Non participants might question the
description of running as a 'sport', but its benefits to fitness and
the modest cost of equipment are unquestionable. A morning
jog or a serious 10-mile effort can follow any route, but certain
areas and pathways are favoured for their even road surfaces,
lack of vehicles and crowds, and relative freedom from air
pollution.
   Obviously these requirements point to the parks, especially
Central Park. Its 30-plus miles of roads provide substantial
variety in distances and difficulty. Suggested routes are detailed
below.
   The fenced reservoir slightly N of the mid-point of the park
has two cinder tracks. Enter the park at **Engineer's Gate**, at 5th
Ave. and E 90th St. The inner track is 1.57 miles long.
   Slightly S of the reservoir is **The Great Lawn Oval**, with a
measured circumference of half a mile and markers at 220yd
(200m) intervals.
   A 6-mile loop follows the main drive around the perimeter of
the park, with frequent opportunities to cut E or W for runs of 1,
2 or 4 miles. Enter at **Engineer's Gate**, or at W 66th St. beyond
the Tavern On The Green restaurant, or just beyond the Zoo.
   Less crowded parks are **Fort Tryon**, **Prospect** (*Brooklyn*),
Riverside, and **Van Cortlandt** (*The Bronx*). **The New York
Botanical Garden** (*also in The Bronx*) is ideal for runners, and is
a worthy destination by itself.
   For river vistas, try the elevated **West Side Highway**,
presently closed to traffic below 42nd St., or the promenades
along the East River, with easy access S from **Carl Schurz
Park**.
   Road races of varying lengths are held every month in the
city. Contact the **New York Road Runners Club** (*9 E 89th St.*
☎ *860–4455*) for dates, times and registration details.
   The following is a list of indoor tracks:

McBurney YMCA   215 W 23rd St. ☎741–9224
92nd St. YMHA   1395 Lexington Ave. ☎427–6000
West Side YMCA   5 W 63rd St. ☎787–4400

Skiing
Cross-country skiing, with rolling terrain and gentle slopes, is
available in **Prospect Park** (*Brooklyn* ☎ 965–6511) and at **Van
Cortlandt Park** (*The Bronx* ☎ 543–4595). Equipment rental,
instruction, and tours to upstate and New England ski centres
are available at **Scandinavian Ski Shop** (*40 W 57th St.*
☎ 757–8524) and **Sportiva Sporthaus** (*145 E 47th St.*
☎ 421–7466).

Squash
Most of the racquetball clubs listed on the preceding pages also
have squash courts.

Swimming
Municipally-owned pools in the five boroughs are open from
late May to early Sept. They tend to be shabby, crowded, and
sometimes rowdy. Visitors are likely to prefer the pools at the
following hotels, some of which are open to outsiders as well as
guests: **Best Western Skyline** (indoor), **Halloran House**,
Harley, **Holiday Inn-Coliseum**, **Parker Meridien**, **Ramada
Inn-Midtown**, **Sheraton City Squire** (indoor), **United Nations
Plaza** (indoor), and **Vista International**. See *Hotels* for
addresses.
  Jones Beach State Park (*on the s side of Long Island*) has the
finest public beach and related facilities in the region, and is less
than an hour by car (*via Southern State Parkway, exiting
s on Wantagh State Parkway*) or special coach from the Port
Authority Bus Terminal. Municipal beaches are nearly always
crowded and the colour of the water is often suspect, even
though certified safe for bathing, but most are within reach of
public transport. **Coney Island Beach** (*S Brooklyn*) is best
known, but **Rockaway Beach**, to the E, is three times as long
with a tenth of the humanity. At its western end is **Jacob Riis
Park**, for long a haunt of uninhibited male homosexuals.
Orchard Beach (*near City Island in The Bronx*), and **Great Kills
Park** (*Staten Island*) are also popular.

Tennis
Commercial tennis clubs usually have equipment shops,
lounges, instructors, and lockers available. Many also offer
saunas, air-conditioning, swimming pools, weekend brunches
and evening parties. Indoor courts are offered by:
Crosstown Tennis   14 W 31st St. ☎947–5780
Gramercy Tennis & Racquetball Club   708 6th Ave.
☎691–0110
The Midtown Tennis Club   341 8th Ave. ☎989–8572
Tower Tennis Courts   1725 York Ave. ☎860–2464
Turtle Bay Tennis & Swim Club   1 United Nations Plaza
☎355–3400
Wall Street Racquet Club   Wall St. (at East River) ☎952–0760
  These are normally open seven days a week from
7.00–24.00; always call ahead to book a court and, if alone, to
arrange a game. All boroughs have municipal courts, but season
permits are required and red tape slows the process. Fanatics
are pleased to know of the **Stadium Tennis Center** (*11 E 162nd
St. in The Bronx* ☎293–2386), open 24hr a day, Oct–May.

Excursions

Unlike the capitals of Europe, New York has no medieval cathedrals or ancient university towns within easy reach. Beyond the inner ring of bleak smaller cities, however, the countryside is dotted with hamlets of Colonial serenity, inviting inns, dairy farms, and a surprising number of stately homes. These places are found in a great variety of natural settings, from hushed valleys to surf-pounded shores. For the following tours a car is essential.

A taste of New England

105 miles round trip NE. One day, preferably with an overnight stop.

Leave the city via the West Side Highway, which goes through several name changes and two toll booths. After the second toll, take the first exit on to the Cross Country Expressway. This merges eventually with the Hutchinson River Parkway, heading towards Connecticut. Leave it at Exit 27, turning left, N, on Route 120 (Purchase St.).

At the next traffic signal, turn right, E, on Anderson Hill Rd. and follow it to the next crossroad, Route 120A (King St.). Turn left, N. Continue past the entrance to the Westchester County Airport on the left. Keep a sharp look-out for Cliffdale Rd. on the right and turn into it. It winds down a steep hill into a bosky gorge with a tumbling brook, and leads on through a neighbourhood of luxurious estates. After a mile, Cliffdale Rd. ends at Route 433 (Riversville Rd.). Turn left, N.

At the intersection with John St., about a mile farther on, is the tall, chunky steeple of the **N Greenwich Congregational Church**, erected in 1896. On the opposite corner is an **Audubon Center**, with nature trails open to the public. Continue N on Route 433 to the first traffic signal, and turn right on Route 22. Just beyond a large modern furniture store is **Smith's Tavern** (*open Wed–Sat 13.00–15.30*). Built at the time of the Revolutionary War, it is now a modest museum of such items as antique dolls' houses and quilts.

Route 22 rolls on over rising and falling hills past country clubs and examples of residential architecture dating back three centuries. Eventually there is **Bedford Village**, settled in 1680 by pioneers from New England. At the fork in the road, park near the tiny schoolhouse (1829) which is now a museum of local history (*open Wed–Sun 14.00–17.00, often closed from Christmas to mid-Feb*). Across the street is a white clapboard Methodist Church (1806) now headquarters of the Bedford Historical Society. The adjacent burial ground was established in 1681.

Bedford deserves an exploratory stroll. Around the triangular village green are the **Bedford Free Library** (1807), the **Courthouse** (1787), and **Post Office** (1838). Side streets have homes of the Dutch Colonial and Greek Revival styles. Most date from after 1779, when a British commander burned all but one of the then existing houses in retribution for rebel resistance. Some of the historic buildings are open to the public (*usually open Wed–Sun 14.00–17.00*) but they are dependent upon volunteers so might be closed at unpredictable times.

You will soon have an opportunity to picnic, and good wholesome fare can be purchased at the delicatessen next to the Post Office or at the **Bedford Gourmet** take-away shop, opposite the cinema. Return to the car and continue through the village on Route 22. Just beyond, bear right at the junction on Route 121, N. If a picnic does not strike your fancy, there is **Nino's**, with good if unremarkable veal, pastas and mussels. Continue on Route 121, which eventually passes the Cross River Reservoir, part of New York City's water system.

Just before the junction with Route 35 is the entrance to the **Ward Pound Ridge Reservation**, 4,750 acres of hiking trails and camping grounds. If you did decide on a picnic, this is the place, but drive around to choose a spot. There are tables, stone barbecues and fields in which to fling Frisbees. In cooler months, deer and racoon are often sighted and cross-country skiing is popular. Return then to Route 35. After about 2 miles, look for the 'State Police' sign and turn left into **South Salem** (settled 1731). Although the hamlet is of mild interest, the primary reason for the detour is to note for future reference the **Horse and Hound** restaurant (*dinner only; for reservations* ☎ *(914)763–3108*), where the chef-owner specializes in game dishes. Follow the street through town, turning left back on to Route 35.

Soon, this crosses into Connecticut and the town of Ridgefield. On the left is the **Inn at Ridgefield**, which offers lodgings and lunch and dinner (*Wed–Sun*). Turn left on Main St., an avenue of majestic trees and splendid 19thC homes. On the right is the **Aldrich Museum of Contemporary Art** (*open Sat, Sun, Wed 13.00–17.00*). Sculptures monumental and whimsical are placed about the lawn and these are on view every day. They and the works within are primarily those by Americans since 1945. There are frequent special shows and equally frequent vacations. Should it happen to be open, a visit is a must. Continue N through the village on Main St. About 2 miles farther on, at the flashing traffic signal, turn right on Haviland Rd. At the next traffic signal, turn right again on Route 7. After half a mile, make a sharp right turn for **Stonehenge** (☎ *(203)438–6511*) – not a megalithic monument, but the finest restaurant in the area. It serves imaginative game dishes and quick-poached trout taken straight from the kitchen's own holding tank. Reservations are essential for weekend dinners and necessary if you want to stay in one of the eight cosy bedrooms overlooking the inn's geese-filled pond. Should this be fully booked or time limited, return to New York via Route 7 and Interstate 95.

Fishing village in the metropolis
40 miles round trip NE. Minimum of half a day.

Pack a bathing suit. Take the West Side Highway to Interstate 95 (E), following that highway as far as exit 8B (City Island–Orchard Beach). The road passes a wildlife refuge as you bear S to **City Island**. A reassuringly ramshackle enclave that is not the slightest bit chic, it has room only for one main thoroughfare, City Island Ave., with short side streets of sturdy detached frame houses for people who live there all year. On the block between Hawkins St. and Carroll St., there are stores full of offbeat antiques, bric-a-brac, and unclassifiable discards. There are also coffee houses intended for leisurely drop-ins. **The Hippie's Place** is one. Another, particularly memorable, is the **Black Whale** (*even in summer it is only open Thurs–Sun, usually 8.30–24.00*). There is a patio out at the back where 15 kinds of tea are served, as well as *espresso* and *cappucino* coffee and a wickedly tempting chocolate angel food cake.

There are numerous seafood restaurants of varying quality.

Those at the foot of the main avenue are bargains with bonus views of the bay and a hazy Manhattan skyline, but they and many others close during the coldest months. **Anna's Harbor** and **Thwaite's Inn** (see *Restaurants*), at the N end of the avenue, are open all year.

After lunch and a stroll, leave by the same road, now following the signs to **Orchard Beach**. This is one of the finest public strands within the city, normally less crowded and littered than the others. There are changing rooms, a playground, snack bars, and ample parking. It takes less than a half hour to return to town by the same route.

The Hudson River Valley
150 miles round trip N. Minimum one long day, preferably two days.

Travel N on the West Side Highway, which becomes the Henry Hudson Parkway and then the Saw Mill River Parkway after it crosses the city line into Westchester County. It is designated Route 9A all the way. Continue through the city of Yonkers and the town of Hastings-on-Hudson, taking exit 17 in Dobbs Ferry, W on Ashford Ave. until it joins with Broadway (Route 9). Turn right, N, and drive on past the commercial district of the village of Irvington. Four blocks beyond Main St., turn left, W, on Sunnyside Lane. At the end, just before the railroad tracks and the Hudson, is **Sunnyside** (■ *open 10.00–17.00*), the home of Washington Irving (1783–1859), author, diplomat and scholar. He always returned to this region, which he called 'Sleepy Hollow' in his novels and stories. The house, gardens and outbuildings have been scrupulously restored, with guides in appropriate 19thC garb. This is part of the Sleepy Hollow Restorations, a group of historic buildings which includes **Philipsburg Manor** and **Van Cortlandt Manor** (see below). Combination tickets can be purchased for all three at a substantial saving.

Return to Route 9 (S. Broadway) and go N, to reach a Gothic Revival mansion called **Lyndhurst** (■ *open May–Oct, Wed–Sun 10.00–17.00*), constructed in 1838 by a mayor of New York, and purchased by the railroad tycoon Jay Gould in 1880. Many original furnishings are in place, generally complementing the vaulted ceilings and stained-glass windows. There are very popular summer concerts in the grounds (☎ *(914) 631–0046 for information*). Picnicking is permitted.

Back on Route 9, proceed N 2 miles beyond the Dewey Thruway, watching for signs to **Philipsburg Manor** (■ *open 10.00–17.00*). Frederick Philipse, a late 17thC Dutch immigrant, was clearly a businessman and entrepreneur of exceptional acumen. This bustling complex of dam, gristmill, granary, bakery, stockyards, shipping wharf, and farmland was only part of his holdings, which at one time totalled 90,000 acres on both banks of the Hudson. Costumed attendants give demonstrations of Colonial cooking, millwork, weaving, and agricultural trades and crafts. You can go on a guided tour, beginning with a short film and then visiting the farmhouse, mill and barn. The **Old Dutch Church** across the street was built by Philipse in 1697. Washington Irving is buried in the nearby cemetery.

Route 9 passes N through Ossining and arrives after 8 miles in Croton-on-Hudson. Turn right at Croton Point Ave., continue to the first traffic signal, and turn right again on S. Riverside Ave. **Van Cortlandt Manor** (*open 10.00–17.00*), the third part of Sleepy Hollow Restorations, is about 100yd down the road. The main house began as a modest lodge erected in the late 1600s and was expanded to its present size by subsequent generations of the wealthy and influential Van Cortlandt family, who lived on this land for over 260yr. The original 86,000 acres have shrunk to 20, but they are well-tended, and the manor has been restored to its 18thC splendour.

Down by the river, past flourishing gardens and fruit trees, is the Ferry House, an inn of the same period that served passengers of the ferry operated by the Van Cortlandts. George Washington stopped by frequently, as did many other prominent figures of the Revolutionary War period. As at the other Sleepy Hollow Restorations, appropriately attired guides and craftspeople give demonstrations of home and farm skills. Frequent special events include a Christmas Candlelight Tour and the Autumn Crafts and Tasks Festival.

Late lunch can be taken in the suitably old-fashioned atmosphere of the 1761 **Bird & Bottle Inn** (*near Route 9, 4 miles N of Garrison* ☎ *(914) 424–3000, open for lunch and dinner Wed–Sun, closed Mon, Tues*). Afterwards drive w on Route 301, s on Route 9D to **Boscobel** (☎ *open Apr–Oct, Wed–Mon 9.30–17.00, Mar, Nov, Dec, Wed–Mon 9.30–16.00, closed Jan, Feb*). This is an early 18thC mansion in the Federalist manner, but with overtones of Neo-Classicism. Many furnishings are original. There are informative guided tours of house and gardens.

Drive N on Route 9D, through Hudson Highlands State Park, joining with Route 9 again a mile N of Wappingers Falls. This leads into the river port town of Poughkeepsie. If time and interest permit, turn E on Route 55 to the **Vassar College** campus. One of the first institutions of higher education for women (opened 1865) and a member of the prestigious 'Seven Sisters' group, it turned co-educational in 1968. The **Taylor Art Gallery** (*open Mon–Sat 9.00–17.00, Sun 14.00–17.00 during the academic year*) is the highpoint, but the other buildings present an attractive and interesting variety of architectural styles. Afterwards, return to Route 9 and turn N.

For evening refreshment at the end of a full day, drive about 16 miles on to Rhinebeck and stop at the **Beekman Arms** (*open all year, meals and room rates moderate*), dating from 1700 and claiming to be one of the two oldest inns in continuous operation in the United States.

Should the next day be a Sat or Sun (May–Oct only), you can see an airshow featuring vintage planes at the **Old Rhinebeck Aerodrome** (☎ *(914)758–8610 to check times*), reached by driving N on Route 9. On other days (or in addition), there are the historic sites in Hyde Park, to the s on Route 9. Near the centre of that sleepy village is the 1898 **Vanderbilt Mansion** (☎ *(914) 229–9115, open June–Aug 9.00–18.00, Sept–May 9.00–17.00*). Most of the works of art and furnishings in it are original. A mile or two s on Route 9 is the entrance to **the home of Franklin Delano Roosevelt** (*times as for Vanderbilt Mansion*). Parts of the house date from 1826, F.D.R. was born there in 1882, and he and his wife are buried in the rose garden.

Two miles further s on Route 9 is an unusual educational institution sometimes called "the other CIA", **The Culinary Institute of America** (☎ *(914) 471–6608 for information and bookings*). The student-chefs operate a coffee shop and a restaurant called the Escoffier Room, both open to the public.

Continue s on Route 9 to Poughkeepsie and take the Mid-Hudson Bridge, picking up Route 9W on the opposite side of the river. In Newburgh is **Hasbrouck House** (*open Wed–Sun 9.00–17.00*), once Washington's headquarters and now restored to an approximation of its original condition. Return to 9W. Just s of town pick up Route 218 through Cornwall, a winding but especially scenic drive high above the Hudson. This road ends at the Washington Gate of the **US Military Academy**, the officers' training college better known as **West Point**. The campus is open to the public all year round. Ask for directions at the **Visitors' Information Center** (*open Apr–Nov daily 8.30–16.30, Dec–Mar Wed–Sun 8.30–16.30*). The **military museum** exhibits uniforms and weaponry from the late 18thC to the present, and dioramas depict important battles. Be sure to stop at the belvedere overlooking the Hudson.

Exit from the main gate at the s end of the reservation, driving through the village and on to Route 9W once again. This passes **High Tor State Park** (🖼 *open June–Sept*) in Haverstraw, with hiking trails, swimming, and picnic facilities. After about 3 miles, watch for the right turn on to Route 303. If it is mealtime, take that road to the **Bully Boy Chop House** (☎ *(914) 268–6555, open for lunch Mon–Fri, and dinner daily*), for uncommonly generous portions of non-gimmicky American food. Alternatively, continue s on 9W, detouring into the business district of Nyack, with antique and bric-a-brac shops.

Pick-up Route 87 (the Dewey Thruway) at the edge of town, driving E across the Tappan Zee Bridge and s into the city.

Shakers and Berkshires
290 miles NE. Minimum two days.

There are numerous opportunities for swimming, hiking, and picnicking along this route, so dress and pack accordingly.

Leave Manhattan via the West Side Highway. This becomes the Henry Hudson Parkway, which joins the Saw Mill River Parkway. Follow the latter to Hawthorne Circle, transferring to the Taconic State Parkway, N, which passes through a sparsely settled countryside of meadows, groves, and green and tawny land with folds like a rumpled blanket. Leave the Parkway at the Route 44 exit, heading E towards **Millbrook**. Watch for the junction with Route 82. Just beyond is Tyrrell Rd. Turn right, s, and follow signs to **Innisfree Garden** (🖼 ☎ *(914) 677–8000, open May–Oct Wed–Sun 10.00–16.00*), the creation of a painter by the name of Walter Beck. A gallery contains a selection of Beck's paintings.

Return to Route 44 and turn right, E, through the small village of Millbrook, an antique hunter's haven. Continue about 10 miles to Amenia, there picking up Route 363 E towards **Sharon**, a charming Connecticut town with white clapboard frame houses beneath sheltering elms and maples. Two miles s on Route 4 is an **Audubon Center** (🖼 ☎ *(203) 364–5826, open Wed–Sat 9.00–17.00, Sun 13.00–17.00*), a wildlife sanctuary with miles of nature walks, a museum, and a herb garden. When you leave, return to the centre of Sharon and pick up Route 41, N, to Lakeville. Once there, turn left, W, on Route 44, crossing once again into New York State and arriving in Millerton. Look for **McArthur's Smokehouse**, by the railway tracks, where superior sausages and other smoked meats are sold. With supplementary supplies from the nearby grocery store, the ingredients of a memorable picnic can be assembled; and the perfect place to eat it is nearby.

To find the spot, take Route 22, N, and after about 8 miles look for the inconspicuous sign directing you to **Boston Corners**, then look for signs to **Bash Bish Falls Reservation**. From the designated parking lot, a woodland path rises towards the gap between two peaks, a brook tumbling by on the right. After less than a mile, a slender waterfall plunges 50ft into a large clear pool, spilling into a series of smaller rock clefts and crevices. Man-made intrusions do not detract from the primitive grandeur of the place.

The road leading from the car park up to a vantage above the falls is a worthwhile detour. Afterwards, return to Route 22 and drive N to **Hillsdale**. At the juncture with Route 23 is **L'Hostellerie Bressane** (☎ *(518) 325–3412 for information and bookings*), an ambitious (and costly) inn of classical Provençal leanings. Only dinner is served, and it is closed at unpredictable times. Turn right, E, on Route 23. This leads back to Massachusetts and through the pretty hamlet of South Egremont, eventually connecting with Route 7. Turn left, N, through Great Barrington and on to **Stockbridge**, 6 miles farther on.

On most counts a quintessential New England village, Stockbridge stops short of touristy clutter. Turn right, E, into Main St. (Route 102). At that corner is the **Red Lion Inn** (☎ *(413) 298–5545* ▯▯ ☞ *108, advance booking essential*). The dining-room serves three meals daily, and there is a convivial tap room downstairs with live music most weekend evenings. The revered illustrator Norman Rockwell lived in Stockbridge much of his life, and many of his paintings are on view at the 18thC **Corner House** (▨ *open Wed–Mon 10.00–17.00*), just down the street. Two blocks in the other direction, W, is the **Mission House** (▨ ☎ *(413) 298–3383, open late May to early Oct, Tues–Sat 10.00–17.00*), built in 1739 and maintained as a museum of domestic Colonial life. The estate of the sculptor Daniel Chester French is 2 miles away, N on Route 102, then S on Route 183. There are daily guided tours of his **house and studio** (▨ *open 10.00–17.00, late May to early Oct*).

The southern Berkshires host a multitude of cultural activities every summer. In Stockbridge, the **Berkshire Playhouse** presents classics and some pre-Broadway try-outs from June–Oct. The **Boston Symphony Orchestra** and other musical ensembles perform at **Tanglewood**, an open-sided 'shed' in spacious grounds in nearby Lenox. The town of Lee is known for the annual **Jacob's Pillow Dance Festival**, in a theatre created by Martha Graham and Ted Shawn. In winter, there are several popular ski resorts, including Bousquet, Brodie, and Jiminy Peak near Pittsfield and Butternut Basin near Great Barrington.

When ready to leave for New York, drive N on Route 7 to Pittsfield, then W on Route 20. Five miles from the centre of Pittsfield is **Hancock Shaker Village** (☎ *(413) 433–0188, open June–Oct 9.30–17.00*), one of the former settlements of the celibate religious sect founded as an offshoot of the Quakers in the 18thC. In accordance with their beliefs, their houses and furnishings were crisp and exquisitely simple. This painstakingly restored village illustrates their crafts and trades, from cookery to 'spirit painting', with admirable clarity. Don't miss it.

Drive W on Route 20, then turn left, S, on Route 22. At Hillsdale, take Route 23 right, W, to the Taconic State Parkway for the return to New York.

Index

Individual hotels, restaurants and shops have not been indexed, because they appear in alphabetical order within their appropriate sections. The sections themselves, however, have been indexed. Streets are listed in the gazetteer and not the index.

Page numbers in bold type indicate the main entry.

Index

Index

Index

Gazetteer of street names

Numbers after the street name refer to pages on which the street is mentioned in the book. Map references refer to the maps that follow this gazetteer.

Streets are listed alphabetically. Numbered avenues (1st Avenue, 2nd Avenue, etc) are listed under **A**. Numbered streets (3rd St., 4th St., etc) are listed in numerical sequence at the end of the gazetteer.

It has not been possible to label every street drawn on the maps, although all major streets and most smaller ones have been named. Some streets that it has not been possible to label on the maps have been given map references in this gazetteer, however, because this serves as an approximate location, which will nearly always be sufficient for you to find your way.

A

Amsterdam Avenue, 112th St., 64; Map 8I3
68th St., 161; Map 6M2
Ann St., 172; Map 2U4
Audubon Terrace, 35, 53, 55–7, 83–4, 95, 101; Map 8F2
Avenue of the Americas *see* 6th Avenue; Maps 2, 5
1st Avenue, 9, 10, 15, 109, 141, 143, 152, 153, 156, 157, 173, 179, 182; Maps 3Q–R5, 5M–R5, 7I–N5, 9I–J5
2nd Avenue, 30, 84, 103, 108, 136, 141, 143, 144, 156, 157, 164, 172, 179, 182, 186; Maps 3R5, 5N–Q5, 7K–L4–5, 9I–J5
3rd Avenue, 14, 94, 136, 137, 139, 148, 152, 156, 159, 165, 166, 169, 172, 173, 178; Maps 2Q–R4, 5N–Q5, 7L–M5
5th Avenue, 10, 11, 13, 14, 15, 30, 31, 32, 35, 36, 42, 45, 46, 47, 48, 65, 67, 74, 76, 79, 82, 83, 84, 85, 88, 89, 90, 93, 94, 95, 99, 102, 103, 107, 111, 115, 122, 125, 142, 152, 154, 156, 157, 163, 165, 166, 168, 169, 170, 171, 173, 179, 180, 182, 183, 184; Maps 2R4, 5M–R4, 7J–N4
6th Avenue (Avenue of the Americas), 10, 11, 13, 36, 43, 44, 63, 98, 102, 121, 166, 170, 171, 184, 186, 187; Maps 2R–S4, 5P–R4
7th Avenue, 9, 10, 15, 30, 43, 66, 79, 107, 121, 124, 125, 155, 156, 158, 159, 163, 167, 185, 186; Maps 2Q–R3, 4N–Q3
8th Avenue, 8, 12, 13, 14,

30, 88, 107, 119, 123, 140, 155, 189; Maps 2Q–R3, 4N–Q3, 6I3, 8E–I3
9th Avenue, 15, 30, 66, 164; Maps 2Q3, 4N–R3
10th Avenue, 116, 159; Map 4N–O2
11th Avenue, 10, 152; Map 4N–O2

B

Bank St.; Map 2R3
Hudson St., 148; Map 2R3
Barclay St., 108; Map 2T4
Barrow St., 43; Map 2R3
7th Ave., 183; Map 2R3
Battery Place, 57, 58; Map 2U4
Bayard St.; Map 3T5
Mulberry St., 148; Map 2T4
Bedford St., 43, 151; Map 2R3
Beekman Place, 74; Map 5O5
Beekman St., 106; Map 2T4
Belt Parkway, 110; Map 13E5
Bleecker St., 42, 43, 156, 182; Map 2R4
7th Ave., 148; Map 2R4
LaGuardia Pl., 155, 160; Map 2R4
Thompson St., 159; Map 2R4
Boardwalk (Coney Island); Map 12F3
8th St., 98; Map 12F3
'Bobkin Lane', 42; Map 2R4
Bowery, The, 40, 57, 67, 87,, 139, 143, 160; Maps 2R4, 3S–T5
Bleecker St., 160; Map 2R4
Broad St., 38; Map 2U4
Broadway, 10, 13, 15, 17, 32, 37, 39, 55, 56, 57,

58, 64, 68, 71, 74, 80, 84, 104, 105, 107, 108, 112, 145, 154, 161, 166, 169, 170, 171, 172, 173, 179, 185, 186, 187; Maps 2R–U4, 4N–O3, 5P–Q4, 6I–M2–3, 8F–I2, 10B2
E Broadway, 42, 146; Map 3S5–6
W Broadway, 27, 105, 152; Map 2T4
Thomas St., 142; Map 2T4
White St., 140; Map 2T4
Brooklyn Avenue, 180; Map 12E3
Brooklyn Bridge, 19, 21, 37, 39, 50, 60, 61, 106, 182; Map 3T–U5
Brooklyn-Battery Tunnel, 60; Map 2V4
Brooklyn-Queens Expressway, 50; Map 3U–V6
Broome St., 27, 40, 153, 164; Map 2S4

C

Cadman Plaza W, 50; Map 3U6
Canal St., 34, 40, 41, 67, 84, 87, 105, 108; Map 2S3–4
W Broadway, 164; Map 2S4
Central Park, 183, 186; Maps 6–7J–N3–4
Central Park S, 46, 115, 117, 121, 122, 124, 157; Maps 4–5M–N3–4
Central Park W, 14, 46, 53, 55, 98, 110, 120, 147, 182, 183; Maps 4M–N3, 6L–M3
Chambers St., 37, 39; Map 2T4
Charles St., 43; Map 2R3
Christopher St., 123, 152; Map 2R3

204

Gazetteer

208

NEW YORK

LEGEND

City Maps

| 0 | 200 | 400 | 600 | 800 Yds |

Major Place of Interest

Other Important Building

Built-up Area

Park

† † Cemetery

† † Named church, church

✡ Synagogue

✚ Hospital

i Information Office

⊠ Post Office

🚗 Car Park

Ⓜ Subway

→ One Way Street

10 ▶ Adjoining Page No.

Area Maps

■ Place of Interest

Built-up Area

Wood or Park

⊙━⊙ Motorway (with access point)

= = = Motorway under construction

━━━ Main Road-Dual Carriageway

━━━ Other Main Road

━━━ Secondary Road

🛡95 Interstate Highway

⬡9 U.S. Highway

㉗ State and Provincial Highway

- - - Ferry

━━━ Railway

✈ Airport

✦ Airfield

▬▬▬ State Boundary

NEW YORK ENVIRONS

0   1   2   4 Miles

Oradell Reservoir

Fair Lawn

Paramus

Bergenfield

Passaic River

Paterson

208

Bergen

Garden State Parkway

4

80

Passaic

17

Hackensack

Engl

Teaneck

46

Clifton

Garfield

Overpeck Creek

Passaic

State Parkway

21

Fort Lee

46

TETERBORO AIRPORT

80

1-9

Bloomfield

17

MEADOWLANDS SPORTS COMPLEX

Jersey Turnpike

North Bergen

3

West New York

Hudson

NEW JERSEY

95

HACKENSACK RIVER

New

Jersey Turnpike

Centre Park

NEW JERSEY HISTORICAL SOCIETY

21

Passaic River

Kearny

New

95

Union City

MANHATTAN

QUEENS BORO BRIDGE

501

Lincoln Tunnel (Toll)

Hoboken

1-9

EAST RIVER

Pulaski Skyway

478

NEW YORK

QUEENS MIDTOWN TUNNEL (TOLL)

NEWARK

1-9

N.J. Turnpike

ROOSEVELT STADIUM

440

JERSEY CITY

78

HOLLAND TUNNEL (TOLL)

CITY HALL

MANHATTAN BRIDGE

WILLIAMSBUR BRIDGE

95

New Jersey Turnpike

Ellis Is.

278

Brooklyn

NEWARK INTERNATIONAL AIRPORT

Turnpike Ext.

STATUE OF LIBERTY

BROOKLYN BATTERY TUNNEL (TOLL)

BROOKLYN BRIDGE

Liberty Is.

Elizabeth

Governors Is.

BROOKLYN HEIGHTS

BROOK AND GAR

UPPER BAY

Bayonne

BROOKLYN ZOO

Prospect Park

NEW JERSEY NEW YORK

27

NEWARK BAY

BAYONNE BRIDGE

Queens Expressway

Fla

SNUG HARBOR CULTURAL CENTER

440

STATEN ISLAND ZOO

Bay Ridge

BROOKLY

278

Brooklyn

Ocean Parkway

278

Staten Island Expressway

Shore Expressway

STATEN ISLAND

VERRAZANO NARROWS BRIDGE (TOLL)

Coney Island

AQUARIUM

J.A. CENTER OF TIBETAN ART

RICHMONDTOWN RESTORATION

GATEWAY NATIONAL RECREATION AREA

LOWER BAY

NEW YORK
SUBWAY SYSTEM

15

ROUTES

—— Broadway - 7th Ave.
(Local/Express/Shuttle)

—— Lexington Ave.
(Express/Local/Local Pelham Express)

—— Flushing
(Local/Express)

—— J.F.K.
(Express)

—— 8th Ave.
(Local/Express/Rockaway Shuttle)

—— Ave. of Americas (6th Ave.)
(Local/Express/Shuttle)

—— Brooklyn/Queens
(Crosstown)

—— Nassau St
(Local/Shuttle)

—— 14 St-Canarsie
(Local)

—— Broadway
(Local/Express/Shuttle/
Nassau St Local)

—— Terminal

· Local Stop

• Express Stop

○ Express & Local Stop

Free Transfers

Special Rush Hour
Express Service

MANHATTAN BUS MAP

16

A selection of crosstown
and uptown routes

route number | via | destination

UPTOWN

M1 5th & Madison Aves
(8 St/4 Ave & 146 St/Lenox Ave)

M4 5th & Madison Aves
(32 St/7 Ave & 193 St/Ft Washington Ave)

M5 5th Ave & 6th Ave
(Houston St/W.B'way & 178 St/B'way)

M6 7th Ave/B'way & 6 Ave
(59 St/6 Ave & South Ferry)

M10 7th & 8th Aves
(Houston St/7 Ave & 159 St/8 Ave)

M11 9th & 10th Aves
(12 St/Hudson St & 133 St/B'way)

M15 1st & 2nd Aves
(South Ferry & 126 St/2 Ave)

M101 3rd & Lexington Aves
(6 St/3 Ave & †93 St/Amsterdam Ave)

M104 Broadway
(42 St/1 Ave & 129 St/Amsterdam Ave)

CROSSTOWN

M19 96th St
(1 Ave/96 St & West End Ave/96 St)

M18 86th St
(York Ave/91 St & West End Ave/86 St)

M17 79th St
(East End Ave/79 St & West End Ave/79 St)

M103 59th St
(York Ave/61 St & B'way/72 St)

M28 57th St
(Sutton Place/55 St & 12 Ave/55 St)

M27 49th & 50th Streets
(1 Ave/47 St & 12 Ave/42 St)

M106 42nd St
(1 Ave/42 St & 12 Ave/42 St)

M16 34th St
(1 Ave/34 St & 12 Ave/42 St)

M14 14th St
(FDR Drive/Delancey St & 10 Ave/15 St)

M13 8th St
(Ave D/10 & West St/Christopher St)

M21 Houston St
(1 Ave/27 St & Hudson St/Van Dam St)